622902

# INDUSTRIAL MENTAL
# HEALTH AND
# EMPLOYEE COUNSELING

# INDUSTRIAL MENTAL HEALTH AND EMPLOYEE COUNSELING

Compiled and Edited
by
**Robert L. Noland**
Professor of Psychology
University of Dayton

**Behavioral Publications**　　　　　**New York**
**1973**

Library of Congress Catalog Card Number 73–157319
Standard Book Number 87705–057–0
Copyright © 1973 by Behavioral Publications

BEHAVIORAL PUBLICATIONS
2852 Broadway—Morningside Heights
New York, New York 10025

Printed in the United States of America

# TABLE OF CONTENTS

# PART III.   MULTIPLE APPROACHES TO EMPLOYEE COUNSELING

## PART IV.   MENTAL HEALTH PROBLEMS OF MANAGERS AND SUPERVISORS

## PART V.   EMERGING COOPERATIVE TRENDS IN LABOR, MANAGEMENT, AND COMMUNITY

# INTRODUCTION

This is, in a sense, the "golden age" for the employee. Or it should be. The physical demands of his job no longer rob him of his youth—or life—at a premature age; he works for fewer hours—in more secure and comfortable surroundings —for more "real" pay; he has more time to expand and maximize his personality in home, civic, and leisure activities.

But it is no accident that the hoped-for "golden age" is for far too many workers the "age of anxiety." Statistics on the variety of work-influencing problems of employees bear mute testimony to the fact that many of today's workers have not been released from the "bonds" which would make—or keep—them adaptive, productive employees.

Just as the technology and machinery of today is drastically different—though retaining some commonality—compared to the past, so too are certain of man's adjustive strengths and weaknesses, sources of satisfactions and stress. Many employees have "paid" dearly for their contemporary employment gains, and they have paid psychologically. Technological advancements have—in many cases—deskilled and routinized their previously pride-invoking skills. In many other cases, the opposite has occurred; a power and systems-centered organizational atmosphere has flooded their senses with rapidly changing conditions to which they are in no way accustomed. We are in the most occupationally revolutionary and stressful period ever experienced in history. Is it any wonder that here and there the stress and strains are showing?

In many businesses and industries the employee problems have other bases. Dramatic social changes, faulty personality development, family problems, personal problems, etc., are representative examples.

Then too there exist a great number of problems related to workers' changing expectations about their treatment by their company—the overall "human relations" climate—and by their immediate supervisors.

The range and origin of problems is, of course, enormous. To one extent or another, however, management must be prepared to assume certain responsibilities in cases where problem employees are involved. The purpose of this book is to provide a comprehensive view of what various companies and individuals have done in anticipating, discovering, understanding, and dealing effectively with problem employees.

This book, then, is concerned with the problem employee. But it takes no reflection at all to conclude that it is normal and, indeed, inevitable that employees experience all kinds of "problems." Just what do we mean, then, by "problem employees"? Just *having* a problem is an insufficient criterion; in fact, the employee *with* a problem may be a *better employee because* of his problem. We will explore this point shortly, but first, what is a "problem employee"?

*A problem employee is one who does not conform to the social-vocational role expected of him at his place of employment.*

From this standpoint, a number of important issues emerge and are placed in a workable frame of reference. For example, physical disability, psychological maladjustment, neurosis, etc., are not in themselves either causes or characteristics of problem employees! Nor is an employee in good physical and psychological health—and a productive person to boot—necessarily a "desirable employee"! Let's explore further what we mean.

Bill and John both lost a leg in Vietnam and have thus incurred a "physical disability." Bill goes back to his office job with a remarkably flexible artificial limb. He still bowls in the company bowling league and even rides his son's go-cart. John was a health major in college and a professional football player prior to Vietnam. He is dejected and morose, claiming that he knows nothing else. He may be said to be—temporarily, at least—occupationally "handicapped." Bill, on the other hand, has a disability but is *not* occupationally handicapped.

One may extend the above principle to cover a variety of abilities or characteristics to show that it is not necessarily the characteristic or presumed problem itself but, rather, the person's perception of and reaction to it, his company's evaluation and handling of it, and the overall social circumstances.

For example, Lawrence works in the Comptroller's office. He has marital problems because of his basically rigid and compulsive personality. He is the epitome of the perfectionist "checker-upper." The psychiatrist would label him abnormal (i.e., "neurotic"). Further, from a mental health standpoint, we would, theoretically, try to get him to change, to "give up" his neurotic drive for perfection. But is he a "problem employee"? Well, he *may* be, but chances are he's a highly efficient and valued member of the organization and the company may well be better off *because* of his unusual characteristics!

The point we are illustrating is that—rightly or wrongly—the *organization* sets the standards of the "problem employee" and the "desirable employee." These standards are *generally* similar to the standards of the "maladjusted" and "adjusted" as set by psychiatrists, psychologists, etc., but there may be many serious exceptions. Many are the persons who were as normal and well adjusted and productive as could be, but were nevertheless labeled "problem employees" and exiled—through transfer; blackballed—through word of mouth or personnel records; or fired. In addition to the organizational expectancies—logical or not—the standards of the immediate supervisor are also key determiners of the employee's adequacy.

There are, after all, "neurotic societies" and "neurotic companies" and "neurotic supervisors," and fairly normal employees may find themselves severely misjudged in such situations. "They" then are "problem employees."

Tom is a healthy and well-adjusted guy who's quite competent in his field. Put him in a situation with (1) an autocratic, oppressive leadership atmosphere; (2) an obsessive profit-motive at the expense of federal laws or Christian decency; (3) an insecure superior; (4) the requirement that after-work hours are "on-call" hours for the company at the expense of his family; and/or (5) a realization that other employees are conforming to these expectations. From one standpoint his conformity would be at the expense of other important values; e.g., personal integrity, proper orientation to time, family adjustment, etc. If, on the other hand, he challenges the status quo, or fails to meet their standards, he's a "problem employee."

But let us not develop too wide a cleavage between the criteria of "problem employees" used by organizations and that developed by mental hygienists such as industrial psychiatrists and industrial clinical psychologists. Nor should we presume to imply that maladjustment in employees is caused solely—or even mainly—by the company. This position would be far removed from the truth of the matter. Look, for example, at some of the possibilities when you relate just the variables of employee mental health and the specific job situation:

(1) Some job applicants have psychological problems at the time of hiring; they may get worse, improve, or stay the same upon employment.

(2) Some employees who may or may not have been maladjusted at the time of employment develop problems at a later date. These problems may or may not be influenced by the job setting.

(3) Some employees show average or superior job performance in spite of—or because of—their problem.

(4) Some employees who are not technically regarded as psychologically handicapped still cannot function effectively under certain work conditions or leadership types.

No further elaboration seems necessary to conclude that the concept of maladjusted or problem employees is an elusive, multifaceted, relative situational designation.

It is near-fruitless to argue over the issue of who's responsible: As long as the employing organization retains troubled employees, it *must* undertake preventative and remedial action to the extent necessary to maintain company objectives and departmental efficiency. The possible approaches available to the company are represented in the articles in this collection.

Part I of this book contains a number of articles designed to explore the relationship between mental illness and industrial variables such as productivity, efficiency, and the economic consequences of job disruption. The articles in Part II of the book are designed to give the reader sufficient historical background in the problem of employee mental health to enable him to understand both problems and trends in current industrial mental health endeavors. The initial article in this section provides an excellent history of occupational mental health. Several following articles delineate the experiences of a number of companies in setting up and offering employee mental health services. Part III contains a number of articles showing the multiple approaches which have been used in the area of employee counseling and industrial mental health services. The work of industrial psychiatry is highlighted, although programs involving clinical industrial psychology, group psychotherapy, and pastoral counseling are included. In Part IV, stress is placed on the mental health of supervisory and managerial personnel, the unique impact of their problems on the organization, and the care which must be taken in dealing with problem employees at these levels of management. The last section, Part V, includes a rather large collection of articles showing recent tendencies for cooperation on the part of labor, management, and community sources. Experiences of unions in bargaining for and setting up mental health services, as well as the use of outside psychiatric services for union employees, comprise the subject matter of this last section. Included also in the papers in this section are evaluational studies related to more recent trends in community mental health services for employees.

It is believed that this collection of readings will serve a useful purpose not only for individual professionals working in this area but also for (1) college students in personnel, industrial management, and industrial psychology; (2) general practitioners in medicine who deal with workers showing psychological problems; and (3) management personnel and industrial training directors in business and industry.

# ACKNOWLEDGMENT

The editor wishes to express his appreciation to the authors of the articles contained in this book. Thanks are offered both for their contributions to the general area of employee counseling and industrial mental health and for approval to reprint their articles in the present collection. To the extent that compilations such as this book of readings are of value to the professional mental health and counseling community, they are so because of the merit of each contributor's paper.

The articles represented in this collection represent important contributions initially published in a number of journals in the United States. Thanks are therefore expressed to editors of the following journals for permission to reprint articles from their publications:

*American Journal of Orthopsychiatry*
*American Journal of Psychiatry*
*American Management Association Bulletin*
*Archives of Environmental Health*
*Bulletin of the Menninger Clinic*
*Group Psychotherapy*
*Harvard Business Review*
*Industrial Medicine and Surgery*
*International Journal of Group Psychotherapy*
*Journal of Occupational Medicine*
*Menninger Quarterly*
*Mental Hygiene*
*Personnel Administration*
*Personnel Journal*

# Part I
# The Industrial Consequences
# of Employee Maladjustment

# 1. MENTAL ILLNESS: SOCIETY'S AND INDUSTRY'S SIX BILLION DOLLAR BURDEN

### Robert N. McMurray

*Organizations have persons who are, to varying degress, fugitives from reality. Thus, conventional modes of dealing with them, including "good intentions," will often be ineffective.*

According to the National Committee against Mental Illness, society's share of the overall cost of mental illness in 1960 was $3,624,831,357. This included expenditures for public, proprietary, and nonprofit mental hospitals; payments for private and psychiatric care; V.A. and other federal agencies' costs; the cost of public institutions for mental defectives and epileptics; the cost of public assistance to the mentally ill and the dollar value of the work years lost by patients in mental hospitals; the wages and salaries lost through absenteeism due to mental illness; and the earnings losses of mental patients.

As an indication of the magnitude of the problem, an estimated 17 million persons, or 10% of the population, are

The author, President of the McMurry Company, is an authority in personnel management, industrial relations, and market research. He began work at age 14 for Armour in the Chicago stockyards and had varied early experience in selling and business administration. After undergraduate work at the University of Chicago, he attended the University of Vienna on a Carnegie Foundation Scholarship and received his Ph.D. in psychology. From 1935 to 1943 he was Chicago representative of the Psychological Corporation of New York. Since 1943 he has headed his own consulting firm with offices in New York City, Los Angeles, San Francisco, San Antonio, and Chicago (the home office). He is well known as a lecturer, advisor, and contributor to business magazines.

currently suffering from some form of mental illness. An additional 5,400,000 persons, or 3% of the population, are mentally retarded. (This latter group alone costs the national economy over 1 billion dollars annually.) Slightly more than one out of every two hospital beds in the U.S. is occupied by a mental patient. The daily resident patient population in public mental hospitals alone in 1960 averaged 539,184 persons. In one year alone, roughly 2½ million men, women, and children were treated for some form of mental disorder. In addition, of all persons who go to general hospitals for treatment for *physical ailments* annually, it is estimated that 6 million are suffering from serious mental and emotional illnesses which are partially responsible for their physical complaints.

Moreover, for every sufferer from serious mental and emotional illness who has been diagnosed or is or has been under ambulatory or hospital treatment (roughly 5% of the population), another victim is at large, unrecognized, and often potentially dangerous. It is probable that as many as 8 million persons belong in this latter category. (This latter group includes many of the cranks, crackpots, eccentrics, fanatics, rebels without cause, recluses, the antisocial and the hypersuspicious.) Much delinquency, many suicides, and alcohol and narcotics addictions are also symptomatic of mental illness. For example, there are estimated to be 3,800,000 problem drinkers in the U.S.,950,000 of whom are chronic alcoholics, and 50,000 are narcotics addicts; 18,330 persons committed suicide in 1959.

## IDENTIFICATION AND CHARACTERISTICS

While there are many symptoms of mental illness, deficiency, and defects, the simplest and most pragmatic indications are that in mild cases the sufferer simply cannot learn or is chronically unhappy and insecure; in more acute cases he is unable to adapt successfully to his environment, and in very acute cases he loses contact to some degree with reality.

Under such circumstances he lives in an unreal world of fantasy and fear. In consequence, his perception of reality becomes faulty: He sees and hears things which do not exist or fails to perceive things in his environment, or what he sees and hears he misinterprets. His behavior often becomes bizarre and inappropriate, dangerously uninhibited or excessively withdrawn and inhibited. He may believe that he is Napoleon or that he is the subject of a nationwide conspiracy whose objective is to kill him. The result, whether the defect or illness is mild or acute, is a basic inability to adjust or a progressive deterioration of judgment and common sense. It is for this latter reason that *there is no necessary correlation between intelligence as measured by tests and judgment.* Often the most brilliant are the most seriously out of touch with reality.

One of the less commonly recognized but serious characteristics of emotional maladjustment and mental illness is their manifestation in the individual's *value system* (what he regards as right, true, worthy, beautiful, and desirable). Each person's system of values is totally unique and is the product of both the environment in which he has developed and his personal needs and motivations. Because these values are strongly personalized and most are highly toned emotionally, their possessor always regards them as "right" and all contrary ones as "wrong." This is in spite of the fact that because the sources of each person's values are highly diverse, many of them are in conflict with one another even within the boundaries of his psyche. (Painful awareness of the existence of conflicting values is minimized in everyone by the mechanism of keeping them confined in so-called "watertight compartments of the mind." This enables the individual to endorse violently inconsistent values without awareness of any conflict. Thus a man may be very pious on Sunday and rob widows and orphans the other six days in the week or profess great patriotism and yet endorse Communist doctrines with complete sincerity. At a more primitive level is the man who says belligerently, "Anyone who says I am not the most peace-loving man in the world I'll take out into the alley and beat to a bloody pulp.")

Senility, often a problem among the aging, poses particular difficulties because the onset of this condition is usually very gradual. Further, while the sufferer becomes increasingly incapable of assimilating any new skills, information, or insights, *he does not forget what he has already learned.* Thus he can often carry on familiar tasks in a well-structured work environment with little apparent loss of effectiveness. However, a careful examination of the sufferer's performance will almost always reveal a greater or lesser degree of deterioration, if not of aberration. The gradual (or sometimes sudden by trauma) damaging of the prefrontal lobes of the cerebral cortex by such conditions as arteriosclerosis induces a state analogous in many ways to alcoholic intoxication, with the drinker's characteristic errors in judgment. (This flawing of judgment often precedes by many years the overt childishness and confusion of the manifestly senile.) The significance of senility lies in the fact that cerebral arteriosclerosis, other circulatory disturbances, and senile brain disease *account for 26% of all first admissions to mental hospitals.* When allowance is made for the fact that only the seriously deteriorated are committed, it may be seen that the incidence of this disorder among the elderly is very great.

A further quasimental illness, also costly in an industrial context, is epilepsy. The *grand mal* attacks obviously incapacitate the sufferer for many types of employment. The major problem to industry, however, is the sufferer from *petit mal.* The person who has only a passing clouding or loss of consciousness. As a result, his condition is not usually apparent to others. Hence, he may be placed in an occupation where he will be a hazard to himself or others, e.g., working with dangerous machinery or as a locomotive engineer. (The engineer of the Santa Fe train wrecked on the outskirts of Los Angeles some years ago with several killed, subsequently reported that he had been having "blackouts" for 29 years.)

## IS CHANGE POSSIBLE?

Most of these defects, deficiencies, maladjustments, and mental illnesses are either inherent (e.g., defect or deficiency), organic (e.g., senility and epilepsy), or functional (e.g., the neuroses and such psychoses as schizophrenia, paranoia, etc.). Unfortunately, little can be done to help the defective and deficient and the senile. Some progress is being made with the epileptic, and psychotherapy is available for the more acutely immature and the neurotic and some of the more serious functional mental illnesses. Nothing, however, offers much promise to change aberrant values, particularly when they are symptomatic of mental illness. They are usually too deeply ingrained. (Most "functional" mental illnesses, the neuroses and psychoses, are, in effect, only bad mental habits, the majority of which were formed early in life and are therefore very resistive to change. This is why even *much psychiatric treatment is palliative rather than curative.* Milieu therapy, for example, seeks to adapt the patient better to his environment and vice versa, often thereby facilitating his adaptation to his environment, rather than to attempt to bring about any significant therapeutic change in the individual himself.)

Paradoxically, perhaps, it *is* sometimes possible to change a person's behavior for better or worse without necessarily altering his basic personality make-up or altering his basic value system. Thus, if an employee is wrongly placed (is "over his head on his job") so that he is subjected to intolerable anxieties and tensions, he may take flight from them into hyperaggressiveness, alcoholism, or hypochondria, to mention only a few possible reactions. These reactions will often be marked by radical changes in his overt behavior. Inversely, not infrequently the acute alcoholic, through Alcoholics Anonymous or some similar supportive agency, can be rehabilitated and restored to usefulness as an employee and citizen. The important point to recognize is that *while the alcoholic's behavior has changed for the better (he no longer drinks), he is still an alcoholic. His fundamental personality has not changed.* Nor, as a rule, have his values: His "recovery" stems from a change in the environment or milieu in which he finds himself. If it has suddenly become more supportive (through the activities of A.A.) or less threatening as a result of a change to a less demanding job, his anxieties and their attendant tensions are allayed. *Hence, he no longer needs alcohol to provide him courage or to dim his awareness of his problems.* However, he, himself, has undergone no inherent change.

Because of the complexity of the roots of human behavior and the fact that many of them are unconscious, the man on the street has little insight into his basic needs and motives even when he is free from serious emotional maladjustment and mental illness. (It is true, that he *thinks* he understands himself, but this is rarely the case. Hence, Socrates' admonition, "know thyself," is, for practical purposes, meaningless.) In most instances, he sincerely believes that what he does is rationally determined, when in actuality his so-called "reasoning" is more often than not a search for rationalizations to justify actions or decisions already taken on quite irrational and unreasoned grounds. It is for this reason that many intelligent and well-educated persons often exhibit such incredibly bad judgment and compulsively repeat the same mistakes again and again.

Although the prevailing American value system holds that man is perfectible and welcomes word of his shortcomings so that he may correct them, this is rarely the case. Most persons, both the mentally sound and those who are to some degree ill, at heart neither welcome attempts to bring about changes in their fundamental make-ups nor are they capable of bringing them about even should they wish to. On the other hand, as far as industry is concerned, it cannot be expected to undertake the therapeutic rehabilitation of its mildly or seriously maladjusted or mentally ill employees: first, because it has no moral obligation to do so (it might as well run a tuberculosis sanatorium); second, because in most instances it cannot do so even should it wish to. (This is in spite of the fact that many personnel people place great faith in "counseling," "the nondirective interview," and similar quasiclinical procedures. (Even the very few companies who employ full- or part-time psychiatrists make no effort to provide therapy for their employees on the job.

In short, costly as they may be, and pessimistic as this may seem, industry must take a realistic view of its mentally retarded, deficient, immature, and ill employees. *It is not going*

*to be able to bring about any significant change in them as persons.*
Their more aberrant behavior may be "contained" and occasionally modified but this is all. If they are "problems" and
most are (included among them are the untrainable, the
stupid, the lazy, the insubordinate, the chronic absentees, the
alcoholics, the hypochondriacs, the day dreamers, the
paranoid, the chronically in debt, the "trouble makers," i.e.,
the psychopathic personalities, the authoritarian personalities,
the accident prone, the senile and confused, the anxious and
indecisive, those with "leftist tendencies," and those whose
lack of judgment indicates that they are in varying degrees
out of touch with reality), it must be accepted as a fact that
they will probably continue to manifest these traits and defend
the values consistent with them. In short, the majority are
to a greater or lesser degree fugitives from reality. In consequence, conventional modes of dealing with them will often be
ineffective.

## EFFECTS OF THE PROBLEM

Management must, therefore, face the fact that it is these
"problem" employees who constitute one of its greatest (albeit
not always recognized) costs. In most instances, it is not only
the employer, but the employee, and even the public as well
who suffer. Among the more common costs to the *employer*
are:
1. Unnecessarily high labor turnover, excessive absenteeism,
   etc.
2. Substandard production.
3. Poor employee morale and internecine strife.
4. Poor public relations.
5. Excessive labor trouble.
6. Ill-advised company policies and practices often leading
   to the failure of the company (when top management
   is mentally ill or senile).
Among the costs to the *employee* are:
1. Chronic job dissatisfaction, with many changes of jobs.

2.  Failure to achieve the goals his intelligence, training, and experience merit.
3.  Job tensions which create psychogenic disorders or lead to fight or flight symptoms (alcoholism, overeating, excessive smoking, etc.)

The *public* loses through:

1.  Personal inconvenience.
2.  Heightened costs.

Obviously, mental illness is not the sole contributor to these conditions, but it is a major one. Its exact cost has never been calculated, but it is estimated to be in excess of 3 billion dollars annually. This, added to society's costs, brings the total to at least 6 billion.

## FACTS AND FALLACIES
## OF HUMAN NATURE

If management is to minimize these conflicts and other costs of mental illness, it must discard many of its outworn and false beliefs about human nature and accept more realistic ones. (Many popular beliefs about the nature of man are of quasitheological origin—principally the Protestant ethic of Calvin and Luther—e.g., man is perfectible, has a free will, etc., and are, in consequence, a part of the prevailing value system of many businessmen. Unfortunately, the fact that such beliefs are widely held does not mean that they are necessarily valid.) In all probability, one of the major reasons why mental illness is so costly to industry is the fact that management and personnel executives persist in retaining beliefs about human nature which are largely or even totally fallacious. One belief alone is probably responsible for the waste of hundreds of millions of dollars. This is the almost universal conviction that all that is necessary to influence people (including the emotionally disturbed) and change their habits and attitudes is to show them *by logic* the error of their ways. Man clings desperately to his illusion that he is "homo sapiens," the rational being, in spite of overwhelming evidence (currently particularly in the field of international politics) that he is not.

In the arena of value conflicts alone, mankind has consistently been his own worst enemy. Fully one-half of man's worst disasters have been self-imposed (religious conflicts and persecutions, the mistreatment or exploitation of minority groups, war and conquest are typical). Man is also notorious for his inhumanity to man. Currently, it appears not unlikely that he will destroy himself completely. To persist in adhering to a value system which sees man as noble, rational, and filled with love, to the exclusion of baser needs and impulses, is to be totally unrealistic. Yet a number of industry's most common convictions include, as already stated, the beliefs that man is not only perfectible, but that everyone (even a Stalin) is basically honest, sincere, and well-intentioned at heart (few in industry know anything of psychopathic personalities—the men who hate) and that attitudes (and the values which they reflect) are susceptible to modification by logic or appeals to the individual's "better nature." It is largely in consequence of these and similar beliefs and the acceptance of concomitant values that so much of present day personnel, employee relations, and industrial relations work is so ineffective. (Actually, from a purely pragmatic point of view, personnel and employee relations have made relatively little progress toward the accomplishment of their major objectives: the reduction of management-worker conflict, the enhancement of employee productivity, the betterment of employee morale, etc., in the 40 years during which they have addressed themselves to these and related problems.)

If management is to cope successfully with problems of this character, it must revise some of its values as they relate to human nature; specifically, it must face the additional facts that:

1.  Actually or potentially at least one-fifth of their employees are or will be victims to some degree of mental disorder, deterioration, or deficit. (It is not one-third because the more acutely ill or deficient are not employable.)
2.  Only in rare instances does the sufferer from mental illness

or deficiency have any awareness that there is anything wrong with *him*. It is always the people and things of his environment which are out of kilter—he distorts his environment to conform to *his* needs.

3. Attitudes of people do change, but these changes are the result of conditions over which it is very difficult, if not impossible, for an outsider to exercise any control. In short, efforts to shape attitudes by counseling, admonitions, formal training, or public or employee relations activities are rarely effective. (There may have been a change in attitudes, but were they produced by the program?)

4. Anxiety and insecurity are endemic in America (next to antibiotics, more tranquilizers are sold—160 million prescriptions are filled annually—than any other type of drug).

5. Although they are not always aware of it, the basic needs of many people who find themselves in a business organization, especially a large one, are for *security, certainty,* and a *predictable future.* It is when they do not find this that trouble starts.

Most important of all, it must be remembered that with the exception of some entrepreneur managers of growth companies, or the independent professional man, nearly all persons who work for wages exhibit to some degree the passivity-dependence syndrome. (Since in the prevailing value system, passivity-dependence is equated with weakness, only the acutely passive and submissive are aware of these tendencies in themselves and even they are prone to rationalize these characteristics in themselves.) The fact remains, however, that dependence with its corollary, anxiety, is almost universal in business and industry (as evidenced in many instances by the vigor with which it is denied). Unless the ubiquitousness of anxiety is recognized for what it is: the nuclear problem of interpersonal relations in business and industry, little or no progress can be made. In addition, allowance must be made for the fact, as pointed out above, that many of the values held by those who are grappling with industry's personnel and industrial relations problems are completely naive, innocent, and lacking in empirical psychiatric substantiation. In consequence, the methods employed to attack these problems are not only ineffective but are often even harmful as well.

## MANAGEMENT
## CREATES THE PROBLEM

If management is to approach its problems of mental hygiene constructively, it must accept the fact that many of them are of its own (albeit unintentional) creation. This is because it has failed to recognize most or all of the following psychological facts of business organization.

It must also be recognized that a business organization requires quite widely differing kinds of people in order to function effectively. The types are:

1. An entrepreneur (usually only one); a risk taker; a decision maker; a tough-minded realist.
2. A group of administrators to carry out the entrepreneur's policies.
3. A staff of technicians and supervisors.
4. Hourly-rated plant, office, and sales personnel to get the job done.

Success at one level or in one type of work does not guarantee success in another. Wrong placement (initially or through promotion) may subject the incumbent to intolerable job pressures. These can arouse latent mental upsets or exacerbate existing ones (e.g., one employee needs a completely structured job; another cannot tolerate it). Incompetent, weak, or incompatible supervision may have the same effect as poor placement. An intolerable (emotionally unhygienic) work environment, particularly one with no challenge or opportunity for self-realization may also create tensions due to frustration, boredom, and monotony. (Again, what one employee finds challenging, another may find very distasteful.) Fortunately, most people, even some who are mildly ill mentally, have a surprising capacity to adapt to jobs for which they are not well suited and to supervision which is less than competent or compatible. (Otherwise, conflict and mental breakdowns would be rampant.)

The key to the minimization of mental health problems in industry is to be found in a pluralistic approach to staffing the organization and dealing with the employees. All new employees or those considered for promotion must be carefully evaluated for:
1. Technical competence.
2. "Will-do" qualifications (stability, industry, loyalty, self-reliance, etc.).
3. Evidence of existing or latent mental as well as physical health problems.
4. Probable compatibility with their superiors.

All present executive, supervisory, and technical employees and "problem" cases at the hourly-rated level should be carefully appraised using patterned merit review techniques to ascertain:
1. Their technical or "can do" competence in terms of the requirements of their jobs.
2. Their qualifications in the "will do" area vis-a-vis their jobs.
3. The extent to which they are personally compatible with their superiors.
4. The extent to which they give evidence of being "problems," and why they are thus classed.

The significant thing for management to remember is that whenever an employee becomes a "problem," no matter how bizarre, contentious, or flagrantly aggressive his behavior, he must be viewed as a "sick" person—not one to be admonished or threatened. (Probably the worst offense committed against employees in industry today is the practice of referring the mentally ill for "counseling" to well-meaning but technically naive amateurs—e.g., supervisors, personnel staff members, the company physician who has had no psychiatric training, or the clergy. If the employee has a heart attack, he is sent to a heart specialist; if he begins to exhibit mental symptoms, all too often all he receives is censure from his superior or "counseling.")

## GUIDELINES FOR ALLEVIATION

If industry is to cope effectively with the mental health problems which confront it, it must face them systematically and realistically. The first fact it must face is that *the employer cannot and should not attempt therapy for those of his people who exhibit evidences of mental inadequacy or illness.* There are several reasons for this:

1. The employer has no more responsibility for the treatment of the *mentally* ill than he has for the treatment of *organic* conditions which are not work induced.
2. Many mental illnesses are very refractory and stubborn; their treatment is very costly and time consuming. Few company medical departments are qualified or equipped to treat such cases and psychiatrists are in short supply. Outside facilities are much better suited to this type of therapy.
3. Any effort to treat even mild mental disorders by non-technically trained personnel is extremely dangerous both to the employer and to the employee. Many mental disorders are very subtle and their manifestations are extremely Byzantine in their symptomology. Hence, only the skilled technician can diagnose them. Amateur diagnoses and treatment, on the other hand, may do irreparable harm. (The worst feature of such inept handling is the fact that the best intended treatment will often produce the worst consequences.)

The second fact which management must face is the importance of prophylaxis in coping with mental illness. Industry can spare itself (and society) a great deal of trouble if it will use ordinary common sense in two areas of personnel administration:

1. *Initial selection:* Many seriously retarded, maladjusted, emotionally immature, and even seriously disturbed persons apply for positions. While not all are obviously potential "problems," a brief test of intelligence, a review of their previous school, service, and employment records, together with personal or telephone checks with previous

employers, will almost certainly reveal significantly aberrant behavior. Regardless of the applicant's explanations and promises to reform, *it is what he has done in the past which is most significant in diagnosing what he will do in the future,* i.e., the extent to which he is likely to become a "problem." (Unfortunately, many of these mental cases do not learn from their mistakes; instead they repeat them again.) It is doing neither the individual, the employer, nor society a favor to employ persons who are clearly potential "problems." It is even possible, in some instances, that employment and the stresses to which it subjects the individual may exacerbate his condition. Nor is he the only sufferer: One mentally deficient or aberrant employee can create many difficulties for his fellow workers, even occasionally for the public.

2.  *Proper placement:* Granting that only those are employed who have at least minimal mental competence and are not seriously immature or maladjusted emotionally, it is still important that everyone hired be reasonably properly *placed.* By this is meant, an effort must be made to *match* the incumbent and the job at least to a reasonable degree in terms of his skills, his level of intelligence, his cultural and educational status, his needs, his motivations and life goals, and his temperament. Furthermore, it must be recognized that *over-qualification* for a job is as deleterious as *underqualification.* If the incumbent is overqualified, he is almost certain to become frustrated (and hence hostile); if he is underqualified, he will inevitably be anxious, insecure, and feel inadequate (with consequent defensiveness and resentments directed against his employer and possibly the development of any of a variety of psychogenic symptoms).

Proper *placement* is not solely a matter of matching the technical and temperamental aspects of incumbent and job: Of equal importance is the insurance that superior and subordinate are *compatible.* If the relationship is not close (the subordinate is simply one of many in a large department), this factor is not too important. It is where the relationship is intimate as in the higher echelons of management (superior and assistant or assistant to) that the character of the relationship becomes critical. To insure compatibility, it is essential that the subordinate:

a.  Conform to his superior's expectations technically.
b.  Meet his superior's expectations socially and culturally.
c.  Be acceptable to his superior personally.
d.  Not be so well qualified that he is a threat to his superior's job security. [Most executives prefer weaker subordinates because they are no threats and they are easier to control (1).]

Where incompatibility exists, both superior and subordinate are under tension: the superior because he often fears his subordinate; the subordinate because he may feel frustrated or because he does not trust his superior. Such tensions often create "problem" relationships and exacerbate tendencies toward mental illness.

The third fact which management must face is the employee's desperate need for security and structure. (This includes most, if not all, members of top management.) As already pointed out, anxiety is endemic in industry. Nothing creates hostility and leads to conflict to a greater extent than does anxiety. If the employees feel threatened in any way, no matter what their positions in the enterprise, their reactions will be either those of "fight" or "flight." As has been found by the study of inmates of mental hospitals, those who are of lower intelligence and come from lower socioeconomic levels tend to react more often to the anxieties and other tensions to which they are subjected by psychotic breaks (fight reactions) than do the more intelligent and better situated economically and socially. These latter (who usually include members of middle and top management) are more prone to react to their anxieties by developing neuroses (flight reactions). Thus, as is regularly the case, plant-level disputes are prone to erupt into violence, often senseless, while members of management turn their aggressions inward. They are the ones who develop psychogenic disorders (ulcers, allergies, hypochondriasis, overeating, etc.), take flight into the bottle or into compulsive random activity, become chronic worriers, or manifest other clearly neurotic symptoms.

The key to these latter conditions, regardless of the level of the employee's position in the enterprise, is the fact that his work assignment is provoking intolerable anxieties in him. These usually come as a result of:

1. The company's failure to provide him with a strong, compatible superior (instead, the latter may be weak, incompetent, vindictive, punitive, unreliable, and authoritarian).

2. It has failed to structure and define his duties, responsibilities, and the scope of his authority with the result that he is afloat in a sea of ambiguity: He does not know what his job is, how well he is doing, or where he is going—all of which creates anxiety.

3. His placement (usually by promotion) in a job where he is clearly over his head—and knows it.

4. His placement in a social (work group) environment where he is not accepted (he is not a member of the in-group) because of his age, nationality, race, or religion, his newness in the group, his technical competence or incompetence, his attitudes toward unions, his place of birth (the "damn Yankees" in the South), his educational or cultural status, and similar conditions. When these sources of rejection or of conflict exist, even where the employee is not subjected to open attack, he is deprived of *the support* provided by membership in and acceptance by the in-group. He is, in consequence, to some degree, an outcast, in "Coventry." This may be extremely anxiety provoking.

5. The failure of management and his supervisor to let him know where he stands and the general outlook for the health of the business is not good (all of which affect his job and economic security). If the hourly-rated employee fears a layoff or an executive anticipates demotion or discharge or the outlook for the continuance of the business is poor, widespread anxieties will arise with their related tensions.

Where anxieties and tensions and their resultant hostilities have been aroused, regardless of their sources, they are almost invariably directed toward management. It is always a convenient scapegoat. Most of the labor strife which bedevils industry has its roots in management's failure to note and correct the conditions outlined above. While most labor strife is *rationalized* on economic grounds, its cause is rarely economic or the result of poor working conditions. (This is evidenced by the fact that companies which pay the highest wages, and often have the finest working conditions, also have the most labor trouble.)

The fourth and most important fact for management to recognize is the fact that the "problem" employee now on the job is often either mentally deficient or ill: Regardless of his irresponsibility, inadequacy, or outright provocativeness, he is not a *willful* trouble-maker: he is handicapped or ill: mentally so. In consequence, the sufferer is not to be blamed, admonished, or threatened. Instead, he must be studied and a systematic effort made to get at the causes of his trouble; not by involved psychiatric analysis but by ascertaining simply:

1. How well he is qualified technically to fit his job.
2. How competent and compatible is his superior with him.
3. How well he knows what his job is, i.e., how well is it structured for him.
4. The extent to which he may be "over his head" on his job in terms of its leadership and decision making demands.
5. How well he is accepted by his peers, subordinates, customers, etc.
6. How clearly and frequently he has been told how well he is doing.
7. How consistent are his values with those of his superior, associates, and subordinates?
8. What evidences are there of mental defect (difficulties in learning, etc.)?
9. What evidences are there of epileptic conditions (observed "black outs," excessive accidents, etc.)?

10. What evidences are there of senile conditions (confusion, disorientation, faulty memory, and other signs that the individual is "failing")?

11. What evidence is there that the employee is reacting to his anxieties with overt symptoms (chronic indecision, worrying, panicking in emergencies, etc.)?

12. What evidence is there that the employee is denying his anxieties by manifesting "fight" reactions (insubordination, defensiveness, disruptive behavior, chronic complaints, charges of persecution, etc.)?

13. What evidence is there that the individual is taking flight from his anxieties by compulsive overwork, alcoholism, overeating, needless travel, overpreoccupation with detail, excessive absenteeism, and any of an assortment of psychogenic (conversion) disorders such as gastrointestinal upsets, allergies, asthma, etc.?

14. What evidence is there that the employee has or is beginning to lose touch with reality (does he make and repeat gross errors in judgment; is he unreasonably erratic and bizarre in his manner and appearance; does he exhibit fixed ideas which conflict with logic and the facts of his environment, etc?

## REMEDIAL STEPS

If this review of the employee's behavior indicates that something is seriously amiss, the first remedial step is to obtain complete and detailed information about his case from his superiors, his associates, and others who are familiar with the total situation. Next, the individual is encouraged to tell his story and present his problems at whatever length he desires. If indicated, psychological tests and a physical examination should be made. If there is reason to do so, the employee's home should be visited and his family invited to present their version of his problems. When these data are collated, it should not be too difficult, on a common sense basis, to determine the extent to which the roots of the trouble lie in:

1. Mental deficit.
2. Physical illness or defect.
3. Job displacement.
4. Emotional maladjustment or mental illness.

Ideally, a clinical psychologist or psychiatrist should be called in to evaluate the data and make a diagnosis and prognosis and prescribe the handling to be given the employee. In practice, relatively few clinical psychologists are available (and many of these know little of industrial conditions or problems) and in the entire U.S. there are currently no more than one dozen practicing industrial psychiatrists. Practically no qualified clinical psychologists and no industrial psychiatrists are to be found outside of the major urban areas. Unfortunately, moreover, as of today relatively few industrial physicians are trained and oriented in clinical psychological or psychiatric theory. In consequence, at least as far as industry is concerned, it is probable that at least 90% of the sufferers from mental deficit, epilepsy, senility, emotional maladjustment, and mental illness will be dependent upon largely untrained and psychologically and psychiatrically unsophisticated personnel to deal with their needs and problems. It is for this reason that the outlook for any substantial improvement in the problem and costs of mental illness and related conditions in industry in the foreseeable future is dim. It is not that remedial techniques are lacking; there are simply not enough trained practitioners.

About all that can be accomplished is to give members of top management and those engaged in personnel and industrial relations work insight into the principal facets of the problem and a recognition of the fallaciousness and futility of:

1. Attempts to change people to facilitate their adaptation to their jobs (by admonition, "counseling," or other than skill training).
2. Attempts to alter employee value systems.
3. Attempts to "reason with" and thereby influence the mentally deficient, the senile, or the mentally disturbed.

If constructive steps are to be taken in industry to cope

with problems of mental deficit or illness, it must be recognized that, as previously pointed out, the greatest hope and the first step must lie in *prophylaxis*. This includes:

1. Careful selection of all new employees to exclude potential "problems."

2. Thoughtful placement of all employees (whether hired from the outside or promoted from within) *to adapt their environments to them (the employees) rather than to force them to fit a job for which they are not suited*.

3. The provision of sufficient job structure and strong, sympathetic, and supportive supervision to keep the employees' anxieties at a minimum. (There must be no ambiguity about the nature of their jobs, there must be a minimum of risk-taking decision-making required, and supervision must provide additional structure and support.)

4. Insurance that there is a reasonable degree of *homogeneity of values* among employees at all levels to insure social cohesiveness and a minimal degree of conflict among employees and employee groups. (Value conflicts tend to lead to the exclusion of the individual from the society of his peers. This can be extremely threatening and anxiety provoking because it deprives the individual of the support and approbation of the members of his group.)

5. Provision of a *psychologically hygienic* job environment, i.e., one which offers:

a. Tolerable working conditions.

b. Acceptable security on the job (here a union may make a very valuable contribution).

c. Outlets for grievances and frustrations (here also a union may be useful).

d. Adequate challenge.

e. Recognition for superior performance.

f. Periodic reviews of the employees' job performance (to let them know where they stand—thus minimizing their anxieties).

g. Information at intervals about the company's business outlook (thus allaying anxieties about job security).

The major portion of the "problem" cases which plague business and industry are not those whose sources are *organic* mental deficit, epilepsy, senility, etc.). It is estimated that at least 80% of the conditions which cause employees to become "problems" are *functional disorders* (emotional immaturity, the neuroses, and borderline and sometimes fullblooming psychoses). These are the same kinds of illnesses which populate all mental institutions (the sufferers differ in the acuteness of their illnesses—in their ability to adapt to their environments—but *qualitatively* their illnesses are highly similar). This provides a clue to a means for the reduction of much maladjustment and internal conflict in industry (e.g., management-labor strife and internecine squabbles within the enterprise).

## HELP VIA TRANQUILIZERS

A promising key to the handling of many "problem" cases may lie in chemotherapy; specifically, in *the wider and more systematic use of tranquilizers.* Their introduction as therapeutic agents in mental hospitals has not only brought about a dramatic reduction in their populations, but they have revolutionized the modes of treatment employed. (Camisoles, continuous baths, and Scotch douches are rarely used and lobotomies are now largely passé.) This is because tranquilizers have made even severely disturbed patients more tractable and readily accessible to therapy. Of greater value is the fact that many patients can now be quickly paroled who previously would have had to be institutionalized for long periods. No one knows exactly how tranquilizers accomplish the improvement they induce; all that can be said is that they often bring about dramatic improvement in cases which otherwise would be regarded as hopeless.

On the assumption that the majority, if not nearly all of the functional mental illnesses which afflict employees, are in part or wholly symptomatic of anxiety, it is reasonable to expect that tranquilizers might well have a favorable therapeutic effect on these cases. (Already, as stated above, thousands of persons are using tranquilizers, with and without prescriptions. Many of these are doubtless employed in industry. Hence, they are, in all probability, already having some effect. It is only because no controlled studies of their influence have been made that there is no general awareness of the magnitude of their potential contribution.)

Much of the conflict encountered in industry and a large proportion of the individual job failures are directly attributable to personal or group insecurity and the manifestations of the symbiotic or dependency syndrome (indecisiveness, inadequacy, autocracy, etc.), together with associated "fight" or "flight" symptoms. It is almost certain that tranquilizers will have a beneficial effect in many emotionally toned relationships. For example, if both parties to a labor negotiation session (normally fraught with marked anxieties and corollary hostilities on both sides) had received a supply of tranquilizers in advance of the meeting, it is probable that the result would be an expedited and more rational settlement of such differences as might arise. It is likewise possible that the harried and harassed executive who has been promoted over his head and thus finds himself in a hell of panic, is indecisive, and anticipates disaster when faced with even a minor decision, could also be appreciably helped. Not only will his anxieties be diminished with a corresponding dimiuntion of the mental symptoms to which they give rise, *but the decisions he does make will be sounder and more clearly reasoned* since they will not be made in a climate of panic.

I do not recommend that tranquilizers be made as available to employees as salt tablets. They should be dispensed only by the company medical department or another qualified physician.

The advantage of medication with tranquilizers lies in the fact that they can be administered by *any* physician, regardless of his competence in the field of psychiatry. While their widespread use as prophylactics to lessen the impact of mental disorder in industry will doubtless be resisted (unions will see their use as some Byzantine scheme of management's to exploit their members), and there may be some potentially troublesome side effects (drowsiness, etc.), their judicious use should, nevertheless, bring about more good than harm.

## CONCLUSION

Mental illness in the aggregate and in industry in particular constitutes one of society's most costly and universally devastating problems. It is probably responsible for more cost, waste of resources, and human misery than any other single condition which afflicts mankind. Because of its peculiar nature (its tendency to warp and distort men's perception and awareness of the problem itself), progress in coping with it has been slow, particularly as it relates to industry. Nor is it likely that there will be any sudden and dramatic breakthrough in the foreseeable future. The problem is too complex and its roots lie too deeply buried in the prevailing culture.

Taking everything into account, *the greatest hope for improvement appears to lie in education.* Just as humanity has learned no longer to place its faith in witch doctors and nostrums in the field of medicine, the public, members of management, and the working population can gain insights which will have prophylactic if not directly therapeutic value. Progress will be slow, but with problems of this magnitude, even infinitesimal improvements are worthwhile. In the meantime, the wider the dissemination of an awareness of the nature and causes of mental illnesses and their symptomology, the more rapid will be the progress toward the conquering of this, one of the worst, albeit unrecognized, scourges faced by mankind.

## REFERENCE

1. Ward, Lewis B., "Do executives prefer weak subordinates?," *Harvard Business Review,* Sept.–Oct. 1961.

# 2. DEALING WITH EMOTIONAL DISTURBANCES IN INDUSTRY

**Samuel B. Kutash, Ph.D.**

The author is Chief, Psychology Service, Veterans Administration Hospital, East Orange, New Jersey.

In recent years, industry and society in general have been exposed to an imposing avalanche of magazine articles, books, and pamphlets—all heavily freighted with psychological and psychiatric terminology—about emotional disorders and mental illness. Needless to say, a host of panaceas for solving the complex and challenging problems of human relationships and human behavior have been offered. For the industrial personnel administrator, who is on the "firing" line as well as the hiring line—and, indeed, for managers and supervisors in general—it is often difficult to resist the temptation to seize on ready-made psychological formulas for dealing with interpersonal situations in industry, and particularly with the so-called problem employee. At times, however, none of these psychological rules of thumb or psychiatric gimmicks seems to work, and a return to a purely rational, common-sense approach is indicated. Some companies have actually employed or used on a consulting basis psychologists and/or psychiatrists in connection with problem employees and have had results varying from the most satisfying to the most disheartening.

26

## MENTAL HEALTH IN INDUSTRY

One of the positive results of the general increase in know-ledge about dynamic clinical psychology and psychiatry has been greater recognition on the part of people in management, labor relations, personnel work, and employee adjustment services of the personality aspects of job adjustment and the importance of the total personality of each employee. A negative result has been occasional instances of undue anxiety on the part of personnel administrators and managements about people with emotional problems, and of unnecessary rejection of many individuals for jobs or promotions when they could actually have been assets of distinct value to the job and the company. *Not all people with anxieties and emotional disturbances are problem employees, and not all problem employees are emotionally disordered.* Industrial psychodiagnosis is a difficult, highly professional technical art and skill, requiring years of psychological and psychiatric training as well as thorough orientation in the problems of modern industry and management. The industrial psychodiagnostician is indeed a specialist.

Many companies have had unsatisfactory experiences with psychological and psychiatric consultations concerning problem employees because the practitioners involved, though otherwise perfectly well qualified, lacked sufficient experience with industrial cases. Other companies have had to contend with practitioners who were not sufficiently trained in psychology, including some who put themselves forth as psychologists after a few courses in a college or university. A fully trained clinical psychologist equipped to diagnose emotional disturbances holds a doctoral degree from a university approved by the American Psychological Association and has had a minimum of two years of supervised internship as well as three additional years of intensive experience. He can then, by passing appropriate examinations in diagnosis, psychotherapy, research, and professional problems of practice, become a diplomate of the American Board of Examiners in Professional Psychology. He is also likely to be a Fellow in Clinical Psychology of the American Psychological Association. As such fully trained professional clinical psychologists and psychiatrists become more intimately involved and concerned with the human problems in industry, we can expect increasingly good results.

Mental health in industry is of central importance not only to our productive capacity as a nation but to our survival as integrated, happy individuals in the Atomic Age. Research on emotional disturbance and mental illness has revealed that all of the major psychogenic disorders—neurosis, functional psychosis, and personality maladjustment—are intimately related to job adjustment, work motivation, and job satisfaction. Those who diagnose and treat these conditions know that every patient is, has been, will be, or should be in a job. More often than not, the early or "prodromal" signs—or perhaps the underlying bases for the difficulty in living happily—become evident in some form on the job, where the employee spends a major portion of his waking life. Very few people are completely without mental or emotional blemishes. Some of these emotional disturbances interfere markedly with an employee's productivity and job adjustment, while other types do not interfere with work performance at all, and may even increase an employee's efficiency in certain jobs. As we shall see, degree of personality disturbance is *not* directly related to job effectiveness.

It is a well-known fact that productive work is a major psychological need of most people. As Carlyle said in *Past and Present,* "Older than all preached Gospels was this unpreached, inarticulate but ineradicable, forever-enduring Gospel: work, and therein well-being." Some of the most frequent immediate precipitants of anxiety attacks, emotional disturbance, or personality decompensation are change in the work situation, the frustration of psychologically inappropriate work, and confrontation with new job requirements and structures which are out of gear psychologically with the employee's self-concept, his personality defenses, and his tried-and-true methods of adjustment. Change in the work situation may result from a transfer, a promotion, a demotion, a change in management's attitude toward the job, or a change in supervision. All of us, the mentally healthy as well as the emotionally disturbed, have certain prerequisites for job happiness and adjustment. When these are conscious, the employee, aided by his awareness of them, is usually able to find a niche in which he can satisfy those within his reach and avoid those that thwart him psychologically or are noxious to him. When these prerequisites are unknown to him and are below the level of awareness, however, difficulties can arise. He may develop emotional symptoms when they remain unsatisfied or unconsciously carry out a self-defeating or unrealistic life plan based on a neurotic pattern.

Clinical psychodiagnostic and psychotherapeutic work with problem employees in industry has highlighted certain common psychodynamic problems and has also focused attention on certain paradoxes that can be understood only on a psychological rather than a logical basis. I shall describe some of these problems and paradoxes and illustrate them by referring to actual cases. Wherever the logical approach to a problem fails, it is usually because of an underlying, hidden psychodynamic conflict between conscious and unconscious goals, which must be handled on a psychological or psychotherapeutic basis.

## DISORDERS THAT HELP AND HINDER

In considering the more common emotional problems of employees, it is most important to distinguish between those disorders that decrease efficiency and employability and those that increase efficiency and employability. An example of the first instance is a highly efficient clerk-typist who worked in a typing pool for four years and was considered outstanding for the amount and accuracy of the material she typed. Never absent and having a good health record, Clara, 33 years old, did so well that she was promoted and assigned to work as secretary to the advertising manager of the large publishing firm that employed her. Shortly thereafter she developed severe anxiety attacks, including palpitations of the heart, fears of fainting, dizzy spells, physical exhaustion, difficulty in getting up in the morning, and a variety of hypochondriacal complaints. Repeated medical examiniations were negative, and Clara did not know of anything that bothered her emotionally. She became self-derogatory, self-critical, and depressed, criticizing severely her inability to concentrate on her work and her inaccuracy in taking dictation or typing letters. Yet she had completed a special brush-up shorthand course in preparation for her promotion and had received approbation as one of the best stenographers in the course. The feelings of depression that disturbed her and the fact that tranquilizers did not seem to help eventually led to her referral for psychological help.

A battery of psychodiagnostic tests, including projective techniques such as the Rorschach ink-blot test, revealed that in early childhood Clara had developed an obsessive-compulsive character neurosis. Her compulsive drive for accuracy and precise repetition of routine activities, and her desire for perfection and speed influenced the more personal things in her life, such as love and social relationships. She tried to win people's approval and to please them by rapid completion of perfect work, just as she had always tried to win her father's approval.

This character structure or personality make-up equipped her very well for clerk-typist or clerk-stenographer jobs, but not for her new assignment. The advertising manager was a man who left quite a bit to his secretary. He expected initiative, flexibility, and decisiveness, and he gave her unstructured, nebulous problems to deal with. Such a problem precipitated her first panic attack. He gave her a batch of letters and asked her to prepare answers for his signature. She became very obsessive about the first letter, doing it over four times. She then became upset and went through the same procedure with the other letters, becoming more panicky all the time. When she was not told exactly what to do, she became so indecisive that she ruminated unproductively and went around in circles.

It was clear that Clara was a liability in this type of job because of the personality structure it required. In the matter of therapy, there was a choice. She could be given short-term help while the company arranged to transfer her back to the type of job suited to her personality, or she could be given long-term psychotherapy designed to change her personality structure so that eventually she could not only hold a higher-level job but be happier in her personal life. In the latter course of action, her unconscious desire to please her father would have to be brought to her awareness and her father-fixation broken.

Personality idiosyncrasies can be successfully sublimated in jobs which are performed in a better-than-average manner. For example, unconscious sadistic impulses may be channeled in butchers, surgeons, and prison guards. Similarly, masochistic feelings may be channeled in people in the various "service to others" occupations: dietitians in company restaurants and people in charge of welfare services for employee groups, for example. More rarely, one runs across such a case in an executive assistant who voluntarily bears the brunt of all criticism and lets his boss take the glory. Histrionic, hysterical characters with shifting ego identifications often make good actors or carry on well in positions requiring an exhibitionistic display of emotion or activity in such fields as public relations and promotion. People with unconscious voyeuristic tendencies sometimes make good photographers, detectives, investigators, auditors, and bank examiners, while people with compulsive drives for achievement often make excellent executives.

For some time, attempts to classify people for jobs or positions were based mainly on intelligence level, educational background, aptitudes, motivation, and direct measurement of abilities. To these factors must be added the personality structure and dynamics of the employee, particularly his unconscious tendencies. The most self-sacrificing, efficient, loyal employee I ever examined was the assistant to the manager of a department store. He did fine work until his boss retired and he was called upon to take over the job. This situation activated a latent complex which was built around his fear of not being able to supplant his powerful father.

## THE SUCCESS SYNDROME AND OTHER PROBLEMS

The employee whose degree of emotional disturbance, disabling symptoms, and anxiety are almost directly proportional to his degree of success is a paradox of sorts. The more successful he is, the more emotionally upset he becomes; the less material and promotional progress he makes, the less upset he is. As he goes up the ladder of success, he is eventually threatened by emotional collapse, yet he constantly strives for ever greater advancement.

C. M., a 29-year-old engineer, married and father of a child, had started with a company shortly after graduating from engineering college. In a period of five years, he had increased his annual earnings from $3,500 to more than $20,000. He was referred for psychotherapy by a friend who was the personnel director of another company on the basis of the following symptoms: He developed panicky feelings in the presence of his immediate superior, toward whom he had mixed emotions. He felt that this man was not taking a keen interest in the business, was resting on his laurels, and was unduly critical. He acknowledged that his boss basically had a lot of character and integrity, and that he respected him for this, but he felt "peculiar" and stupid in his presence. He could not dictate in front of his boss and felt as if the office were closing in on him. The more understanding the boss became, the less comfortable the patient felt. He reached the point where he could not stay in the office and spent all of his time in the field. His anxiety attacks finally became intolerable, and he felt compelled to quit the job.

During the course of psychotherapy, it bescame apparent that this young man could be effective only when fighting an uphill battle against odds and stiff competition. Being accepted was threatening to him, and he always had to "gum up the works." His ambitious push came to the front when he was struggling against a superior antagonist; when confronted by a kindly, accepting superior, however, he had extreme feelings of guilt. Too much contact with a paternal figure activated feelings in him that threw him into panic.

Another example of the "success syndrome" is the case of a man who was referred for treatment because he had developed severe phobic fears of a dramatic and disabling nature five months after his promtion  to a top executive position in a large industrial corporation—a position for which he had striven for 12 years. He had panicky feelings when riding the elevator to the floor where his new office was located. He suffered from acrophobia of such severity that he could not take planes for business trips and was afraid to go near the window of his office because of an impulse to jump out. The underlying basis of these symptoms was revealed in part by the first dream he reported to the therapist:

> This took place on the roof of a high building. I found myself on a platform jutting out over the edge of the building. The platform resembled an aircraft carrier. There seemed to be benches for sitting down all around the periphery of the plat-form, but each time I tried to sit down the bench moved precari-ously toward the edge and I was afraid I'd fall over. I looked over the edge of the platform and got woozy, so then I tried to get into the building proper, but the door wouldn't open. There was no way to get off the platform and I was there all alone. I woke up in a cold sweat.

Here was a perfect example of fear of the "dizzy heights"—the feeling of aloneness at the top, the fear of falling, the threatening fact that there was no place to go except down. In short, this man felt too insecure to tolerate success and being on top. Psychotherapy revealed that it all went back to early conflicts related to psychosexual problems.

Many emotional problems among executives are in the category exemplified by the man who has a record of steadily increasing achievement based on a lifelong pattern of activity and much hard work, but who suddenly goes into a depressive phase around the involutional period and begins to feel extremely depressed, suicidal, and guilt-ridden. He shows psychomotor retardation and inability to concentrate on his work and may suffer outbursts of tearful self-recrimination. This patient is often severely ill, and drastic measures may have to be taken to tide him over the period of depression—hospitalization, intensive supportive psychotherapy, and sometimes electric shock treatment. Many of these psychotic depressive episodes are self-limiting, provided the patient is carried over the dangerous suicidal period successfully. After recovery he may return to work and be as efficient and valuable as he was before the illness.

Other executives develop paranoid conditions in which they have exaggerated suspicions that others are out to get their jobs. They become intolerant of their most loyal subordinates and inadvertently sacrifice the company's welfare to preserve their seemingly threatened status. This is part of a not-too-rare serious psychiatric illness of later life.

## THE PERSONAL ROOTS OF WORK PROBLEMS

In attempting to provide psychotherapeutic aid to a person in industry who is handicapped in his job by his personality, we must consider his total life situation. Often, the cause of the difficulty lies not in the work situation but in highly personal aspects of the home or family situation. Such cases are best handled by referral to private practitioners outside of the work situation, so that the problems can be treated on a confidential basis. For example, numerous instances of job maladjustment involve such problems as marital difficulties, psychosexual disorders, alcoholism, and personal bereavement. These matters cannot possibly be handled successfully within the company itself, even if psychological counselors or psychiatrists are employed on a full-time basis.

One such case involved an industrial relations executive of a well-known firm. This man, T. L., developed some very spectacular symptoms, which started with a gradually increasing difficulty in concentrating on his work and went on to fear of imminent collapse and panic at the sound of a siren. He was a devoted, self-sacrificing perfectionist who put in many hours of overtime, was unusually conscientious, and yet always felt that he was failing in his job. He had a never-ending fear of impending disaster, including fantasies of making a mistake and getting fired, although his work was considered satisfactory.

T. L. considered himself unable to handle some of the problems in his job and felt powerless to do anything about this deficiency. His feelings of inferiority were quite marked: When called by a superior for a conference, he always felt that he was going to be excoriated for doing something wrong, whereas usually only routine matters were discussed. What bothered him most were obsessive thoughts which distracted him from his work, and the fact that things were piling up; he felt that he would be unable ever to catch up unless he could clear up his emotional unrest. Having previously taken some psychology courses, he sought help "in order to prevent a catastrophe," as he put it. He feared that he might be "going crazy" because of his "peculiar thoughts."

After the initial psychotherapeutic sessions, T. L. confided with great shame and anxiety that he was partially sexually impotent, seeming to have lost interest in his attractive wife. He was of the Catholic faith, 30 years old, and the father of three young children. He was constantly obsessed with sexual thoughts and berated himself because he "lusted for other women," yet when he attempted intercourse with his wife during the safe period it was unsatisfactory. He began to think of himself as inadequate and "queer."

In addition, he had the peculiar symptom of going into a panic every time he heard a siren and feeling compelled to run home—no matter where he was or what he was doing—in order to be with his wife and children. He had the phobic fear that he would be killed by an atomic bomb before he could go to confession, and that he would burn in Hell because he would not have confessed his lustful thoughts; to counteract this threat he went to confession as often as possible. He continued to have these fears even though he knew that we were not at war and that it was unlikely that the siren meant an atomic attack. During the middle of the fifth psychotherapy session, a fire engine happened to pass by the office, with its siren sounding, and he immediately grabbed his hat and ran home before I could stop him. In a later session, he heard a siren again about 10 minutes before the end of the hour, but this time I took his hat and coat and urged him forcefully to sit down and discuss the matter. He became quite panicky—beads of perspiration ran down his face, and he became pale and extremely jittery.

This "fear of the atomic bomb" complex was relieved only after certain personal data had been revealed. The patient, it seemed, had at an early age been interested in entering the priesthood and had attended a parochial school. During adolescence he gave up this plan, much to the disappointment of his mother, and even turned against the Church. While serving with the army, he saw much action. During a bombing on the battlefield in which many of his buddies were killed, he got down on his knees and prayed. He vowed that if he got out alive he would never marry and would return to the Church and study for the priesthood. This "chastity vow" was forgotten after he returned home safely and was not recalled until the therapy session, in which he once more became conscious of it. Through his impotence, he had been unconsciously carrying out the chastity vow and punishing himself through his symptoms for his previous violation of it. The phobic fear of the atomic bomb proved to be really a fear of the wrath of God—of sudden drastic punishment from Heaven. He had felt compelled to be with his wife and children to demonstrate that he was not having "lustful" thoughts. There were, of course, other complications, but these highlights bring out the point that highly personal problems—which can be brought out only in private, confidential sessions—are often at the root of job difficulties.

## THERAPEUTIC ECONOMY
## FOR INDUSTRY

Men of management and industry often ask the pertinent question of whether psychotherapy must necessarily always take a long time, or whether it is possible to bring about important changes in people with short-term treatment. Largely in response to the needs of industry, attempts have been made to handle patients on a short-term basis. We have found it possible to achieve fully satisfactory results by making modifications in methods of psychodiagnostic exploration, by limiting therapeutic goals, and by streamlining the technical tools of therapy—in a sense, retooling. We now practice "therapeutic economy" by aiming at an early goal of vocational adjustment so that the patient can achieve a satisfactory work experience as soon as possible. In some cases, in the course of achieving this goal, dramatic fundamental personality changes and restructuring take place. In other cases, the patient and therapist have the choice, as a result of favorable results thus far, of deciding whether or not to undertake long-term intensive psychotherapy or psychoanalysis to achieve more lasting and far-reaching satisfactions in life, including increased vocational, social, sexual, and personal happiness. Relatively few patients need such an extensive personality overhauling; many can stop treatment at the point of re-establishing their creative work possibilities, which in turn produces other changes in "chain reaction" fashion.

## CONCLUSION

Psychologists have learned that satisfactory work experience is often the greatest force in mobilizing emotional energies to meet creative challenges, and that resolving emotional conflicts concerning work and vocation is among the most rewarding methods of healing emotional illness. Ideally, no man who has shown his worth in productive work should be cast out when transitory emotional disorder throws him out of gear. We must repair our human resources as well as our machines. This approach will encourage each employee to seek help for those emotional conflicts which he cannot solve alone and will provide industry and professional psychology and psychiatry with the knowledge needed to prevent irreparable emotional breakdown.

# 3. EMPLOYMENT AND MENTAL ILLNESS

Nyla J. Cole, M.D., Dixie Covey, M.A.,
Richard L. Kapsa, M.D., and C. H. Hardin Branch, M.D.

In the past decade, treating a patient within his social setting has become the new look in psychiatry. To this end, state institutions have been progressively decentralized and are being replaced by community-based systems of care—with the emergence of day and night hospitals, halfway houses, family therapy, and so forth. These changes are motivated by a growing conviction that the degree of recovery from a mental illness will be enhanced if the patient's ties to the everyday realities of living are maintained as much as possible. This shift in treatment philosophy has naturally led to an increasing interest in the community practices and attitudes that influence adjustment (5), especially the social factors that enhance or deter patients' functioning within their capabilities. In this frame of reference, adequate job opportunities for the mentally ill have become a deserving topic of concern.

Actually we have little information about the vocational

This project was conducted by the Department of Psychiatry at the University Medical Center, University of Utah, Salt Lake City, Utah. This publication and previous publications have been supported by the Research Foundation of the National Association for Mental Health and were made possible largely by contributions from the estate of Mr. H. C. Coleman of Pennsylvania.

The authors here thank the staff of the United States Employment Service, Salt Lake City, Utah, and the employers interviewed for their kind collaboration with the research team.

experiences of mental patients. Recent exploratory research does suggest, however, that business attitudes may be more flexible than we have assumed. For example, from a telephone survey conducted in 1960, Bieliauskas and Wolfe found that only 8% of the employers in both large (1) and small (8) firms refused to consider hiring such people. Olshansky (4), utilizing personal interviews, indicated similar results, with 25% refusal. While one might doubt the validity of expressed attitudes over actual practices, Landy and Griffith (3) recently tested positive responses by requesting job placement, with greater than 50% success; this report, however, was not based on a random sample.

While these results may seem to give grounds for some optimism about the job outlook for ex-patients, their predictive usefulness in a practical situation is clouded by certain limitations. Research on employment practices has usually been conducted by asking samples of businessmen whether they "would hire" or "have hired ex-mental patients." In the first place, such questions beg for the socially appropriate affirmative answer. In the second place, this approach deals with the mentally ill population as a stereotype and allows no room for the expression of social variance in defining this broad diagnostic group; yet the Star survey showed that one can reasonably expect hiring practices to vary according to individual definitions. Third, while the assumption is made that people generally admit their psychiatric history, it is probable that most avoid giving this information (4, 7, 8). In practice, then, employers usually evaluate a job candidate without knowledge of the psychiatric label and make hiring judgments on other bases: e.g., job skills, observable personal behavior during an interview, and so forth.

With these thoughts in mind, the study to be reported here was designed to provide some information about the hiring practices of the business world. A series of questions was explored. Given job applicants who display various types of personality difficulties, which ones will probably be hired and which will not? Which ones will be identified as mentally ill? Are there significant interrelationships between such identification and hiring judgments? And what is mental illness, as far as the businessman is concerned?

## PROCEDURE

The data in this study are based on the statements of a sample of 67 employers.[1] The hiring official of each business was personally interviewed with a standardized protocol. Fifteen personality descriptions, printed on individual cards, were presented to the interviewees as potential employees, each specified as having equal job training and skill. Each vignette was designed to represent the behavioral symptoms of a specific psychiatric problem but *no mention* of this fact was made to the employer. These descriptions are reproduced in Appendix A. The employer was requested to sort all the cards in response to each of the following questions, in this order of presentation:

1.  Which ones would you hire?
2.  Assuming all these men were currently working for you, which ones would you expect to (a) promote; (b) keep; (c) replace when possible; or (d) fire immediately?
3.  Which ones are normal and which are not normal?
4.  Which ones are mentally ill?

[1]The 67 employers represent the combination of two sample groups. One was obtained from a random sampling system supplied by the Utah State Employment Service and is composed of 58 employers in Salt Lake County businesses; this first sample, originally 94, was reduced by 10 refusals, 10 listed businesses which had no employees, 14 firms no longer in existence, and 3 listed divisions of a single company combined because of centralized management. Because the authors were interested in whether unionized businesses might follow different hiring policies, an additional random sample of 10 companies (one refusal) was drawn from a listing of all union companies in the county. Since separate analyses of the two groups indicated no significant differences in their responses, the two samples were then combined. The size of the firms are: 34 employed fewer than 10 people; 16 had 11 to 50 workers; 17, more than 51. In terms of education, 23 hiring officials had no more than high school education; the remainder, some college education or more.

5. How do the persons you have called "not normal" differ from being "normal" or "mentally ill"? What do you mean when you use the term *mental illness?*

Statistical analysis was done by use of appropriate techniques and computation of percentages.

For clarity of presentation the results are presented under two general topic headings:

I.  Employment Judgments and Employer Diagnosis.
II. Employer Definitions of Mental Illness.

## RESULTS

### I. Employment Judgments and Employer Diagnosis

Of the 15 psychiatric problems portrayed as job applicants, the respondents hired a total of 29%. The relative standings of the individual vignettes are shown in Figure 1. As one might expect, persons whose profiles represented the more severe functional disorders were rarely employed; the simple schizophrenic is last on the list: only 6% hired. Character problems involving acting out against others appear next in unpopularity: e.g., antisocial reaction, 16%; dyssocial reaction, 24% hired. The more acceptable people are those whose emotional difficulties distressed primarily the patient: e.g., passive-dependent personality; 70%; phobic reaction, 57%.

While more severe standards operate in hiring, attitudes toward keeping an employee appear somewhat more accepting. Although only 29% of the total group were hired, 37% were either kept and/or promoted when specified as currently on the job. Figure 2 shows that the rank order of retention roughly reduplicates the initial hiring judgments, with the passive-dependent again at the top of the list with 85% retention and the simple schizophrenic at the bottom with 4%.

On employer diagnosis, 25% of the patient descriptions were regarded as normal, 36% not normal, and 39% mentally

DIAGNOSIS
PORTRAYED

PERCENT HIRED

0  10 20 30 40 50 60 70 80 90

| | |
|---|---|
| PASSIVE-DEPENDENT | 70% |
| PHOBIC | 57% |
| CYCLOTHYMIC | 45% |
| CONVERSION | 39% |
| SOMATIZATION | 34% |
| DEPRESSIVE | 28% |
| ALCOHOLIC | 25% |
| PASSIVE-AGGRESSIVE | 24% |
| OBSESSIVE-COMPULSIVE | 24% |
| DYSSOCIAL | 24% |
| EXHIBITIONIST | 18% |
| ANTISOCIAL | 16% |
| CHRONIC UNDIFFERENTIATED SCHIZOPHRENIC | 13% |
| PARANOID SCHIZOPHRENIA | 10% |
| SIMPLE SCHIZOPHRENIC | 6% |

**Figure 1:  Percentage of Employers hiring each of 15 personality descriptions illustrating different psychiatric syndromes.**

ill. The differential frequency with which each vignette was placed in these categories is illustrated in Figure 3. In general, there is a positive relationship between the decision (a) to hire; (b) to retain the employee; and (c) to label the person described as normal. Conversely, comparison of Figure 1 and Figure 2 with Figure 3 indicates that negative employment judgments roughly parallel the label of mental illness. On an individual basis, using the average distribution of responses as the standard, the passive-dependent personality, who was predominantly hired and also retained, was significantly labeled as normal ($p > .001$). Similarly, patient descriptions which were firmly called mentally ill (schizophrenic reaction, paranoid type, $p > .001$; sexual deviation, exhibitionist, $p > .001$; schizophrenic reaction, simple type, $p > .01$; obsessive compulsive reaction, $p > .01$; schizophrenic reaction, chronic undifferentiated type, $p > .02$) are the same people who received the highest incidence of negative employment ratings.

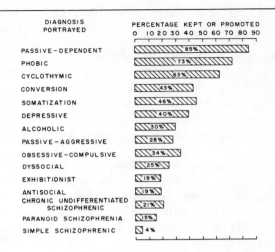

**Figure 2: Percentage of Employers keeping or promoting each of the 15 personality descriptions illustrating different psychiatric syndromes.**

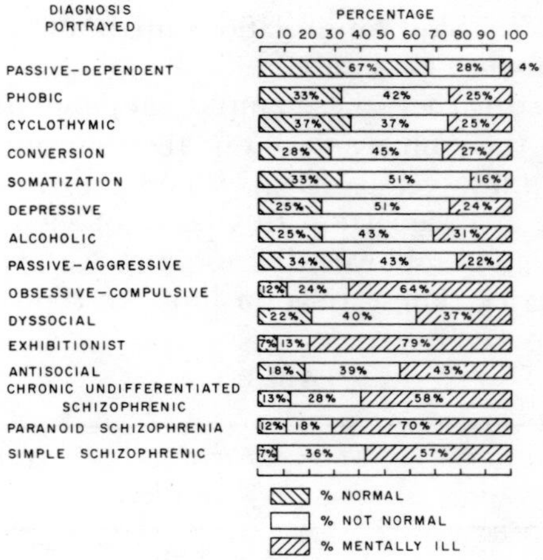

**Figure 3: Percentage called normal, not normal, or mentally ill by employers, in each of 15 personality descriptions illustrating different psychiatric syndromes.**

The amount of education these employers had did influence diagnosis. On the whole, those with a high school education (or less) saw less normality in the vignettes but about the same frequency of mental illness when compared to those with higher level schooling. In some instances, differences in diagnostic labeling appeared between the two groups. However, because of the small numbers involved, the interrelationships between education, diagnosis, and hiring practices cannot be accepted with any confidence and are therefore not reported.

Interrelationships between employment attitudes and diagnosis were next examined. Table 1 shows the differential frequency with which these respondents hired, or planned to keep, each person whom they categorized as normal, not normal, or mentally ill. The normals were hired at a rate significantly greater than those called not normal $(p > .001)$; and, in the same fashion, the not normal group were hired more often than those designated mentally ill $(p > .001)$. Normals have a 1.5 to 1 chance of employment, the ratio reversing for not normals to 1 chance in 3, and for the mentally ill to 1 chance in 7.5. The same relationships hold for the question of job continuance $(p > .001)$.

As indicated earlier, these employers generally set stricter standards in their hiring decisions than on questions of job continuance (29% versus 37%). When the three diagnostic groups were analyzed from this point of view, it was clear that retaining an employee did not improve proportionately in each category. These relationships are reported in Table

TABLE 1

| Employer Diagnosis | Number Hired | | | Number Kept | | |
|---|---|---|---|---|---|---|
| | Yes | No | Ratio | Yes | No | Ratio |
| Normal | 153 | 98 | 1.5: 1 | 177 | 74 | 2.4: 1 |
| Not normal | 94 | 268 | 1: 3 | 134 | 228 | 1: 1.7 |
| Mentally ill | 46 | 346 | 1: 7.5 | 57 | 335 | 1: 5.9 |
| | 293 | 712 | | 368 | 637 | |

TABLE 2

| Employer Diagnosis | Hired (%) | Kept(%) |
|---|---|---|
| Normal | 61 | 71 |
| Not normal | 26 | 37 |
| Mentally ill | 12 | 14 |

2. While both the normals and not normals show at least a 10% improvement in being kept over being hired, the mentally ill group changed little, only 2%.

The internal consistency with which these businessmen made consecutive employment judgments was also compared with the three diagnostic categories. The results are given in Table 3. With the normal and not normal groups, if an employer decided to hire the individual described, he also decided to retain him when that question was raised, with 88% and 87% consistency, respectively. However, with the mentally ill, the internal consistency dropped to 52%, a no better than chance relationship. The unreliable fashion in which consecutive employment judgments were made may reflect the uncertainty and doubt these businessmen felt in trying to evaluate the job potential of this group.

When given a series of vignettes depicting various types of mental illnesses, this sample of employers agreed with our professional meaning of the term 39% of the time, placing 25% of the remainder in a normal, and 36% in the not normal category. Expressed employment judgments are highly related to employer diagnosis. If the individual was considered normal, this was paralleled by a favorable job response. If defined in the employer's mind as not normal, negative employment decisions sharply increased and became the overwhelming response for the group called mentally ill. Next, while decisions to continue employment generally improved over decisions to hire, this improvement does not include the mentally ill category. And last, while these businessmen were highly consistent in making consecutive employment

**TABLE 3**

| Employer Diagnosis | No. Hired | Percentage Hired Who Were Kept |
|---|---|---|
| Normal | 153 | 88 |
| Not normal | 94 | 87 |
| Mentally ill | 46 | 52 |

decisions when evaluating the normal and not normal groups, the internal reliability disappeared in evaluating the mentally ill.

## II. Employer Definitions of Mental Illness

Differences in hiring or retaining were related to employer diagnosis. The bases upon which the categories of not normal and mentally ill were defined were obtained by simply asking employers to give their ideas on how the personalities they called "not normal" differed from being "normal" or "mentally ill." Interjudge agreement on the defining characteristics of the responses to these questions is 96% for mental illness, 94% for not normal. In order of importance, as determined by frequency counts, these characteristics are listed in Table 4.

The outstanding employer attitude toward the "not normal" category was the ease with which he could identify with such problems ("only a quirk," "we've all got something like that") and his hopeful outlook for the future of this group. He saw them as essentially normal but with problems that interfered with the display of their basically sound psychologic structure. Although the businessman recognized their problems and thought they might need some kind of help, their general performance was regarded as relatively acceptable and their prognosis, in time, was good.

The optimistic outlook and the easy understanding exhibited with the "not normal" category were replaced by an uneasy lack of self-confidence which showed in the ideas

**TABLE 4**

| Responses (%) | Defining Characteristics of Not Normal |
|---|---|
| 24 | Qualitatively different than mental illness. |
| 23 | Not pervasive, limited to one area of personality function. |
| 16 | Quantitatively different than mental illness, not as serious. |
| 11 | Too prevalent in general population to be called mental illness. |
| 8 | Doesn't present any serious interference with interpersonal relationships in job performance. |

presented about "mental illness." The inappropriateness or lack of control attributed to the behavior of this group (i.e., ". . . their problem controls them") further increased the distance between the mentally ill and the employer. As one man said, "You get the feeling that when you tell them something, they don't understand what you're saying in the way other people do. . . . You're just never sure, and you have to be careful about giving responsibility in business. With some of them you'd never know exactly what they might think or do."

When making a job decision, the employer naturally chooses the individual he defines as the healthiest. When the worker is recognized as "not normal," employment attitudes become more restrictive, but the businessman still seems realistically to accept the necessity of living with a certain number of problems—so long as he himself can identify with what he considers to be minor and changeable. With his definition of mental illness, however, the employer usually has more severe behavioral disorders in mind, and given this limited definition, his lack of job optimism becomes explicable. This finding might be underscored. These employers seemed to identify mental illness in terms of degree of deviancy from normal personality, largely psychosis, and also associated this interchangeably with negative employment ratings.

## TABLE 5

| Responses (%) | Defining Characteristics of Mental Illness |
|---|---|
| 78 | Irrational or illogical thinking. |
| 37 | Behavior inappropriate, unpredictable. |
| 33 | Qualitatively different symptomatology than the not normal. |
| 28 | Serious interference in job performance and interpersonal relationships. |
| 24 | Immoral, unethical. |
| 24 | Illness more serious, quantitatively different than the not normals. |
| 18 | The problem controls the person. |
| 16 | Needs treatment, hospitalization; prognosis only fair. |
| 12 | Inappropriate emotional reactions. |
| 9 | Problems chronic in nature. |
| 6 | Pervades personality. |

## CONCLUSIONS

If the responses of these employers can be taken as a reasonable index of business attitudes generally, work opportunities for mental patients carry a dismal prognosis. In addition, it would appear that the general formula of mental illness roughly equaling psychosis has changed little since the Star survey (6) some years ago, at least in this population group. Considering the current trend toward advising discharged patients to "discuss their mental illness frankly," one would wonder whether this recommendation is the best course or whether it simply introduces confusion because of the different meaning the label holds for psychiatric and business personnel.

These data also emphasize the problems a psychiatric patient—who needs and *is able* to work—faces in an open, competitive labor market. Most employers seemed unaware of the fact that some of the mentally ill may actually be the better job candidates. For example, the description of an obsessive-compulsive reaction was usually *not* hired (75%); yet, this diagnostic category includes a number of better performers than the run-of-the-mill population. That the burden of a psychiatric problem is not necessarily related to inadequate work performance—and in some instances may be a distinct advantage—remains an area for continuing education efforts.

A group of social circumstances conspire to skew the information an employer has about work and mental illness. Most discharged patients avoid mention of their psychiatric history. Those who are asymptomatic, and by definition more able to perform adequately, are predominantly the ones who remain unidentified to the business world. At the same time the chronic psychotics with disease residua—and variable work capacity—become the mentally ill the employer really knows about; these people then become the yardstick for measuring work performance of the group as a whole. Thus, as time passes, businessmen receive a continuous reinforcement of the idea that mental illness means on-the-job dificulties, despite educational efforts to the contrary.

Most businessmen are sincerely interested in and concerned about their employees. They are practical, empirically schooled in dealing with people and problem situations, and present a realistic approach to managing specific mental illnesses when encountered. Their experiences with acute or chronic adaptive difficulties reflect a tolerance and general know-how that, by and large, are successful. Only when confronted with overwhelming illness (for example, a chronic paranoid psychosis) is their person-to-person common sense impaired. In this situation, the uniform request was for more information on mental illness and for help regarding management on the job. Their desire should prove an asset as we pay more attention to this area of life adjustment.

# APPENDIX A[2]

## Passive-Dependent Personality

Mr. N. was as friendly as a puppy, eager to please and to hang on every word. He was the type who is the first to rush and pick up whatever anyone has dropped. From personal acquaintances the interviewer knew Mr. N. was well liked but considered to be a little henpecked. However, he appeared none the worse for his wife's nagging. Actually he liked his current job and felt it was a good one, but his wife had insisted he apply for this one because he "needed to think of the family and make more effort to better himself." So, Mr. N. applied.

## Phobic Reaction

Mr. P., a shy, slender person, was retiring but likable. He spoke slowly with a slight stammer which disappeared as he felt more at ease. However, he remained nervous throughout the interview and seemed to be trying too hard to make a good impression. When questioned about his nervousness, he admitted he had been having some trouble the past year. In particular, he had found himself unable to stand being enclosed in small places. Because his previous job had been on the eighth story of a large building he had had to quit because he could not stand to ride on the elevator several times a day.

## Cyclothymic Personality

Mr. Q., an amusing fellow who produced an idea a minute, had a huge collection of jokes and funny remarks which made the interview very enjoyable. At one time, as a matter of fact, he had considered being a comedian—but had discarded the interest because of the interference with home life, etc. When asked if he were always in such good spirits, he said, "No, I am really a moody person." He stated that he had had periods of mild depression when he felt irritable and down. Generally, these periods only lasted about a week or so; then he would bounce back and feel on top of the world again. As long as he could remember, these cycles had been repeating themselves. Most of his family were the same type of people.

[2]The diagnostic labels used for these vignettes were assigned by their author (N. J. Cole). To check the adequacy of labeling, four psychiatrically trained personnel were asked to match the personality descriptions to the diagnosis employed.

Interjudge agreement of these four individuals was highly significant ($p < .001$).

## Conversion Reaction

Mr. S., a round-faced, slightly plump, neatly dressed man, had a pleasant, agreeable personality. In five minutes the employer felt more as if he had known him for years. He recounted some of his work background and personal life easily. However, there was one jarring note. On his last job Mr. S. told how he began having fainting spells and periods when his right arm would become paralyzed. He commented blandly that this always seemed to happen when the work load became heavy and he had to work under pressure. When questioned about medical care, Mr. S. said he was seeing a doctor regularly.

## Somatization

Mr. M. was a thin, slow-moving fellow who picked at a mole on his face during the entire interview. His voice was a little whiny. Apparently his wife had sent him to apply for a new job because the salary was better, and "They had so many medical bills." On questioning, Mr. M. said he had had a lot of physical troubles, but the doctors had recently given him a clean bill of health. The illness included headaches and stomach troubles, for which he now took pills. As an additional aid, Mr. M. had put himself on a strict health food diet to build up strength.

## Depressive Reaction

Mr. H. was an unhappy man—his face wore a sad look. He spoke clearly, but very slowly. He seemed preoccupied with worry after worry, whether he could meet the medical bills from his wife's last illness, etc., and said he wondered whether he had done something wrong to cause all his troubles. Although he was currently employed with a good salary, he wanted to change employment because he felt too pressured and worried at night about mistakes he might have made during the day at work. However, he knew that when he checked for mistakes he could not find any. Tears appeared when he talked about his feelings of failure.

## Alcoholic

Mr. B. was a confident fellow with a friendly smile on his face. On his application form he indicated that he had been fired from his previous job for excessive drinking. On questioning, it appeared that about every three months he would not show up for work—sometimes for a day or so, sometimes for a week, because he had been on a drinking binge. He was quite willing to discuss this situation and promised that he would not repeat. He blamed the trouble on his wife's relatives meddling with his marriage.

## Passive-Aggressive Personality

Mr. D. appeared eager for the job. He was friendly and talkative. On his application he stated that he had once been in jail overnight for disturbing the neighborhood during a fight with his wife. Questioning drew out the fact that he had been fired from his previous job—because he argued with his boss when given orders he did not like. Mr. D. recognized he had a violent temper, used to fight at the drop of a hat, but felt he now could control it.

## Obsessive-Compulsive Reaction

Mr. K. was a very self-centered individual, neither friendly nor unfriendly. He spoke in a definite fashion and seemed rather sure of himself. In discussing his relationships with other people he stated he had no dificulty getting along, but preferred to work alone: "Then I can do a good job and do it right." During the interview it was noted that his hands were red and chapped. On questioning he said he might as well admit that he was afraid of dirt and germs, and frequently had to wash his hands because of this—sometimes 30 or 40 times a day. Since this sometimes made him slow with his work he usually stayed late to finish.

## Dyssocial Reaction

Mr. L. should have been a salesman—he was enthusiastic, a "go-getter," a persuasive speaker. After half completing his application card, he was on friendly terms with those around him. He had noted on the card that he had once been arrested. When questioned, he first laughed and said it was for "going through a red light." He then switched his story and earnestly confessed he had overdrawn his checking account on several occasions and someone had pressed charges. "I just can't keep track of the balance . . . that darned guy had my paycheck attached, can you imagine? Oh well, it's over now and my wife keeps the budget. Can you imagine? They called it writing bum checks, and that's not it at all!"

## Sexual Deviation, Exhibitionism

Mr. J. was friendly and easy to talk with—and obviously got along well with others because of his agreeable attitude. It came as a surprise that he had lost his previous job following an arrest with a one-month sentence in the county jail. The story given was that he had been picked up for exposing himslf on a street corner to some woman passing by. There had been no previous occasions of arrest.

## Antisocial Reaction

Mr. R. seemed a little restless during the interview and on a few occasions showed some impatience with the questions he had to answer. In general, however, he appeared to be an amiable, sincere person whose personal charm far out-weighed his occasional bursts of irritability. On his application he left a blank where police records were asked for, but when he found this information would be checked he suddenly became disarmingly frank and admitted he had been involved in armed robbery "a time or two," and mentioned a few lesser offenses. He said he had been on parole for two years with no additional arrests. He blamed "bad breaks" and "rowdy friends" for his past behavior and added that, if people would just quit hounding him about the past and provide him with some "good breaks," he knew he would go straight.

## Schizophrenic Reaction, Chronic Undifferentiated Type

Mr. E. was difficult to interview. He talked very slowly, searched for words, and seemed to lose his train of thought. Occasionally he smiled or laughed aloud for no obvious reason. He indicated that he preferred to work by himself, rather than with a bunch of people. When asked about his previous work, he said he had quit because his back began to hurt him, his head felt funny, and he thought there might be fumes coming from the nearby traffic that was causing the difficulty.

## Schizophrenic Reaction, Paranoid Type

Mr. C. was an intense person. He seemed to have had a fair education—he used a lot of big words, but sometimes he was a little difficult to follow. When asked about his previous job he became angry and stated that his previous boss was unfair, played favorites, and that he had certain "proofs" of it. However, he refused to say what these "proofs" were and clammed up. Mr. C. later frankly stated he did not trust people, and vaguely referred to the idea that the world might be soon coming to an end.

## Schizophrenic Reaction, Simple Type

Mr. I. was a very quiet person. During the interview his mind seemed to be miles away. When questioned, he said he had always been shy around people, even a little afraid of them, and consequently he stayed to himself as much as possible. Much of his time was apparently spent daydreaming. He showed little interest in the job description, asked no questions about it. Just before he left he suddenly announced that he should tell the employer that if he took the job, it would only be a stop-gap, that he was sure he would become famous soon—and would have to quit when his "chance" came.

# REFERENCES

1. Bieliauskas, V. J., Wolfe, H. E. The attitude of industrial employers toward hiring of former state mental hospital patients. *Journal of Clinical Psychology,* 1960, **16**, 256–259.

2. Cole, Nyla J., Brewer, D. L., Allison, R. B., & Branch, C. H. H. Employment characteristics of discharged schizophrenics. *A.M.A. Archives of General Psychiatry,* 1964, **10**, 314–319.

3. Landy, D., & Griffith, W. D. Placement of the emotionally handicapped. *Journal of Rehabilitation,* 1958, **24**, 17–18.

4. Olshansky, S., Grob, S., & Malamud, I. T. Employers' attitudes and practices in the hiring of ex-mental patients. *Mental Hygiene,* 1958, **42**; 391–401.

5. Redlich, F. C., & Pepper, M. Social psychiatry. *American Journal of Psychiatry,* 1963, **119**; 637–641.

6. Star, Shirley A. The public's ideas about mental illness. Presented at the Annual Meeting of the National Association for Mental Health, Sheraton-Lincoln Hotel, Indianapolis, Indiana, November 5, 1955.

7. The employment adjustment of veterans with histories of psychosis and psychoneurosis. Monograph, Veterans Administration, TR 22-1, Washington 25, D.C., January 1963.

8. Wolfe, H. E. The attitude of small industrial employers toward hiring former state mental patients. *Journal of Clinical Psychology,* 1961, **17**, 90–92.

# 4. IDENTIFYING EMOTIONAL DISTURBANCE IN PERSONS SEEN IN INDUSTRIAL DISPENSARIES

Beatrice M. Rosen, B.S., F.A.P.H.A.,
Ben Z. Locke, M.S., F.A.P.H.A.,
Irving D. Goldberg, M.P.H., F.A.P.H.A.,
and Haroutun M. Babigian, M.D.

*The authors discuss the extent to which nonpsychiatric physicians working in industrial dispensaries detected emotional problems in their patients. They examine the nature and degree of disability resulting from these problems and the resources used by the physicians in their treatment.*

Growing professional interest in the role of the general medical physician in the treatment of patients with mental or emotional problems has been demonstrated by increased emphasis on psychiatric training of the general practitioner

Mrs. Rosen, Mr. Locke, and Mr. Goldberg are associated with the National Institute of Mental Health, 5454 Wisconsin Avenue, Chevy Chase, Maryland 20013. Mrs. Rosen is a statistician in the Register Development and Studies Section, Biometry Branch. Mr. Goldberg is Acting Chief of the Register Development and Studies Section and Chief of the Evaluation Studies Section, Biometry Branch. Mr. Locke is Assistant Chief of the Center of Epidemiologic Studies. Dr. Babigian is Associate Professor of Psychiatry and Preventive Medicine and Community Health and Director of the Division of Preventive and Social Psychiatry, University of Rochester School of Medicine and Dentistry.

This article is adapted from a paper presented at the 96th Annual Meeting of the American Public Health Association, held in Detroit, Michigan, November 11, 1968.

Tables reflecting data in this report are available on request from Mrs. Rosen.

55

and in a variety of recent studies on this subject (1, 4–8, 11–15, 17–22). Such studies have shown the extent to which non-psychiatric physicians in private or group practice in the United States and abroad have detected psychiatric distur-bance in their patients.

This report focuses on the extent to which nonpsychiatric physicians, employed in industrial dispensaries, detected emo-tional problems among employees, the nature and degree of disability resulting from these emotional problems, and the resources used by the physician to treat these patients. Two established companies in an industry of a highly technical nature located in Monroe County, New York, agreed to pro-vide data from dispensaries serving five plants and administra-tive units with an employee population of approximately 20,000. Each dispensary reported data for a one-month period. The periods covered were from mid-November 1965 to mid-February 1966 and September and October 1966. Information reported on each person seen during the study period pertained to his first visit of that month. The proce-dures for collecting the data varied slightly among the dispen-saries to fit the routine procedures of each dispensary.

The study form used to record the data was divided into two parts. First, information on the characteristics of the dis-pensary population was recorded. This included data on age, sex, marital status, socioeconomic characteristics, years employed, presenting problem, medical diagnosis and number of visits during last 12 months. In general, except for identifying information which was recorded by a clerk, this section of the study form was completed by a nurse or a physician at the time of the employee's visit to the dispensary.

If the patient was judged to have an emotional problem at the time of the visit, the physician completed the second portion of the form, dealing with that emotional problem. This section included information on the physician's impres-sion of the patient's "psychiatric" diagnosis, level of impair-ment, length of time patient was bothered by problem, pre-vious psychiatric care, and type of mental health care provided by the dispensary.

If the patient had recovered from such a disorder and was

judged not to have an emotional problem at the time of the visit, the section dealing with his emotional problem was not completed. Findings for this report are presented in two parts. First, information on employees diagnosed to have an emotional problem (the first section of the form) is related to the total dispensary population. Secondly, specific information relating only to the patients with emotional problems is discussed (second section of the form).

This analysis focuses on the dispensary population 20–64 years of age. Two hundred and seventeen persons under 20 years of age or 65 years and over were excluded from the study due to the difficulty of interpreting the findings of an "employed" population in these age groups. A few patients (.4%) were stated to have a "mental, psychoneurotic personality" disorder (ICD, 1957) but no data on a current emotional problem at the time of the visit was provided (24). These patients were excluded from the "emotional disorder" group.

In interpreting the findings, it is important to bear in mind that dispensary personnel were not requested to probe for emotional disorders, but rather to carry on their medical practice in the customary manner. No attempt was made to validate diagnoses or data supplied by the dispensaries. Demographic information was well reported for each patient, but information on previous psychiatric care and other aspects relating to their emotional problem was frequently incomplete. Seasonality also may have affected the findings of the study since the reporting period occurred only during the fall and winter months.

# FINDINGS

## Comparison of Emotional Disorder Cases with the General Clinic Population

Of the 3,165 patients 20–64 years of age seen during the reporting period in the cooperating industrial dispensaries,

153 or 4.8% were considered by dispensary physicians to have had an emotional, psychiatric, mental, or personality disorder and are designated in this paper as the "emotional disorder" group. The proportion of patients who were determined to have an emotional disorder was lowest for the younger patients and increased for each age group, from 2.5% for patients 20–29 years of age to 8.1% for those 50–64 years of age. This increase may have been due in part to the fact that older patients who were more likely to have been employed for many years were better known to physicians and the fact that files of their past illnesses and visits were well documented and maintained in the dispensary.

Data by sex show a proportion with emotional problems of 5.3 of every 100 men and 4.1 of every 100 women with relatively higher proportions for men than women in all age groups except 20–29 years of age. However, differences between both the overall and age-specific percentages, by sex, were not statistically significant; therefore, additional data by sex are not presented here.

In terms of marital status, the relative frequency of emotional disorders was particularly high among separated and divorced persons (10.3%) but low among both the single (4.4%) and the married (4.8%).

Information was analyzed for two socioeconomic factors —the employee's occupation and his residence in terms of socioeconomic ranking. Within each occupation group, the proportion of patients with emotional disorders was generally high for those of high occupational status—8.2% for managers and 5.8 for professionals. Service workers, which generally included protective personnel, elevator operators, porters or other such workers requiring relatively little training, also showed a relatively high proportion with emotional disorder, 6.1%, though they represented a relatively small group.

*Similarly, relative frequencies were also highest for those living in census tracts of high socioeconomic ranking (6.8%* compared to 4.1 to 5.0% for other socioeconomic areas). This ranking was based on the classification of urban, suburban, and rural census tracts in Monroe County into five major groupings using five census variables to develop a composite index for each tract: median value of owned homes; median rental value; percentage of skilled, semiskilled, and unskilled workers; median years of education of adults; and percentages of sound dwelling units (23).

In general, the proportion with emotional disorders was higher for those employed five years or longer compared to those employed for a shorter time. This was the case for all occupation groups except salesmen and service workers, but again, few in these occupation groups were represented in this study. The higher proportions for employees with longer duration of service are due in part to the older ages of these employees where the relative frequency of emotional disorder was shown to be higher, and, as stated before, to the fact that employees working for the company for several years were usually better known to the physicians in the dispensary.

Clinicians were asked to indicate which of the following major reasons induced employees to come to the dispensary: accident or injury, physical symptoms, emotional symptoms, preventive measures, to seek advice or counseling, or for other reasons. Among the "emotional disorder" group, 52% went to the dispensary for physical reasons, such as accident, physical symptoms, and preventive measures, in contrast to 89% of the remaining patients, that is, the "nonemotional disorder" group. On the other hand, about 39% of the "emotional disorder" group had emotional symptoms (31%) or sought advice and counseling (8%) compared to 1% of the "nonemotional disorder" caseload. Of all patients who came to the dispensary because of emotional symptoms, 84% were included in the "emotional disorder" group. In contrast, the advice seeking patients generally were not judged to have had an emotional problem since only 39% were so classified. Proportions of patients with emotional disorders were largest among older patients regardless of presenting problem, but particularly so for those coming to the dispensary for emotional symptoms or to seek advice or counseling.

Physicians were expected to indicate the medical diagnosis for all dispensary patients requesting care, including those with emotional disorders, which were classified according to the International Classification of Diseases (24). Among the somatic conditions reported for the "emotional disorder" group, the most frequently diagnosed ones were the digestive, circulatory, and allergy, and endocrine disorders.

As expected and as shown in other studies, "emotional disorder" cases generally had more visits during the previous 12 months than the general patient caseload (11–13).

### "Emotional Disorder" Patients

We have provided an overview of the demographic and medical characteristics of "emotional disorder" cases compared with the general caseload of these industrial dispensaries. The following section deals primarily with the "emotional disorder" group and focuses on the nature and extent of emotional problems in this group.

In addition to providing a general medical diagnosis, physicians were asked, but not required, to assign a broad psychiatric diagnosis to those patients considered to have an emotional, psychiatric, mental, or personality problem. While it is recognized that the assignment of specific psychiatric diagnoses is difficult, it is assumed that nonpsychiatric physicians can recognize psychiatric disorders and are able to assign such disorders into broad diagnostic groupings. The extent of this capability is the subject of a future phase of this study.

The fact that physicians were not required to assign a psychiatric diagnosis probably accounted for a substantial portion of the 37% of cases in which the space for recording the psychiatric diagnosis was left blank. Nevertheless, physicians judged that 7% of the cases had psychotic disorders, 32% were psychoneurotic, and 17% had personality disorders. The percent with personality disorders was appreciably higher for the older than younger patients. In addition, 6% were diagnosed with other or unspecified psychiatric disorders. Age, and/or perhaps length of time on the job, may have been factors in assigning a psychiatric diagnosis to a patient since relatively more of the older patients than the younger ones were given specific diagnoses.

In terms of presenting problems, patients diagnosed in this study as psychotic and psychoneurotic were equally likely to come to the dispensary for physical or emotional symptoms (about 35% came for each) but few came for accident or injury, for advice or counseling, or for preventive measures. In contrast, study patients diagnosed with personality disorders came at approximately the same relative frequency for each major category of "presenting problem." Also, unlike the psychotics and psychoneurotics, a substantial proportion of persons with personality disorders came because of accidents or injuries or for preventive services.

When physicians were asked how long they believed their patients were bothered by their emotional disorder, they reported that more than half of their patients were bothered for five or more years, regardless of their psychiatric diagnosis.

Doctors were asked to judge the degree of psychiatric impairment of the "emotional disorder" group. Impairment was reported for 88% of the cases. Of these, 15% were considered severely impaired, 43% moderately, and 37% mildly impaired, while 5% showed no functional impairment. In terms of diagnosis, the impairment was considered severe or moderate for 80% of the psychotics, and 85% of those with personality disorders, but for only 51% of the psychoneurotics. Although differences were small, impairment was more serious for older patients than younger ones and for those with problems of long (five years or more) rather than short duration.

Physicians were asked to indicate if "emotional disorder" patients had had previous psychiatric care and, if so, what kinds. Such care was reported for 56% of the patients. Of these, 15% received care in more than one facility. A total of 86% had some form of outpatient psychiatric or ancillary service and 25% inpatient psychiatric care; 12% had both types. Of those with known care, 35% had seen a private psychiatrist, but very few had received services in a mental health clinic or family agency. The use of a private psychiatrist rather than a clinic or a social agency is an indication of the broad medical insurance made available to personnel of these companies as well as their high socioeconomic level. For the

44% for whom previous psychiatric care was not reported, it was not possible to determine how many had no prior care and how many had care of an unknown type.

As might be expected, patients with psychotic disorders were more likely to have had previous care and in more than one type of facility than those with other psychiatric diagnoses. In addition, almost all the psychotics (9 of the 10 psychotics with known care) had seen a private psychiatrist in contrast to about 40% of those with psychoneurosis and 21% of those with personality disorders. Further, 6 out of 10 of the psychotics but only a third each of the psychoneurotics and those with personality disorders were reported to have been hospitalized at some previous time. It might be noted that the item on previous care was completed for almost all of the psychotic group compared to slightly more than half of the psychoneurotics and about three-quarters of those with personality disorders, reflecting to some extent the greater likelihood of psychiatric care for the more serious disorders.

Dispensary physicians were asked to indicate if they had ever provided mental health care in terms of supportive therapy, suggestions for environmental changes, and/or the prescription of drugs for the patients they considered to have had emotional disorders. For those for which a response to this question was given, 96% had received supportive therapy, 66% were given drugs, but only 12% received suggestions for environmental changes. Of these patients, 65% had received more than one type of care at the dispensary, most frequently a combination of supportive and drug therapy. The only exception was among the psychotic group in which supportive therapy was frequently provided without other forms of care.

## DISCUSSION

This paper, which is concerned with patients coming to a medical dispensary, represents one of several recent studies by Locke and associates designed to investigate the extent to which persons are seen and identified by nonpsychiatric physicians as having emotional disorders. The proportion of dispensary patients in this study considered to have an emotional problem, 5 per 100 patients, is lower than the 15% reported in a study of general medical group practice (13) and the 9 and 17% found in two studies of patients of private practitioners (11, 12). Although the experience observed among the study population is not necessarily reflective of the total employed population in these companies, the relatively low frequency of diagnosed emotional disorders may have been attributable to a basically low-risk, stable, and employed population working in well-paid, prestigious establishments. Further, employees in these companies were initially screened through job interviews and physical examinations, thus eliminating some persons with overt psychiatric problems. Other factors contributing to the low frequency may have been the encouragement by these companies of adequate health care oriented toward prevention and the partial subsidizing of good insurance coverage. In addition, the companies have been supportive of employees with emotional problems and assist such persons in eliminating stressful on-the-job situations even if this means changing jobs. Nevertheless, an employee with such a problem may naturally fear for his job security or promotional opportunities if his condition were known to his employer.

Another finding of interest which has also been substantiated in a variety of psychiatric settings is the relatively high proportion of separated and divorced persons with emotional disorders (10). If the findings among the dispensary population reflect the experience of the total employed population of these companies, then it would appear that a secure employment environment does not alter that association.

Also suggestive of further study is the relatively high frequency of emotional disorder among those of high socioeconomic status attending the dispensary. Previous studies reflecting utilization of psychiatric services indicate that persons of lower socioeconomic status generally had significantly higher rates of utilization (2, 9).

There are a number of interrelated factors which may

account for the study observation of a relatively high frequency of emotional disorders among the high socioeconomic group:

1. Those included in the high socioeconomic group were generally employees of long standing and, hence, their medical histories were more likely to be known to the dispensary.

2. The employees in the high socioeconomic group tend to be more medically sophisticated and more accepting of the companies' expressed liberal attitude towards emotional disorders.

3. Managers and professionals are trained to be cognizant of the influence of emotional disorders on job performance. Thus, they are more closely associated with dispensary medical personnel and have a direct and more personal relationship with the physician.

4. The relatively lower proportions for the nonprofessional worker may reflect to some extent a lack of trust in the dispensary physicians, particularly in terms of discussing emotional problems. This lack of trust could be related to the employees' concerns of job security and advancement as well as their limited medical sophistication.

Therefore, it is difficult to assess the extent to which each of the above factors contribute to the relatively high frequency observed in the upper socioeconomic group. Stresses associated with responsible positions can also contribute to this phenomenon.

As stated earlier, the findings reported in this study reflect the extent to which emotional problems were diagnosed by industrial dispensary physicians who were requested to conduct their practice in the customary manner, and not as a case finding project. In the second phase of analysis, the ability of dispensary physicians to identify patients with emotional disorders will be studied. Patient data from this study will be matched to the Monroe County Psychiatric Case Register (3, 16). This matching procedure will identify the group of dispensary patients who received prior or subsequent psychiatric care. Included will be both those considered to have emotional disorders, as well as those who were not considered to have an emotional problem at the time of the study. This phase of the study will also provide a gross index of the proportion of persons judged to have an emotional disorder who did not receive psychiatric care. Subsequent matchings should make it possible to determine whether or not it is more likely to be reported to the psychiatric register if one had been considered by the dispensary physician to have an emotional disorder in contrast to the patient group not so considered.

Two other studies, also centered in Monroe County, New York, will be the focus of similar matching to the Monroe County Psychiatric Case Register. One involves patients of private nonpsychiatric physicians, and the other patients attending general medical clinics operated by general hospitals in Monroe County. All three studies, each involving different but major types of general medical care in the County, will provide an overview of the ability of nonpsychiatric physicians in a variety of settings to identify persons with emotional disorders.

The study finding that only 5% of the employees who came to these dispensaries were considered to have an emotional disorder may have several important implications. If a matching comparison of these cases with those in the psychiatric case register indicates that the "emotional disorder" group was underdetected, a need for further training of physicians in the identification of persons with emotional problems might be indicated. On the other hand, if there is little or no indication of underdetection and if the findings for the dispensary group represent those for the total employed population in these companies, one could infer that a stable, well-compensated working environment, accompanied by good health care, is conducive to a mentally healthy employee population. Although this hypothesis is generally not questioned, we are not aware of any other studies conducted to actually investigate this hypothesis.

## SUMMARY

This study examines the extent to which nonpsychiatric physicians, working in industrial dispensaries operated by companies in a highly technical industry, detected emotional problems in their patients, the nature and degree of disability resulting from these emotional problems, and the resources used by the physician in the treatment of these patients.

Major findings are as follows:

1. Of the 3,165 patients 20–64 years of age seen during the reporting period, approximately 5% were considered to have an emotional problem at the time of the dispensary visit.

2. Higher proportions of patients with emotional disorders were noted among the older patients compared to younger ones, for those separated and divorced, for those of high socioeconomic status, and for those employed five years or longer compared to those employed for shorter periods.

3. Among patients for whom a psychiatric diagnosis was reported, 32% were diagnosed as having psychoneurotic disorders; 17%, personality disorders; and 7%, psychotic disorders.

4. Among those for whom impairment was reported, the degree of impairment was judged to be severe or moderate for 58% of the cases, mild for 37%, and no functional impairment for 5%.

5. Previous psychiatric care was reported for 56% of the patients. Of these, 86% had some form of outpatient psychiatric or ancillary service and 26% inpatient psychiatric care; 12% had both types. Among those receiving outpatient care, 35% were seen by private psychiatrists while very few were served by mental health clinics.

6. Dispensary physicians reported that at some time they provided supportive therapy to 96% of the "emotional disorder" patients for whom this item was reported, drugs to 66%, but suggestions for environmental changes to only 12%.

## REFERENCES

1. Cooper, B., Brown, A. C., & Kalton, G. A pilot study of psychiatric morbidity in general practice. *J. Coll. Gen. Pract.*, 1962, **5**, 590–602.

2. Gardner, E. A., & Babigian, H. M. A longitudinal comparison of psychiatric service. *American Journal of Orthopsychiatry*, 1966, **36**, 818–828.

3. Gardner, E. A., Miles, H. C., Iker, H. P., & Romano, J. A cumulative register of psychiatric services in a community. *American Journal of Public Health,* 1963, **53,** 1269–1277.

4. Gurin, G., Veroff, J., & Feld, S. Americans view their mental health. New York: Basic Books, 1960.

5. Hollingshead, A. B., & Redlich, F. C. Social class and mental illness. New York: John Wiley & Sons, 1958.

6. Kessel, N. The neurotic in general practice. *Practitioner,* 1965, **194,** 636–641.

7. Kessel, N., & Shepherd, M. Neurosis in hospital and general practice. *Journal of Mental Science,* 1962, **1108,** 159–166.

8. Kessel, W. I. N. Psychiatric morbidity in a London general practice. *British Journal of Preventive and Social Medicine,* 1960, **14,** 16–22.

9. Klee, G.D., Spiro, E., Bahn, A. K., & Gorwitz, K. An ecological analysis of diagnosed mental illness in Baltimore. In R. R. Monroe, G. D. Klee, & E. B. Brody (Eds.), *Psychiatric epidemiology and mental health planning,* American Psychiatric Association Psychiatric Research Report 22, Washington, D.C., April 1967.

10. Kramer, Morton. Some implications of trends in the usage of psychiatric facilities for community mental health programs and related research. Public Health Service Publication No. 1434, Washington, D.C.: U.S. Government Printing Office, 1966.

11. Locke, B. Z. Patients, psychiatric problems, and nonpsychiatrist physicians in a prepaid group practice medical program. *American Journal of Psychiatry,* 1966, **123,** 207–210.

12. Locke, B. Z., & Gardner, E. A. Psychiatric disorders among the patients of general practitioners and internists. *Public Health Reports,* 1969, **84,** 167–173.

13. Locke, B. Z., Finucane, D. L., & Hassler, F. Emotionally disturbed patients under care of private nonpsychiatric physicians. In R. R. Monroe, G. D. Klee, & E. B. Brody (Eds.), Psychiatric epidemiology and mental health planning, American Psychiatric Association Psychiatric Research Report 22, Washington, D.C., April 1967.

14. Locke, B. Z., Krantz, G., & Kramer, M. Psychiatric need and a demand in a prepaid group practice program. *American Journal of Public Health,* 1966, **56,** 895–904.

15. Mazer, Milton. Psychiatric disorders in general practice: The experience of an island community. *American Journal of Psychiatry,* 1967, **124,** 609–615.

16. Miles, H. C., & Gardner, E. A. A psychiatric case register. *Archives General Psychiatry,* 1966, **14,** 571–580.

17. Robertson, R. L., & Shriver, B. M. The general practitioner training program of the National Institute of Mental Health: Fiscal years 1959-1962. *Journal of Medical Education,* 1964, **39,** 925–934.

18. Roth, V. E., Rury, J. L., & Downing, J. J. Psychiatric patients in a general

practice. *General Practice,* 1959, **20**, 106–110.

19.  Shapiro, S., & Fink, R. Methodological considerations in studying patterns of medical care related to mental illness. *Milbank Memorial Fund Quarterly,* 1963, **41**, 371–399.

20.  Shepherd, M., Cooper, B., Brown, A. C., & Kalton, G. W. Minor mental illness in London: Some aspects of a general practice survey. *British Medical Journal,* 1964, **2**, 1359–1363.

21.  Shepherd, M., Fisher, M., Stein, L., & Kessel, W. I. N. Psychiatric morbidity in an urban group practice. *Proceedings of the Royal Society of Medicine,* 1969, **52**, 269–274.

22.  Stein, L. Morbidity in a London general practice: Social and demographic data. *British Journal of Preventive and Social Medicine,* 1960, **14**, 9–15.

23.  Willie, C. V. Socioeconomic and ethnic areas in Syracuse, N.Y. Unpublished Ph.D. thesis, Syracuse University, 1957, pp. 162–222.

24.  World Health Organization. International classification of diseases. Vol. 1. Geneva, Switzerland: World Health Organization, 1957.

# 5. AN APPROACH TO MEASURING THE COST OF MENTAL ILLNESS

Ronald W. Conley, Ph.D., Margaret Conwell, Ed.M., and Mildred B. Arrill, M.A., M.S.W.

Using a new conceptual framework, the authors present a comprehensive estimate of the cost of mental illness. They identify and quantify components of this cost that add up to almost $20 billion annually. Almost half the cost, they note, is borne by persons other than those whose emotional difficulties actually cause the loss. Because of its relevance for policy decisions in regard to mental health programs, the authors also discuss the relationship between the costs of mental illness and benefit–cost analysis.

Few diseases are as destructive of the welfare of so many as mental illness. In 1966 almost 2.6 million individuals received psychiatric attention; 38% of these were cared for as inpatients in hospitals for persons with emotional or psychiatric disorders. Undoubtedly many millions more required treatment but failed to receive it. Although estimates of the prevalence of mental illness vary greatly, the most frequently cited estimate is in the vicinity of 10%.

Efforts to quantify a part of the cost of mental illness have been made by Dorothy Rice (4) and Rashi Fein (2). Fein concluded that the loss of earnings among the institutionalized mentally ill plus the cost of care for both the institutionalized

The authors are with the National Institute of Mental Health, where Dr. Conley is Economist, Planning Branch; Mrs. Conwell is Statistician, Program Analysis and Evaluation Section, Division of Mental Health Service Programs; and Mrs. Arrill is Chief, Program Analysis and Evaluation Section, Division of Special Mental Health Programs. Dr. Conley's address is 5454 Wisconsin Avenue, Chevy Chase, Maryland 20203.

and the noninstitutionalized mentally ill were $2.4 billion in 1952 (2). Rice expanded this approach by taking account of mentally ill persons among the noninstitutional population who are "unable to work" or who suffer "work loss" days and by placing a value on the loss of the services of mentally ill homemakers. She calculated that the cost of mental illness was a little over $7 billion in 1963 (4).

In this paper we advance the work of Fein and Rice in two ways. We present a more comprehensive estimate of the cost of mental illness by estimating the reduction in productivity among the employed mentally ill and by taking account of the costs of a wider range of treatment services. In addition, we estimate the distribution of this burden between the mentally ill and the nonmentally ill. Another of our purposes is to show that the conceptual framework we have devised to describe the cost of mental illness is equally suitable for the more important task of evaluating the effects of treatment.

Before proceeding, however, several limitations of estimates of the cost of mental illness should be emphasized. To begin with, no precise measure of the cost of mental illness is possible, or is ever likely to be. One problem is that there is great uncertainty as to the appropriate criterion of mental illness. A little less or a little more tolerance as to acceptable behavior may mean the exclusion or inclusion of several million persons in the mentally ill population.

Another problem is that the available data are grossly inadequate. In part, this is because much of the existing information is not collected. But more importantly, the concept of the "cost of mental illness" hypothesizes an impossible "with and without" situation. We can never know with certainty what would have happened had mental illness not existed. A final problem of measurement is that some losses caused by mental illness are difficult to quantify (e.g., loss of homemaking services) and others are impossible to quantify (e.g., loss of feelings of personal worth).

A second limitation of estimates of the cost of mental illness is that they have relatively few uses. They cannot properly be used, as they sometimes are, to justify increased expenditures on programs to aid the mentally ill. Increased expenditures are justified only if additional services are expected to reduce the cost of mental illness. These "costs to save costs" will be discussed below. The only purpose for which estimates of the cost of mental illness can be used is to describe the size and the dimensions of the problem—i.e., what type of costs are incurred, who bears the burden, and what is being done about it—and so to stress the seriousness of the problem and the importance of seeking new methods of treatment.

## THE COST OF MENTAL ILLNESS

We define the cost of mental illness as the loss of well-being suffered by society as a result of this disease. The total cost of mental illness can be usefully subdivided into the cost that results from a reduction of productive activity among the mentally ill; the cost of treating the mentally ill; the cost of illegal and other undesirable behavior that can be attributed to the effects of mental illness; and the intangible psychic loss that so often accompanies mental illness, e.g., the fear, frustration, and despair that arise from idleness and rejection. The first three of these categories are defined as the material or tangible costs of mental illness, i.e., the reduction in resources that society has available for the satisfaction of human wants as a result of the disease.

### Cost of Reduction of Productive Activity

The largest material cost of mental illness is the decrease in productive activity that can be attributed to it. This has three components: loss of output, loss of homemaking services, and loss of unpaid work.

We estimate that mental illness reduced marketable output by $14.3 billion in 1966.[1] A little over one-fourth of this loss was due to the inability of the mentally ill to work. The bulk

---

[1] A table showing the data that are used in this article and our estimating procedures is available on request from the Biometrics Branch, National Institute of Mental Health. This table will be contained in the proceedings of the 1967 Conference on Mental Health Statistics, to be published by the National Institute of Mental Health.

of those unable to work was concentrated among the half million persons confined in mental institutions at any moment of time during the year. The remainder of the loss of output was attributed to the excessive absenteeism, longer and more frequent spells of unemployment, withdrawal from the labor force, and inefficiency on the job caused by mental illness and the acceptance by the mentally ill of jobs that are less productive than they would otherwise have obtained.

Needless to say, the latter part of this estimate is highly speculative. Although we believe that the assumptions upon which it is based are conservative, we wish to stress that it is based on a broad definition of mental illness. It includes the potential Ph.D. who collapses under the pressure of graduate work and becomes a store manager as well as the quarrelsome and dissatisfied worker who is fired from one job after the other. Although we are aware that not everyone will agree with the use of a definition of mental illness that is this broad, it has at least the virtue of focusing attention on the part of the population that may benefit from mental health services.

Mental illness may reduce current output in still other ways. A few workers may withdraw from the labor force in order to provide nursing care for a mentally ill relative, although this is more or less offset by the fact that others may be forced into the labor force to provide or supplement a family income that has been reduced through the loss of the earnings of a mentally ill member or a large expense for treatment of mental illness. In addition, a few workers, among both the mentally ill and the nonmentally ill, suffer from work-impeding injuries caused by the accidents and aggressive behavior that can be attributed to the illness of the former. Moreover, some workers suffer from a psychosomatic illness which impedes their work effort. Finally, mental illness may not be an insignificant cause of death. Many deaths by suicide can be traced to mental illness; obesity, which in some cases can be traced to emotional disorder, has dangerous effects on health; and death is occasionally one of the sequelae of the accidents and antisocial behavior that can be attributed to mental illness.

Mental illness also reduces future output. Mentally ill parents are often unable to provide adequate care and training for their children—thus impairing their future talents and attitudes. Mentally ill children are sometimes unable to take full advantage of developmental opportunities, especially if psychiatric care is not available to them. Idleness among mentally ill adults may cause deterioration of skills. Savings and hence capital formation may decline slightly because of lower incomes among the mentally ill and the use of resources for the care and treatment of their afflictions.

Most of these additional factors affecting present and future output also affect future production of homemaking services and other unpaid work, topics which are discussed below. For reasons that are obvious, we were unable to quantify the effects of these additional aspects of the cost of mental illness.

Conservatively, we value the reduction in homemaking services among mentally ill women who are totally unable to carry on this activity because of their illness—the great majority of whom are in institutions—at $970 million in 1966. The value of homemaking services was further reduced because the efficiency with which some mentally ill homemakers carried out their duties was impaired and because the wives of some of the mentally ill found it necessary to seek paid employment to supplement their family's income. On the other hand, many mentally disturbed women chose to function in the less demanding role of homemaking who would have sought remunerative employment if they had not been ill. Thus, in some cases mental illness increases the provision of homemaking services.

The net effect of the conflicting influences is uncertain. Conceivably, mental illness could increase the provision of homemaking services. Because of the large institutional population, however, it seems probable that there is, on balance, a substantial loss. We assumed, therefore, that the net loss in the value of homemaking services due to mental illness was $970 million in 1966—i.e., that all but the first of the above-mentioned effects of mental illness on the value of the homemakers' services just offset each other.

Unpaid work done around the home such as painting and

yard maintenance, and unpaid work done outside the home such as voluntary time given to charitable organizations, is as much a part of the productive capacity of individuals as remunerative employment or homemaking. Unpaid work should also include the value of any reduction in recreational activities. In short, any activities that serve to increase people's well-being should be considered as productive activity and any reduction in these activities due to mental illness should be counted as a cost of mental illness.

The effect of mental illness on unpaid activities is conflicting. Clearly, some persons are impeded or prevented from carrying on these activities, but others, unable or unwilling to engage in remunerative work, have more time for it. We believe, once again because of the large institutional population, that the net effect is negative. Therefore, a speculative but probably conservative value of $240 million, about a fourth of the reduction in the value of homemaking services due to mental illness, will be placed on the loss of unpaid work around the house due to mental illness.

## Cost of Treatment and Prevention

We estimate that almost $4 billion was spent on the treatment and prevention of mental illness, our second major category of cost, in 1966. Treatment for mental illness is defined as any special therapeutic, medical, and nursing care and maintenance provided to the mentally ill to cure, arrest, or alleviate their illnesses, to assist them to cope with their environment, or to rehabilitate them into useful activity. We normally distinguish between treatment received in inpatient facilities and treatment received in outpatient facilities. Prevention of mental illness refers to efforts to prevent persons from becoming mentally ill.

Slightly over $2.5 billion was spent on inpatient care in the United States in 1966. Almost half of this expenditure was for the operation of state and county public mental hospitals. Most of the rest supported mental health care in Veterans Administration hospitals, private mental hospitals, and inpatient services in general hospitals.

These costs are slightly overstated since they include purchases of food, clothing, and lodging. Expenditures for food and clothing are not a part of treatment cost, even if received in an institution, since these items are required by persons whether they are mentally ill or not. Moreover, to the extent that being in an inpatient facility reduces the cost of housing for some individuals, this reduction should be subtracted from the cost of providing living quarters in the inpatient facility in order to find the net incremental cost to society.

We estimate, probably conservatively, that the cost of operating outpatient facilities in 1966 was slightly greater than $1 billion. Almost all outpatient care was provided by outpatient psychiatric clinics and psychiatrists in private practice.

During 1966 considerable amounts were spent by federal, state, and local governments on the development of mental health facilities ($121 million), training of mental health personnel ($94 million), and research in mental illness ($113 million). These expenditures are a cost of treating and preventing mental illness in the future but will not be reflected in the direct costs of services since they are not costs to the personnel providing the service. In theory, these costs should be capitalized and depreciated over future years. If it is assumed, however, that they serve as a proxy for the depreciation of past expenditures, they may properly be included as an element in the current cost of mental illness.

The management expense of operating government agencies concerned with mental health is also a part of the cost of providing mental health services. Although we were unable to determine the cost of managing state mental health agencies, it cost almost $20 million to operate the National Institute of Mental Health in 1966. (This is exclusive of research, training, and development of services.)

Before concluding the discussion of the treatment and prevention cost of mental illness, we should emphasize that we have not identified all of the ways in which mental illness is treated or prevented. For example, we have not included preventive mental health services rendered by school psychiatrists, teachers, pastors, policemen, and parents. Nonetheless, we believe that we have covered the most important elements of the cost of mental illness, both in size and in relevance to future activities in the mental health field.

## Cost of Illegal and Other Undesirable Behavior

The cost of illegal and other undesirable behavior to which some of the mentally ill are prone is another part of the cost of mental illness. Illegal behavior refers to the thefts, assaults, homicides, etc., that can be attributed to mental illness. Other undesirable (but not illegal) behavior takes several forms. Because of their illness, some of the mentally ill may be more likely than the average to be involved in accidents at home or on the job. Also, the attitudes and behavior of the mentally ill may lead to divorce, disharmonious family relationships, excessive gambling, promiscuity, illegitimacy, alcoholism, or drug addiction. The list of the undesirable social consequences of mental illness could be greatly extended.

Illegal activities and accidents that can be attributed to mental illness impose a cost on society by causing property loss, personal injuries, and occasional fatalities. In addition, illegal activities raise the cost of law enforcement and incarceration, and excessive accidents may invoke increased efforts for accident prevention. The harmful effects of the other forms of socially undesirable behavior are obvious, even if complex. Among these harmful effects are an increase in personal unhappiness, a reduction of both present and (through the improper care of children) future productivity, an adverse effect on present and future attitudes, and so on down the list.

We did not attempt to estimate from the limited data available the cost of the illegal and other undesirable behavior that can be attributed to mental illness; only scattered clues are available as to the magnitude of this figure. It is estimated, for example, that there are approximately 14,600 mentally ill persons who are in hospitals exclusively for mentally ill offenders (3). The true number of mentally ill offenders is considerably greater than this, however, since many institutions care for other mentally ill persons along with mentally ill offenders. As another example, it is estimated that many male narcotics addicts support their habits by stealing merchandise valued at $30,000 or more per year; female addicts often resort to prostitution. As still another example, it has been suggested that alcoholism contributes to over half of all fatal automobile accidents and a fifth of all industrial accidents.

Before leaving this topic, it would perhaps be wise to stress that a measure of the cost of undesirable behavior caused by mental illness depends crucially upon the criterion used to define mental illness. A very broad definition of mental illness might class any asocial activity or abnormal carelessness as indicating an underlying mental illness. In this case, the cost of the undesirable behavior attributed to mental illness would be enormous. If, on the other hand, only the more severe forms of mental disorder are accepted in the definition of mental illness, then there is some evidence that the disease may inhibit criminal tendencies (1).

Although no single definition of mental illness can be said to be more correct than all other definitions, we would, in general, prefer a broad one. This is not because we wish to magnify our measure of the cost of mental illness, but because we wish our estimates to encompass all of the costs that might be reduced through the provision of mental health services.

## Intangible Losses

The enormous intangible losses that are associated with mental illness is our final major cost category. Mental illness and its effects often leave its victims insecure, bewildered, frustrated, embittered, and sometimes hostile. When mental illness causes a family head to be chronically unemployed, for example, or addicted to drugs, or an alcoholic, the entire family may suffer a reduction in self-esteem and an increase in anxiety due to deprivation. The psychic suffering often caused by broken or unhappy marriages, whether or not as a result of mental illness, is well known. Of course, it is not possible to obtain a meaningful measure of the intangible losses due to mental illness.

## DISTRIBUTION OF THE COST

A substantial portion of the cost of mental illness is borne by persons other than the mentally ill and their families. Of those costs which we identified and quantified for 1966, we estimate that almost half, over $9 billion, was borne by the general population. This amounts to about $48 per person or $240 for a five-person family.

Since the general population includes the mentally ill and the nonmentally ill, the actual burden on persons other than the mentally ill and their families would be somewhat less than that borne generally. Because of the limitations of the data, we did not believe it worthwhile to guess at the part of the cost of mental illness that falls exclusively on persons other than the mentally ill and their families. Nevertheless, since a relatively small proportion of the population is actually treated for mental illness or suffers a large reduction in earnings because of this disease during the course of a year, it follows that the great bulk of the portion of the cost of mental illness that is borne by the general population falls on persons other than those whose illness is actually responsible for the cost.

Losses in earnings due to mental illness are shared by the general population in two ways. First, the loss in taxes that results because of the reduction in earnings must be offset by proportionately higher taxes on other earnings (assuming a constant level of government services). Second, mentally ill persons whose earnings are drastically reduced by their illness must be provided sustenance by society through transfer payments—i.e., social insurance, public welfare, private insurance, or charity.[2] Altogether, we estimate that

---

[2]Transfer payments for sustenance are not net social costs of mental illness (see above), since the costs to the general population are about offset by the gain to the recipients.

approximately 45% of the loss of earnings due to mental illness in 1966, about $6.4 billion, was borne by the general population. Although we were unable in this estimate to take account of support funds provided by private insurance companies or private philanthropy, these amounts are probably small.

Any changes in the value of housekeeping services and other unpaid work done around the home that are traceable to mental illness must, for the most part, be borne by the mentally ill and their families. In a few cases, outside agencies may provide household help to a home because of the inadequacies of a wife or mother. Of greater concern to the general population, however, are the future consequences of the inadequate care and training provided to some of the children of the mentally ill.

The great bulk of the cost of treating the mentally ill, almost $3 billion, is borne by the general population. Almost three-fourths of this sum is expended through governmental agencies. Private insurance carriers, private industry, and private philanthropy account for the remainder.

Although we were unable to quantify the cost of the illegal and other undesirable behavior of the mentally ill, the non-mentally ill share fully in the consequences of this behavior. For almost every accident, assault, or theft committed by a mentally ill person, there is a nonmentally ill victim. The possible consequences of disrupted family relationships—neglect of children, embitterment of adults, loss of income—often overflow onto the rest of society.

The nonmentally ill share even in the intangible costs resulting from mental illness. Few persons are so insensitive as to feel no compassion or sorrow for the plight of the mentally ill.

## CONCLUSIONS

In summary, we identified and quantified components of the cost of mental illness that summed to almost $20 billion for 1966—about 3% of the gross national product. Almost half of this cost was borne by persons other than those whose emotional difficulties actually caused this loss. There are, however, many imperfections in our estimates other than those that have already been described. Only token allowances were made for the value of the loss of homemaking services and unpaid work around the home. No attempt was made to quantify the cost of the undesirable and illegal behavior caused by this disease or the intangible losses that result from it. Nor did we attempt to calculate the cost of premature death or suicide associated with mental illness. Finally, many of the estimates of the components of the cost of mental illness were based on questionable assumptions and are subject to later revision.

Our estimate of the cost of mental illness must, therefore, be viewed and used with caution. Our reasons for presenting it are:

1.  We believe that the estimate, in and of itself, is useful. No similarly comprehensive overview of the cost of mental illness and its distribution in society has yet been published. Despite their limitations, we believe the data are sufficiently accurate for the limited purposes for which they can be used.

2.  For policy-making purposes, we believe that it is better to estimate, even if speculatively, the total cost of mental illness rather than rely only upon that part of the total cost that can be based on relatively firm data, as is often done. Not only does the latter approach fail to depict accurately the nature and seriousness of the problem but it is likely to be used as if it were a measure of the total cost. From the standpoint of allocating resources, it is as much of a mistake to underestimate as to overestimate a problem.

3.  Finally, we believe that the comprehensive conceptual framework that we use to describe the cost of mental illness may be of value to others who are studying the effects of mental illness or the effects of any other physical or mental deficiency. The framework is easily expandable if it is desired to incorporate additional types of costs or to identify additional persons, agencies, or other groups

who bear a portion of these costs. Next year, for example, we hope to factor out that part of the treatment cost of mental illness being financed through medicare and medicaid.

## Costs to Save Costs

Reduction in the costs of mental illness can be achieved through programs to prevent, cure, or ameliorate the illness and programs to rehabilitate its sufferers. The decision to extend preventive, treatment, or rehabilitative services to the mentally ill, however, does not depend upon the total cost of mental illness but upon the reduction of this cost that can be achieved by a particular course of action. If the reduction in the cost of mental illness that is being incurred will be greater than the cost of a prospective mental health program, then in general that program should be instituted unless another program can be shown to give even greater returns per dollar spent on treatment for the same group of patients. If an existing program can be shown to be adding more to the cost of mental illness than it is reducing this cost, then the program should be curtailed. This approach is frequently termed benefit–cost analysis, where the benefits are the reductions in the costs of mental illness that were being incurred before the treatment program was inaugurated.

Since it is a comparison of benefits and costs that is relevant for decision-making purposes, we will conclude this paper with a number of observations on the relationship between the costs of mental illness discussed above and benefit–cost analysis, and some of the limitations of benefit–cost analysis.

1. The conceptual framework that we have devised to measure the various costs of mental illness can, and in fact should, be used to measure the benefits of treating the mentally ill since the latter are the changes in the former—e.g., the increased earnings attributable to the improved functioning of the mentally ill after treatment

are equivalent to the reduction in the loss of earnings due to mental illness that existed prior to treatment.

2.  It is usually less difficult to estimate the reduction in total cost of mental illness due to a specific program (the benefits) than to estimate the total cost of mental illness. The patients are known and the effects of treatment can be observed. Nevertheless, exact measures of the benefits of treatment cannot, in the vast majority of cases, be obtained for the same reasons that precise measures of the total cost of mental illness (see above) are unobtainable.

3.  It is not always necessary to have complete or precise measurements in order to arrive at a positive decision through the use of benefit–cost analysis. As long as the part of the benefits that can be approximated exceeds the cost of treatment, as is often the case, then treatment should be rendered. As a result many treatment programs can be justified on the basis of measurable returns alone. On the other hand, in the case of treatment programs where the measurable returns are less than costs, a value judgment about the importance of intangible returns must be made explicitly or implicitly before they can be said to be justified or not justified.

4.  Benefit–cost ratios are specific for particular groups of patients and particular modes of treatment. High benefit –cost ratios will be maintained for additional patients. Whether a program should be expanded or not depends upon the benefit–cost ratio for the anticipated additional patients (i.e., the marginal benefit–cost ratio), and not the benefit–cost ratio for previous patients (i.e., the average benefit–cost ratio).

5.  An optimal program to combat the effects of mental illness will encompass a wide range of treatment and preventive services. Mental illness has many causes, takes many forms, and has differing effects depending upon socioeconomic grouping. The services that are most desirable for one person will often differ substantially from what are most desirable for another. However, benefit–cost analysis is of limited value in determining the optimal mix of mental health programs because of the difficulties of obtaining

precise measures of marginal benefits. In many cases, the likely errors in the measures of benefits will be greater than the calculated differences in benefits among different mental health programs. Hence, benefit–cost ratios for particular programs are frequently misleading guides as to the optimum mix of mental health programs. In these cases, the judgments of professionals in the field are better policy guides.

6.  Since it is the general population which bears the bulk of the cost of treating mental illness, benefit–cost analysis as a decision-making tool is greatly strengthened if the benefits that accrue to the general population are separated from those that accrue solely to the mentally ill. If the benefits received by both the general population and the mentally ill can be shown to be greater than costs they bear, then the desirability of treatment is assured. That the benefit–cost ratio for both groups will often be greater than one can be inferred from our earlier estimate that almost half of the costs of mental illness are borne by the general population.

7.  Finally, we wish to introduce another cost concept: the cost of the neglect of the mentally ill. This is the loss of well-being suffered by society as a result of not treating mentally ill persons for whom the benefits of treatment would have exceeded the cost. It is equal to the difference between what the benefits and cost of treatment would have been had it been rendered. This measure emphasizes that it costs society more to not treat mentally ill persons who can be helped than it does to provide them with the treatment they need. We suspect that a substantial portion of what we have described as a cost of mental illness could be more aptly described as the cost of our neglect of many of the problems of the mentally ill.

## REFERENCES

1. Brill, H., & Malzberg, B. Statistical report on the arrest record of male ex-patients, age 16 or over, released from New York State hospitals during the period 1946–48. New York State Department of Mental Hygiene, undated (processed).

2. Fein, R. *Economics of mental illness.* New York: Basic Books, 1958, pp. 57, 87.

3. National Institute of Mental Health. Office of Biometry, unpublished data.

4. Rice, D. Estimating the cost of illness. Washington, D.C.: U.S. Department of Health, Education and Welfare, Health Economics Series No. 5, Public Health Service Publication No. 947-6, 1966, p. 81.

# 6. SOME ECONOMIC ESTIMATES OF JOB DISRUPTION: FROM AN INDUSTRIAL MENTAL HEALTH PROJECT

**Walter W. Winslow, M.D., Kaney Hayes, Ph.D.,
Leslie Prentice, M.Ed., William E. Powles, M.D.,
William Seeman, Ph.D., and W. Donald Ross, M.D.**

As long as 20 years ago a claim was made that "psycho-neuroses and pathological emotional attitudes of employees toward their employment, their foremen, and their fellow workers and machines were responsible for a greater loss in dollars and cents than accidents and contagion" (1). But this claim has not yet been substantiated by reports from cost accounting.

Attempts to estimate the costs of ill-health in the industrial setting would seem to have obvious value for the justification of expenditures on preventive measures (2, 3). However, few published results of such attempts could be found in a search of the literature on occupational health in general, or industrial mental or emotional health in particular (4–6).

Rather large cost figures have been suggested as accruing to the consequences of absenteeism, accidents, and alcoholism, the three A's of industrial mental ill-health, without explana-

Submitted for publication December 3, 1965; accepted April 20, 1966.

From the Department of Psychiatry and the Department of Environmental Health, University of Cincinnati, College of Medicine.

Reprint requests to the Kettering Laboratory, University of Cincinnati College of Medicine, Eden Ave., Cincinnati 45219 (Dr. Ross).

tion from detailed accounting as to how these sums were derived (7–13). If companies have been calculating such costs, they have not yet made their methods of estimation available in the literature covered by the authors of this paper.

Burr, in two papers stressing the investment value of periodic examinations for executives, has made some convincing calculations that the early discovery of one rectal carcinoma may have recouped the total costs of the annual examination of 1,458 executives (3, 14). Maxwell (15) compared 48 problem drinkers in one industry with 96 matched controls. He discovered greatly higher absence and accident rates and sickness benefit payments about three times that of the control subjects. Howard and Hoag (16) present figures on the diminution of absence-days due to nonoccupational illness, and of sickness payments, in the four years following establishment of a plant medical department. In dollar figures, their findings are even more striking since wages (hence sickness payments) rose 50% during this same period of time.

Dr. Robert Kehoe, to whom this issue is a tribute, encouraged a team conducting a five-year project in Industrial Mental Health at the University of Cincinnati, College of Medicine, to include among its goals the estimation of costs pertaining to maladjustments at work. It was hoped that some net gain, in comparison with the costs of financing the operations of the team directed toward prevention, could be demonstrated. Dr. Kehoe also encouraged the team to make use of consultants in the behavioral sciences. Even with an economic consultant familiar with cost accounting methods used in business, the members of the team found such great difficulty in assigning specific cost figures to the company, the employee, and the community, especially for the preventive costs themselves, that they were not surprised that so little along these lines had appeared in the literature.

However, some methods were worked out by estimating conservatively the costs of certain absences from the job, some undisputed failures in productivity, and the operation of medical and compensation programs. It appears worthwhile to present illustrations of at least some of the costs which can be related to particular samples of problem employees. Illustrations will also be presented of changes in costs, over time, for other employees, in relation to whether mental health recommendations were made by the team and whether or not these recommendations were carried out.

# METHODS

## Sampling

Although 325 employees within two working populations totaling 3,600 were subjects in this study, the methods of calculating economic values will be illustrated on only three matched samples of 19 employees each. The same method will be employed to illustrate cost changes, over time, on a sample of 89 employees, subdivided according to whether or not team recommendations had been made, and whether the referral was, or was not, carried through. The overall methods and the findings pertaining to other aspects of the mental health research project have been presented elsewhere (17–21). The total project was in no sense any attempt to transform human values into dollar values. Rather it was an experiment in secondary prevention, with attention to human problems at an early stage. This was accompanied by an attempt to get some measurements of "ounces of prevention" and "pounds of cure."

The calculated costs of two "problem" samples were compared with a "problem-free" sample since it would be incorrect to assume that no costs accrue concerning the "problem-free" sample of employees. This will be apparent in the presentation of results. Furthermore, to estimate cost changes related to remedial intervention, it is necessary to compare costs of at least two comparable samples at two separate time periods. For example, the cost changes, over time, of the employee sample which accepted remedial intervention were compared with cost changes, over time, of the employee sample which did not accept remedial intervention. Again, it would be incorrect to assume that the baseline costs of any one sample would not vary, over time, due to random or uncontrolled factors.

The first sample on which these economic estimates were calculated was comprised of 19 employees, with a variety of manifestations of job-disruption detected by the personnel or medical departments. These 19 employees shared the common feature to observers in the work environment and to the research team of having some evidence of excessive or frequent drinking of alcoholic beverages. The other two samples, each containing 19 employees, were obtained by matching, individual for individual, from among other employees under study by the team according to sociocultural background, age, marital status, and number of children. They were not matched for income. The item of rate of pay turned out to be an interesting dependent variable.

These three samples will be designated by the following labels: "suspected problem drinking," "miscellaneous problem," and "problem-free." The miscellaneous problem sample was chosen from a pool of employees presenting such problems as short- or long-term absenteeism, repeated accidents, manifestations of interpersonal friction or inefficiency on the job, or frequent visits to the medical department but without evidence of problem drinking. The problem-free sample was obtained from a pool of employees who had been considered by the personnel department to be free from work problems. These samples were drawn from only one of the companies in the study, thus minimizing the differences in cost that might be related to the working environment or fringe benefits.

The sample of 89 employees followed, over time, in relation to recommendations (recommendations, none; recommendations, not followed through; and recommendations, followed through) was divided about equally between the two companies for the total sample (47–42), and for each subsample (24–20, 11–12, and 12–10).

The subsamples, for separate calculation of economic values

during the first half of the mental health study ($T_1$), and again during repeat examinations 27 months later ($T_1$), were comprised of 44 employees for whom no recommendations had been made by the mental health team, 23 for whom recommendations had been made but who had not followed through, and 22 who had followed through on the referral, wholly or in part.

Members of this team had found in a previous study a highly significant correlation between reduction of psychiatric impairment and the following through of a psychiatric consultant's recommendations (19). It seemed worthwhile to compare the cost estimates of the sample of individuals for whom no psychiatric recommendations were made (the majority of whom had been recognized as not presenting a psychiatric disorder), with the sample of employees who had not followed through on the team's recommendations, and with the sample of employees who had done so.

Cost comparisons were also calculated on the same 89 employees after dividing the sample into two subsamples based on clinical diagnosis. Forty-eight employees who were considered "normal" by the clinical team were compared with 41 employees who had been given a clinical psychiatric diagnosis (Table 1).

## Cost Accounting

Two of the authors (K. H. and L. P.) spent considerable time gaining a first hand knowledge of the administration and accounting methods employed in each of the companies in which this study was done. They ferreted out hidden costs that could be related to various kinds of job disruptive behavior. For example, an employee involved in an accidental injury resulting in two days of lost time accrues a measurable cost to the company and to himself. Not only does the company have to replace the employee for two days, but personnel time is involved in the medical department, administering medical aid and keeping records. Personnel time is also needed to record the incident and fill out the appropriate compensa-

## TABLE 1
### Cost comparison

| | Cost to Company | Cost to Employee | Cost to Insurer |
|---|---|---|---|
| Cost of impaired productivity | $100 -$ Percent potential $\times$ Annual salary | | |
| Costs of interpersonal friction | Number of grievance procedures $\times$ Processing costs | | |
| | Number of disciplinary procedures $\times$ Processing costs | | |
| | Number of garnishment procedures $\times$ Processing costs | | |
| Costs of absenteeism | Number of days absent with pay $\times$ Base daily wage | Number of days absent without pay $\times$ Base daily wage rate $-$ Sick benefits paid | |
| Costs of health and accident problems | Number of compensation claims $\times$ Processing costs | | Amount paid annually by Workmen's Compensation Bureau |
| | Number of hospital-medical-surgical claims $\times$ Processing costs | | Amount paid annually for weekly sick benefits |
| | Number of clinic visits $\times$ Average cost per visit + Cost due to lost time | | Amount paid annually for employee and family hospital-medical-surgical expenses |

tion claim forms, not to mention the salary loss to the employee, even if he is partly compensated by the Workmen's Compensation Bureau for this.

Four general areas of cost accounting, involving 12 separate items, were applied to each employee in the study. The method of cost finding will now be described in more detail, under four general headings: (1) cost of impaired productivity, (2) costs of interpersonal frictions, (3) costs of absenteeism, and (4) costs of health and accident problems.

*Cost of impaired productivity.* A Supervisor's Efficiency Rating Scale was constructed by one of the team members. This was comprised of eight 5-point scales on employee attitude and performance, a check list of common problems, and an overall estimate of efficiency. The Rating Scale was administered by a team member who interviewed the employee's immediate supervisor. Correlation coefficients were calculated for each of the eight scales, and the scale relative to "percent potential utilized" correlated well (r.87) with the average of all scales, and with the scale rating "overall effectiveness" (r.74). One of the scales presented the question, "What percent of the employee's potential is represented by his actual performance?" The scale item, "percent potential utilized" was converted into a dollar figure by applying the following formula:

$$100 - \frac{\text{percent}}{\text{potential}} \times \frac{\text{annual}}{\text{salary}} = \$ \underline{\qquad\qquad}$$

The figure obtained represents the apparent economic loss to the company resulting from impaired productivity of an employee as evaluated by an immediate supervisor. It is recognized that this is not an "objective" measurement. However, it is an estimate based on the judgments of representatives of management, made independently of the psychiatric assessments or of any bias toward trying to demonstrate a relationship of costs with any mental health grouping. The supervisors did not even know which of the employees whom they were rating were in "problem" or "problem-free" samples.

*Costs of interpersonal frictions.* It would be impossible to estimate all of the costs arising out of interpersonal frictions within the working environment, but in this study three areas representative of some interpersonal difficulties were evaluated—grievance procedures (Levels 2, 3, 4), disciplinary and garnishment procedures. Dollar costs were estimated by interviewing administrative personnel involved in these proceedings and obtaining a consensus as to how much time, and how many personnel, clerical and administrative, were involved for each of the proceedings. Dollar figures were obtained by multiplying the amount of time involving each person by his daily wage rate. If the employee was involved in the proceedings his time away from work was also taken into account.

$$\frac{\text{Time (hrs)}}{8} \underset{\text{consumed by procedure}}{} \times \underset{\substack{\text{each individual}\\\text{involved in}\\\text{proceedings}}}{\text{Daily wage of}} = \$ \underline{\hspace{2cm}}$$

These were considered to be costs to the company.

*Costs of absenteeism.* Absenteeism represents a loss to the company if the absence is with pay, a loss to the employee if without pay, and a cost to the insurer if the employee is compensated for the absence under a sickness benefit plan. Dollar costs were calculated by multiplying the daily wage rate by the number of days absent with pay (for the company) and by multiplying the number of days absent without pay (for the individual employee). If the employee was compensated for his absence by a sickness benefit plan, this amount was subtracted from the employee's losses. The formulas below were used to calculate absence cost figures.

Cost to Company:

$$\underset{\substack{\text{Days}\\\text{absent}\\\text{with}\\\text{pay}}}{} \times \underset{\substack{\text{Base}\\\text{daily}\\\text{wage}\\\text{rate}}}{} = \$ \underline{\hspace{2cm}}$$

Cost to Employee:

$$
\begin{array}{c}
\text{Days}\\
\text{absent}\\
\text{without}\\
\text{pay}
\end{array}
\ \times\
\begin{array}{c}
\text{Base}\\
\text{daily}\\
\text{wage}\\
\text{rate}
\end{array}
\ -\
\begin{array}{c}
\text{Employee}\\
\text{weekly}\\
\text{sick}\\
\text{benefits}
\end{array}
\ =\ \$\underline{\hspace{2cm}}
$$

Costs to the insurer, which are ultimately company and employee costs, were arrived at by recording the total amount of benefits paid to each employee for the one year period under study. All types of absences were included here.

*Costs of health and accident problems.* Cost figures were estimated for the processing of compensation claims and hospital-medical-surgical benefit claims by estimating the number of clerical and administrative personnel involved, and the amount of time occupied by them when assigned to this particular task. The formula used was very similar to the one applied to grievance, garnishment, and disciplinary proceedings.

Medical clinic visit costs were estimated by dividing the yearly operating costs (salaries and overhead) of the clinic by the total number of clinic visits per year, giving a mean cost per medical clinic visit. Added to this was the estimated time, and its related cost to the company, that an employee would be away from his job while attending the medical clinic.

$$
\begin{array}{c}
\text{Number}\\
\text{of}\\
\text{clinic}\\
\text{visits}
\end{array}
\ \times\
\begin{array}{c}
\text{Mean}\\
\text{cost}\\
\text{per clinic}\\
\text{visit}
\end{array}
\ +\
\begin{array}{c}
\text{Mean}\\
\text{cost of}\\
\text{employee}\\
\text{time loss}
\end{array}
\ =\ \$\underline{\hspace{2cm}}
$$

These were also considered to be company costs.

Health and accident costs to the insurer included the annual amount paid to the employee to compensate him for losses resulting from injury or illness to himself and to his family.

Total costs to the company, the employee, and the insurer for each sample under the study, were calculated and recorded for comparison.

# RESULTS

A breakdown of costs to the company, including the average "percent potential" ratings and absence data, is presented in Tables 2 and 3. In Table 4 total and mean costs to company, employees, and insurer are listed for comparisons between six samples of employees, three of these also being compared over time. Table 5 illustrates costs in relation to a grouping based on whether a psychiatric diagnosis was made after a clinical interview.

The Kruskal–Wallis one-way analysis of variance and the Mann–Whitney U test were used to test the significance of the comparisons derived from the data which these tables summarize.

First it might be mentioned that the salaries (base daily wage) for the three samples of employees in Table 2 were significantly different ($p < .01$) due to higher salaries in the problem-free sample (mean = \$21.60) than in the suspected problem drinking sample (mean = \$17.40) and the miscellaneous problem sample (mean = \$19.00). The latter two samples were not significantly different in salaries ($p = .1469$). This was the interesting dependent variable when these samples had been matched for some key personal variables. Apparently the company was already paying a higher base daily wage rate to the problem-free employees than to the suspected problem drinking employees without taking into account explicitly the kind of cost estimations from which we derived the data summarized in Table 2.

Because of the differences in salary rates we calculated, for comparison, the total costs to the company both on the basis of actual individual salaries for these employees (Table 2) and on the basis of a mean salary for all 57 employees. Both methods of calculating total costs to the company demonstrated significant differences between the problem-free, the miscellaneous problem, and suspected problem drinking samples ($p < .01$ for individual and $p < .02$ for mean salaries).

## TABLE 2
### Calculated costs to company

| | Suspected Problem-Drinking Sample | Miscellaneous Problem Sample | Problem-free Sample |
|---|---|---|---|
| Compensation claims | 194.00 | 194.00 | 38.80 |
| Grievance, level 2 | 4.55 | 9.10 | — |
| Grievance, level 3 | 100.20 | 150.30 | — |
| Grievance, level 4 | 1,279.40 | 1,279.40 | — |
| Disciplinary warnings | 103.80 | 51.90 | — |
| Garnishee warnings | 48.65 | 20.85 | 6.95 |
| Hospital-medical-surgical claims | 297.00 | 660.00 | 231.00 |
| Days absent with pay | 221.00 | — | 38.00 |
| Medical clinic visits | 1,010.16 | 1,225.44 | 426.42 |
| Percent potential costs | 28,143.00 | 27,233.00 | 15,740.00 |
| Total | 31,401.76 | 30,823.99 | 16,481.17 |
| Subtotal | 3,258.76 | 3,590.99 | 741.17 |
| Mean | 1,652.00 | 1,622.00 | 867.00 |
| Percent Potential | 67 | 71 | 86 |
| Mean days absent | 33 | 15 | 2 |

## TABLE 3
### Calculated costs to company from $T_1$ to $T_2$

| | Recommendations None | | Recommendations Not Followed Through | | Recommendations Followed Through | |
|---|---|---|---|---|---|---|
| | $T_1$ | $T_2$ | $T_1$ | $T_2$ | $T_1$ | $T_2$ |
| Compensation claims | 395 | 300 | 388 | 165 | 126 | 72 |
| Grievances, level 2, 3, 4 | 318 | 100 | 1,288 | – | 8 | 50 |
| Disciplinary warnings | 69 | 35 | 25 | 17 | 26 | 69 |
| Garnishee warnings | 7 | 5 | 21 | 19 | 49 | 48 |
| Hospital-medical-surgical claims | 759 | 1,089 | 594 | 759 | 264 | 396 |
| Medical clinic visits | 1,536 | 1,259 | 745 | 600 | 530 | 551 |
| Percent potential costs | 51,343 | 39,473 | 24,904 | 30,427 | 28,526 | 27,695 |
| Days absent with pay | 2,890 | 2,333 | 1,394 | 1,910 | 2,478 | 897 |
| Total | $57,317 | $44,594 | $29,359 | $33,897 | $32,007 | $29,778 |
| Mean | 1,306 | 1,013 | 1,276 | 1,474 | 1,455 | 1,353 |
| Percent potential | 77 | 83 | 77 | 75 | 71 | 73 |
| Mean days absent | 10 | 8 | 12 | 13 | 13 | 8 |

**TABLE 4**

Cost comparisons

| | | Suspected Problem Drinking Group I (19) | Miscellaneous Problems Group II (19) | Problem Free Group III (19) | Recommendations None Group A (44) | | Recommendations Not Followed Through Group B (23) | | Recommendations Followed Through Group C (22) | |
|---|---|---|---|---|---|---|---|---|---|---|
| | | | | | $T_1$ | $T_2$ | $T_1$ | $T_2$ | $T_1$ | $T_2$ |
| Cost to company | Total | $31,402 | $30,824 | $16,481 | $57,317 | $44,594 | $29,359 | $33,897 | $33,007 | $29,778 |
| | Mean | 1,652 | 1,622 | 867 | 1,306 | 1,013 | 1,276 | 1,474 | 1,455 | 1,353 |
| Cost to employees | Total | 8,238 | 4,051 | 524 | 6,316 | 3,594 | 2,502 | 3,462 | 1,980 | 2,193 |
| | Mean | 433 | 213 | 28 | 144 | 82 | 108 | 150 | 90 | 99 |
| Cost to insurer | Total | 7,099 | 4,716 | 1,935 | 9,249 | 4,982 | 5,329 | 5,606 | 2,113 | 2,159 |
| | Mean | 373 | 248 | 162 | 210 | 113 | 231 | 243 | 96 | 98 |

**TABLE 5**
**Clinical diagnosis and costs**

|  | No. Clinical Diagnoses (N = 48) | Clinical Diagnoses (N = 41) |
|---|---|---|
| Compensation claims | 189.00 | 348.00 |
| Grievances | 50.00 | 100.00 |
| Disciplinary warnings | 52.00 | 69.00 |
| Garnishee warnings | 49.00 | 24.00 |
| Hospital-medical-surgical claims | 1,485.00 | 726.00 |
| Days absent with pay | 1,319.00 | 3,921.00 |
| Medical clinic visits | 1,532.00 | 865.00 |
| Percent potential costs | 42,967.00 | 54,661.00 |
| Total | 47,644.00 | 60,714.00 |
| Mean | 992.00 | 1,480.00 |
| Percent potential (mean) | 83 | 72 |
| Days absent (mean) | 7 | 12 |

To test this another way, nine employees in each of the three samples were matched also for salary (daily wage rate) and again a statistically significant difference in total costs was demonstrated ($p < .02$).

It is interesting to note in Table 2 that the approximately equal total costs to the company for the two problem samples are almost twice the total costs for the problem-free sample, when costs based on the percent potential are included. Furthermore, the approximately equal subtotals for the problem samples, without including percent potential, are more than four times the costs for the "problem-free" sample ($p < .001$). In other words, the "percent potential" estimates, based on management's judgments of the employees, although contributing to the large total cost figures, are not needed to show that the "problem-free" employees are less costly to the company than the employees in the problem samples.

It was also calculated that the yearly medical clinic visits, the percent potential figures, and the yearly days absence totals were significantly different in the three samples of Table 2 ($p < .01$, $p < .01$, and $p < .001$), indicating some of the differences accounting for the total cost differences.

The costs to the employees and the costs to the insurer for the same three samples (suspected problem drinking, miscellaneous problem, and problem-free), as summarized in Table 4, were significantly different ($p < .001$ and $p < .001$). The suspected problem drinking employees appeared to be about 16 times as costly and the miscellaneous problem employees about 8 times as costly to themselves (in loss of pay) as the problem-free employees. Similarly, the costs to the insurer appeared to be about 3½ times as high in the suspected problem drinking sample and about 2½ times as high in the miscellaneous problem sample as in the problem-free sample.

Inspection of Tables 3 and 4 gives the impression that employees for whom no recommendations were made and employees who followed through on recommendations decreased in costs to the company from $T_1$ to $T_2$, and that these employees who did not follow through on recommendations increased in such costs. However, the statistical calculations did not indicate other than random variance over time in these different samples.

Table 5 illustrates significantly greater total costs and lower percent potential ratings accruing to a sample of employees for whom a psychiatric diagnosis had been considered appropriate when compared to a sample of employees who also had been interviewed and had not been considered by the clinical team to fit into any psychiatric diagnostic category ($p < .05$).

## COMMENT

Our cost findings relative to the suspected problem drinking employee confirm the observations of Maxwell (15), who reported that problem drinkers had significantly higher absence rates and accident and sickness benefit payment rates than a control group of employees. Furthermore our data indicates that the suspected problem drinking employee has a significantly greater number of medical clinic visits, is rated lower (percent potential) by his immediate supervisor, and is paid a lesser salary than the problem-free employee.

It would be unrealistic to assume that the problem-free sample was composed of the average or normal employee; more likely he approached the ideal or supernormal. For the sake of comparison, if we place the problem-free employee at a hypothetical 100% efficiency (actually rated at a mean of 86%), the suspected problem drinking employee would, at best, be working up to only 77% efficiency, about a "three-quarter man." Others (8, 22) have called the problem-drinking employee a "half man," using somewhat different criteria, but perhaps our sample of problem-drinkers, being only suspected and probably still in the early phases of their illness were somewhat less impaired than the more commonly observed problem-drinking employee.

Some may be tempted to conclude immediately that the problem-drinking employee and other problem employees are too costly to be kept in the working group and that the wise solution would be to discover and dismiss them as soon as possible. Experience does not support this. It is very difficult to discover any but the most grossly impaired alcoholic, particularly if fellow employees, and even supervisors, know it is the policy of the company to dismiss problem-drinking employees upon discovery. A policy of this kind often results in the alcoholic being even more carefully hidden. If a company were to start a "witch hunt" with these groups to decrease costs, it would eventually eliminate many valuable employees who might be in a temporary, reversible, state of impairment and, as recent experience demonstrates, have a reasonably good chance of making a recovery.

Economic analyses of the three samples (recommendations none, recommendations not followed through, recommendations followed through), involving cost changes over time ($T_1$

to T²) and outcome of recommendations, did not demonstrate any significant degree of change. Thus, we were unable to establish the economic value of remedial intervention in this particular study.

Reasons why the recommendations followed through sample did not show a significant decrease in costs are not apparent but this may be related, at least in part, to the rather short interval of 27 months which is probably too short a time to demonstrate the kinds of changes we had hypothesized.

The authors would like to re-emphasize that this study, which was only part of a larger study on secondary prevention, is not an attempt to place dollar values on human problems but rather to demonstrate in as specific a way as possible the economic impact of problem drinking and perhaps other emotional illnesses, with the hope that data of this nature will encourage both labor and management to implement all of the known treatment methods toward rehabilitation of these employees. It is also an attempt to take out some of the guesswork when estimating the costs of problem employees.

## CONCLUSION

1. Suspected problem-drinking and other-problem employees are significantly more costly to the company, themselves, and the insurance carriers than problem-free employees.
2. Employees who have been given a psychiatric diagnosis by a clinical team are significantly more costly to industry than employees for whom a psychiatric diagnosis did not seem warranted.

## SUMMARY

A method of calculating specific costs to industry stemming from job-disruptive behavior is presented. Costs to the company, the employee, and the insurance carriers were calculated based on the following indices:

1. Cost of impaired productivity.
2. Cost of interpersonal frictions as manifested in grievance, disciplinary, and garnishment procedures.
3. Cost of absenteeism.
4. Cost of health and accident problems as manifested in compensation and hospital-medical-surgical claims, and medical-surgical and weekly sick benefit payments.

Costs were calculated for suspected problem-drinking, miscellaneous-problem, and problem-free samples, and cost changes over time were examined for three employee samples based on whether remedial intervention was recommended, followed through, or not followed through.

Evidence is presented which demonstrates the significantly higher costs to industry accrued by problem-drinking and other-problem employees. However, this study did not demonstrate the economic value of secondary prevention or early remedial intervention within the relatively short span of follow-up which was possible in this project.

## ACKNOWLEDGMENT

This study was supported in part by Mental Health Project grant No. MH 287, U.S. Public Health Service.

G. R. Ashman, Ph.D., who was formerly Senior Psychologist on this project and Assistant Professor of Psychology, Department of Psychiatry, University of Cincinnati, constructed the Supervisor's Efficiency Rating Scale.

## REFERENCES

1. Burlingame, C. C. You can drive a horse to water. *Mental Hygiene,* 1945, **29**, 208–216.

2. Shepard, W. P. *The physician in industry.* New York: McGraw-Hill Book Co., 1961.

3. Burr, H. B. Business objectives and procedures. *Archives of Environmental Health,* 1962, **5**, 192–200.

4. Brehm, P. A. Cost analysis of a medical department in industry. *Industrial Hygiene News Letter,* 1949, **9**, 6–7.

5. Fein, R. *The economics of mental illness.* New York: Basic Books, 1958.

6. Schwartz, L., Tulipan, L., & Birmingham, D. J. *Occupational diseases of the skin,* ed. 3. Philadelphia: Lea and Febiger, 1957.

7. Ferguson, C. A., et al. *The legacy of neglect.* Fort Worth, Texas: Industrial Mental Health Associates, 1965.

8. Henderson, R. M., & Bacon, S. D. Problem drinking: The Yale plan for business and industry. *Quarterly Journal of Studies of Alcoholism,* 1953, **14**, 247–262.

9. Maisel, A. Q. (Ed.). *The health of people who work.* New York: National Health Council, 1960.

10. McMurry, R. N. Mental illness, society's and industry's six billion dollar burden. *Personnel Administration,* 1962, **25**, 4–18.

11. Menninger, W. C., & Levinson, H. Industrial mental health: Observations and perspectives. *Menninger Quarterly,* 1954, **8**, 1.

12. Plummer, N., & Hinkle, L. E., Jr. Sickness absenteeism. *Archives of Industrial Hygiene,* 1955, **112**, 218–230.

13. Schulzinger, M. S. *The accident syndrome.* Springfield, Illinois: Charles C. Thomas, 1956.

14. Burr, H. B. Westinghouse management health examinations—Their investment values. *Journal of Occupational Medicine,* 1960, **2**, 80–91.

15. Maxwell, M. A. A study of absenteeism, accidents and sickness payments in problem drinkers in one industry. *Quarterly Journal of Studies of Alcoholism,* 1959, **20**, 302–312.

16. Howard, M. N., & Hoag, A. E. Value and operation of an industrial medical program. *Archives of Industrial Hygiene,* 1951, **3**, 375–385.

17. Lipinski, E., et al. Occupational accidents: Some psychosocial factors in the accident syndrome. *Canadian Psychiatry Association Journal,* 1965, **10**, 299–307.

18. Powles, W. E., et al. "Without the will": Problems of motivation in secondary prevention in industrial mental health. *Journal American Psychiatry Association,* to be published.

19. Ross, W. D., et al. Report on the follow-up study, industrial mental health project of the College of Medicine, University of Cincinnati (N.I.M.H. Grant OM-287), June 1960.

20. Ross, W. D., et al. Five year report, industrial mental health project of the College of Medicine, University of Cincinnati (N.I.M.H. Grant OM-287), August 1964.

21. Ross, W. D., Powles, W. E., & Winslow, W. W. Secondary prevention of job-disruption in industry. *Journal of Occupational Medicine,* 1965, **7**, 314–320.

22. Ross, W. D. *Practical psychiatry for industrial physicians.* Springfield, Illinois: Charles C Thomas, 1956.

# Part II
# Emerging Trends
# in Industrial
# Mental Health Programs

# 7. OCCUPATIONAL MENTAL HEALTH: REVIEW OF AN EMERGING ART

**Alan A. McLean, M.D.**

The emerging field of occupational mental health is concerned with both the psychiatrically ill employee and with factors in the work environment which stimulate mentally healthy behavior. This report traces historical influences which have contributed to present practices, discusses current activities, surveys selected publications, and considers possible implications for future developments.

Historical material has been largely drawn from the pages of the *American Journal of Psychiatry,* its annual reviews, and definitive articles which, since 1927, have been addressed periodically to industrial and occupational psychiatry. Other disciplines have increasingly contributed, however, broadening our base of knowledge beyond clinical concepts and applications. From the behavioral sciences, occupational medicine, and toxicology have come publications and programs of significant interest to those concerned with mental disorder and mental health in the work setting. Much of this material will also be considered.

Dr. McLean is Program Director, Center for Occupational Mental Health, Inc., 120 Grand Street, White Plains, N.Y.

This review was prepared under contract for the National Clearinghouse for Mental Health Information, National Institute of Mental Health, Bethesda, Maryland.

Center consultants who participated in the preparation of this review include: Ralph T. Collins, M.D., Richard A. Dunnington, M.A., David H. Goldstein, M.D., Harry Levinson, Ph.D., John MacIver, M.D., and Graham C. Taylor, M.D. Members of a subcommittee of the American Psychiatric Association Committee on Occupational Psychiatry, chaired by Simon Auster, M.D., edited the final draft.

## HISTORICAL REVIEW

For a century or so prior to 1870, a primary aim of industrial leaders seems to have been the highest possible production at the lowest possible cost. The worker was employed as a source of physical energy, and little consideration was given to his well-being. He knew no material security and "earned too much to die and too little to live" (85).

Around 1850 the average life expectancy of the factory worker was 32 years. In many locations, particularly in England and on the Continent, children started working at age six, putting in the same 12 hours a day as did their fathers.

In this period the relationship between factory hand and industry was characterized by suffering—materially, bodily, and mentally. There probably was a certain kind of adjustment based upon their current interpretations of tenets of Christianity which saw suffering as an essential condition of life, labor as a punishment, and happiness as not to be achieved in this life.

The rise of the labor movement was the expression of a challenge to this philosophy that was developing throughout all the ranks of the society. Comfort and ease, even perhaps happiness, were to be attainable. It was in this context that concern with occupational mental health first appeared.

While nothing appears in the literature until the 1940s concerning his activities, C. C. Burlingame in the first annual review of psychiatric progress on "Psychiatry in Industry" (14) notes that his activities in 1915 at the Cheney Silk Company constituted the first full-time function of the psychiatrist in industry. Neither in this article nor in the many later references to Burlingame in this pioneering role is there a detailed outline of his functions.

In the first issue (1917) of the journal *Mental Hygiene*, Herman Adler, previously chief of staff of the Boston Psychopathic Hospital, reported on patients for whom unemployment had been a serious problem (1). Males between the ages of 25 and 55, these individuals were grouped into three classifications: "paranoid personalities," "inadequate personalities," and the "emotionally unstable."

Three years later, Mary Jarrett reported a follow-up of this same group, observing that 75% were successfully adjusted from an occupational point of view (43).

Few articles appearing in the literature prior to Adler's 1917 report could properly be included in the emerging field of industrial or occupational psychiatry. Both his work and Jarrett's appear to have resulted from the stimulus of E. E. Southard, Director of the Boston Psychopathic Hospital and Professor of Neuropathology at Harvard.

In 1919 Southard was asked by the Engineering Foundation of New York to investigate emotional problems among workers. Working with a clinical team that included a social worker and a psychologist, he found that "62 % of more than 4,000 cases reached the discharged status through traits of social incompetence rather than occupational incompetence" (43). These statistics are still quoted today as a valid representation of a continuing industrial pattern.

The following year Southard commented as follows:

> Industrial medicine exists, industrial psychiatry ought to exist. It is important for the modern psychiatrist not to hide his light under a bushel; he must step forth to new community duties. It seems to me that as psychiatrists we should be able to help this movement wherever it becomes practically possible. The practical possibilities of helping lie in connection with the fact that the majority of our male patients have come out of industry in some capacity. Some investigations of the individual patient with respect to their industrial status and future should be made. I think that we will have a place in the routine of industrial management not as a permanent staff member (except in very large firms and business systems) but as consultants. The function of this occasional consultant would be preventative rather than curative of the general condition of unrest (81).

Thus was set down in Boston some 45 years ago an operating philosophy for the psychiatrist—and, indeed, in later days for the clinical psychologist—in industry.

**1920–1929**


The first "Review of Industrial Psychiatry" in the *American Journal of Psychiatry* in April 1927 (80) summarized the literature to date, defined the field, and traced its development. Mandel Sherman, its author, considered the psychiatrist's rightful area of concern to be the "individual's adjustment to the situation as a whole." The psychiatrist also is said to "attempt to forestall maladjustments by aiding in developing interests and incentives."

The stimulus for the development of industrial psychiatry until that time is traced to: (1) the work of the psychologists in the industrial field, whose studies of abilities and intelligence were felt to fall far short of considering the whole man; (2) the adjustment problems of men in the armed forces during World War I; (3) the propaganda efforts of the mental hygienists," here including Southard; and (4) the introduction of scientific methodology into psychiatry.

By scientific methodology, Sherman meant the study of the individual and his vocation from the standpoint of "development of conflicts in his early life." He attributed this approach to the mental hygienists and termed it a contribution of American psychiatry. He went on to discuss a second "methodological" approach: "Another method stems from the European psycho-analytic method, finding conflicts due to lack of adequate expression of two primary instincts, sexual and self-preservative." Citing W. A. White's paper "Psycho-analysis in Vocational Guidance," he notes that vocational choice often results from drives developed early in life. He further notes that W. Stekel has used three groups to classify vocational choice: (1) those who developed strong positive identification with father, (2) those rejecting a hated father, and (3) "the sublimation group."

Sherman cited other methods of explaining intrapsychic conflicts manifest in the work situation. He included the "instinct theory" of O. Tead, whose subsequent books on industrial management became classic, and a theory of "reveries." The latter contribution came from Elton Mayo in 1922, well before the famous "Hawthorne experiments" at Western Electric Company which he led.

The penchant of psychiatrists of the time to classify patterns of emotional reaction did not escape those with industrial interests. In addition to Adler's attempt, which did not meet with general acceptance, Pruette and Fryer spoke of the "repressed" and the "elated" as two categories of disturbed worker.

At the conclusion of this first review of the field, Sherman said that among the various methods of industrial psychiatry, the most successful procedure used to aid the individual in readjusting to industry had been one which attempted to analyze the total situation—the early life history, the social situation, the worker's motives and incentives in addition to the immediate difficulties at work. "Classification of maladjusted individuals into types or groups has been of little help." His final plea was for vocational guidance during the formative years to obviate many later industrial maladjustments.

The year 1922 saw the introduction of the first full-time psychiatrist in an American business organization of which we have a full description; Lydia Giberson was employed by the Metropolitan Life Insurance Company (31). In 1924, a mental health service was introduced at the R. H. Macy department store. V. V. Anderson, in 1929, summarized-this program in the first book on industrial psychiatry (3). In a paper at the 80th annual meeting of the American Psychiatric Association, also in 1924, Osnato discussed current concepts of the industrial neuroses, by which he meant post-traumatic reactions (68). His primary concern was in distinguishing between "malingerers and hysterics."

In the 1920s the greatest stimulus to the study of industry as a social organization came from Professor Mayo. Psychiatrists then and now acknowledge his influence on their thinking about the individual and his environment. Professor Mayo became interested in studies on fatigue and monotony at the Harvard Physiology Laboratory. In 1923, he was asked to investigate high labor turnover in a textile mill. He noted that, with the introduction of rest periods for workers in monotonous jobs, morale rose and labor turnover decreased.

In 1927, Mayo and his associates undertook a study of working conditions at the Hawthorne Plant of the Western Electric Company in Chicago. In several years of study at this location, 20,000 employees were interviewed and small experimental groups of workers were intensively observed as changes were made in their work situation. These studies demonstrated the tremendous importance of human interaction as an integral part of the work situation, and that dissatisfactions arising in or out of the plant become entwined, influencing each other and affecting work production.

Mayo's classic volume, *The Human Problems of an Industrial Civilization* (56), describes this work, as does the book *Management and the Worker* by Roethlisberger and Dickson (76).

The Hawthorne studies concluded that an industrial enterprise has two functions: economic and social. Production output was felt to be a form of *social* behavior, and all the activity of a plant may be viewed as an interaction of structure, culture, and personality. If any one of these variables is altered, change must occur in the other two. Reactions to stress on the part of individual employees arise when there is resistance to change, when there are faulty control and communications systems, and in the adjustments of the individual worker to his structure at work (62).

During the first World War a series of papers from the Industrial Fatigue Research Board in England began to focus attention on the psychological components of industrial accidents (34), on fatigue, and on psychiatric illness in the work setting (23). Little mention was made of these studies in American literature until some two decades later. Basic concepts of accident proneness and our first indications of the prevalence of psychiatric disorder in an industrial population came from this work.

The applications of psychiatry to industry in this country during the 1930s are well described in Rennie, Swackhamer, and Woodward's 1947 paper, "Toward Industrial Mental Health: An Historical Review" (73).

**1930–1939**

The depression years were characterized by quiescence in the field; even the annual review was dropped from the *American Journal of Psychiatry*. The major clinical activities were those of Giberson (31–33) and Burling (10,11), the only psychiatrists operating full-time programs. Some interest continued to be shown by industrial medicine (22). Mayo's work, which continued well into this decade, was the most significant research of the period.

**1940–1949**

World War II had tremendous impact upon clinical applications of the psychiatrist, and to a lesser degree the clinical psychologist, in industry. Concepts of psychoanalytic psychology were introduced and applied. Expectations of industry were high, perhaps unrealistically so, and to a certain extent psychiatry and psychology were "oversold." Yet during the war years greater and more sophisticated applications in the mold of Southard, Sherman, and White could be seen (7, 8, 53, 55, 59).

Of the many papers during these years, three will illustrate the pattern of publication during the early 1940s. In a 1944 editorial in the *American Journal of Psychiatry*, C. Macfie Campbell stated that the war had "swept the psychiatrist out of his hospital wards and his administrative routine." It was to be hoped, he said, that the psychiatrist would continue "devoting more attention to that portion of social living which occupies the major portion of an individual's life—his job." He went on to conclude: "Industry turns out two main commodities, material goods and human satisfactions. The wholesome or unwholesome structure and the stability or instability of our modern industrial community may well depend upon the amount of attention given to the latter commodity" (20).

In 1943, Rosenbaum and Romano discussed "Psychiatric

Casualties among Defense Workers" (77). They pointed to the need for industrial physicians to concern themselves with the recognition of emotional factors underlying behavior, which so frequently resulted in inferior output, high sickness rates, high labor turnover, and absenteeism—"of prime importance under wartime conditions which cannot countenance impaired efficiency."

Among the many articles describing mental health programs in wartime industry, those concerning the Oak Ridge, Tennessee, industrial community subsequently received major attention (14–17). With available psychiatric assistance, primarily through "emotional first-aid stations," a minimum of on-the-job treatment resulted in conspicuous on-the-job improvement. As in publications prior to the war, psychiatrists outlining their wartime experiences noted that the causes of emotional disturbance in industry lie primarily in the individual or in the home or nonwork social surroundings, rather than in the job situation.

Following the war, with the sharp cutback in defense industries which had employed psychiatrists, many industrial mental health programs came to a halt. Interest in the rehabilitation of the psychiatrically handicapped veteran gave impetus to the development of civilian programs such as that at Eastman Kodak Company. Successful application of psychiatric skills in the armed forces during the war stimulated the interest of several psychiatrists to broaden their scope of practice and to include preventive concepts born of their experiences in the service.

The federal government initiated action with the Vocational Rehabilitation Act Amendments of 1943, and the Office of Vocational Rehabilitation issued a pamphlet, "The Doctor and Vocational Rehabilitation for Civilians" (84). Stimulus was given to the training of clinical psychologists in greater number, primarily in programs of the Veterans Administration. Many were subsequently to work in industry.

Roffey Park was established by British industry immediately after the war as an industrial rehabilitation center for "neurosis cases." During the ensuing decade, some 8,000 cases were treated. In the introduction to the volume describing this work, Ling states that "Maladjustment to work has been a major factor in the ill health of many of these men and women" (60).

At the Central Institute of Psychiatry in Moscow, Melekhov and his associates also dealt specifically with psychoneurotic World War II patients. An article outlining the rehabilitation of these patients appeared in *Occupational Therapy and Rehabilitation* in 1947 (60).

In the United States, problems of workmen's compensation were receiving increasing attention, since the courts had by then ruled a wide variety of illness compensable. According to Burlingame's annual review in 1949 (17), coronaries occurring on the job following occupational stress, hypertension, cancer, and tuberculosis activated by employment, suicide caused by job-related depression, and "paralysis by fright" had all been awarded claims. This trend has in the 1960s received closer attention as awards increase for psychiatric disability unrelated to physical accident.

The first fellowship program for training psychiatrists for work in industry was announced in 1948. Under a grant from the Carnegie Corporation, and under the direction of Leighton and Burling, seven psychiatrists were trained at Cornell University's New York State School of Industrial and Labor Relations (13).

The late 1940s also saw the publication of books by Tredgold (82), Ling (54), Brodman (6), and Rennie, Burling, and Woodward (72). These and other monographs focused professional interest on the role of the psychiatrist in industry.

Along with continuing concern for the effects of the emotionally disturbed employee on his work environment and the early recognition and treatment of his symptoms came increased attention by psychiatrists for specific problems such as alcoholism, accidents, psychosomatic reactions, the aging worker, the executive and his emotional problems, emphasis on techniques of management education, and the structuring of the work environment. These areas were receiving increasing attention from several of the behavioral science disciplines during the same period.

## 1950–1955

In the early 1950s, Dershimer assumed responsibility for the annual reviews in the *American Journal of Psychiatry* (24–27). From 1943 to 1955 he was chief psychiatrist for the du Pont Company. His pessimistic notes listing few of the current publications complained about the lack of acceptance of the psychiatrist in business and industry. The reasons, he felt, were that: (1) psychiatrists have no knowledge of the realities of private enterprise; (2) they belittle the practical knowledge of the field of human relations possessed by industrialists; and (3) they resort to "name calling" when industry fails to demand their services.

One trend Dershimer identified was the increasing tendency to treat psychoneurotic employees while they continue at work. Dershimer wrote that, even though the job may be stressful, "end results are better when patients are helped to meet their responsibilities." At du Pont, he implied, such an approach was then common.

The first few years of the decade saw publication of a series of significant documents. From the Tavistock Clinic in London came the first volume of the Glacier Metal Company studies, led by Jaques (41). Both the methodology and the research results of this pilot application of psychoanalytic concepts to organization behavior had considerable influence on the development of subsequent programs. Jaques' later concepts of equitable wage payment based on the time span of responsibility inherent in any job were mainly published in the late 1950s but had their roots in the earlier work (39, 40, 42). The reactions of the management of the Glacier Metal Company were subsequently reported by the chairman of its board of directors, Mr. Wilfred Brown (9).

Kalinowsky's psychiatric study of war veterans in Germany (44), Pokorny and Moore's "Neuroses and Compensation" (70), Burling, Lentz, and Wilson's volume on the hospital

(12), Ross' excellent psychiatric text for the industrial physician (78), and the Group for the Advancement of Psychiatry's definitive statement on the role of the psychiatrist in industry (35) are but a few representative samples of U.S. publications.

During these same first few years of the 1950s, Mindus conducted a six-month survey of industrial psychiatry in Great Britain, the United States, and Canada for the World Health Organization and later developed his own concept of industrial psychiatry (63). The surgery resulted in the most extensive report on programmatic activities in the field (64). The author visited plants, universities, institutions, agencies, and union facilities, summarizing his observations and relating them to prior experiences in the Scandinavian countries.

National committees in the United States included those of the American Psychiatric Association, which served as a clearinghouse of information and represented the official professional viewpoint, that of the Group for the Advancement of Psychiatry, which continued to evaluate current developments in the field, and, while less active at this time, those of the American Medical Association and the Industrial Medical Association.

This period, as reflected in the literature, saw concern for management and executive education with more formalized techniques than previously existed. Laughlin's work with government executives (47–49), lectures and seminars sponsored by individual companies and by community agencies such as local mental health associations, and "sensitivity training" as exemplified by programs of the National Training Laboratories received considerable attention from psychiatry. A psychoanalytic view of work and employment (69), significant research on industrial accidents (79), concern with executive mental health, with labor union programs, and with the rehabilitation of the previously hospitalized psychiatric patient were all subjects of discussion.

## 1956–1959

Training for psychiatrists, industrial physicians and executives expanded, particularly with the stimulus of the Menninger Foundation and an enlarging number of other sponsoring agencies including the University of Cincinnati, Cornell University, the National Association for Mental Health, and the American Psychiatric Association. Interest on the part of the lay and business press in industrial mental health programs became heavier with feature articles in papers such as the *Wall Street Journal*, syndicated stories by a writer for the Associated Press, and articles in *Business Week, Fortune*, and the *Saturday Evening Post*.

New full-time psychiatric programs were begun at International Business Machines Corporation, America Fore Insurance Group, the Metropolitan Life Insurance Company, and elsewhere. At Metropolitan, Giberson, now reporting to an executive vice-president, was no longer associated with the medical department where a psychiatrist was added. With the death of Walter Woodward, the program at American Cyanamid was discontinued in favor of outside psychiatric consultations. The short-lived program at General Electric Company in Cincinnati was discontinued in favor of a part-time consultant. James Conant, a clinical psychologist, was added to the medical staff of the General Electric Company at Hanford, Washington, to concentrate on management education and clinical consultation on a full-time basis. Research activities under Ross at the University of Cincinnati and Levinson at the Menninger Foundation were instituted.

Books included McLean and Taylor's *Mental Health in Industry* (59) and Menninger and Levinson's *Human Understanding in Industry* (61). By this time articles and monographs concerning the psychiatrist and clinical psychologist in industry, publications by them and others about mental health problems in the world of work were issued frequently. The majority of citations in a recent bibliographic definition of the field, which included nearly 2,000 items, appeared during the late 1950s and early 1960s (67).

Alcoholism, automation, absenteeism, rehabilitation, research, post-traumatic neurotic reactions, the psychological fulfillment of the individual in the work setting, the ever-present, generally descriptive discussions of psychiatric applications in business and industry—these were frequent concerns in the literature.

## 1960–1965

The first half of this decade has been marked by continuing growth and expansion of interest in the field. On the international level, a world-wide interest in the mental health implications of the industrial setting was evident in the content of papers read at the 14th International Congress on Occupational Health held in Madrid in 1963. More than 40 presentations were concerned with the psychological problems of the industrial environment. The 1964 annual meeting of the World Federation for Mental Health, held in Bern, had its entire program devoted to mental health in industry. The First International Congress on Social Psychiatry in London in 1964 included many formal presentations on this topic.

In this country, surveys indicated more than 200 psychiatrists and 150 clinical psychologists active in industry. New professional organizations were created, including the Occupational Psychiatry Group and the Center for Occupational Mental Health, Inc. The former, in New York City, consists of 75 industrial medical directors and psychiatrists who meet five times a year for formal discussions followed by a social hour and dinner. The latter, a nonprofit organization, was incorporated in 1963 to collect and disseminate data in the field and develop research and educational programs and services for the expanding activities of those interested in occupational mental health.

Significant events in the early '60s included the omission of the word "Physically" from the title of the President's Committee on the Handicapped, with its subsequent emphasis on the "mentally restored" and mentally retarded worker. Legal implications from the Carter vs. General Motors case (86), where a psychosis was held compensable in the absence of specific physical or psychological trauma, stimulated increased psychiatric attention to matters of workmen's compensation.

Concern for the social and psychological implications of

automation has been reflected in seminars and symposiums, a major one being held under the sponsorship of the Group for the Advancement of Psychiatry in 1964. Regular sections of the American Psychiatric Association's annual programs included papers on employment and rehabilitation as well as round-table discussions on occupational stress, compensation, automation, and research (57, 58).

In the program area, new ones continue to develop and old ones to grow. In the universities these range in focus from the pure behavioral science research activities of the Institute for Social Research of the University of Michigan (30), through the studies on job satisfactions and psychological growth of Herzberg at Western Reserve (36, 37), to the clinical analysis of the organization and application of group dynamics by Argyris at Yale (4, 5).

Typical of the activities in medical and psychiatric centers are those of the Allan Memorial Institute of Psychiatry of McGill University (18) and the Menninger Foundation. The Industrial Relations Center of the former institution conducts a consultative and educational seminar program (19, 72). The Division of Industrial Mental Health of the Menninger Foundation conducts research on the relationship between man and the organization and also operates a fellowship program for psychiatrists in industrial psychiatry and an educational program for industrial physicians and executives (52).

Industry itself currently has a full range of programs, from part-time outside consultants to full-time staff personnel. Their activities may be based in the medical departments or personnel departments or they may report directly to a senior executive. Their work may consist of straightforward clinical evaluation or treatment with varying regard to the circumstance of the work setting, of clinical consultation, education, training, policy consultation, research, or a combination of these; the last arrangement is most common with those spending a major part of their time in the work setting.

The professional literature of recent years demonstrates a continuing concern on the part of medicine, management, unions, the behavioral sciences, and psychology for the mental health of people at work. As expressed in publications, interest has most recently been focused on automation, accidents, psychosomatic reactions, alcoholism, job adjustment, and work satisfaction, rehabilitation, compensation claims, industrial mental health programs, motivation for work, and symptoms of psychiatric illness which disturb effective performance.

Journal articles and books vary in their content from psychodynamic speculations to precise engineering studies of man-machine relationships. Many writers continue the earlier trend of exhorting and directing others to develop better mental health programs or to become interested in psychiatric problems. Carefully executed clinical research is rare and not often seen in the literature. However, many clinical programs of fair sophistication have not seen the light of the printed page, the feeling of some companies being that conduct of clinical programs and the results of behavioral science research within the organization are properly proprietary. Additional reluctance has stemmed from professionals conducting such programs who feel that outlines of their activities are not proper subjects for the scientific literature. And, of course, many journals discourage such purely descriptive articles in favor of those reporting research results. It is fair to say that the literature does not accurately represent the level of activity in the field.

In the periodical literature, in addition to the occasional individual papers, special sections relating to occupational mental health are appearing from time to time. The greater portion of one issue of *Industrial Medicine and Surgery* (June 1963) was devoted to "The Worker in the New Industrial Environment" while a previous issue dealt extensively with "Emotional Problems of Executives" (May 1963), and one complete issue was concerned with "The Impact of Psychiatry on American Management" (November 1962).

This half decade has also produced a number of major publications covering all aspects of occupational mental health. On the clinical side, there is a new textbook by Collins (21). The American Medical Association issued a guide for employability after psychiatric illness (38). Levinson's *Emo-*

*tional Health in the World of Work* (50) appeared in early 1964
to aid executives' understanding of behavior, and the American Psychiatric Association's Committee on Occupational
Psychiatry issued *The Mentally Ill Employee* (2), a management-
oriented guide, in early 1965. Research publications include
monographs by Levinson and associates (52), by the staff of
the Institute for Social Research of the University of Michigan
(30), and a volume on the *Mental Health of the Industrial Worker*
by Kornhauser (45). A unique publication is a study of industrial mental health by a group of Harvard Business School
graduate students, entitled *The Legacy of Neglect* (28).

Publication of a regular newsletter in occupational
psychiatry was undertaken by the American Psychiatric
Association's Committee on Occupational Psychiatry in 1960.
This was recently superseded by *Occupational Mental Health
Notes,* a monthly information bulletin put out by the National
Clearinghouse for Mental Health Information in connection
with its bibliographic and abstracting activities.

## LABOR UNION ACTIVITIES

In May 1964 a conference on Labor and Mental Health
was held in New York City, sponsored by the Community
Services Division of the AFL-CIO. Organized labor and mental
health professionals were about equally represented at this
meeting, the first of its kind and the first formal step by the
national labor movement to develop a mental health policy.

While this was a major advance in the field, it did not appear
de novo but took place against a background of several decades
of interest by individuals and groups in the labor movement.
As far back as 1944, Clayton W. Fountain of the United Auto
Workers addressed the American Psychiatric Association on
"Labor's Place in an Industrial Mental Health Program" (29).
While confirming the interest of the unions in the workers'
mental health, he stated that to be acceptable to labor, any
program developed must not be paternalistic, nor should it
be used to undermine the grievance procedure or in any
other way subvert the union movement. These cautions con-

tinue to influence labor's attitude towards industrial mental health programs and have resulted in few programs being developed under joint sponsorship. Where a company has successfully established a program that avoids these pitfalls, the union will often work with it in close collaboration, but formal participation is avoided.

In 1957 labor movement interest in mental health crystallized around the formation of the National Institute of Labor Education, an organization under the joint directorship of union leaders and mental health professionals. The purpose of this group was to stimulate research and program development in the area of labor and mental health. As part of this program, two documents (65, 71) have been published to serve as guides to interested professionals.

Development has accelerated in the program area. Although as far back as 1946 the Labor Health Institute of Teamsters Local 688 in St. Louis had a psychiatric service as part of its comprehensive health program, it was supported by money from a negotiated fund for general medical care rather than through a specific clause of a collective bargaining agreement (83). The latter pattern did not appear until 1959, when Retail Clerks Local 770 in Los Angeles obtained a contract providing funds for psychiatric services. Since that time a number of other programs have appeared. There has generally been something innovative about each of them. An early one was established by the United Mine Workers of America, which contracted with a private mental hospital in Virginia to serve their members and dependents through a program of traveling clinics. As the demand for service grew, these clinics became permanent establishments in several communities, partly supported by a retainer from the United Mine Workers and partly from fees from nonunion patients (65).

More recently, four union locals in Chicago have collaborated to establish a psychiatric clinic at the Union Health Center and have included in its design two training programs in the recognition and handling of emotional problems, one for their general physicians and one for union leaders. A recently initiated program is located at the Sidney Hillman

Health Center of the Amalgamated Clothing Workers of America in New York City (87). An outgrowth of a physical rehabilitation project, this project has sent its staff out into the factories where they work with union representatives and into the union halls where they are visible and immediately available to all workers. Cooperation by management has been uniformly high.

The most recent development in this area, and a particularly important one because of its trend-setting features, is the mental health benefit program recently negotiated by the United Auto Workers with the automobile and agricultural implement manufacturers (66). This contract represents a shift from the traditional labor emphasis on prepaid programs in its provision of limited-coverage health insurance of a traditional type. From the point of view of the industrially oriented psychiatrist, it also unfortunately loses the potential benefits of a program tied in with the work setting.

Despite the variation in the programs described here, it is clear that the pattern of union provision of services has been set. The labor movement, in part feeling that management has been neglectful of its responsibilities in this area of health services and also recognizing its own broader responsibility to its members as part of its general concern for their welfare, is continuing to press for mental health services of a kind best suited to its particular needs (75).

## OCCUPATIONAL MEDICINE

Physicians in occupational medicine are increasingly concerned with the mental health and illness of employees. They themselves feel their role in industry is one of the most important contributions to the field of occupational mental health. Their effectiveness in dealing with occupational illness is manyfold greater than in times past. No longer is the occupational physician the surgeon restricting his role to repair of the occupational injury. His concern with proper placement in accord with both the physical *and* the emotional make-up of the employee has led to an increasingly effective role. While it is true that his assessment techniques vary with his competence and his resources, he has made successful application of much recent research and experience.

The physician in industry has, over the past few years, seen remarkable advances in insurance coverage for treatment of psychiatric illness among employee groups. Where possible, he has lent his support to this trend. In spite of resistance from some insurance carriers, many responsible employers include psychiatric care, either to the same extent as care for physical illness or at a reduced level, in their employee benefit plans. Pressure from union groups has been an increasingly potent factor in support of this trend.

## OCCUPATIONAL MENTAL HEALTH DEFINED

From the foregoing, it would appear that occupational mental health may be defined in several ways. In the narrowest sense, it is concerned solely with the psychiatrically ill worker whose symptoms interfere with his effective functioning on the job. This is the purest clinical concept of the field. In a broader sense, occupational mental health is concerned with thought, feeling, and behavior—both healthy and unhealthy—as it occurs in the work organization or as it relates to the performance of a job. In this larger context, the field deals with factors in the work environment which support mentally healthy behavior as well as those which may be involved in triggering the development of symptoms of emotional disturbance.

The literature of occupational mental health has increased in breadth, scope, and content. Through it, the clinician has contributed a great deal to our understanding of the individual's motivation for work, his suitability for various occupational roles, and the influence of work on his physical and mental health (46).

The volume of sophisticated study from the behavioral sciences is equally great in its contribution to our understanding of work groups, interaction patterns at work, job satisfaction, employee attitudes and morale, and of the corporate subculture in which the individual functions. From all this work one might conclude that if there is such a field as occupational mental health at all, it cuts across and through occupational medicine, social, clinical, and industrial psychology, cultural anthropology, social psychiatry, and psychiatry proper. An indication of this may be obtained from a listing of the subject matter most frequently cited in a partially annotated bibliography published by the National Clearinghouse for Mental Health Information (67): accidents; absenteeism; alcoholism; the executive, his role and psychopathology; industrial health and occupational medicine; organized labor and the unions; leadership and supervision; motivation and incentives; specific occupations. Also, industrial mental health programs; occupational roles and status; the relationship between specific personality variables and the work setting; specific psychiatric illnesses as they relate to the job (traumatic neurosis, psychosomatic reactions, and organic brain syndromes are most often discussed); rehabilitation of the physically and psychiatrically disabled; psychodynamics of personality functioning in relation to work; the roles of psychiatrist, psychologist, industrial physician, and behavioral scientist; the meaning of work; and the structure, function, and environment of the work organization.

## IMPLICATIONS FOR THE FUTURE

The future development of occupational mental health can perhaps best be seen when envisioned in the context of the change in the world of work during the past century. Today there is a high degree of industrial mechanization and automation, a skilled and educated work force, an acceptance of the results of research from the physical and behavioral sciences, improvements in the health and longevity of the population, and legal advances and accelerating change in work style as well as in the social and cultural environments.

Changes in our society have altered the ways in which people satisfy their economic, social, and psychological needs. They have required people to find new ways of obtaining job security, new social devices for protection against injury, sickness, and death, new modes of developing skills, forms of recreation, and sources of emotional support.

The extended family unit can no longer be relied on for support as its members are less likely to be found living in the same area, where they can turn to each other for social activities and mutual aid. Even where the geographic problem does not exist, social class mobility—a comparatively common phenomenon—may often make it impossible to turn to the extended family. Nor can one rely on neighborhood or community roots for psychological sustenance in a nation where 20% of the population changes residence annually.

Instead of a geographical orientation point, many now have developed a corporate orientation point. They identify themselves with an organization—a company, church, university, or government department. The work organization frequently provides the thread of continuity for a family moving from one area to another and may become a psychological anchor point for it. Often a man's social friendships arise from his work associations. Old Navy men have long had a ready bond of friendship, and two strangers who work for a nationwide organization are likely to have much in common (51).

While people have increasingly begun to turn to work and the employing organization for many of these lost supports, even in work some sources of gratification and support are being lost. Rapid technical changes have altered the composition of work groups and work tasks. Occupational and status achievements are somewhat tenuous when skills can readily be made obsolete or when their social value can depreciate rapidly, as occurs with technical changes and new industrial developments. When skills become obsolete, they not only lose their meaning as instruments of economic security but also of psychological security, for a man loses an important method of mastering some part of his world.

Many of the services formerly performed by small entrepreneurs are now carried out by larger units of production and marketing; for those who were part of the smaller group, these changes contribute to the loss of a sense of group purpose about work and of group solidarity. Movement from a small business to a larger enterprise usually means some loss of personal freedom. It also results in relatively less recognition of the individual as an individual and relatively more of the individual as part of the organization. It gives added weight to the importance of the relationship between a man and his work organization as a way for the man to gain social power. Within that relationship, however, the individual seeks increasing individual recognition, consideration, and responsibility and seeks support from his supervisors to obtain them.

Programs of clinical application in industry have begun in the past few years to apply a variety of techniques in support of the mental health of people at work. Many of these applications represent advances over the previous role of evaluator of the employee with mental illness. From psychiatry proper we have major advances in theory and practice. Tremendous strides have been made in occupational medicine as well as the other medical specialties. The behavioral sciences are contributing new research results, concepts, and methods of relating to the health of employees and managers—and, indeed, of companies and organizations.

Mindus stated in 1952:

> I do not think that in the present situation the industrial psychiatrist exerts very great influence on management policies. I doubt if he ever will do it. But it is quite obvious that where the management had learned that they could benefit from discussing their problems with a good psychiatrist their points of view always were broadened and they developed a much more careful and understanding attitude (63).

Perhaps we are not clear as to what he meant by "policies," but recent developments indicate a beginning in the application of clinical concepts to the ongoing policies of corporate organizations. Depending on one's definition of "policy," one will attribute varying influence to the clinician and to the behavioral scientist. Does a change in employee benefit plan to include coverage of mental illness as well as physical illness involve a policy alteration? And what does this reflect of a growing union interest in mental health? Does the increased recognition by company management of unconscious process in motivating its employees' behavior represent a policy change? Does the involvement of the clinical consultant in top management staff meetings which determine policy represent such an influence? How is the increasing freedom of the clinician or the behavioral scientist to initiate research activities within the organization to be regarded?

Because of the widespread reluctance to publish work in these areas, referred to earlier, it would appear that these activities have to a large extent developed independently as isolated phenomena in different centers. It is a reasonable assumption that the milieu that fostered their initial appearance will continue to provide a fertile environment for future development along lines already established. Within the limitations of the general area of concern of the mental health professional, and his primary goal of the maintenance and improvement of mental health in the occupational setting, there are at least several new directions in which developments can be expected to take place. The profound changes being introduced into the work setting, mainly as a result of automation, will require a familiarity with the process of change and the stresses consequent to it, together with the knowledge and ability to apply techniques for alleviating them (74).

Management's increasing perception of the industrial organization as an element in the organic unity of the social order and of the work setting as an integral part of man's life will lead to a growing recognition within industry that developments on the industrial scene that may appear to be of only limited consequence to the person at work can, in fact, have considerable impact on his performance. Thus, not only do job loss, obsolescence of skills, or early retirement resulting from many of the changes taking place in industry require major reorganization of the individual's life after they occur, but the threat or imminence of these developments can seriously affect his on-the-job functioning. Consequently, the clinician and behavioral scientist will be asked to develop programs for helping ease these transitions and to provide services where difficulties develop.

Union activities in mental health are still too new and too limited to provide more than a suggestion of the likely direction programing will take. Their primary concern has been with the provision of service to their population and will probably continue to be focused mainly in this area. However, limited exploration of the work setting and its potential place in a union mental health program has begun. The returns from this approach, even in these early stages, would suggest that for at least some unions, this will become a major area of development.

The role of the comprehensive community mental health center in occupational mental health is yet to be defined. The relative lack of interest in the area demonstrated by its omission from state planning in all but three states would suggest that development of this role will be primarily on an individual basis, reflecting the concern of the interested staff member. One potential asset of the community mental health center for activity in this field is its third-party position, which may enable it to provide services in areas of labor-management conflict where an impartial evaluation is necessary.

The shift in clinical emphasis from routine diagnostic evaluation in the industrial medical department or in the office of the consulting psychiatrist and psychologist to the broader areas of activity described above has made it necessary for the professional interested in this field to become familiar with an extensive body of knowledge not required of many of his colleagues. The behavioral science contributions to an understanding of group process and mental health education, the legal issues in workmen's compensation, the problems of psychotoxicology, and, most of all, the nature of the industrial environment are all subjects about which some understanding is necessary for successful work in industry. It is likely that formal training programs in occupational mental health will have to be developed before widespread acceptance of the clinician can be expected from industrial organizations.

Previous material in this paper suggests the wealth of current research activities relating to the mental health of the American worker. It appears that we may not only expect expansion of research efforts but can anticipate greater application of research results in the ongoing affairs of industrial organizations.

A closer working relationship between university-based research programs and organizational personnel practices has been suggested and appears more frequently in practice. This has led to the training of the behavioral scientist for work as a salaried member of company personnel staffs and develops further the utilization of research data from the campus *and* from within the employing company. From academia we see increasing evidence of concern for the use of the results of research studies. From the viewpoint of the behavioral sciences which participate in organizational mental health programs, the direction of the future appears to be away from pure research on campus and toward the in-company study, with application of research results to the ongoing affairs of the company.

## SUMMARY

In the past decade there have been more clinicians quoting behavioral science research, more behavioral scientists quoting clinicians, and greater application of the theoretical frames of reference of each of the several disciplines to practical problems within industry. Occupational medicine has largely emerged from its cocoon of emergency surgery and compensation cases with the recognition that, like internal medicine and general practice, half of its case load is made up of patients with emotional problems, either overtly displayed or in the guise of psychosomatic reactions. Borrowing concepts and clues from psychiatry, psychology, and the behavioral sciences, industrial medical directors and their staffs have taken steps toward more active involvement with the policies of their organizations—policies recognized as influencing the health of employees.

Becoming involved with the physician in industry, some behavioral scientists have been studying not only the prevalence of psychosomatic disease in industrial populations, but also the influence of the industrial environment on these illnesses. Indeed, health concepts have been applied to the industrial organization itself with the "corporate personality" regarded as "sick" or "well." Factors within its subculture have been studied as one studies the individual personality. It is common to hear a group of social scientists with industrial interests discuss the "health" of a work group, a company, or an industry.

The relationship of job satisfactions to mental health has been widely suggested, even assumed, although still unproved. Identification with the work organization—or with one's labors —has received great attention from occupational medicine, clinical psychology, psychiatry, and behavioral science. The centrality of interest seems to have focused recently on psychosomatic reactions. The next common area of concern appears to have been the industrial accident with its illusive "human" etiology. More recently the garden varieties of emotional reaction—the psychopathology of everyday life and its relation to the work process, to the exercise of various types of authority, to the cohesive influence of the work group, and to productivity—have been discussed.

Finally, we see a common interest in the fulfillment of the individual in the work setting. From each discipline come expressions of concern, research efforts and suggestions, and operational programs for allowing greater understanding and fulfillment of the psychological needs of the individual at work. Each discipline has contributed. Each considers itself properly concerned. Indeed, many proprietary feelings continue in each specialty as to *who* should be looked to by industrial management, *who* should be responsible, *who* should direct the efforts of the others, *who* may "rightly" have the moral, ethical, and social responsibility to study and influence these many factors which in turn can be related to the mental health of the industrial employee at whatever level.

Both the clinical disciplines and the behavioral sciences will play an increasing role in fostering healthy employees and healthy companies through increasing influence on the policies and procedures of corporate organizations.

The evidence points to an expanding role for the clinician as well as for the behavioral scientist, but with less concern for the purely clinical function of examining patient-employees. Greater emphasis is suggested at the present time on preventive health programs, research, management education, and concern with policies influencing employee mental health. It is by now apparent that the trend toward prevention originally foretold by Southard, Jarrett, Adler, Campbell, and Giberson continues as the main concern of occupational mental health.

## REFERENCES

1. Adler, H. M. Unemployment and personality. *Mental Hygiene*, 1917, 1, 16–24.

2. American Psychiatric Association Committee on Occupational Psychiatry. *The mentally ill employee: His treatment and rehabilitation: A guide for management.* New York: Hoeber Medical Division, Harper and Row, 1965.

3. Anderson, V. V. Psychiatry in industry. *American Journal of Psychiatry,* 1944, 100, 134–138.

4. Argyris, C. *Personality and organization.* New York: Harper Brothers, 1957.

5. Argyris, C. *Understanding organizational behavior.* Homewood, Illinois: Dorsey Press, 1960.

6. Brodman, K. *Man at work–The Supervisor and his people.* Chicago: Cloud, 1947.

7. Brody, M. Dynamics of mental hygiene in industry. *Industrial Medicine*, 1945, 14, 760.

8. Brody, M. Neuropsychiatry and placement of industrial workers. *Connecticut Medicine*, 1945, 9, 84–88.

9. Brown, W. *Exploration in management.* New York: John Wiley and Sons, 1960.

10. Burling, T. Personality and the economic situation. *American Journal of Orthopsychiatry*, 1939, 9, 616–622.

11. Burling, T. The role of the professionally trained mental hygienist in business. *American Journal of Orthopsychiatry*, 1942, 11, 48.

12. Burling, T., Lentz, E. M., & Wilson, R. N. *The give and take in hospitals.* New York: G. P. Putnam's Sons, 1956.

13. Burling, T., & Longaker, W. Training for industrial psychiatry. *American Journal of Psychiatry*, 1955, 111, 493.

14. Burlingame, C. C. Psychiatry in industry. *American Journal of Psychiatry*, 1946, 103, 549–553.

15. Burlingame, C. C. Psychiatry in industry. *American Journal of Psychiatry*, 1947, 104, 493–496.

16. Burlingame, C. C. Psychiatry in industry. *American Journal of Psychiatry*, 1948, **105**, 538–540.

17. Burlingame, C. C. Psychiatry in industry. *American Journal of Psychiatry*, 1949, **106**, 520–522.

18. Cameron, D. E., & Ross, H. G. *Human behavior and its relations to industry.* Montreal: McGill University, 1944.

19. Cameron, D. E., & Ross, H. G. *Studies in supervision.* Montreal: McGill University, 1945.

20. Campbell, C. M. The psychiatrist and industrial organization. *American Journal of Psychiatry*, 1943, **100**, 286–287.

21. Collins, R. T. *A manual of neurology and psychiatry in occupational medicine.* New York: Grune and Stratton, 1961.

22. Culpin, M. Psychological disorders in industry: Symposium on industrial medicine. *Practitioner*, 1936, **137**, 324–333.

23. Culpin, M., & Smith, M. The nervous temperament. (Government Publications—Medical Research Council Industrial Health Research Board, Report No. 61.) London: H. M. Stationery Office, 1930.

24. Dershimer, F. W. Psychiatry in industry. *American Journal of Psychiatry*, 1952, **108**, 536–538.

25. Dershimer, F. W. Psychiatry in industry. *American Journal of Psychiatry*, 1953, **109**, 524–526.

26. Dershimer, F. W. Psychiatry in industry. *American Journal of Psychiatry*, 1954, **110**, 527–528.

27. Dershimer, F. W. Psychiatry in industry. *American Journal of Psychiatry*, 1955, **111**, 534–535.

28. Ferguson, C. A., Fersing, J. E., Allen, A. T., Baugh, N. P., Gilmore, G. A., Humphrey, J. W., McConnell, F. E., Mitchell, J. S. W., Sauer, J. W., & Scott, T. J. *The legacy of neglect: An appraisal of the implications of emotional disturbances in the business environment.* Fort Worth, Texas: Industrial Mental Health Associates, 1965.

29. Fountain, C. W. Labor's place in an industrial mental health program. *Mental Hygiene*, 1945, **29**, 95.

30. French, J. R. P., Jr., Kahn, R. L., & Mann, F. C. (Eds.) Work, health and satisfaction. *Journal of Social Issues*, 1962, **18**, 1–129.

31. Giberson, L. G. Psychiatry in industry. *Personnel Journal*, 1936, **15**, 91–95.

32. Giberson, L. G. Emotional first-aid stations. *Personnel*, 1939, **16**, 1–15.

33. Giberson, L. G. Pitfalls in industry for the psychiatrist. *Medical Women's Journal*, 1940, **47**, 144–146.

34. Greenwood, M. A report on the cause of wastage of labour in munition factories. (Government Publications—Medical Research Council.) London: H. M. Stationery Office, 1918.

35. Group for the Advancement of Psychiatry, Committee on Psychiatry

in Industry. The application of psychiatry to industry. GAP Report No. 20, July 1951.

36. Herzberg, F., & Hamlin, R. M. The motivation-hygiene concept and psychotherapy. *Mental Hygiene*, 1963, **47**, 384–397.

37. Herzberg, F., Mausner, B., & Snyderman, B. *The motivation to work.* New York: John Wiley and Sons, 1959.

38. Howe, H. F., & Wolman, W. Guide for evaluating employability after psychiatric illness. *Journal of the American Medical Association*, 1962, **181**, 1086–1089.

39. Jaques, E. Some principles of organization of a social therapeutic institution. *Journal of Social Issues*, 1947, **3**, 4–10.

40. Jaques, E. Standard earning progression curves. *Human Relations*, 1951, **11**, 167–190.

41. Jaques, E. *The changing culture of a factory.* New York: Dryden Press, 1952.

42. Jaques, E. *Measurement of responsibility.* Cambridge: Harvard University Press, 1956.

43. Jarrett, M. C. The mental hygiene of industry—Report of progress on work undertaken under the Engineering Foundation of New York City. *Mental Hygiene*, 1920, **4**, 867–884.

44. Kalinowsky, L. B. Problems of war neuroses in the light of experience in other countries. *American Journal of Psychiatry*, 1950, **107**, 340.

45. Kornhauser, A. *Mental health of the industrial worker.* New York: John Wiley and Sons, 1959.

46. Lapinsky, E. The future of health in industry. *Industrial Medicine and Surgery*, 1965, **34**, 71–77.

47. Laughlin, H. P. An approach to executive development: Five years experience with analytically oriented groups of executives. *Diseases of the Nervous System*, 1954, **15**, 12.

48. Laughlin, H. P. Seminars with executives on human relations in the United States Government. *International Journal of Group Psychotherapy*, 1954, **4**, 165.

49. Laughlin, H. P., & Hall, M. Psychiatry for executives: An experiment in the use of group analysis to improve relationships in an organization. *American Journal of Psychiatry*, 1951, **107**, 493–497.

50. Levinson, H. *Emotional health in the world of work.* New York: Harper and Row, 1964.

51. Levinson, H. The future of health in industry. *Industrial Medicine and Surgery*, 1965, **34**, 321–334.

52. Levinson, H., Price, C. R., Munden, K. J., Mandl, H. J., & Solley, C. M. *Men, management and mental health.* Cambridge: Harvard University Press, 1962.

53. Ling, T. M. Roffey Park Rehabilitation Center. *Lancet*, 1945, **1**, 283.

54. Ling, T. M. (Ed.) *Mental health and human relations in industry.* New York: Paul B. Hoeber, 1955.

55. Lott, G. M. Emotional first-aid stations in industry. *Industrial Medicine*, 1946, **15**, 419–422.

56. Mayo, E. *The human problems of an industrial civilization.* New York: Macmillan Co., 1934.

57. McLean, A. A. Occupational psychiatry. *American Journal of Psychiatry*, 1964, **120**, 654–657.

58. McLean, A. A. Occupational psychiatry. *American Journal of Psychiatry*, 1965, **121**, 659–662.

59. McLean, A. A., & Taylor, G. C. *Mental health in industry.* New York: McGraw-Hill Book Co., 1958.

60. Melekhov, D. E. Rehabilitation of psychoneurotic World War II patients in the U.S.S.R. *Occupational Therapy*, 1947, **26**, 388–393.

61. Menninger, W. C., & Levinson, H. *Human understanding in industry: A guide for supervisors.* Chicago: Science Research Associates, 1957.

62. Miller, D. C., & Form, W. H. *Industrial sociology.* New York: Harper and Brothers, 1951.

63. Mindus, E. Industrial psychiatry in Great Britain, the United States, and Canada. Report to the World Health Organization, Geneva, 1952.

64. Mindus, E. Outlines of a concept of industrial psychiatry. *Bulletin of the World Health Organization*, 1955, **13**, 561–574.

65. Morrow, J. K., King, J. P., Chiles, D. D., & Painter, T. E. The bituminous coal country: A psychiatric frontier. *West Virginia Medical Journal*, 1959, **55**, 164–167.

66. *National Association for Mental Health Reporter,* October 1964, **13**(7).

67. National Institute of Mental Health: Selected bibliography on occupational mental health. (Public Health Service Publication No. 1338.) Bethesda, Maryland: National Clearinghouse for Mental Health Information, 1965.

68. Osnato, M. Industrial neuroses, *American Journal of Psychiatry.* 1925, **82**, 117–131.

69. Pederson-Krag, G. *Personality factors in work and employment.* New York: Funk and Wagnalls, 1955.

70. Pokorny, A. D., & Moore, F. J. Neuroses and compensation. *American Medical Association Archives of Industrial Hygiene and Occupational Medicine,* 1953, **8**, 547–563.

71. Reiff, R., & Scribner, S. Issues in the new National Mental Health Program relating to labor and low-income groups: Report no. 1. New York: National Institute of Labor Education, 1963.

72. Rennie, T. A. C., Burling, T., & Woodward, L. E. *Vocational rehabilitation of psychiatric patients.* New York: Commonwealth Fund, 1950.

73. Rennie, T. A. C., Swackhamer, G., & Woodward, L. E. Toward industrial mental health: An historical review. *Mental Hygiene,* 1947, **31**, 66–68.

74. Rennie, T. A. C., & Woodward, L. E. *Mental health in modern society.* New York: Commonwealth Fund, 1948.

75. Riessman, F. New approaches to mental health treatment for labor and low-income groups: Report no. 2. New York: National Institute of Labor Education, 1946.

76. Roethlisberger, F. J., & Dickson, W. J. *Management and the worker.* Cambridge: Harvard University Press, 1939.

77. Rosenbaum, M., & Romano, J. Psychiatric casualties among defense workers. *American Journal of Psychiatry,* 1943, **100**, 314–319.

78. Ross, W. D. Practical psychiatry for industrial physicians. Springfield, Illinois: Charles C Thomas, 1956.

79. Schulzinger, M. S. *The accident syndrome.* Springfield, Illinois: Charles C Thomas, 1956.

80. Sherman, M. A review of industrial psychiatry. *American Journal of Psychiatry,* 1927, **83**, 701–710.

81. Southard, E. E. The modern specialist in unrest: A place for the psychiatrist in industry. *Mental Hygiene,* 1920, **4**, 550.

82. Tredgold, R. F. *Human relations in modern industry.* New York: International Universities Press, 1950.

83. Tureen, L. L. The role of the psychiatrist in a prepaid group medical program. *American Journal of Public Health,* 1959, **49**, 1373–1378.

84. U.S. Federal Security Agency, Office of Vocational Rehabilitation: The doctor and vocational rehabilitation for civilians. Washington, D.C., 1947.

85. Van Alphen de Veer, M. R. *Success and failure in industry: A psychomedical study.* Assen, The Netherlands: Van Gorcum and Co., 1955.

86. Waters, T. C. Mental illness: Is it compensable? *Archives of Environmental Health,* 1962, **5**, 178.

87. Weiner, H. J., & Brand, M. Involving a labor union in the rehabilitation of the physically and mentally ill. *American Journal of Orthopsychiatry,* 1964, **34**, 342–343.

# 8. EMPLOYEE COUNSELING IN INDUSTRY: OBSERVATIONS ON THREE PROGRAMS

**Harry Levinson, Ph.D.**

In the course of the Menninger Foundation Survey of Industrial Mental Health (1), there have been frequent questions about the details of various kinds of "emotional first-aid stations" in industry. In response to these queries, two leading psychiatric programs (2) and a psychiatric clinic for the treatment of alcoholism (3) were described previously. This paper describes and discusses three formal counseling programs in industry which are "psychological" in orientation, in contrast to "psychiatric" or "social work." The three programs have in common an emphasis on nondirective counseling, commonly identified with psychology, rather than on treatment or casework.

These programs were selected first, because their respective companies, organizational structures, methods and objectives are sufficiently varied that together they represent a broad sample of such counseling practices in industry; and second, because of their historic, pioneering roles in industry. One of the three, that of Prudential Life Insurance Company, is now defunct. The other two, those of the Western Electric Company and the Caterpillar Tractor Company, are currently in operation.

A brief report from the Menninger Foundation Survey of Industrial Mental Health. The author is the Director, Industrial Mental Health, The Menninger Foundation.

## THE THREE PROGRAMS

### Western Electric

After interviewing some 20,000 employees in the course of the now classical experiments (4) at the Hawthorne (Chicago) plant of the Western Electric Company from 1927 to 1932, the investigators reported two discoveries (5), both significant although elementary knowledge to anyone with clinical training: (1) The complaint, as stated, was frequently not the real source of the individual's difficulty. Consequently, action based on the *manifest* content of the complaint did not assure that the underlying difficulty would be eliminated. (2) With the opportunity to express themselves freely, the employees were able to more clearly formulate their complaints, and in many cases the complaints disappeared entirely. In addition, many employees developed a new enthusiasm for their work as they talked out their problems and lost some of their tensions.

These considerations led to the development of the Western Electric counseling program, formally organized in 1936 as part of the Industrial Relations Branch, which became the precursor of all other nonpsychiatric industrial counseling programs. Inasmuch as the interviewers who had participated in the research were supervisors and other plant employees, it was perhaps only natural that those who became counselors should also come from the ranks. Forty such persons, 20 men and 20 women, made up the original counseling force. Contemporary counselors are specifically employed for the job, but, like their pioneer predecessors, have no formal preparation as counselors. They are supervised and given in-service training by six supervisors under the direction of the Chief of the Personnel Counseling and Training Division (6).

Employees are counseled by persons of the same sex. Each counselor is assigned a given territory within the plant where he serves between 300 and 400 employees. He seeks to integrate himself in the work group, relating himself to everyone in the same impartial way, but remaining outside the social relationships which are organized around the work itself. He is deliberately not given any formal authority lest, on one hand, such authority become a barrier to free communication between counselor and counselee, and, on the other hand, lest an authoritative person outside the immediate work relationships undermine the position of the supervisor.

Thus the counselor becomes familiar with the employees, the shop processes, the social relationships in the shop, and supervisory and administrative practices, but he does not enter into the power relationships of the shop. He makes himself available to the employees and supervisors in informal contacts on the floor of the shop or in a small interviewing room where the employee can talk in privacy. Most counselees are seen from one to five times. Some are counseled for a year or more.

Counselors are concerned exclusively with "bringing about adjustments and changes in employee (and supervisory) attitudes through the interviewing method itself" (5). Interviewing in this case means to maintain a neutral, confidential listener's role. The orientation is nondirective, no probing, no implication of analyzing the employee. But the counselor may, by asking questions, "direct the employee's thinking into those areas which he needs to take into account in order to achieve an adequate adjustment" (4). The counselors do not diagnose, give advice, or prescribe. W. J. Dickson, who set up the counseling program, felt that, "This procedure avoids many of the problems of transference which arise in clinical interviewing which would be difficult for a layman to handle" (4).

Being neutral means absolute confidentiality. All the records which the counselor keeps are his property, not that of the company. It also means that he can in *no way* take action upon any difficulties, complaints, or grievances which he learns about in his interviews, seek to create changes within the organization, or make referrals.

In attempting to bring about adjustment, the "counselor's sole object is to lead the employee to a clear understanding of her problem such that she herself comes to realize what action to take and then assumes responsibility for taking it" (4). He enhances the employee–supervisor relationship when either the employee or the supervisor adjusts more effectively to the work situation (6), or when both employee and supervisor, after talking to the counselor individually, find their relationships more congenial. Through his teaching contribution to supervisory training, through generalized "feedback" on employee's reactions to policies and practices, and through interviews with management representatives as they come to his section, the counselor communicates problems of the social structure. The major focus, however, is on the adjustment of the employee.

Dickson claims (5) the following advantages for this kind of counseling: emotional release and relief of tensions; stimulation of the employee to re-examine his ideas, beliefs, and fantasies with a view toward reappraising them; creation of a stabilizing force for the employee in the employee–counselor relationship; avoidance of attaching a stigma to the employee who seeks counsel by relating the counselor to an entire work group; provision of counsel without disrupting normal work routine; early detection and dissipation of emotional disturbances.

## Prudential Life

In October 1948, twelve years after the Western Electric program had been initiated, the Prudential Life Insurance Company established a counseling center in its Newark home office (7).

The Prudential program differed in several ways from that of Western Electric. Its staff was made up of "people with prior specialized and professional training in interviewing conducted for the purpose of helping clients solve problems" because "it is easier to take professionally trained people and teach them something about the company than it is to draw employees from the ranks and try to teach them the techniques of counseling" (8). Dr. John A. Bromer, a psychologist, was director of the center. Two other psychologists and a social worker comprised the staff. There was only one center for counseling. Counselors did not initiate contacts with employees. Clients were not necessarily assigned to counselors of the same sex. The counseling center was avowedly and publicly a mental hygiene service.

The goals of the Prudential program were improved morale, greater job satisfaction, and increased friendly relations between the company and its 11,000 home office employees (7). "When members of the home office feel the desire or the need to discuss something in their day-to-day work situations or anything else that troubles them, we want them to be able to do so," the personnel vice-president wrote the employees (9). All employees were eligible to use the center. The focus was on normal people who were "interested in improving their understanding of themselves and others or in learning how to get along better with their fellow men" (8).

The counseling center was responsible to the vice-president in charge of personnel, but was separate from personnel administration. It had neither administrative responsibility nor authority.

As at Western Electric, the center kept no formal records and such notes of its interviews as it did keep were strictly confidential within the center itself. It had no contact about the employee-client with anyone else in the company.

Although its orientation was basically nondirective, direction and interpretation were sometimes used, following the methods suggested by Super (10). It was Bromer's thinking that nondirective counseling avoided the anxieties and hostilities which he felt were likely to be aroused by more clinically oriented diagnostic and evaluative programs conducted by clinical psychologists and psychiatrists (8). Persons whose problems might be dealt with more adequately by psychiatric or case work services were referred for such services. Employees who sought answers to specific questions about community resources, training opportunities, or administrative routines within the company were given direct answers. Budget planning and financial advice were given, as well as vocational guidance and counsel on emotional problems. The counseling staff administered and interpreted interest and aptitude tests. Results of these tests could be referred to the personnel department upon the request of the employee if he were seeking a job change.

In its first full year, 331 clients visited the center for 983 counseling sessions, ranging from 1 to 20 consultations per client (7). More than half of those who sought the center's help were men, although two-thirds of the employees in the home office were women. Although most of the clients who used the center were rank and file employees, managers and supervisors, proportionally speaking, made greater use of it. More than half of the problems brought for discussion involved the job or work situation. By the end of 1952 the counselors had seen 1,500 people representing one-sixth of the working group. In addition, the staff was frequently consulted by executives on ways of handling personnel problems.

## Caterpillar Tractor

The Caterpillar mental health program grew out of the interest of Dr. Harold Vonachen, medical director of Caterpillar Tractor Company, and Dr. M. H. Kronenberg, manager of medical services at the Peoria plant. The program was designed jointly by these men and a team of psychologists and psychiatrists from the Cornell Medical Center (11). A mental health section was created in the medical department (13, 14). From its inception in 1945 it was conceived as "a comprehensive program endeavoring to cover all phases of human behavior for the improvement of mental health."

The present staff of the mental health section includes the director, an industrial psychologist, two other industrial psychologists, and a clinical psychologist. Each of the industrial psychologists has also had some training in nondirective counseling and has some acquaintance with projective techniques. Counseling techniques range from the permissive and nondirective to authoritative advice. Local psychiatrists serve as consultants. The contemporary work of the section falls into three major areas—selection and placement, employee counseling, and supervisory development.

The current functions of the counseling service are:

1. to administer minor psychotherapy;
2. to consult with supervisors on the management of employee problems;
3. to furnish psychological test data with interpretations to company physicians;
4. to assist in arranging transfers, job changes, and medical leaves of absence for persons with emotional difficulties;
5. to assist employees and management in referrals of severe emotional adjustment problems to private and community care;
6. to consult with physicians and supervisors relative to post-treatment rehabilitation and adjustment of employees who have undergone severe mental and emotional disturbances;
7. to maintain case records on all reported cases of employee adjustment problems.

All interviews are confidential. All test information and all counseling information are regarded as medical information and accessible therefore only to persons in the medical division. Only progress and behavior on the job are discussed with supervisors.

Employees may go to the mental health section for counseling of their own accord, or they may be referred by physicians, supervisors, or their personnel office. In 1954 there were 4,239 consultations with employees or with management about employees. No counselee has to appear for interviews after the initial contact. He may terminate counseling at any time. All kinds of company records are used to guide the counselor: safety, personnel, medical, and foremen's. With the employee's knowledge and consent, contacts are made with the plant and family physicians, social agencies, and the counselee's family, if the counselor feels it necessary. Severe emotional problems are referred to the family physician first with the recommendation of additional referral to a psychiatrist. Employees who demonstrate psychotic disturbances on the job are escorted home, or, with the help of the family, to the hospital.

The unique aspect of the work of the mental health section is its collaboration with the personnel office. Every applicant is routinely given psychological tests by members of the mental health section. These include the Cornell Word Form and a modification of the Cornell Selectee Index (15). If there are indications from the latter test that the applicant has severe psychological problems which might make him unemployable or which would require that his placement be given more consideration than usual, one of the psychologists in the mental health section sees him in a personal interview. About 15% of the applicants are so seen for an evaluation of the severity of their problems and for recommendations regarding their placement. Applicants who are thus interviewed may be recommended for general placement within the organization, for a limited placement, or not recommended at all. If the mental health section decides that Caterpillar should not employ the applicant, this decision is regarded as a medical decision and interpreted to the applicant as such. He is then advised, on the basis of his test results and interviews, about the kind of work he might profitably seek.

A study (11) of more than 500 case histories of persons referred for consultation from January 1, 1948, to May 15, 1953, disclosed that out of 130 cases which were sufficiently detailed for analysis and evaluation 82% of the persons improved in various degrees and in the remaining 18% there was no evidence of improvement in the employee's emotional health.

## DISCUSSION

The historic contribution of the Western Electric program was that this company was among the first to recognize the importance of the personal tensions and feelings of its employees. Furthermore, the company recognized the importance of providing an avenue for the discharge of tensions and for the expression of feelings. This implied that such feelings were regarded as natural, that they were accepted as the usual customary behavior of all human beings, and that they were of such importance that the company was willing to provide for their relief as it would provide for the relief of medical emergencies. Taken together, all this tended to create a greater feeling of dignity on the part of the employee.

The merits of the Western Electric approach, as with any other approach, depend upon the situation to which it is adapted. The counselor in such a situation thoroughly knows the work environment and everyone in it. By enabling employees to ventilate their problems, he makes it possible for many to better mobilize their own strengths. At the same time the limitations of his listening technique preclude his getting into dangerous areas beyond his competence. The technique itself militates against any manipulation of the employee and this readily apparent advantage must make the employee feel quite comfortable about talking to a person whom he perceives much as "a friend in need." Seeing the counselor for help becomes a matter of casual everyday talking as one would talk to any interested friend. Another advantage is the opening up of an additional anonymous channel of communication with management.

Western Electric has a medical department and a personnel department which carry the responsibility, respectively, for treating and referring persons who are ill and for evaluating and placing job applicants and employees. Western Electric does not want its counselors to have anything to do with these other aspects of the company functioning because a counseling service in that company which operated differently than the present method would tend to create other problems. To expect diagnostic and referral services, vocational guidance, or other clinical activity from the Western Electric type of program is to expect something for which the program was not designed.

To the Western Electric precedent Prudential added the status and proficiency of a professional staff. The implication here was that not only were an employee's tensions or feelings important enough to warrant the company's providing a way for their expression, but they were sufficiently important to provide a person professionally skilled in understanding and eliciting feelings. Furthermore, the Prudential program gave recognition to the fact that often, despite its therapeutic advantages, the expression of thoughts and feelings alone was not enough to solve a given problem. Two things were added therefore. First, the Prudential program brought the social resources of the community to bear on the problem. Second, it provided an objective evaluation of the employee's aptitudes and interests, when needed, so that he might better determine the direction in which he would like to go. Finally, the Prudential program gave full recognition to the fact that people's everyday tensions and feelings are related to their health by clearly defining its work as mental hygiene.

As at Western Electric, there were certain things which the Prudential company handled outside the counseling service such as morale studies and medical problems. Prudential clearly defined the role of the counseling service as dealing with employees' emotional problems in a counseling relationship. They did not envision a more broadly clinical kind of situation, preferring that clinical problems be dealt with by the medical department.

The Western Electric and Prudential programs operate almost as autonomous units within the respective companies; that is, in contrast to most other operations of the business organization, their highly confidential relationships together with their limited contacts outside their own services preclude any detailed supervision of or knowledge of their work on the part of management or other departments in the same organization. This kind of autonomy is extremely important to counselors and those who are being counseled. Yet there are certain dangers. For example, it is easy for such a department to become isolated, and isolation can mean the gradual withering and ultimate death of any program. It is critically important that continuous efforts be made to acquaint the rest of the organization with the work of the counseling service and with its contribution to the mission of the business organization.

The structure of the Caterpillar program provides another

avenue for avoiding the danger of isolation, through its integration of medical, personnel, training, and supervisory functions. As was the Prudential program, it is directly tied to the community and thereby able to coordinate company and community facilities in the interest of the employee with problems. It also has constantly available to it, as tools in the counseling process, all the objective measures of job adjustment and job potential, both physical and mental, that the company provides.

The Caterpillar approach has two other major advantages: (1) Direct contact between the counselors and supervisors, where there is an exchange of information about any given problem (without violating confidences) and cooperation in its solution, permits a certain amount of environmental manipulation in the interest of the troubled employee. (2) By being a part of the medical department, the counseling service has the advantage of the traditional acceptance of the medical department by the employees as a source of help (16).

Transcending the major advantages and limitations of the three programs is the degree of daring required of the three corporations in establishing their programs. Certainly the industrial relations climate of 1936 was not one conducive to a departure such as Western Electric's program. Nor had the climate improved by 1945 and 1948 to the point where either Prudential or Caterpillar would feel compelled to institute counseling services because others were doing so. The experience gained by the three corporations has helped provide important guides for those who will follow.

## SUMMARY

The pioneer counseling programs of the Western Electric Company, the Prudential Life Insurance Company, and the Caterpillar Tractor Company are described and discussed. These programs differ widely in scope, method, degree of integration within the parent organization, and in the type of business they serve. They have in common a primarily nondirective approach to the adjustment of the employee to his work.

# REFERENCES

1.  Menninger, William C., & Levinson, Harry. The Menninger Foundation survey of industrial mental health. *Menninger Quarterly*, 1954, **8**, 1–13.

2.  Levinson, Harry. Consultation clinic for alcoholism. *Menninger Quarterly*, 1955, **9**, 15–20.

3.  Levinson, Harry. What can a psychiatrist do in industry? *Menninger Quarterly*, 1955, **9**, 22–30.

4.  Roethlisberger, F. J., & Dickson, William. *Management and the worker*. Cambridge: Harvard University Press, 1940.

5.  Dickson, W. J. The Hawthorne Plan of personnel counseling. *American Journal of Orthopsychiatry*, 1945, **15**, 343–347.

6.  Palevsky, Mary. *Counseling services for industrial workers*. New York: Family Service Association of America, 1945.

7.  Palevsky, Mary. Prudential's employee counseling service cuts down high cost of worry. *National Underwriter*, 1950, **29**, 16–17.

8.  Bromer, John A. A new approach to employee counseling. Paper presented to a graduate seminar in industrial engineering, Columbia University, March 1950 (mimeographed).

9.  Personal communication to Prudential Life Insurance Company's home office staff from F. Bruce Gerhard, vice president, October 8, 1948.

10.  Super, Donald E. *Appraising vocational fitness*. New York: Harper and Brothers, 1949.

11.  Vonachen, Harold A., Mason, Joseph M., & Kronenberg, Milton H. Study of five years of employee counseling in an industrial medical program. *Archives of Industrial Hygiene and Occupational Medicine*, 1954, **10**, 91–131.

12.  Vonachen, Harold A., et al. A comprehensive mental hygiene program at Caterpillar Tractor Company. *Industrial Medicine*, 1954, **15**, 179–184.

13.  Weider, Arthur, & Mittlemann, Bela. Personality and psychosomatic disturbances among industrial personnel. *American Journal of Orthopsychiatry*, 1946, **16**, 631–639.

14.  Weider, Arthur. Mental hygiene in industry—A clinical psychologist's contribution. *Journal of Clinical Psychology*, 1947, **3**, 309–320.

15.  Mittlemann, Bela, & Brodman, Keeve. The Cornell Indices and the Cornell Word Form: Construction and standardization. *Annals of the New York Academy of Science*, 1945, **46**, 573–577.

16.  Evans, Chester K. The consulting psychologist in industry. *American Journal of Orthopsychiatry*, **16**, 623–630.

# 9. INDUSTRIAL PSYCHIATRY— FIVE-YEAR PLANT EXPERIENCE

## Gerald Gordon, M.D.

An experimental investigation was carried out in a large chemical plant to learn whether there was a psychiatric problem in the industry of sufficient magnitude to interfere with production, and what could be done about it.

F. W. Dershimer, M.D., pioneered in the introduction of psychiatry to the du Pont Company, beginning in 1943. Twenty-five years of research had led him to the formulation of new concepts of mental health, and of the cause, transmission and psychopathology of mental illness. From these he evolved shortened, simplified measures for treatment and prevention. These seemed to have useful applications in industry (1-2).

The work reported here has been—and still is—an independent attempt to check on the validity of his theories, and to demonstrate whether his results could be duplicated by another psychiatrist.

Between January 1947 and December 1948, 7% of the plant personnel were seen in psychiatric consultation as a result of referrals by the plant physicians, supervision, or the employees themselves. These individuals all had emotional difficulties sufficient to interfere with their well-being and productivity. This group by no means contains all the mentally sick employees in the plant. Our continuing experience and that of other observers suggest that there are probably three or four times as many more patients as have been seen.

The author is Psychiatrist, E. I. du Pont de Nemours & Company, Wilmington, Delaware.

Presented at the Annual Meeting of the E. I. Du Pont de Nemours & Company Medical Division, Wilmington, Delaware, October 1952.

Statistical analysis of the patient group reveals that this is a fair sample of the plant population as to age, service, health, responsibility, and social and economic status.

Certain features did distinguish this patient group from the average employee group. They contributed predominately to the problem of absenteeism; they had, as a group, a significantly greater percentage of the major and submajor accidents than the rest of the plant. They furnished an excessive proportion of the industrial and personnel relations problems. They had contributed grossly to the dispensary attendance and had taken a disproportionate amount of time on the part of the physicians, nurses, supervisors, and shop stewards.

Review of medical records and other data which could be gathered indicated that these emotionally sick individuals, early in the course of their employment, had set a pattern of poor productivity which had persisted grimly throughout the years without regard to type of job, personality of the boss, location of work, or any other extraneous circumstances, so long as no corrective steps were taken.

The records disclosed that many well-intended efforts had been made to help these people. Disability wages had been paid for sickness after sickness, medical attention had been lavish, and 40–50 days lost on disability wages per year for 13 years were not rare. Dispensary visits for medical and surgical conditions would frequently run 30-40 per year.

The collected data necessary to properly evaluate these cases provided some indication that proper compilation of such data into one record could give an objective means of recording and evaluating the performance of an employee early in the course of his employment. Where this would suggest a potential failure, corrective measures could be instituted early so that rehabilitation might be more successful.

The data indicated, too, that the mentally sick, the failing, employee is not a different kind of human being. He cannot be described by size, shape, or personality. The common characteristic is his failure to meet his basic responsibility for living and working productively.

Contrary to common belief, he is not being made sick by

bad heredity, by material insecurity, by greater responsibility, by world tension, or any of the many excuses for nervousness. Complaints about bosses or working conditions usually proved groundless when investigated. The real cause of the difficulty in the nervous patient is that he is not being required to behave properly and probably never was required to do so through childhood and adolescence.

The symptoms presented by the usual patient were those well known in the common anxiety state, plus a story of considerable social, domestic, and working friction.

Lack of job security did not contribute to the emotional illness. On the contrary, many of the long service employees, who had as near complete job security as possible, were most anxious and insecure in their jobs. Not one single person blamed his difficulties on material insecurity even where this existed in fact. The very real material insecurity was not infrequently the result rather than the cause of the mental illness. In spite of an adequate income, evasion of reality had resulted in economic straits. The patient would usually have something on which to blame his sickness. This self-diagnosis, like other forms of self-diagnosis, as has been recognized by the medical profession for centuries, is misleading and dangerous.

Injuries or toxic exposures, which involved the emotionally sick employee, were particularly serious problems. In cases where the trauma had healed completely or there were no residual effects from the toxic exposure, a policy of continued treatment, reassurance, and appeasement led only to prolongation of the patient's complaints. Removing an employee from an area where he had received such exposure upon the basis of the patient's own diagnosis of the disability resulted only in fixing the patient's symptoms. Individuals have reported that since they were removed from a hazardous area, no one would ever convince them that they had not been harmed by the substance to which they had been exposed. They reasoned that management would not have moved them unless management, also, believed that the injury or toxic hazard caused their continued symptoms.

A definite superstitious fear of the emotionally sick employee was found among supervision and some medical men, most of society having been completely overawed by him. This has, in the past, led to a policy of appeasement and efforts to remove the individual from the stresses and strains of life, yet it was common observation that the subsequent history of many of these individuals showed repeated difficulties. Many nervous patients recovered spontaneously by the time the 13 weeks' disability wage period had expired. One clearcut paranoid schizophrenic was found who had been hospitalized for his disabling mental illness on three different occasions during a period of 10 years. In each instance, apparently quite cured, he returned to work within a few days of the expiration of his pay for disability.

Efforts to cure the patient by changes in the environmental conditions only prolonged the disability and set the stage for recurrent illness. The daily dispensary records on these patients, going back over many years, revealed the utter futility of symptomatic treatment. The backache would give way to diathermy, but was immediately followed by gastric ulcer symptoms. This yielded to antispasmodics, but was replaced by headaches. When aspirin solved this problem, nervousness ensued. Phenobarbital calmed the patient down for a while. Soon, job failure made supervision pass him off to another area with a glowing recommendation, but his happiness with the new job was ruined by the distress shift work caused him. That was easily handled by another transfer, but the lifting of heavy barrels in the new area quickly resulted in backache which again required hours of time in the dispensary for diathermy. The records of many individuals showed symptoms referable to every major system in the body.

Occupational therapy has long been known as a useful adjunct to other forms of treatment in the mental hospitals. Industrial physicians and nurses, as well as management and supervision, are in a position to experiment with the effect of real occupational therapy in the case of the problem employee.

After a case was studied and the diagnosis of emotional sickness was made, standard corrective practice required the employee to return to full regular duty at the same job. This was routine except where serious organic contraindications were present, such as a bleeding gastric ulcer or the rare case of a dangerous psychotic. The experience in this plant showed this to be a safe procedure, since most of the cases had been thoroughly studied for their various illnesses by outside specialists and the plant doctors, and many had been hospitalized for diagnostic studies. Where indicated, supervision was contacted and recommendations made that all excuses for poor performance be henceforth disregarded. It was emphasized that under no circumstances should the supervisor allow himself to become involved in an argument as to whether the patient was ill. This was held to be strictly the responsibility of the plant physician. The supervisor was to concern himself solely with the man's behavior on the job. His work performance was to be required to be the same as that of all other workmen in the group. Failure to require this usually prolongs the illness. There were, of course, exceptions to this. We have no data to indicate that any injustice, either medically or morally, was ever done to any employee through this course of action. These same recommendations were made in the same way to management for the treatment of salaried personnel.

One employee, exposed to toxic fumes early in the year, who has no residual defects, is still in and out of work with various psychosomatic complaints. The above recommendations had been made to his supervisor, but the man reports that they are being very kind to him, permitting him to take it easy. He will probably continue to be sick and nonproductive until he is required to be otherwise.

Where supervision failed to follow the medical recommendations and insisted upon coddling and appeasing the employee, failures usually resulted. One patient, who had been put to work with a backache of nervous origin, came in complaining bitterly because his foreman was always asking him how he felt. He went on to say, "I feel lousy, and I don't want to talk about it. I wish you would get that foreman off my neck." Supervisors were not the only offenders; they complained about the physicians following a policy of appeasement and coddling. This type of comment was heard: "I give a man a reprimand for poor work, and he goes crying to the hospital with a bellyache. Somebody sends him home. How can I straighten him out without some cooperation from the hospital?"

The complaints of both the physicians and the supervisors were well founded in many cases. The solution to this dilemma already exists in the strict division of areas of responsibility. When the supervisor maintains his authority in the field of production and the physician maintains his authority in the field of health, and neither tries to usurp that of the other, this problem ceases and the employee benefits.

Misunderstandings frequently arose because both groups did not have the same records available and were consequently getting different pictures of the problem. Further work is being carried out in cooperation with one of the plant personnel men in an effort to evolve a form of record which will contain the necessary data for an objective evaluation of the employee's overall performance. The need for such records became even more apparent when the evaluation of the results of the psychiatric experiment was attempted. Supervisors frequently commented that the idea of expecting people to work and earn their daily bread was nothing new, but that this realistic approach could also help individuals recover from illness was new.

The physician, too, found it difficult to overlook the symptoms of the suffering individal, since his training had been to minister to the comfort of his patients. Our data indicate that requiring a patient to meet his responsibilities, regardless of the symptoms of his psychosomatic ills, creates no hazard to his physical health compared to the very real danger to his mental health where his symptoms permit him to evade his obligations. It must be emphasized that there are few, if any, malingerers. It is impossible to "imagine" symptoms, nor are a patient's symptoms ever "in his head." The weak, sick, complaining employee usually feels just as badly as he reports. Whereas the patient with pneumonia is helped by nursing, the patient with an emotional illness is driven into further sickness, suffering, and disability by this same nursing. Using this form of therapy, the physician cannot hope to be liked by the patient. It was found, however, that this same disgruntled, angry employee would sometimes report back two years later stating that he was grateful for the treatment he had received. He recognized that, for many years, he had needed someone who would treat him in this realistic, mature fashion and stop his persistent evasion of reality.

The author's military experience bears out these observations. A training camp had been set up in the combat theater. Patients who had resisted all possible forms of therapy and who were found to be medically well were sent to this camp for a course in basic training. No excuses were accepted for not soldiering. The commanding officer of this camp reported that many men, after completing their training and returning to active units again, came back to visit on their leave and expressed gratitude to him for finally being made to perform like men. As long as the door of the psychiatrist's office was held open for soldiers to escape from their duty, quite reasonably they took advantage of it, and many remain, to this day, sick wards of the state. When the door was closed, they became honorable soldiers again and are now self-respecting independent citizens. It is understood that the observations of World War II are being applied successfully in Korea at this time.

Many conferences were held with groups of supervisors in the effort to encourage them to carry out what appeared to be, at first, a course of action which would make the patient worse. In those areas where supervision persisted in following these recommendations, however, absenteeism was reduced, fewer accidents were encountered, and personal problems were minimized, with an apparent improvement in morale.

Early in the course of this program, objections were raised by the union, which was critical of the course of action. The union officers did their job by making their objections known, but were extremely open-minded to reasons and data. The results were watched carefully and, so far as is known, no official complaint was ever made to management about the psychiatric program. There has been no union committee in the psychiatrist's office for over a year. Occasionally, a shop steward will drop in to get psychiatric help in the handling of some person with a grievance. A member of management, who cooperated most closely with the author in this program of occupational therapy, was recently promoted and transferred to another plant. At his farewell dinner, a present and letter of appreciation were given to him by the union in recognition of his straightforward policies in dealings with them.

The weakest part of any psychiatric research is the evaluation of results. This paper is subject to the same criticism. In order to minimize this defect, cases were considered improved only in those instances where definite objective evidence of better performance was available. Such factors as improved attendance, better safety performance, and cooperativeness were used as criteria where possible. Objective factors always superseded the psychiatrist's opinion and records. The hazards of even this type of evaluation are illustrated by this incident. One of the patients was reported by his supervisor, voluntarily, about six months ago, as being "a star pupil" who had become a fine, productive workman and was no longer a problem to the boss since he had been seen by the psychiatrist. A similar glowing report was made later. Very recently, the same employee was seen in another physician's office with a note from the same supervisor asking what was wrong with the man, since every time he was asked to do a job he complained he could not do it "because of spasms or something."

Two-thirds of the entire patient group for the period studied are still actively employed in the plant. Personal interviews with the present supervisor and management revealed that about half of the patients were considered to have improved. Some of this group had accepted psychotherapy, some had not. Where the patient had accepted therapy, a distinctly higher rate of improvement was found.

Unknown to the author at the time, an experiment was performed in the group which probably had the worst safety record in the entire company. The superintendent of this group was severely criticized for this poor safety performance, it having been made clear to him that such performance would no longer be tolerated. He, in turn, demanded the same performance from the supervisors and they, in turn, from the workmen. The result was a world's record of safety performance in this group with the identical personnel and working conditions.

This study has opened up many avenues for future exploration. The failures show that by no means do we have in psychiatry a panacea for all the ills of industry. The work does, through its minor successes, indicate a direction which, at the moment, and in the opinion of the author, seems to offer hope for improving a situation which is far from satisfactory. On the basis of such criteria as we now feel indicate the quality of morale, the data seem to show that the picture in this plant has improved.

## SUMMARY

1. A psychiatric problem exists in industry which involves at least a quarter of the working force.
2. The emotionally sick employee causes an excessive number of injuries, absenteeism, and industrial and personnel relations problems. This performance will usually continue until some action is taken to see that it stops.
3. The emotionally ill employee superficially does not differ from the average normal employee except in the degree of his individual productivity.
4. Management and supervision can successfully rehabilitate many emotionally sick employees by requiring normal performance. The sickest individuals seen are those who have had the most done for them.

5. It is possible early to identify the potential problem employee by properly centralizing and correlating pertinent data.

6. In the author's opinion, the psychiatrist's chief function is to make a diagnosis of the emotionally sick employee and give medical support to management for what is at present an unpopular course of action.

## ACKNOWLEDGMENT

This project could not have been carried out without the support and cooperation of Management. E. E. Evans, M.D., the Medical Director, and the other plant physicians worked closely and cooperated most helpfully with this work. Mr. Ivan Viele, a plant personnel man, has done much to assist the author in accumulating and studying those items of personnel data which contribute to the evaluation of employee productivity. Mr. Wallace MacKinnon, of the Organic Chemicals Department, assisted in the setting up of the form for the collection of data and did the mathematical calculations for the statistical analysis. Dr. F. W. Dershimer was in consultation with the author throughout the entire work and contributed immeasurably to its fulfillment.

## REFERENCES

1. Dershimer, F. W. A study in the cause and prevention of functional mental disease. *American Journal of Orthopsychiatry*, 1938, **8**, 2, 302.

2. Dershimer, F. W. The influence of mental attitudes in childbearing. *American Journal of Obstetrics and Gynecology*, 1936, **31**, 3, 444.

# 10. OCCUPATIONAL PSYCHIATRY THROUGH THE MEDICAL PERISCOPE

### C. A. D'Alonzo, M.D., F.A.C.P.
### Allan J. Fleming, M.Sc., M.D.

Occupational psychiatry, as a branch of occupational medicine, appears well rooted for a continuing growth. At least three other manufacturing companies, namely, Eastman Kodak, General Electric, and American Cyanamid, employ a full-time psychiatrist on the medical staff, and the number of part-time psychiatrists in this specialty is continually increasing. The psychiatric program began at the Du Pont Company in 1943 with the acquisition of a full-time psychiatrist. In 1946, a second was added, and the present staff still consists of two full-time specialists in this field.

Occupational psychiatry, in our Company at least, has been well received by management. At the present time most employees accept it readily as a matter of fact. There are, to be sure, still a few die-hards who view it with reluctance. As to the reasons for this persistent reluctance, we believe that the main discrepancy lies within the field of psychiatry itself.

For years the psychiatrist was known as an "alienist." As such, he obviously had to alienate something or somebody. Then, the court scene familiar to us all, of two well-known psychiatrists, both leaders in their field, of unquestionable

Dr. D'Alonzo is Corporate Medical Director and Dr. Fleming is Medical Director of E. I. du Pont de Nemours and Company, Wilmington, Delaware.

reputation, each on opposing sides and rendering as divergent a view as is possible—one stating with an air of certainty that, in his opinion, a suspect is insane in the legal sense of the word, and hence unaccountable for his acts; the other that the suspect is sane and can differentiate right from wrong, and is thus responsible for his acts! Little wonder that an employee, with due consideration for that kind of background situation, would not willingly submit to psychiatric evaluation! Would you, yourself, not ponder about submitting to it? Therefore, if employees are reluctant to accept it, we can but chiefly blame the psychiatrists themselves for the dilemma. The institution of an educational program to overcome this distaste is in order.

The aim of occupational psychiatry certainly differs in no respect from that of any other branch of psychiatry—the aim of all is the treatment and cure of the signs or symptoms resulting from emotional or mental conflict. Moreover, the psychiatrist in industry conducts research into the factors necessary to prevent severe emotional disturbances; he trains plant physicians in techniques for handling psychiatric problems, and consults with plant physicians on individual cases, or group behaviors, which are, or are suspected of being, of occupational origin; and he advises management regarding the proper methods of handling emotionally disturbed individuals or groups.

To be successful, occupational psychiatry should function as a unit of an occupational Medical Department. Its function, just as with any other unit, must be to contribute to the occupational health program in general. Figure 1 shows all of the functions of an occupational Medical Department, of which occupational psychiatry is another unit.

There are, to be sure, differences between psychiatry as it is practiced in: (1) a mental institution, (2) an office of the private psychiatrist, and (3) industry. Two and three should differ but little. The chief variances as viewed by us are noted in Figure 2. The points of differentiation are clear. Every successful occupational physician practices psychiatry

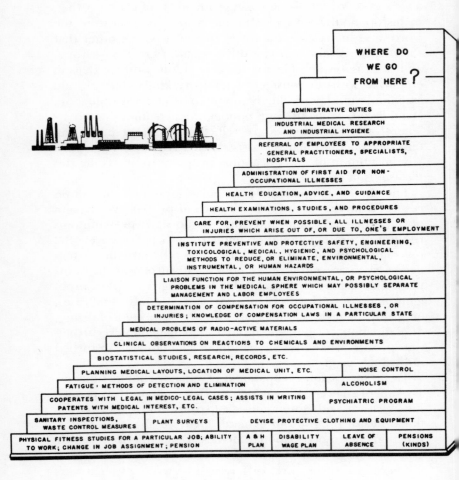

**Fig. 1.** The functions of an occupational medical department.

## TO A GREATER EXTENT

## TO A LESSER EXTENT

1 – DEALS MORE WITH WORKING POPULATION ——→ LESS WITH INSTITUTIONAL POPULATION

2 – CONCERNED MAINLY WITH NEUROSES ——→ LESS WITH PSYCHOSES

3 – INTEREST IS CHIEFLY IN TRAINING PROPER HANDLING OF EMPLOYEES, AND PREVENTIVE RESEARCH. ←— LESS INTEREST IN PSYCHOANALYSIS, OR FREUDIAN PRINCIPLES.

4 – CHIEF CONSIDERATION IS ON THE JOB "HYPOSENSITIZATION" TO PROBLEMS ——→ LESS INTEREST IN HOSPITALIZATION IN THICK-CARPETED INSTITUTIONS, WITH THE SEPARATION BY TIME, AND WITH THE SUBSEQUENT NECESSITY OF RETURNING TO JOB ANYWAY TO FACE THE INITIAL PROBLEM

5 – MAIN THERAPY IS FRONT LINE THERAPY ——→ LESS CONCERNED WITH THERAPY BY SEPARATION

6 – CONCERNED CHIEFLY WITH PSYCHOTHERAPY ——→ AND LESSER NEED FOR CHEMOTHERAPY

Fig. 2. Occupational psychiatry.

although he may not call or recognize it as such. Therefore, since he is nonetheless practicing psychiatry, it might just as well be fully appreciated. Similarly, it might just as well be good as bad. Nothing is to be gained by closing one's eyes to a field which is essential.

Physicians in industry have been somewhat disappointed by some practicing psychiatrists who seem to blame all or most of the troubles of an employee on the parents. It is convenient and face-saving to place the blame on someone else. When possible, the parents should be consulted before establishing their guilt. No judge would do otherwise.

A fair amount of what is considered as needing psychiatry is often lack of discipline, training, responsibility, adjustment, maturity, bigness, or honesty. Fancier diagnoses sometimes channel the disorder into some other direction. A shift of symptoms and not a cure results.

The main psychiatric factors among employees are as follows:

1. Improper discipline during childhood and youth ("momism," at home, or on the job).
2. Job adjustment and responsibility; the need of all people to face reality with its attendant successes and failures; learning to accept criticism and to compensate for defects.
3. Family problems.
4. Health worries.
5. Miscellaneous fears, phobias, anxieties, etc.

Insofar as the education of employees in industry and the need for orientation in this particular field are concerned, the following items are listed as of prime importance in overcoming the hesitation in employees' minds:

1. Psychiatric records, as is the case with all medical records, are confidential, and are so treated and kept.
2. The chief intent of the occupational psychiatrist is to assist employees in ways and means of handling common problems and conflicts, and not of telling them, as many employees believe, that they are or are not "crazy." The function of occupational psychiatry is to promote and maintain mental health and mental efficiency.

3. The relationship of the employee to the occupational psychiatrist carries with it the same doctor–patient relationship that prevails in any other branch of medicine. The psychiatrist may inform a department or division that a particular employee needs hospital treatment, or special therapy, or that specific steps should be taken to right an obvious organizational wrong, but the psychiatrist is not at liberty to discuss the more personal aspects resulting from the interview.

4. Employees should be educated to the fact that there is no fear of the loss of their job simply because they require or desire consultation with a psychiatrist, and that they will not in the future be side-tracked organization-wise for "having needed a psychiatrist."

The Freudian psychiatrist, or the psychoanalyst, will be somewhat disappointed and frustrated in occupational psychiatry. The main basis of the latter is, as a matter of fact, more practical and factual, and deals more with the phases discussed above. The emotional difficulties encountered are those based on existing problems in everyday life, and not with fantasies or reveries of the past. It is obvious that the occupational psychiatrist must be well versed, and have experience and knowledge in the field of occupational medicine as well as regarding the manufacturing industry. Familiarity with the employee's industrial environment, management, and groups is essential.

The psychiatrist, regardless of his particular field, can contribute to the advance of occupational psychiatry in various ways. These are briefly summarized as follows:

1. By taking a realistic viewpoint toward the fact that one-half of the waking day of the employee is spent at his job, and that often the occupational psychiatrist will know much more of the facts about an employee than the personal psychiatrist can ever hope to learn by subjective history, the latter being often no more than a record of the delusions of a patient.

2. By getting down to a more sensible approach to the needs

of the patient, and not making big issues about little things, which often, having found their way into the lay press, give the impression that no two psychiatrists ever agree, and that a personal evaluation is a fluctuating affair, depending on which particular psychiatrist is seen. Some employees have spoken to us of the opinion that psychiatry is a field not based on fact or science. We believe that the psychiatrist himself is partially to blame for this concept.

Cooperation should exist between the occupational psychiatrist and the personal psychiatrist in both diagnosis and treatment to the end that the needs of the patient will be more fully and intelligently served.

We entertain sincere doubts about the general need of institutional treatment for the psychoneuroses. Often, these particular employees are required to make a dual adjustment upon their return to employment. First, they must overcome again the same dislikes and face the same realities, and fall into the same disciplines, to which they may possibly have objected before being separated from their employment by a span of time. And, second, they must overcome the stigma, which unfortunately still exists in nonmedical minds, of "having been in a mental institution." Moreover, considering the number of psychoneurotics among the population, any hope of solving the overall problem by institutional care and treatment appears futile.

These remarks are recorded because occupational psychiatry is a growing field, is being more and more readily accepted by employees, is losing its unfavorable stigma, and is serving a real need. More and more people are directly asking or seeking referral to the occupational psychiatrist.

On the other hand, the private practitioner of psychiatry need have no concern as to infringement on his field. One can but recall the fear of private medical practice when occupational medicine began. It is now generally accepted that occupational medicine has enlarged and expanded every phase of the work of the general practitioner and the specialist. Those of us in industry can readily see that the same situation now prevails in the newest field of psychiatry—occupational psychiatry.

It is our firm belief that both the need and the scope of the work of the private practitioner of psychiatry will be increased and more adequately expanded through the efforts of the industrial psychiatrist. Not only will there be ample room for both fields, but also the needs of the patient will be more fully realized and appropriate therapy more successfully instituted.

# 11. MENTAL HEALTH IN INDUSTRY

**Louis Belinson, M.D.**

Mental health is an all-inclusive term; mental—a word which tends to induce anxiety—and health—a word which can today be construed as an anxiety reducer. Though we may speak quite freely about mental health and mental illness, we cannot actually separate the two. Both health and illness are parts of the same state of adjustment and stability of the individual. The subject today follows the advent of pioneering studies in the field of human behavior. Medicine has for many decades been concerned with the toxic and environmental hazards of workers and has stimulated industry to concern itself with better physical protection of workers.

## CONTRIBUTIONS

During World War I, the effectiveness of workers in England became the concern of the government, and studies were done in the area of sociological and psychological aspects of the various types of jobs (3, 10). In this country, one of the early references to the employment of a psychiatrist in industry was in 1916, when the operators of a silk mill sought to evaluate the emotional adjustment of the workers (5). Three

Dr. Belinson is Deputy Director, Division of Mental Diseases, State of Missouri; Clinical Assistant Professor of Psychiatry (part-time), University of Missouri School of Medicine, Columbia, Missouri; and Lecturer in Hospital Administration, School of Medicine, Washington University, St. Louis, Missouri. The author's address is Division of Mental Diseases, State of Missouri, 722 Jefferson Street, Jefferson City, Missouri.

Presented at the Winter Meeting of the Central States Society of Industrial Medicine and Surgery, St. Louis, Missouri, December 5, 1959.

years later, the Engineering Foundation of New York designated a psychiatrist, Dr. Southard, to do a careful analysis of some 4,000 cases. He reported that social incompetence rather than occupational incompetence brought about the discharge status of 62% of the workers (1). Russell Frazer in a survey of the mental health of more than 3,000 workers from 13 different factories (in Great Britain) found that from one-fourth to one-third of absenteeism was due to illness caused by nervous disorder (11). The Metropolitan Life Insurance Company added a psychiatrist in 1922 (5). In 1925, a Dr. V. V. Anderson analyzed the personnel of a large New York department store and reported that 20% of the group could be called problem cases, owing to maladjusted personalities, poor physical condition, or disability for the particular jobs to which they were assigned (2).

Perhaps the outstanding series of studies were the contributions of Elton Mayo and his associates from the Harvard School of Business Administration. To his group, we owe the present day practice of "rest periods." Initially, this modification in working conditions was intended for workers whose jobs had a high degree of monotony. The most significant value of his work at the Hawthorne (Illinois) Plant of Western Electric, some 32 years ago, was the concept that human interrelations are an integral part of the work situation (3). The plant operates in both an economic area, bringing forth a product, and a social area, where there is created and distributed job satisfaction. For effective and productive plant operation, then, we have a triangle with (1) the structure, (2) the culture, or climate, and (3) the personality of the worker firmly linked together.

## ORGANIZATIONAL STRUCTURE

While it may tend to clarify our thinking to delineate a progressive movement as if it occurred as an isolated phenomenon, we must ever be mindful of the fact that there are many developments which contribute concurrently and make specific advances possible. I am now referring to the entire field of administration and management. It was not too many years ago that the great majority of our larger organizations were autocratic in administrative operation. The individual family or group who owned the organization or plant or factory were primarily concerned with the success of the operation as measured by profits and the necessity, of course, to protect the investment. It was only when management became more democratic—that is, when more individuals began to share in the total administration of the organization—that the interrelations between individuals began to enter the thinking and planning for the total program.

We owe much of our present understanding of administrative structure and organization to the field of political science. Here we find that, by virtue of political expediency and changes in political fortunes, organizations had to be built, dissolved, and rebuilt every one or two or four years. While they were political organizations, they contained the inherent structural relationships of any organization. Political science gave us the organizational plan with its chain of command and channels of communication. This was the beginning of a vast body of knowledge which now has accumulated through experimentation, research, and practical application.

This was followed by the development of scientific management, which provided us with the concept of job descriptions with its levels of authority and levels of responsibility and statements of qualifications and experience. It made possible the recruiting of the right man for the particular job.

With this background, the field of psychology added its skills and contributed the role that the leader plays in utilizing the table of organization and job descriptions. The value of good leadership, the qualities of a leader, and the study of techniques of leadership were invaluable contributions during this period. More recently we have reached what might be called the fourth phase. This has been contributed by the social scientists, or sociologists. The social scientist has pointed to the fact that the interrelation of the three previous contributions with the actual workers in the plant constitute a team. The worker must be considered a member of the team. In fact, the social scientist repeated what Elton Mayo had indicated—that we must not confine ourselves to the product but must consider the productive worker as well. Great amounts of time, effort, and money are expended to improve the product. A significant amount of interest, time, effort, and money must be given to improve the producer of the product so that we will not lose from our ranks, as Dr. Southard pointed out many years ago, two-thirds of our workers because they could not get along with their supervisors and fellow workers (1).

## THE WHOLE WORKER

Today we have begun to realize that a person cannot ignore either his concern with social, financial, and spiritual obligations or his very personal likes, dislikes, attitudes, and temperamental traits when he comes through the office door or factory gate.

Millions have jobs—millions work. Work is healthy. Human beings need to work—to give of themselves, to be productive, creative, to contribute to a total effort. Whether one can see the total process or only the finished product, the act of doing for a cause—a goal—gives meaning to living. The fact that we are compensated for our services all too frequently obscures the deeper significance. Surely we expect to be paid—to have money to procure the necessities and comforts of life; but work itself enriches our lives, particularly so if the job is satisfying, stimulating, and instills pride. Pride in one's job is not confined solely to the positions requiring technical skills.

There are, of course, many, many variables when one questions the suitability of a particular person to a job. I would hazard a guess that most of us came to our present jobs without major logical decisions involving careful evaluation of aptitude, temperament, and the other factors involved. Actually, personal needs which may not reach full awareness tend to make one more comfortable in one type of work than another. We look for such jobs. Recognizing this in recent years, psychologists have developed a variety of aptitude tests, hoping to leave less to chance and intuition and more to careful analysis.

Let me emphasize that, while one may illustrate specific problems by situations which are unusual and perhaps abnormal, this in no way means that we are concerned only with workers who are emotionally or mentally ill. Actually, our concern is for the better adaptation of the normal worker to his job situation.

The goal of occupational health or mental health in industry should be to promote and maintain the highest degree of physical, mental, and social well-being. This will bring health and happiness to people at work.

## PERSONAL ADJUSTMENT

It can correctly be stated that a worker can be a bit fearful, a bit forgetful, a bit suspicious, a bit compulsive, irritable, and angry and still be very much a normal person. When confronted by stress and strain in the form of worries, whether they be precipitated in the home or at work, there may be an exaggeration of these particular traits. In other words, he may become more fearful, more suspicious, or lose his temper more easily. For many workers, these particular qualities may appear and disappear. For others, they may be a part of the personality make-up of the individual.

Besides the foregoing traits, all human beings in maintaining what might be called psychic equilibrium or staying on an even keel resort to mental mechanisms with which many of us are familiar. Some of these are *rationalization*, which simply means to "save face"; *projection*, to "blame others"; *identification*, to "copy others"; *overcompensation*, an example of which is a "sullen loser"; *sublimation*, shifting some need or urge to a more acceptable area, e.g., hostility drained off in competitive sports; *displacement*, a device noted when one "scolds subordinates" after a run-in with the boss; *isolation*, the use of a protective measure such as a "phobia"; and *conversion*, noted when a "headache develops" in the face of an unpleasant task.

These are very helpful and enable many, many persons to ride the punches and handle unexpected setbacks and the like. When a person begins to depend upon one such mechanism for all his conflicts and anxieties, however, he begins to lose flexibility. The very device which was an asset can become a serious liability and make increasingly difficult the adjustment of the worker to his family, friends, and co-workers. Again, these are normal mental mechanisms which can become distorted in emphasis and lead to difficulty in adjustment.

If the utilization of traits mentioned previously and the mental mechanisms just described fail to protect, in a sense, the integrity of the individual, then additional subconscious defense mechanisms come into play without any awareness on the part of the individual.

So frequently do we find individuals precipitated into a sea of turbulence and uncertainty by the development of conflicts which apparently cannot be resolved. The presence of a conflict, with oscillation to and from each possibility, creates anxiety as a product. Anxiety is what we call that very uncomfortable feeling that grows and finally engulfs us when we cannot reach a decision.

If we could reach a decision, the need for a defense mechanism would no longer exist because the anxiety would disappear.

In order to protect this individual from such a disturbing situation which is progressively impairing his relationship to everyone about him, however, the human organism may develop any one of several defense mechanisms which are known to all of us. The person may show chronic maladjustment, or he may develop a psychosomatic disorder or sufficient changes in his make-up to constitute personality disorders involving both patterns and traits. Under stress, he may instead begin showing neurotic symptoms involving conversion reaction, phobias, obsessions, etc. Or he may develop a psychosis. It is true—a psychosis is a defense mechanism attempting to protect the integrity of the organism from what seems to be overwhelming disaster, but actually the defense mechanism adopted may be far worse than the real difficulty.

I shall not go further into a description of the particular way in which these mechanisms operate; they are surely very important, however, in the overall picture of mental health in industry—whether we are dealing with someone already employed or are interviewing an applicant for a job.

## PSYCHIATRIC SERVICES

Successful personnel management, recruiting techniques, and good working relationships in any plant are dependent upon some understanding of the foregoing. I hasten to add that it is not the responsibility of the unit supervisor or personnel officer or executive to attempt to do psychotherapy. However, by virtue of his close relationship with the worker and his knowledge of not only the particular employee but what is expected of him in the job, very successful handling of many such difficulties which do not involve any deep-seated problems may be made possible. I know most seminars and workshops in human relations and employee relations have stressed this point.

Generally speaking, when a mental health or psychiatric unit is established, the medical department seems to be the ideal place. It is considered a neutral zone in many management programs and permits a degree of confidentiality that could not be expected elsewhere. A medical department may consist of only a nurse and a doctor on call or a part-time physician. With increasing needs, one finds a full-time physician specializing in industrial medicine with a psychiatrist in consultation. In larger operations, there may be a full-time psychiatrist who specializes in industrial psychiatry. Today, with the fuller acceptance of the vital needs in this area, we find not only a psychiatrist and a psychologist employed, but human relations experts, business administration and management consultants, personnel officers, plant physicians, industrial nurses, and social workers with industrial social work experience.

It is my understanding that industry for general health purposes of its employees employs 5,000 full-time physicians, with another 10,000 on a part-time basis, and another 10,000 on emergency call (13).

The mental health program in an industrial plant can be conceived of as an operation tying together the general health programs and the human relations techniques and procedures practiced by all supervisory personnel.

There is a rather definite agreement on the scope of the services rendered by a psychiatrist (6–8, 12). These include:

1. Dealing with major psychiatric disturbances of workers in terms of diagnosis and disposition in the community;
2. Dealing with minor psychiatric disorders of workers in terms of diagnosis and superficial or brief therapy;
3. Advising on selection and placement of new workers who have psychiatric disorders or problems;
4. Advising and assisting in the rehabilitation and placement of employees who are or who have been psychiatrically ill;
5. Teaching and training medical department personnel concerning psychiatric and mental health aspects of industrial medicine;
6. Taking part in mental health education programs for employees.

## COMMENT

It is not unusual, however, when a large organization finds it of value to add to the medical department an industrial psychiatrist that as long as two years may elapse before that highly qualified person is fully accepted as a resource and utilized by management whenever the occasion arises.

In order, then, for the organization to develop to the highest degree its product, constant and continuing concern must be given to the productivity of the worker. Industry, then, must accept responsibilities to maintain a working climate which is conducive to good mental health.

In psychiatric practice, whether it be in private practice or in a clinic situation, the troubled person is usually aware of his unhappy relationship with other people. A situation has developed in spite of what he has tried to do and over which he is able to exercise less and less control. This frustrating situation involving those about him is confined not only to his own family and relatives but also to the neighborhood, his friends, and, perhaps most important for this subject today, his fellow workers and supervisors in the plant in which he works.

Problems are a mixture of environmental stresses and personal needs. Very frequently they appear in one or more large categories such as sickness, financial difficulties, marital adjustment problems, and concern over the children. Actually, these simply may be the overt manifestations of efforts on the part of the individual to handle not only the mental mechanisms for equilibrium, but the defense mechanisms of more serious maladjustments.

What, then, can be described as symptoms of poor mental health in industry? These symptoms, which collectively are estimated to cost from 3 to 12 billion dollars annually, are absenteeism, excessive turnover, alcoholism, industrial accidents, lowered productivity, and labor strikes.

The insecurity, anxiety, restlessness, irritation, and sensitivity of the unhappy, dissatisfied worker produces, in effect, an emotional contagion which frequently cannot be resisted by a good number who are susceptible, and the state of tension begins to spread. Thus, it is most urgent that these individuals be given every opportunity to obtain psychiatric help.

Some of the more frequent factors that seem to undermine morale and, in turn, mental health are poor or bad supervision, work which is repetitious and has a high component of monotony, the lack of job security, and temperamental incompatibility of the worker and his job.

The full support of management should exist in the endeavor to support this employee in his hour of need. Each worker represents a sizable investment in time, effort, and money as witnessed by the amount of training that has been provided. Salvaging one employee into a more productive worker is not only an extremely satisfying service to a human being, but, more than that, it does and will accrue to better mental health for all of his co-workers.

## CONCLUSION

In closing, let me point out that the mounting interest in vocational rehabilitation as it relates to the emotionally and mentally ill has drawn the psychiatrist much closer to the specialty of industrial psychiatry. The restoration of a man to his job and rebuilding his security and self-esteem serve to preserve our family, life, stabilize our communities, and lessen the probability of the need of future psychiatric care. The productive worker is a taxpayer. Mental health programs in industry are good business.

## SUMMARY

Over the past 40 years, industry has shown increasing interest in the emotional problems of the worker. Pioneered by the significant contributions of Elton Mayo and his associates, this area of personnel relations has come to be the key to success or failure in industrial progress.

The objective of mental health activities in industry is to promote health and happiness of people at work. The most important way to seek this goal is not the provision of psychiatric services, but the planning of work tasks and patterns of individual organization which do not run counter to human emotional needs.

By these definitions, a number of professions become involved in industrial mental health. The psychologist and the psychiatrist earn a place through their specialized knowledge of human behavior. The expert in human relations, business administration, and management is also a key person. The personnel officer, the plant physician, the industrial nurse and social worker, management and labor all deal with the human problems and health of the individual worker.

# REFERENCES

1. Jerrett, M. C. Mental hygiene of industry. *Mental Hygiene*, 1920, **4**, 867.

2. Anderson, V. V. *Psychiatry in industry.* New York: Harper and Brothers, 1929.

3. Mayo, E. *The human problems of an industrial civilization.* New York: The Macmillan Company, 1933.

4. Roethlisberger, F. J., & Dickson, W. J. *Management and the worker.* Cambridge, Massachusetts: Harvard University Press, 1940.

5. Giberson, L. G. A wartime survey of industrial psychiatry. *M. Clin. North America*, 1942, **26**, 1090.

6. Cameron, D. E. Psychiatry in industry. *Canadian M. A. J.*, 1945, **53**, 540.

7. The application of psychiatry to industry. G. A. P. Report 20, 1951.

8. Mindus, E. Industrial psychiatry in Great Britain, the United States and Canada, Report to World Health Organization, 1952.

9. Menninger, W. C. Men, machines and mental health. *Mental Hygiene*, 1952, **36**, 184.

10. Markowe, M. Occupational psychiatry. *Journal of Mental Science*, 1953, **90**, 84.

11. Mindus, E. Outlines of a concept of industrial psychiatry. *Bulletin of the World Health Organization*, 1955, **13**, 561.

12. Ling, T. M. Mental health in industry. *Bulletin of the World Health Organization*, 1955, **13**, 551.

13. Is there a doctor in the plant? *Journal of the American Medical Association*, 1957, **63**, 1139.

14. Levinson, H. Emotional first aid on the job. *Menninger Quarterly*, Sept. 1957.

15. Duval, A. M. Psychiatry and the everyday work of the foreman. *Advance Management*, 1957, **22**, 15.

16. Laughlin, H. P. A psychiatric contribution to the development of executives. National Institute of Mental Health, U.S. Department of Health, Education, and Welfare, Washington, D.C.

17. A review of mental health in industry—1957. National Institute of Mental Health, U.S. Department of Health, Education, and Welfare, Washington, D.C.

# 12. REVOLUTION
# IN MENTAL HEALTH

### Wilbur J. Cohen

Like the Industrial Revolution of a century ago, there is a revolution in mental health which is not only revamping the methods of dealing with mental illness but is affecting American society as a whole.

This is a time of great social change. Automation and new technologies are rapidly changing man's world. The crisis of the cities and needs of the poor demand that society find new ways to deal with its problems. Change is even occurring in the back wards of long-term mental institutions that once housed the so-called "hopeless" patients.

The changes within state hospitals are a major indicator of the important revolution in mental health. In 1945 there were 450,000 patients in public mental hospitals in the United States. In 1950 there were 500,000; and in 1955, the number climbed to 570,000.

And then in 1955 a turning point came—not a symbolic turning point but a real one. The upward trend began to reverse itself. During 1967, the decline was the sharpest to date—down by 26,000 patients in one year to 426,000. This significant trend has occurred at a time when the American population has grown tremendously. If the upward trend of 1945 to 1955 had continued there would be more than 700,000 patients in our mental hospitals today.

This, in itself, is one of the great success stories of our time, but it is only the beginning. Beneath this dramatic exam-

Mr. Cohen served as Secretary of the Department of Health, Education, and Welfare from March 1968 to January 1969.

ple of change are several important innovations that are direct-ing the development of mental health programs.

Perhaps most dramatic is the advent in this decade of the psychoactive drugs: the tranquilizers, the antidepressants, and the antipsychotics. Each year sees more progress in developing new drugs, refining the ones we have, and understanding how they work. Secondly, there is the development of com-munity facilities for psychiatric care—clinics, general hospitals, aftercare, and rehabilitation programs. This past year, for example, more patients were admitted to general hospitals for psychiatric illness than to state mental institutions.

But more important than both of these developments has been the change in community attitudes. Mental illness is rec-ognized by the public as an illness that can yield to treatment. These important changes have led to the development of today's community mental health centers.

## THE BOLD NEW APPROACH

Since the passage of the Community Mental Health Centers Act in 1963, Federal funds have been made available to 276 centers. The National Institute of Mental Health, which administers this program, expects 500 centers to be in opera-tion by 1970, growing to 2,000 within the next decade. This will mean that even fewer people will be treated in state hospi-tals and more mental health care will be provided locally.

Since the emphasis of community mental health is on return-ing the emotionally disturbed to their homes and their jobs, the impact on industry is significant. More employees can receive prompt attention for their mental problems and return to work sooner. More people will be receiving treatment as they stay on the job.

In the new centers, five basic services will be offered to

every resident: inpatient treatment, outpatient treatment, partial hospitalization, emergency services, and consultation and education. These services—provided in a coordinated program—represent the public health approach to treatment and prevention of mental illness and related problems such as alcoholism, drug abuse, suicide, and delinquency. The modern approach reduces the disability caused by illness and involves many elements of the community in the restoration of the patients.

Of the centers, 40% will provide new inpatient services, while 32% will have enlarged inpatient services—with new physical facilities, enlarged staff, or both.

More than half the centers now being built will provide partial hospitalization in areas where no such service previously existed.

New outpatient services will be offered at 45%, while another 40% will improve and expand these services, including individual and group psychotherapy, family therapy, and drug treatment.

Half the centers will provide new emergency services; a third more will increase these services beyond their present level.

Finally, 40% will have new consultative services, and a similar percentage will expand their existing services. These are services that are offered to schools, churches, courts, juvenile authorities, welfare agencies, and to industry.

One of the outstanding characteristics of the program is that it pulls together and coordinates all existing services. In too many communities in the past, the interests of individual agencies often took precedence over the interests of the patient and his family.

## INDUSTRY'S ROLE
## IN THE MENTAL HEALTH

The revolution in mental health has serious implications for businessmen and managers in industry. Managers and personnel officers are already noticing change generated by the reduction of hospital populations and the growth of community outpatient mental health services.

The development of such services is changing the nature and direction of treatment for mental illness and has important bearing on managerial decisions to allow more liberal sick leave for disturbed workers. Where once custodial care was the only choice for persons who did not respond to treatment, today's treatment methods—including drugs and other therapies—can change the behavior of a patient so that he can live and work in his community.

It is this emphasis on a return to functioning, rather than cure, that should make it possible to provide job protection for workers who are mentally ill as effectively as for workers who are physically ill. Most industries have liberal sick leave policies for workers who become ill. However, workers who suffer from psychiatric disorders rarely have similar advantages and protection.

Decisions are made every day about mentally ill workers by medical, managerial, and public agency personnel from their narrow and specialized points of view. Under these fragmented procedures, it is today possible for a worker to be refused reinstatement on his job by management or ruled "unable to work" by the Employment Service, and at the same time be denied social security or other benefits on the grounds that "no permanent disability" has been demonstrated.

Mentally or emotionally ill workers must be allowed to work, when they are able, either through modifications of industry's methods to access employability or by adjusting work assignments; or benefit programs must be amended to provide for them. As community treatment expands and custodial care declines, there will be greater demands on medical departments in industry to make decisions concerning the ability or disability of mentally ill employees. Unfortunately, most industries do not have the trained or experienced staff to make these difficult decisions.

Community mental health center staffs can provide consultation services to fill what is now a partial vacuum, not only by acting as a third party when questions arise, but also as a professional group through which referrals can be made and treatment provided.

The traditional psychiatric diagnosis of a patient is not a completely reliable basis for determining his ability to remain at work; nor can reinstatement to employment, under today's treatment methods, depend on "proof of cure" or "recovery."

New methods of appraisal and new guidelines are needed to assess the employability or disability of a worker. Each appraisal must be made about a specific person in relation to a specific job and his capacity to function in that particular circumstance.

## THE INDUSTRIAL ENVIRONMENT

Community mental health centers can help managers provide better services for their employees. But treatment is only part of the problem. There is growing recognition today that the relationship between a man's work and his mental health is basic to human satisfaction and productivity.

The national mental health program is today concerned with man and his total environment, because it is in the subtle interplay among biological, biochemical, physical, psychological, and environmental factors that the key to prevention can be found. The concern with the industrial environment is not new to the field of occupational mental health, but there is still much to be done.

One example of a specific problem that lends itself to greater cooperation between mental health centers and industry is alcoholism. Considering the size of the problem, industry has initiated few alcoholism control programs, but those it has started have been comparatively successful. Studies have shown that when industry makes an intensive effort with employees who have drinking problems, the recovery rate ranges between 65 and 85% as contrasted with a general public recovery rate of 30% or less.

## CENTERS CAN MEET CHALLENGE

Community mental health centers present an unparalleled challenge and opportunity for industry to overcome long time neglect of the problem of alcoholism. The range of services provided by community mental health centers is precisely the range of services required for dealing with alcohol problems. Managers can work with staff at community centers to develop effective alcoholism control programs.

Managers can also do much to improve the work environment and thereby improve the mental health of their work force. Sometimes, for example, jobs can be reshaped to provide greater work satisfaction. Sometimes the organization structure or labor-management relations need to be re-examined to increase employee morale, motivation, and productivity. Some of these steps may call for extensive research.

On the other hand, the work environment can also be improved by changes in attitude on the part of management. Providing job security based on high standards of excellence in work performance is one example. Another is the need for individual recognition and the opportunity for career development and growth. Another is the need for maximum employee participation in the life of the organization. Finally, there is the need for managers to adopt and maintain a straightforward and direct approach to decision-making in dealing with their employees. Studies have shown that where management policy is unclear, employees undergo unnecessary emotional upheaval and stress.

## INDUSTRY'S COMMUNITY RESPONSIBILITY

The psychiatrist and the business man or industrialist do not generally enjoy sound working relationships, but the time has arrived to establish a relationship that can be mutually beneficial.

The consultative service of a community mental health center can open the door to this kind of communication. Centers can provide consultation directed at prevention as well as toward better treatment.

There needs to be a greater acceptance of the concept of mental health consultation in the industrial setting. There needs also to be an increased interest in and knowledge of occupational mental health on the part of psychiatrists, psychologists, and other mental health professionals.

Never before has this country really tried to prevent and control mental disorders from a public health point of view. We are now engaged in such an effort on the premise that mental illness is a public health problem.

As industry begins to accept this idea as part of its community responsibility, it can make many important contributions to the mental health of its employees, and therefore to the efficiency of the work force. One area in which it can take the lead is the vital area of research.

There are certain kinds of research that only industry can initiate. There is great need for comprehensive statistical data on absenteeism, accidents, alcoholism, job turnover, and the amount of production scrapped because of faulty workmanship. These data and many more can be supplied by industry and related to mental health programs. Using the findings of such investigations, health professionals can make their aid and consultation more effective.

In its research programs, the National Institute of Mental Health supports research in the causes, diagnosis, treatment, prevention, and control of mental illness and the promotion of mental health. Events have moved into the laboratory and this laboratory has become the world.

The process of urbanization and industrialization, for example, is affecting our entire nation. The problems of metropolitan areas are problems of stress, of crowding, and of increased leisure time. Automation is creating surplus manpower that is relatively unskilled and undereducated.

New leaders are emerging in our urban communities. Some are representatives of the poor, the young, and minority groups. Some are representatives of large industries, trained in the new techniques of management and skilled in interpersonal relationships.

## NEW LEADERS MEET CHALLENGE

All of these new leaders, particularly the civic-minded business men, are playing a greater role in planning and sponsoring vital community services, including mental health services.

They are increasingly putting the stamp of their abilities and interests on the quality of services where they live and work.

We have to look to new leadership to develop new partnerships, to establish new patterns of service that will raise the quality of life for all of our people. For it is on the capacity of Americans to lead healthful, productive, meaningful lives that the future of our society depends.

# Part III
# Multiple Approaches
# to Employee Counseling

# 13. THE ROLE
# OF THE PSYCHIATRIST
# IN INDUSTRY

**Gerald Gordon, M.D.**

*Psychiatric principles can be applied to organizational effort. They can assist in establishing realistic organizational and personal goals.*

Management is a difficult art and a highly complex and responsible function. Its purpose as defined in a company publication (1) "is to bring cohesion and vitality to human effort within its purview, transforming ideas and materials into units of greater value."

Management is a creative and necessary function for a complex, highly developed civilization. If it fails, then civilization as we know it fails and we may well return to a subsistence level of life. It operates in a world of uncompromising reality, the competitive market place.

It is the role of the psychiatrist in industry to assist management in the discharge of these heavy responsibilities in a manner best promoting the general welfare of the people and the organization they compose.

Dr. F. W. Dershimer (6), our retired Director of Psychiatry, characterized the industrial setting as "one of the most realistic

Dr. Gordon was formerly Chief, Psychiatric Section, Medical Division, E. I. Du Pont de Nemours and Company. He is a member of the American Medical Association, the American Psychiatric Association, and the American Academy of Occupational Medicine. He is certified in Occupational Medicine by the American Board of Preventive Medicine.

situations in our modern world. As such it is the testing ground on which the strengths and weaknesses developed by the early training of individuals become clearly apparent. The reactions of men and women in this real world disclose faults and virtues of school and home as did army life during the war. They bring out also the factors that cause functional mental disorders in so-called normal people. Psychiatric observations of these factors should in time supply us with data by means of which we can diagnose important causes of psychiatric conditions and go on to develop effective measures for preventing them."

Crawford H. Greenewalt (3), president of the Du Pont Company, delineated the problem between the individual and the organization as "how best to preserve the creative power of the individual in the face of organizational necessity. The problem exists whatever the purpose toward which the organization is directed, whether it is the Du Pont Company, Princeton University, the U.S. Marine Corps, the Church of the Latter Day Saints, or Tammany Hall.

## CREATIVITY VERSUS CONFORMITY

Much has been written and spoken about the negative or repressive influence of the organization on the individual for conformity; but little note is taken of either the individual's influence on the organization, or the potentiality for constructive influence by the organization in the life of the individual.

In order to function at all management must have people who are sufficiently disciplined to follow instructions. At the same time the individual must be free, independent, creative, and responsible, for the irresponsible conformist can be as much a threat to the integrity of the organization as the irresponsible nonconformist. In the same speech, Mr. Greenewalt went on to say:

> The problem, moreover, is not solely one of protection for the individual—it is in some respects one which involves protecting the organization itself from the stagnation created by those

who find that "conformity," like vice, can first be endured, and finally embraced. The unhappy fact is that conformity is for some an alluring state, a condition representing the course of least resistance. All too many, I am afraid, reach a point at which they seek refuge in protective coloring, with security replacing accomplishment as the primary goal.

When this happens, instead of the individual becoming the victim of pressures within the organization, it is the organization that falls prey to organization men. A comfortable sense of ease may bring solace to an individual, but to the organization itself it brings only a descent to mediocrity.

These basic concepts of man's relationship to his working environment set the stage for the psychiatrist's role in industry to promote the well-being of both the individual and the organization, for there is no inherent conflict. Mentally healthy people will create a healthy organization and conversely a healthy organization will present an atmosphere in which people can mature and find real satisfaction from living.

A well-run company can provide a decidedly potent curative atmosphere.

## THE PSYCHIATRIC ROLE

The psychiatrist's job as a therapist in industry is an important one but should be relatively minor. Certainly he will be faced with the host of emotional disturbances seen in society at large and will be called upon to advise and counsel with individuals and supervisors both for personal and family problems. The psychiatrist's competence in these areas is presumed.

The purpose of this paper is to discuss how psychiatric principles can be applied to groups of people working together in a business organization. Since prevention is the ultimate goal of all industrial medicine, it is equally valid for the occupational psychiatrist.

Since emotional illness has its roots in the early experience of the individual, true prevention is impossible in industry, but there are curative forces in the work place which can be utilized to promote health and at least prevent further illness.

The practical problems created by human behavior are the province of both management and psychiatry and both in their own way have knowledge to apply. The psychiatrist is not the only expert, for sound management personnel have a vast background of experience as well as profound intuitive understanding of human behavior.

The psychiatrist is apt to be more expert in understanding the unconscious underlying motivations and can assist management and supervision in controlling the environment in such a manner that man can find the greatest real satisfactions possible.

In order to fulfill this obligation the psychiatrist in industry must recognize and accept that he operates in the same framework of reality as does management.

Dr. Dershimer (4) reports frequent observations made to him by industrialists and industrial physicians that "the kind of psychiatry that supplies an endless variety of excuses to individuals seeking to escape from responsible behavior, can never be accepted with safety in competitive industry."

## PERSONALITY VERSUS ENVIRONMENT

People bring to their place of employment a well-established personality composed of deeply ingrained systems of values and behavior patterns, all based on highly individual training experiences throughout their years of living. They are motivated to seek and do those things which satisfy inner feelings and desires and avoid those things not satisfying.

Even the most weird and bizarre behavior makes some sort of sense to the individual engaging in it. It is difficult for the nonprofessional to realize, let alone accept, that painful, unpleasant, and self-destructive satisfactions, are motivated and sought after as avidly by some as others seek success, happiness, and survival. It seems unreasonable that self-destructive behavior should be able to exist in the presence of an all-pervading biological will to survive; but it can, and more often than is generally recognized, it is a prime, though unconscious motivating force, based on sick (unrealistic) values. It takes an overwhelming training experience to convert inborn biological survival mechanisms into self-destructive force. Few people commit suicide outright; a large number do it piecemeal throughout their lives until they die of some stress disease.

Once established, human personality is a persistent characteristic. Its rehabilitation requires a training experience almost as profound as the one which created the deviation in the first instance.

A child who learned from his experience that sickness or merely unpleasant symptoms were accepted by his parents as substitutes for correct performance evolves into a kind of adult who uses sickness as a shield against the usual stresses of his daily life.

If he were taught that work is an imposition upon mankind in general and himself in particular, he will feel bitter and resentful; and will do only the very minimum his management will tolerate. If he had learned that work can be a major source of gratification, he will enjoy the same job others find monotonous or intolerable.

If he learned that life should adapt to him rather than he to life, he will be one of those individuals who can stand very little in the way of frustration or denial.

Dr. Rudolph Dreikurs (5), a psychiatrist active in child guidance work, has made the profound observation that "those who cannot stand much always have to put up with so much more."

Generally speaking it is not the job or external circumstances which make for human satisfaction. Samuel Butler in *The Way of All Flesh* sums up man's relationship with his environment by writing:

> All our lives we are engaged in the process of accommodating ourselves to our surroundings; living is nothing else than this process of accommodation. When we fail a little we are stupid. When we flagrantly fail we are mad. A life will be successful or not, according as the power of accommodation is equal to or unequal to the strain of fusing and adjusting internal and external chances.

The adult human is more likely to be a victim of himself than of his present environment. More important than the problems he faces is the manner in which he handles them. The way he meets the stresses of life is in turn a function of the human values he holds. Perhaps the most devastating area of confusion is whether he expects to adapt to life, or life to him.

The following case history illustrates the operation of underlying motivations in dictating human behavior to achieve an end. In this instance, it was an inefficient and cumbersome technique but ultimately "successful."

> A young woman employee caused repeated difficulties in her work area including much unnecessary lost time for minor emotional illness. Her behavior made no sense to her supervisor nor did any effort on his part seem to improve her performance. Eventually her employment was terminated. On her exit interview with the plant physician, she was obviously gleeful and exclaimed how she was persuaded against her wishes to come to work with us by relatives who were delighted with their own employment. "Now," she said, "I'm going into nursing school which is what I always wanted to do."

This may or may not have been her real motive, or necessarily a valid one, but whatever her value standards, they drove her to fail in one job and seek another. Unfortunately, if she were to go at her nursing career the way she behaved on her previous job, she would find no happiness there either.

A more realistic course for this girl would have been to have had the courage to set her own course and resist the blandishments of her well-meaning family, rather than force her employer to make her decision for her.

Such maladaptive performance is not willful perversity or malingering but merely an accurate reflection of her own unrealistic but fixed-value standards.

Patterns of this sort become clearly evident within the first few years of employment. Management often fails to note and act on the evidence because it is unaware that all human behavior is motivated to ends which are mysterious not only to management but to the individual himself. By failing to act appropriately, management neglects a duty and an opportunity for service to both the individual and the organization. Instead, it nurtures a growing body of ineffective individuals who place an unfair burden on themselves and on the more productive members of the organization as well as increasing management's burden.

The word "neglect" is used because it is a form of negligence to ignore or even reward unacceptable performance. If the maladaptive behavior patterns are studied, it appears that the individual is almost deliberately even though unwittingly creating difficulties, thereby tacitly calling attention to his need for guidance.

Unfortunately such clues to real motivation are often overlooked or misinterpreted, sometimes through indifference, but more often through a kind of well-meant sympathy masquerading as humanitarianism. But neither course of action does much to rehabilitate the failing human, for ultimately people usually do what they find rewarding. Where men fail to act in their own best interests which usually are not very different from the interests of the employer, the rewards set by management should be re-evaluated.

Few of us are inclined to exert ourselves more than circumstances demand. Where there is no challenge, there is no response. All too often management is getting exactly the kind of performance it asks for, often unwittingly rewarding and encouraging the very unproductive behavior it bemoans.

Murray Sidman (6) has shown clearly in experimental behavior research that laboratory animals will do precisely what they find rewarding. He describes an experiment in which he was teaching a pigeon to peck at a lighted disk by giving it access to a food tray for a few seconds each time it pecked. He noticed the pigeon instead of pecking at the disk was moving its head in the opposite direction, away from the disk. He remarks that this was strange behavior but found a prosaic answer. "I noticed that the food delivery mechanism was slightly defective and was delivering food to the bird, not when it pecked the disk, but when it withdrew its head after pecking. This delay of a fraction of a second was enough to change the bird's behavior radically. But the bird was doing what it was actually being rewarded for. The fact that it was not what I wanted it to do was a function of the inadequacy of my own technique."

It is a bitter truth but the kind of performance we get from others, our children, wives, friends, employers, and employees, is often the truest reflection of our real requirements of them. All people have their share of both sound and not so sound unconscious motivation and value standards to lead them astray.

## TESTING GOALS AND VALUES

It is in this area that psychiatric objectivity should assist management. As value standards are realistic and promote well-being, so will the individual find satisfaction and genuine contentment with life; as they are unrealistic, the individual will be disgruntled, unhappy, and ill. The organization will reflect its people.

Management in consultation with the industrial psychiatrist can do much to improve the lot of many by investigating and testing the effects of realistic policies on human welfare and morale.

Much can be done on a broad scale to improve the lot of these individuals by establishing more realistic goals for them and letting them find for themselves the deeper satisfaction arising from more creative and productive living based on sound human value standards.

Human organizations, simply because they are human, are dynamic and constantly fluctuating; thus they require a continual sampling and re-evaluation of overall goals and values.

Social evolution, being a relatively slow process, needs highly refined techniques for earliest recognition of failure at a time when correction is relatively easy. As poor standards creep in, they are accepted more generally. As Disraeli said "Custom may not be as wise as law, but it's always more popular."

Naturally standards set by man will be less than perfect. But a willingness to experiment and learn from failure is the mark of a truly creative, healthy individual. The best judgment based on the facts available at any given moment, the courage to act responsibly, admitting error when results show defective judgment, and a willingness to try again, is the best man can expect of himself.

Occupational psychiatry is a new field which has still to prove itself. The psychiatrist working in industry has an unparalleled opportunity to learn about real human values, motivating forces, and man's capabilities; and an opportunity to help the organization and its people. He is not the only expert, for sound management people are also skilled. Thus there exists a situation of mutual reinforcement in which each can guide the other to the ultimate benefit of mankind and the human institutions he creates.

## REFERENCES

1. *This Is Du Pont. The story of management.* Wilmington, Delaware: E. I. Du Pont de Nemours and Company, 1961.

2. Dershimer, F. W. Constructive forces on the job. *Mental Hygiene*, 1948, **32**, 373–381.

3. Greenewalt, Crawford H. The individual in the organization. Address at Princeton University, March 10, 1961.

4. Dershimer, F. W. Psychiatry in industry. *American Journal of Psychiatry*, 1953, **109**, 524–526.

5. Dreikurs, Rudolph. *The challenge of parenthood.* New York: Duell, Sloan and Pierce, 1958.

6. Sidman, Murray. A Symposium Presented by the Child Study, Treatment and Research Center of the Woods School, Langhorne, Pennsylvania, May 17, 1961.

# 14. PSYCHIATRIC PRINCIPLES APPLICABLE TO INDUSTRY

### William C. Menninger, M.D.

Psychiatry makes no assumption that it has all the answers to human behavior, or even that it knows how to communicate its point of view. However, the psychiatrist's study of personality, how it works, and how it develops, is the basis of his ability to help people. This knowledge should be equally useful to those in other fields who are working with people and are responsible for them, such as in industry.

What are some of the basic principles and concepts by which psychiatrists operate to help people who are unhappy and distressed?

## 1. THE ACCEPTANCE OF THE VALIDITY OF PSYCHOLOGICAL DATA

There's a kind of a lip service to this principle in all fields, so much so that most people regard themselves as amateur psychologists. Their "blind spot" lies in failing to recognize that there are a lot of *scientific* data in this area.

Particularly is this true of medicine. The chief emphasis in the training of the physician is, and always has been, on the body. The patient is too often looked at as a kind of disease, instead of from the psychiatric point of view as an individual, as a struggling organism with certain equipment

When The Menninger Foundation presented seminars for industrial executives and physicians earlier this year, Dr. William C. Menninger, general secretary of the Foundation, was asked to present the orientation lecture at each. This article was adapted from the remarks he made on those occasions.

in a changing environment in which he uses whatever equipment he has to struggle with whatever the forces are in that environment. Few medical schools teach enough psychology, sociology, or anthropology to help the student grasp this idea of psychological and social factors in illness. There's a tendency for the physician, if there isn't something *physically* wrong with a patient, to say, "There's nothing wrong. Just go play golf and forget it." Platitudes! Often there is no recognition that even if a headache is entirely psychological in origin, it's still very much a headache.

This lip service also applies often to industrial leaders; many of them at very high levels have blind spots for psychological facts of life. An enormous amount is spent on research in developing businesses in terms of chemistry, physics, and many other aspects. But, with very few exceptions, industries have never set up any kind of research programs into the human relations, into the personalities of people and how they work in their organizations.

Why shouldn't they? For example, industry has a very expensive interest in safety. Millions are spent to reduce accidents. Yet most accidents aren't due to machine failure and the like. They're due to people—people who have had quarrels at breakfast, sleepless nights, or other kinds of difficulties that manifest personality problems in the form of accidents. The amount spent on studying the personalities of people who are likely to have accidents is an extremely small portion of the total investment in safety.

The role of psychiatry in business and industry has been extremely limited because psychiatry to date hasn't had much to offer. (There are only four full-time psychiatrists and one half-time psychiatrist in all industry. Perhaps 200 more have a nominal relationship with business, most of them treating employees who become disturbed and are referred by the company.) But there are so many specific examples of emotional problems—from the extremes of behavior such as alcoholism to the ways we live in our everyday lives, all of which can be understood—that it is evident that the validity of psychological data isn't yet very well accepted.

## 2.  A HOLISTIC CONCEPT OF PERSONALITY

Personality, the word, is now so misused that it can be the attribute of a perfume, or refer to an animal or to a picture. From the point of view of psychiatry, the individual is thought of in terms of muscles and bones, of enlarged tonsils and bow-legs, of many loves and hates, of eccentricities and aspirations, of his heart and lungs, of the way he walks and talks—all as a unity. Perhaps most simply put, personality is all that a man is, all that he has been, and all that he hopes to be. Those three things combined, including his physical parts, comprise his personality. It is, therefore, a very concrete concept of this *unity* of the individual instead of the group of parts.

There is a high degree of variation in personalities because of the many factors which influence their development. Certainly there isn't any such thing as a "normal personality." If we do want to use the term, we can conceive of only a range of normality; if we think of it as applied to an individualist, it fits none of us. Perhaps if we were normal, we would be very drab. Unless we have some unusual qualities, some excesses, some very conspicuous differences, we are only mediocre.

## 3.  THE ANATOMY OF THE PERSONALITY

Theoretically, there are two major areas of personality. The first is the *conscious*, the part of all of us that has to do with cognitive thinking; it is a storehouse of some of our knowledge, the powerhouse that makes our voluntary muscles act, it includes a portion of our memory and all that we are aware of about ourselves.

The second, much more forceful, area is the *unconscious*. We cannot reach it by voluntary effort, but it is the powerhouse of our instinctive drives, of our psychological energy system, of our deep-seated emotions that arise spontaneously. In the literal sense, the unconscious is illogical, it is timeless, it stays the same from birth to death. It is also the storehouse of many feelings, experiences, even memories, which become forgotten. No one remembers his first two or three or four years in life, but they are tremendously significant in the development of the personality. These early feelings and experiences have been "repressed" from conscious life. But they still remain, even though we are unaware of them, and they wield great power.

The theory of there being these two major portions of the personality permits psychiatrists to make sense of what they hear and see in people. Most of us really can't adequately explain much of why we do certain things or the origins of many of our interests, hates, prejudices, and loves. We can consciously "rationalize" how we feel about them, but to learn the real reasons why they are there is a difficult job, even for those who specialize in trying to understand people.

## 4. THE PHYSIOLOGY OF THE PERSONALITY

Psychiatrists assume the energy system which drives men has two major instinctive drives. One is the constructive, creative, or love drive. The other is the hostile, destructive, aggressive drive. These also are entirely theoretical constructs, but how they are modified by early childhood experience and how they then manifest themselves through the unconscious in what we do as adults give a basis for understanding behavior. Their source is the unconscious, and they are active throughout life.

Oversimplified, the psychiatrist's assumption is that the major difficulties of all of us arise because these two drives are not fused in such a way as to help us get along with other people. For some reason we don't appropriately fuse these two drives, and perhaps don't even recognize sometimes that we should. But hate is only neutralized by love. The constructve, creative person is he who can use his aggressive drive for the force behind the initiative. The tempering by the love drive makes his initiative something constructive, rather than being destructive by only being directly expressed as aggression.

## 5.  THE HOMEOSTATIC QUALITY, OR EQUILIBRIUM-MAINTAINING ASPECT, OF THE PERSONALITY

The development of any symptom represents an attempt by the individual to maintain a kind of an equilibrium. In a sense, it's an attempt at self-cure. With any physical illness, we mobilize all kinds of defenses: temperature, white blood cells, etc. A psychological symptom is an attempt to heal, as fever is an attempt to heal. The mobilization of anxiety is the attempt of the individual to meet and overcome some kind of a threat, whether it is bacteria or his mother-in-law. Symptoms of behavior are ways of coping with an external situation, or sometimes an internal situation, to meet conscious and *unconscious* personality needs. Very often it is a fantasied external situation, an unreal one. But if we accept psychological data as valid, whether the individual has an organic or emotional stomach ache, it is just as real to him. As we get some understanding of the personality's anatomy and physiology, we understand the symptoms.

## 6.  THE SIGNIFICANCE OF PERSONALITY DEVELOPMENT

Great weight must be given to the influence of early life experiences, some well beyond our memories, that shape the personality. Psychiatrists are certain, for instance, that we learned as little children long before the time of our conscious adult memory can now recall. How one relates himself to people is learned, pretty largely, before the time our conscious memory can recall. That behavior pattern depends on how he related to his parents, siblings, and early associates. Most of us learned a technique and a way of dealing with frustrations long before we can remember. In the same way, we devised ways of learning how to accept reality and social adaptation. Most important in how we can relate ourselves to people is how those first people treated us, whether they rejected us or neglected us, whether we were deprived or loved, how much we were loved, how we were loved.

For instance, the experience a baby has in its nursing procedures is extremely important in what happens to his personality. This process is the main focus of life over a period of a year or so, one that occurs many times a day. It can be fraught with great difficulty, when complicated by inadequate breast milk, for example. Psychiatrists believe it is during this time that a child sets a pattern of reaction to receiving and to accepting, a reaction pattern that continues perhaps all through his life. Such patterns can be changed, but they're usually fairly permanent personality aspects for every one of us.

Psychiatry recognizes that such experiences in early life can leave us vulnerable, as adults, to certain kinds of stresses. Two men go through the same kind of experience, and one can take it and one can't. Perhaps it's because the first fellow is working with a particular kind of a superior and he never got along with his father. He wouldn't admit it, or maybe if he did admit it he wouldn't admit that it had injured his ability to get along with father figures. The second man didn't have any trouble and goes through well. But this early "Achilles heel" experience for the first man with his father made it difficult or impossible for him to relate to such people.

We now know that, even if neither man as an infant or child had any real difficulties of major proportions that made him vulnerable in a particular area, both will begin to bend if subjected to stress long enough and severe enough. This wasn't known for a long time. It was assumed that certain well-integrated people ought to be able to take anything indefinitely. But again and again it has been shown that individuals who had had no indication of pathology whatever in their family lives, in their hereditary backgrounds, or in themselves could be put under stress long enough to begin to bend. During war many persons break without regard to I.Q., to heredity, to social background—just acute stress.

# 7. THE IMPORTANCE
## OF THE ENVIRONMENT
## IN HEALTH AND DISEASE

Because any personality has the potential of complete emotional breakdown, psychiatry places great significance on the role of environment—not only the childhood environment, but also the psychological and social noxious influences in adult life. It isn't just bacteria and bullets that bowl people over. It's very often bad relationships with other people. Psychiatrists take into account the total environment in which a man lives—all the people he's associated with and, in terms of the definition of a personality, also the kind of relationships that existed prior to the present. Only as those are known can the reactions to them be really understood.

## 8. THE INFLUENCE OF ONE PERSON ON ANOTHER IN TERMS OF HIS RELATIONSHIP TO THAT PERSON

In medicine, this is known as interpersonal relations between the physician and the patient. It is axiomatic with a psychiatrist working with a troubled person that he will have feelings about that patient, the patient is going to have feelings about the doctor, and that those exchanges of emotions influence each person enormously. They influence the treatment as well as the therapist's hope that he's going to influence the patient. Two people cannot get together in a relationship in which this exchange of emotions is not present. It is essential, therefore, to recognize that what is going on can't be understood just by hearing what's said, but only by learning what the two people feel about each other.

It is most important for any person in a helping role to see his own blind spots, to take into account, if he can (and this is a little like lifting one's self with his bootstraps), the significance of his own prejudices and defenses. If I am ignorant about myself and if I then bump into a patient who has problems in the same area as mine, obviously I'm not going to help him.

As a result of our ignorance of ourselves, we use various kinds of techniques to deal with people. Some are unpleasant techniques, like the "brush off," or jumping to conclusions, or having a know-it-all attitude. Sometimes we are subject to a "bad day," perhaps because of the person sitting near us, or maybe because of other factors in our lives: "I just don't want to have anything to do with you; I'm unusually annoyable today." Without any attempt on our part to understand our annoyance, it will become vindictive and hostile. We must try to find out what's going on within ourselves and to know as much as possible about ourselves, in order to be as objective as possible to other persons.

Psychiatry has had a number of "miracle" drugs recently. They aren't really miracles at all, though they're going to be of some help. The most important therapeutic devices psychiatrists have are their own personalities, what they know about them, and what they know about how to use them in relation to other people. As they know themselves and as they have a basis for understanding the other person's problem, then they are in a position to help him.

These eight points are basic principles in the practice of psychiatry. They headline some of the knowledge essential in understanding people. Hopefully, they apply to the understanding of all people and, hence, are potentially important to those in other fields, such as industry.

# 15. DEVELOPING A COMPANY PSYCHIATRIC PROGRAM

Robert L. Meineker, M.D.

Despite a considerable number of reports (1–5), both professional and popular, testifying to the benefits of occupational psychiatry, attempts to introduce and develop a company psychiatric program are usually met with resistance so severe that there are still relatively few in existence, and many are only embryonic. This paper attempts to explain some of the etiology of this situation by use of psychodynamic observations made during almost two years of full-time experience acquired developing such a program. It discusses various methods of applying psychiatry to industry, and offers practical suggestions on how psychiatry might simultaneously improve health and business profits through more constructive regulation of the working environment.

## SOURCES OF RESISTANCE

In the field of occupational health, just as in the community, general hospital, or medical profession, there is superficial recognition of the usefulness of psychiatry; but this is frequently undermined and negated by a great lack of knowledge about psychiatry, as well as by fears, emotional blind spots, and prejudices on the part of the average doctor, manager, or worker. Doctors in the community and within the company

Dr. Meineker is Psychiatrist, America Fore Loyalty Group, 80 Maiden Lane, New York, New York.
Submitted for publication February 12, 1962.

medical department may sabotage psychiatry unknowingly just as they do in their private practices, medical schools, or hospitals. Employees avoid psychiatry because of fear, the "stigma" attached, and lack of cultural conditioning. As medicine becomes more intimately involved with business, management often develops feelings of rivalry set off by the conviction that the medical department is struggling for power after a fashion common to rival factions in management. With the best intentions, management may use the medical department as a scapegoat or may increase confusion by lack of communication with the department. There is confusion about what is good for people, due not only to ignorance and social tradition, but to personal idiosyncrasies and neuroses of some men in key positions. Sometimes the fact that industry exists for man, not simply for profit, is lost sight of. These situations suggest the kind of obstacles that demand, yet obstruct the development of occupational psychiatry.

## DEALING WITH RESISTANCE

It is obvious that communication and education are the cornerstones on which the psychiatrist might base his treatment of these problems. However, in the beginning, the psychiatrist usually has few or no established channels of communication within the company. Indeed, communication is nearly impossible because of the huge disparity in point of view between management and psychiatry. Just as certain socioeconomic segments of the population cannot use psychotherapy because of lack of conditioning and understanding, so business is not quite ready for psychiatry. Psychiatry is a complicated field about which there is much misunderstanding because it deals with the vast area of people's feelings, thinking, and interpersonal relations. These matters are often intangible and complicated by keen sensitivity and defense mechanisims. Traditionally, a psychiatrist is most helpful when a patient comes to him with a problem. He can work best from the passive, consultative position. Resistance problems during treatment can be managed most effectively in a patient who has been willing to undergo treatment and who acknowledges the psychiatrist as helpful.

Industrial management does not seek psychiatry as a remedy for problems because it does not have a suitable frame of reference. The occupational psychiatrist, in an atmosphere characterized more by fear and suspicion than by respect, must play an unaccustomed, assertive role to establish in management an appreciation of his value and methods of operation. This inevitably entails frequent demonstration of problems. The resulting exposure aggravates management and thereby produces more resistance despite the corrective motives underlying the activity. All of this is at once a prelude and a pattern for the practice of occupational psychiatry. Consequently, while communication and education will be ultimate activities of the occupational psychiatrist, he will have to utilize the clinical tactics of the psychotherapist to overcome resistance before he can work on his objectives openly.

In the introduction of a psychiatric program into a company, the psychiatrist should take into consideration the history of the development of the company, its management policies, and the special kinds of psychological conflict generated by the specificity of the organization's activity. Besides revealing what the company needs, this knowledge should guide him in choosing an approach that will be more successful in utilizing existing trends and avoiding head-on collisions with prejudice and resistance.

## COMPANY DYNAMICS

Historically, it appears that there are two fundamental situations under which psychiatry has been introduced into a company. These situations are dictated to a large extent by the structure and activity of the company. They greatly influence the type and emphasis of the psychiatric program to evolve.

The first situation occurs in companies usually large, diversified, and widely dispersed, and often involved in the development of new technical processes requiring research and ingenuity. Management has been forced by practical considerations of size, production efficiency, union pressure, compensation insurance, and need for inventiveness and originality in developing its product to be interested in personnel matters and the efficiency of its human work force. These companies tend to view workers as groups or forces rather than as individuals. Their expectation from medicine is to get the most efficient work output from the individual. The research orientation has favored the development of strong personnel and industrial-relations departments which overshadow the medical, are oriented by statistics more than emotional conviction, and are devoted to education and research rather than medicine or paternalism as means of realizing their goals. In this situation management welcomes the public-health, statistical, group-approach side of psychiatry and psychology, but uses these tools for its own purposes rather than those of the individual. Problems are handled more by educational programs and alteration of the rules used to regulate the group than by treatment of the individual.

The other situation occurs in companies that are somewhat smaller, older, less dispersed, and engaged in work demanding less originality. Management is apt to be oriented around one or two men whose decisions are often the final word. There are many traditions or customs in each department, and change is viewed with apprehension. The individual supervisors have known their workers more personally. There is more tendency toward indulgence of inefficiency so that change will not have to be instituted. Security is strongly accentuated. While there is high toleration of individual idiosyncrasy, there is strong reaction against group change. There is distrust of training, education, statistics, new methods, machines. Administration is handled more through personal contact and friendship than general policy or directive. Directives come more often after the fact. In this situation, personnel and industrial-relations departments and education facilities are relatively weak, underdeveloped, reactionary, and regarded with suspicion. The medical department usually will have been set up by management for medical care of the individual employee. Management looks to the doctor as its personal physician, rather than as physician to the company. Consequently, the level of individual medical care and facilities will be high and there will be relatively little emphasis on the individual's relation to the group. The objective will be to make the individual comfortable and safe, rather than to get the greatest efficiency out of him. This is also true of psychiatric programs stimulated by unions, which are more interested in patient care than in the general running of the company. In these situations, psychiatry is more apt to be introduced by the medical department (as part of better medical care for the individual) than by management. It will, therefore, be clinically oriented and regarded with suspicion and resistance by management.

## PROMOTING OCCUPATIONAL PSYCHIATRY

The two situations just described represent extremes. Most companies and their occupational psychiatry programs fall between the points of view represented. However, two objectives of mental health activities in industry have emerged. One is to promote the health and happiness of people at work, sponsored by the doctors, social scientists, etc., and the other is to get the most efficient operation from the employee, sponsored by the management-initiated programs. Actually, these two goals are quite congruent because it is only when a person is operating most efficiently that he is most happy and feels most worthwhile. However, the difference in approach can cause a good deal of argument and misunderstanding. It is up to the psychiatrist to effect congruity.

In companies falling in the first category described above, the development of a statistical approach to measure work output and efficiency, plus training programs and education, may often be undertaken before individual clinical activities. Psychiatry will probably be sold to management more easily in terms of facts and figures with emphasis on ways to increase group efficiency and save money. Development of good clinical service for the individual will trail, but must be pushed;

such development may well be the most difficult and acute problem in this type of company.

In companies in the second category, development of a good clinical program will probably have to pave the way for environmental and group approaches. Programs will be more likely to be sold through an individual, friendly approach leading to emotional conviction rather than through facts and figures.

For most companies an intermediary approach is advisable. Since there is growing appreciation of direct clinical psychiatric service to the individual, providing examination, diagnosis, and treatment of symptoms and untoward behavior, the clinical approach is probably the one through which the operation and benefits of psychiatry can be best illustrated. In addition, the individual clinical approach is closer to the pursuit of medicine as opposed to the pursuit of management and is needed in all occupational situations to prevent distortion of good mental-hygiene practices.

## APPROACHES
## TO OCCUPATIONAL PSYCHIATRIC PRACTICE

The following two examples illustrate the clinical psychiatric approach. Such cases influence the individual, management, and the community and, therefore, are of basic importance in initiating occupational psychiatry.

> A middle-aged woman, a clerical worker, was absent four or five days a month and was reporting to the medical department almost daily for treatment. In addition, she was consulting five doctors in the community, and was overmedicated. She was making life extremely difficult for her family and her employer, not to mention herself. In about five sessions of psychotherapy, plus consultation with some of her doctors and nurses, it was possible to bring about a marked change in her behavior so that her feelings of illness decreased. She was able to handle her problem at home more efficiently, and, for the next four months, she did not report to the medical department nor was she absent.

> A man only 45 years of age had suffered a coronary. Despite nine months of treatment, which resulted in a return to normal

of his laboratory test results, he was still unable to work. The
psychiatrist discovered he was suffering from a depressive reaction. By working with him and his wife, it was possible to get
him into treatment with a competent psychiatrist. After three
months of treatment, the patient was back on the job, apparently
working somewhat better than he had for a long time.

Even though results are not always so happy, a good deal
of benefit does derive from this sort of service. Not only are
individuals helped to feel better and therefore to work more
efficiently, but also there is an improvement in their morale
so that they want to work and are not participating in an
unconscious sit-down strike. The improvement is contagious,
too, reassuring other disturbed members of the work group,
offering them help by example as well as by relieving them
from dealing with a disturbed person.

As beneficial as clinical service is, it is not the only important
contribution psychiatry can make to industry. Since the industrial psychiatrist's principle aim, in cooperation with other
members of the industrial medical team, is to keep employees
operating at maximum efficiency rather than to cure their
illnesses, his attention must be shifted from individual to group
considerations. Consequently, new approaches to diagnosis
and management which are essentially group-oriented are
required.

Uncomfortable emotional symptoms or unprofitable
behavior result from a combination of interacting factors
which cannot be treated exclusively and directly with the
individual alone, the way an inflamed appendix can. Emotional problems arise when deeply imprinted habits and rigidly
structured drives within the individual come into contact with
environmental stresses. Often these habits and drives are not
subject to the conscious control or awareness of the individual.
As a result he cannot alleviate the conflict by direct action.
It is impossible to reconstruct personality quickly. Consequently, regulation of environmental influence on the
individual is of paramount importance in securing and
improving mental health. Through management, industry

provides a unique situation in which environmental factors can be manipulated more easily than in the community in general.

From this orientation it is obvious that good management is one of the essentials of occupational mental health. Psychiatry alone could not make a strong organization, but the psychiatrist can be helpful as a consultant to management, particularly in those areas where people must interact. He has professionally collected and organized experience with human behavior and interaction into forms of observation, diagnosis, and prescription which can lend themselves readily to utilization by management.

## NEEDS OF MANAGEMENT FOR PSYCHIATRY

Some of the more common interpersonal problems which may beset management will no doubt be all too familiar, since they have existed from the time business organizations began; these problems are as follows.

1. Valuable employees quit, are ill, or are not performing well because of lack of recognition, promotion, or reward.
2. Lack of communication between various groups of management and between management and the general working group, results in the crippling of individual security and wasted effort.
3. Policies for handling incapacitated or incompetent people are ill-defined and inconclusive, increasing their incompetence and demoralizing others. In connection with this, it is noteworthy that, in most cases, it is not kind to spare people frank evaluation.
4. There is poor evaluation and recording of the employees' efficiency.
5. Overconcentration on the part of top management on technical details allows insufficient time to develop major policy and procedure, not to mention training and the esprit of the company.
6. The business is unable to attract brilliant young men of the highest caliber.

7.  Incomplete recognition of work capacity often results in conscientious employees being pushed to the breaking point or, in the reverse situation, in employees who feel that they do not have enough to do because no one watches them.
8.  There is insufficient recognition of the importance and impact of education and training.

These problems are indigenous to all business because they arise primarily from personality conflict. They are problems which cost much in efficiency and on which psychiatry might offer considerable elucidation. While they can never be eliminated entirely, they can be reduced. Absentee, accident, sickness, and turnover rates are helpful indicators of the severity of these problems.

## ROLE OF THE
## OCCUPATIONAL PSYCHIATRIST

Some of the ways that psychiatry might be utilized to help management in its efforts to deal with these problems are as follows.

1.  It can provide psychiatric consultation to troubled employees, augmented, as appropriate, by communication and clarification of their problems to management, their physicians, families, and other agencies for business, personal, medical, and family problems.
2.  It can provide psychiatric consultation to management on matters relating to production efficiency of people at all levels in the company. Here the scope is broad and infinitely varied. Activities would include participation in selection, placement, transfer, promotion, separation, and retirement of employees, appraising those factors in the individual's personality which bear on his fitness or unfitness for work, clarifying his strengths and liabilities. The general effort should be to clarify both the manifest and latent content of problem situations so that the true motivations and relationships are apparent. Management would carry on from this point in making decisions.

3.  It can provide psychiatric consultation to physicians in the medical department in situations where diagnosis is in question or treatment is hindered by untoward emotional attitudes.
4.  It can promote and participate in the design and development of education programs at all levels of the company.
5.  It can discover and help in the management of mental health problems in the company through observation of workers and working conditions, and following statistics dealing with absenteeism, turnover rates, accident rates, and efficiency rating.
6.  It can maintain relations with other industries, public health departments, departments of labor, and management, educational, and research organizations on matters pertaining to occupational psychiatry.

## Relation to Management

Generally, it is my opinion that the establishment of clinical psychiatric service in the medical department, aimed at helping the individual with problems which reduce his work efficiency, is the best way to initiate a company psychiatric program and should be its nucleus. Without adequate clinical psychiatric service and control, group methods and statistics may be precipitously taken over by management for its own purposes, leading to some misuse and the development of new mental-health hazards.

At the same time I believe that better results for the group come from good environmental management than from direct application of clinical psychiatry, and that, in the last analysis, it is management than must handle problems. Good management is the thing that makes healthy industry. Psychiatry can best offer its help in the occupational situation through education and consultation requested by management for problems involving people. It should be emphasized that psychiatry does not seek to set policy itself or operate by making rules. Rather, it aims at resolving conflict by increasing communication and clear understanding of all aspects of a problem. It fosters those things that will increase self-realization. It attempts to promote a constant interplay between originality and conformity to provide progress without sacrificing stability. It tries to broaden the business mind so that there may be understanding of the relationship between business, society, and the individual. Psychiatry is a support, a friend, a counselor, not an unfriendly power or threat. The primary interest is making people happier and more productive through improving their understanding of themselves and their relations to others.

## SUMMARY

Despite strong testimony in favor of occupational psychiatry, its growth is meeting much resistance. Causes for this are discussed in terms of general social problems that delay utilization of psychiatry. Group dynamics and attitudes toward psychiatry in very large companies involved in research are contrasted with those in companies whose activities are more routine. Two objectives with respective methods of occupational psychiatry emerge: One is to get the most efficient operation from the employee group by environmental psychiatric approaches, and the other is to promote the health and happiness of the individual by clinical psychiatric service. While establishment of sound individual clinical psychiatric service in the medical department is probably the best way to initiate a company psychiatric program, it is good management that makes healthy industry. It remains for clinical psychiatry to ease resistance and pave the way for the environmental approach. Industrial problems wherein psychiatry might simultaneously improve health and business profit through more constructive regulation of the working environment are enumerated.

## REFERENCES

1. Belinson, L. Mental health in industry. *Journal of Occupational Medicine*, 1961, **3**, 336.

2.  Proctor, R. C. Psychiatry in an industrial setting. *Archives of Environmental Health*, 1961, **3**, 63.

3.  Himler, L. E. Place of psychiatry in industry. *Journal of the Michigan Medical Society*, 1950, **49**, 75.

4.  Industry is the psychiatrist's new patient. *Business Week*, February 18, 1956.

5.  Ellison, J. Psychiatrist on the assembly line. *Saturday Evening Post*, February 11, 1961.

# 16. PSYCHIATRIC TREATMENT— BRIEF PSYCHOTHERAPY PROCEDURES FOR THE INDUSTRIAL PHYSICIAN

Leonard E. Himler, M.D.

## THE TRANSITION FROM STANDARD MEDICAL PROCEDURES TO INDIVIDUALIZED PSYCHOTHERAPY

It is admitted that psychotherapy in industry—as in private practice—is still more of an art requiring a constant intuitive response to the patient than it is an exact science. The tactics must be flexible and subject to change at any point in the therapy.

Ordinarily a patient expects the physician to tell him what to do, and in return for doing as he is told he expects the physician to cure him. In psychotherapy the patient must be taught to play a more responsible role, and the physician must be prepared to prescribe himself as therapy. In this role he functions variously as a guide, confidant, counselor, teacher, friend, and protector.

Industrial physicians sometimes drift into psychotherapeutic relationships without having formed any comprehensive plan which is based soundly on goals and objectives applicable to their individual setting. Work under pressure and the need to accomplish as much as possible in the limited time available may make careful application of even limited psychotherapy seem impossible. As a result, the physician may feel it imperative to fall back on quick intuitive impressions in an attempt to give the patient prompt relief from at least his most pressing difficulties. There are few industrial physicians who would

The author's address is Mercy Hospital, 4038 Jackson Road, Ann Arbor, Michigan.

not derive benefit from better application of the techniques of brief psychotherapy to their daily work.

Most employees coming to the Medical Department will think of themselves as suffering from some physical handicap, illness, or injury. At first they may tend to ascribe any discernible emotional disturbances to difficult external situations or to the behavior of others. Many will be unaware of the difficulties within themselves which have contributed to the problem.

It follows that the physician must first meet the employee on his own ground, tentatively accepting the patient's own view of the problem. When an adequate survey of the physical factors has revealed no cause for the patient's complaints, it becomes necessary as a first step to explain how feelings and emotions may give rise to disturbances of bodily function.

When the employee blames external environmental conditions, it is necessary to explore with him both how this external problem has arisen and what possibilities there are of finding a satisfactory solution for it. Here the physician observes how realistically the patient is able to discuss his problem, whether he is able to face issues squarely or projects the blame elsewhere, and how far he may be torn between alternatives that are quite incompatible with each other.

Some patients provide a remarkably clear picture of the psychogenesis of their difficulties. Others, in spite of a quite rational account of the external events, seem incapable nevertheless of grasping the emotional importance of the occurrences and situations they describe. Here the physician must listen with ears sensitized to any hints of the patient's affective attitudes toward the events that he is relating.

A quick survey of the patient's life and work history will furnish the physician some knowledge concerning the normal satisfactions open to him, along with some of the past and present obstacles. Opportunity may present itself to relate some of the problems and symptoms occurring on the job to similar experiences occurring in the home or in the patient's adjustment elsewhere. By watching for hints of emotional reactions under various circumstances, it will be possible to piece together a fairly good impression of what constitutes the individual's most disturbing problem. The physician should try to sense the dominant trend and trace the disturbed affect back to its earlier sources.

The plan of therapy involves moving from a tentative acceptance of the patient's own view of his problem to a gradually widening exploration of related emotional experiences. The key revelations which tend to work themselves to the surface in the discussion form the basis of the unique shared relationship which constitutes the core of the therapy. Improved insight and self-understanding, with release from fear and other hampering emotions, lead to resetting of goals more in harmony with the patient's real situation.

## AN APPROACH TO THE TREATMENT OF PSYCHONEUROTIC REACTIONS IN INDUSTRY

As in private practice, half of the work of industrial physicians is concerned with emotionally upset individuals and those with some degree of neurosis. Neurosis occurs as a failure of the ego to perform its daily functions of securing adequate gratification of basic needs for security, social relationships, and love under the existing external conditions. Neurotic tendencies lie latent in every person. When the individual is exposed to difficulties beyond his powers of adaptation, these latent tendencies may result in an acute neurotic state.

When an acute neurotic disturbance develops under the pressure of unusually difficult external conditions, the ego's functional capacity is only temporarily impaired. In such cases the therapeutic task consists in first reducing the intensity of acute anxiety or other incapacitating emotions. As the patient's confidence in himself is restored, he will be able to face the situation and make a more effective adjustment to it. If such acute reactions are not properly treated they are likely to become chronic.

The industrial physician frequently sees individuals who have developed hostile attitudes and impulses under the impact of unsolved problems and a mounting sense of frustration. If the central problem can be solved or ameliorated, frustration will subside and the resultant hostile impulses should disappear. It is often possible to eliminate hostile impulses by digging behind and uncovering the problems which gave rise to them without focusing attention directly upon the hostility itself.

More than palliative treatment is not possible for workers who exhibit chronic neurotic reactions or who have warped or weak ego structure, whether constitutional or acquired. In such cases, supportive therapy can best meet the patient's need for assistance by actual guidance of his daily routine of activities. "Inferiority feelings are not traced back to their origin but are combated with reassurance; guilt feelings are not explained but are assuaged by permissive attitudes; anxiety is relieved by the physician assuming a protective role. Permanent change in personality structure is not expected. The effectiveness of such purely supportive treatment is often limited, and repeated contacts over a long period may be required" (1).

Disturbed experiences in interpersonal relationships as a cause of emotional disorder, acute or chronic, make up a large part of the daily practice of industrial medicine. A majority of such neurotic conditions may be viewed as failures of adjustment by individuals to social living.

The conflict between help-seeking dependence and self-assertive rivalry finds expression in such disorders as peptic ulcer and hypertension. Patients in the former group defend themselves against their immoderate need to be loved by an exaggerated display of efficiency and accomplishment; and the latter are caught between their hostile competitive tendencies and their passive dependent wishes.

The aggressive protest of an alcoholic against his dependent cravings may take such disturbing forms that he may be rejected as beyond the physician's sphere of responsibilities. "If the physician overcomes this irritation and feeling of hopelessness, and looks for the rationale behind the disturbing behavior, he will discover that this aggressive protest is only an excessive—(but at the same time, a futile)—manifestation of the very incentive that must be utilized in helping him learn to play a more independent role. At first the alcoholic is so ashamed of his intense dependent cravings that he must use all his aggressive energy in attempts to deny them. If some of these dependent needs can be satisfied in the transference relationship that is established, the intensity of the dependent cravings may be diminished, and shame will be replaced by insight into the universality of the need for dependent gratification" (1).

Industrial physicians are aware that emotionally disturbed persons, whether recognized as such or not, exert a tremendous influence on others, not only in the home as fathers and mothers, but also as fellow-workers, foremen, executives, and union leaders.

Psychoanalytic principles and techniques can be applied to the treatment of persons suffering from the various types and degrees of emotional disturbance encountered in industrial medical practice. The plan of treatment must be based on a dynamic-diagnostic appraisal of the employee's personality and the actual problems he has to solve in his life situation, both at home and at work.

## PRINCIPLES AND TECHNIQUES
## OF BRIEF PSYCHOTHERAPY

"Brief psychotherapy is treatment consisting of one, two, or three interviews. Its efficacy depends upon (1) the physician's ability to see at once the precipitating difficulty in relation to the patient's total personality; (2) the capacity of the patient's ego for insight and his ability to use this insight to make changes in his life; and (3) the ready confidence of the patient in the physician whose role fitted the particular case" (1).

Psychoanalysts have found that therapeutic results can be achieved without the patient's recalling all important details of his past history. It should be remembered that the neurotic employee is suffering not so much from his memories as from his incapacity to deal with his actual problems of the moment. The past memories have merely prepared the way for the present difficulties.

Simple "confession" by the patient of matters about which he previously had been unable to speak to anyone is found in practically every therapy. Through his confidence in the physician's objective, noncondemning attitude, the patient becomes able to confess disconcerting personal matters, and often gains immediate symptomatic relief. The therapeutic effect of confession does not depend on giving the patient insight into his deeper motives. The emotional reassurance and satisfaction which the patient derives from this relationship with the physician may lead to a disappearance of his symptoms.

In such therapy the physician uses his opportunity to help the patient see intellectually and at the same time *feel* the irrationality of his emotional reactions and thus make a new settlement of the old problem. Because the physician's attitude is different from that of the authoritative person or persons of the past, he gives the patient an opportunity to face again and again, under more favorable circumstances, those emotional situations which were formerly unbearable, and to deal with them in a manner different from the previous response.

Freud defined "transference" as the reaction to the therapist as though he were not himself but some person in the patient's past, i.e., some person who has at some previous time played an important role in the patient's life. In a wider sense, the term refers to irrational repetition of stereotyped reaction patterns which have not been adjusted to conform to the present situation. In the so-called "transference relationship" the physician is representative of a figure of importance from out of the patient's past.

It is obviously impractical in the industrial setting to employ free association to bring about a repetition of the whole childhood situation with all its conflicts. The physician must rather concentrate interest on that phase of the transference situation around which the central conflict gathers. The physician uses the positive attitudes of the employee toward him to establish rapport and keep the curative process in motion.

An employee whose disturbance is due to ambivalence toward his father may displace onto the physician only the role of the good father, while his fear and hostility may be displaced onto his supervisor. It is not necessary for such a person to go through the experience of repeating these negative feelings, this time against his physician, in order to overcome them. It is necessary, however, that he be aided and advised regarding his animosity and that he see the relationship to his earlier conflict. In the transference situation, the patient is first given an opportunity to see the same emotional conflict he had toward his father, and then to find a new, less neurotic solution for this conflict.

It is a fundamental part of all psychotherapy to teach the patient that his neurotic reactions are in accord with old, outmoded patterns, and to help him acquire new ways of reacting that conform more closely to the new situation. This is the part of the therapy that is called "reality testing." The function of therapy is thus one of facilitating a learning process.

Sometimes a patient's symptoms disappear almost dramatically with only brief contacts. This so-called "transference cure" is the result of the relief the patient derives from thus unburdening himself of his difficulties. It may within a period of time make possible a better adjustment to the real life situation, and with continued improvement the patient no longer requires the emotional support from the physician.

The physician must decide if his function is to be primarily supportive, which may or may not involve changing external conditions through transfer, leave of absence, etc., or if uncovering or insight therapy is indicated. Permanent change of the ego through insight and the emotional experience of the transference situation involves prolonged and complex reactions which go beyond the province of the industrial physician.

In general it is best to choose and space the interpretations in such a way as to focus the patient's attention upon only one problem at a time. When therapy consists primarily of giving emotional support, as in the industrial setting, there is little need of interviews more frequently than may be necessary to maintain this sense of reassurance and encouragement. In well-conducted therapy as much or more happens in the intervals between interviews as in the interviews themselves.

In brief psychotherapy the patient's attention should be focused upon his real present problem and should be turned to disturbing events in the past only for the purpose of throwing light upon the motives of irrational reactions in the present. Therapeutic change is based on the increased capacity of the ego to deal with the emotional constellations which were unbearable in the past. Patients gain the ability to face their intolerable insecurity only because of their great confidence in the physician. The therapeutic result is a process of emotional re-education in which old unsettled conflicts are re-experienced in a new, permissive setting, and with a new, constructive ending. By repetition, these corrected reactions gradually become automatic.

## AIDS IN CONDUCTING
## A DYNAMIC-DIAGNOSTIC APPRAISAL

The accumulated historical data, examinations, and dispensary notes usually constitute a satisfactory groundwork for brief psychotherapy when this is required in the industrial setting. It would be extremely useful if medical examiners also incorporated descriptions of personality factors as these arise in their routine contacts with employees. The need for attention to emotional disturbances, in any event, should be determined by positive evidence of their presence, not merely by the absence of organic findings.

Some physicians have difficulty in the management of the transition phase when it becomes necessary to shift emphasis from physical factors to the associated emotional aspects of the patient's disorder. This phase is best handled by explaining simply that the absence of a physical disease does not preclude functional impairment which can be just as troublesome, and that treatment requires exploration of possible causes in more detail. The patient should be given the clear impression that he shares responsibility with the therapist in this task.

The following are examples of the type of questions which are helpful in handling this opening phase of the contact:

Did anything unusual happen when the trouble first started?
Just what in your opinion was the cause?
Do you think you have been working too hard lately?
What seems to make the trouble better (or worse)?
Do you have more difficulty on or off the job?
Is this trouble tied up with anything else that is bothering you?
Does worrying seem to make it worse?
Have you been under any extra strain or tension recently?
Do you know of anyone else who had symptoms just like yours?

The intrapersonal conflicts which may have been revealed by the patient's responses to these questions should be worked through, with the goal of making conscious as much understanding of the relationship of symptoms to stress as the patient can accept. The physician at the same time gains an impression of the depth, complexity, and chronicity of the emotional element in the patient's situation. Confirmatory evidence of neurotic development will be revealed in further answers to questions such as the following:

Is is hard for you to relax at times? How?
How well do you sleep? Are you rested when you wake up?
Do you consider yourself "nervous?" In what way?
Do you think you are becoming a "worry-wart?"
Do you "blow up," get "high-strung," or lose your temper over trifles?
Do you think you have an "inferiority complex"?
Are you a perfectionist?
Is it hard to keep up with all the demands made on you?
What things make you blue or get you down?

While listening to the patient's account of his personal tensions, stresses, insecurities, frustrations, and anxieties, the physician will be in a position to appraise the relationship of off-the-job problems to the individual's efficiency and interpersonal relations on the job.

In the discussion concerning the work environment, the physician should note any tendency to bring in personalities, especially supervisors. Amplification of attitudes toward authority, fellow-workers, attendance, accidents, and other job-related problems may be explored with inquiries of the following type:

Does your job cause any special strains? Give examples.
Is your supervisor putting on too much pressure?
Are you satisfied with the way you are treated?
Do you get appreciation for what you do?
Is anyone picking on you? Is it a personal matter?
Do you find it hard to take orders sometimes?
Have you noticed if any other employees feel as you do?
Do you think the rules (attendance, safety) are too strict?
Have you had trouble of this type on other jobs?

The industrial physician of necessity is forced to restrict attention to the patient's home problems to those which show some direct relationship to efficiency at work. The decision as to where to draw the line is by no means simple, even on a minimal basis. Some of the more significant home, family, and social problems and personal habits can be revealed through questioning along the following lines:

Do you have trouble getting away from home in the morning?
Do you think you have a well-balanced daily routine (work, rest, relaxation, avocation)?
Is it hard for you to keep on a regular schedule?
Does your family realize what you are faced with?
What does your wife think is the cause of your condition?
Do you have any worries about anyone in your home?
Do you get out enough?

Is the smoking and drinking you do related to your symptoms?

What help have you been able to get from people you have consulted (family doctor, minister, priest, relatives)?

The feeling of relief which comes after ventilation of his major areas of conflict may make the patient more amenable to suggestion. The physician should utilize this opportunity to point out what the patient can do for himself. The type of questioning which enlists the patient's participation and encourages him to proceed toward attainable goals is illustrated as follows:

Does this clear things up better for you?

What do you see ahead that you can do for yourself?

Would you like me to talk this over with your supervisor?

Is there anything more you think the company, Medical Department, or supervisor should do about this matter?

Should your own physician be consulted?

Do you think we need to call in a nerve specialist?

Has it helped you to talk the whole thing over?

Tell me what you are going to do about this matter now.

Will you let me know in a few days (weeks) how things work out?

Follow-up interviews (including those which the physician initiates himself) should include a brief review of the main features of this therapy which the patient has been carrying out. Reinforcement of the patient's efforts at self-help can be made with positive suggestions and reassurances, as follows:

Are you satisfied with your progress?

What else do we have to do to improve your condition?

Have you come to any more conclusions regarding the cause?

Are you sure you understand your condition better now?

Have you reason to believe you can manage things from now on?

Are you getting along satisfactorily with your supervisor now?

Do you have your cofidence back?

What do you think should be our next step?

Will you let me know if you need further help?

## SUMMARY

Psychotherapy in the industrial medical setting should be planned and carried out in accordance with sound psychodynamic principles. The industrial physician will require skill in making diagnostic appraisals focused primarily on presenting problems and symptoms, with minimal investigation of past conditioning experiences and unconscious motivation. Brief psychotherapy in this specialized relationship utilizes a variety of techniques, including nondirective questioning, confession, reassurance, suggestion, referral, and follow-up contacts, all dedicated to the practical objective of emotional re-education as may be required for each individual case.

## REFERENCES

1. Alexander, Franz, & French, Thomas M. *Psychoanalytic therapy–Principles and application.* New York: The Ronald Press, 1946.

2. Deutsch, Felix, & Murphy, William F. *The clinical interview–Volume I: Diagnosis.* New York: International Universities Press, 1955.

3. Menninger, Karl A. *A manual for psychiatric case study.* New York: Grune & Stratton, 1952.

4. Miner, Roy W. Psychotherapy and counseling. *Annals of the New York Academy of Sciences*, 1955, **63**, 319.

# 17. THE GROUP PSYCHOTHERAPIST IN INDUSTRY: A PREVENTIVE APPROACH

**Marvin A. Klemes, M.D., and Verne J. Kallejian, Ph.D.**

The treatment of patients in groups has become an important modality of psychotherapy primarily due to steadily increasing demands for help with emotional problems in the presence of limited facilities. However, as we have utilized the method, it has become apparent that group psychotherapy is not merely an expedient substitute for individual treatment, but has unique advantages in its own right (1). Many of these advantages are not confined to the *therapeutic* group, but can be attained in other kinds of group situations as well. Valuable learning experience can accrue to members of nontherapeutic groups when such groups are directed toward an appropriate concern with the emotional as well as the intellectual development of the membership.

By supplementing his clinical training with specific information about important groups in the community, the group psychotherapist can apply his abilities outside of the clinical setting. He can offer to the individuals of the community services that will enable them to lead more effective lives and set in motion forces that may obviate the future need for formal treatment. This shift in focus of interest from the therapeutic to the preventive is accompanied by a change

This paper is based on the authors' research and training experiences in experimental programs sponsored by the Institute of Industrial Relations, University of California at Los Angeles.

in role from that of psychotherapist to the more diverse one of consultant.

An area in which the preventive approach can be utilized with far-reaching effects is the field of business and industry (2). Since most people spend half their waking hours at work, this is a most important area in considering the preservation—if not restoration—of mental health. For many people work is a source of great pleasure and deep satisfaction. Frequently, however, it is the arena for friction, strife, discontent, and frustration, as mirrored in statistics of turnover, absenteeism, accidents, illness, and alcoholism. Too often one's vocation is solely a means to an end and is intensely disliked *per se*. It is not surprising, then, that in such a milieu many basic needs are not being met, frustrations from other areas are intensified, and additional stress is constantly being placed on an individual's capacity for maintaining emotional homeostasis.

Management's concern with the emotional health of its employees reflects the growing recognition that productivity in the broadest sense is intimately related to the effectiveness of interpersonal relations, the level of morale and job satisfaction, the degree of cooperative group effort, the problem-solving skills of key personnel, and the uninterrupted flow of communications—all of which variables are indices of the emotional well-being of plant personnel. Consequently, enlightened management is incorporating more and more into its traditional consultative and training programs services which take advantage of the knowledge and skills derived from clinical experiences. Ways in which these clinical services are utilized are as follows:

1. Supervisors are trained to be more effective leaders by increasing their sensitivities to the needs of their subordinates.
2. Staff personnel are helped to deal better with human relations problems.
3. The skills of industrial trainers, who in turn have training responsibilities, are sharpened.

4. Key personnel in top management are trained to work more effectively together as well as with and through subordinates.

## OBJECTIVES AND PROCEDURES

The primary objective of the programs to be described is to increase the personal effectiveness of individuals in dealing with problems in human relations. This objective is met by helping individuals gain greater insight into themselves and others, develop a sensitivity to the dynamics of group behavior, become aware of the defenses they employ, learn more effective ways of dealing with conflicts and tensions, and implement their emotional understandings with useful skills.

Although our efforts are preventive rather than therapeutic, the *principles* and *techniques* of analytic group psychotherapy are utilized with appropriate modifications. As in group psychotherapy, the depth or superficiality of the procedure depends on the frequency of meetings, the size of the group, the degree of motivation and sophistication of the individuals involved. In the industrial setting, some additional variables must be considered. The consultant must be aware of the "philosophy," reactions, and degree of support of other persons in the administrative hierarchy apart from the group with which he deals. The atmosphere of the group will vary. It depends upon whether meetings are on "company time" or the individual's time; whether meetings are within the physical setting of the plant or away from it; whether attendance is voluntary or compulsory (no matter how labeled).

The line of demarcation between psychotherapy and preventive procedures is not always a sharp one. Our main interest in preventive practice is in helping group members gain insight into *how* they act and react rather than *why*. Interpretations are never on a deep or dynamic level. For example, a group is encouraged to inquire into how individuals react to aggressive or critical members of the group and to explore the resultant effects upon the group's activity, rather than to be concerned about the environmental and emotional antecedents of such behavior.

Usually, the services of a consultant are requested when the responsible member of the group becomes aware that increasing interpersonal tensions result in impaired performance.

## ILLUSTRATIONS OF TRAINING PROGRAMS

The types of programs that can be instituted vary over a wide range and can be organized in various settings. Some are conducted under the aegis of a university and bring together personnel from various plants; others are conducted within the plant itself. Two in-plant programs will be described.

1. The most frequently utilized program involves the formation of *a new group organized specifically for purposes of training.* The members are drawn from different areas in the plant and have no on-the-job relationship with one another. Formal "status differences" are minimal. The initial objective of the consultant here is to establish a permissive atmosphere and maximize the flow of communication between all members of the group. The amount of structure which is introduced into the group meetings, especially at the beginning, depends on the sophistication of the participants and the amount of previous information they have been given regarding the nature and purpose of the program. The consultant makes a constant effort to increase the group's interest in—and attention to—its own processes, including the interpersonal feelings which exist, the barriers to communication which develop, and the forces which determine the group's operation. These insights enable the group to determine its own needs and to act appropriately upon them. In such a setting, valuable emotional as well as intellectual learning takes place. For example, members of the group often experience intense satisfaction in feeling free to evaluate critically the behavior of the consultant or other members of the group; this easily leads

to a concern about methods for dealing with hostility in inter-personal situations.

As problems are discussed, it is not uncommon for marked interest to center around such topics as interviewing, counseling, dealing with "difficult" individuals, and group leadership. When appropriate, discussion is supplemented by the use of films, didactic material, and "role playing"—a nonclinical adaptation of psychodrama.

2. Working with a "natural work group" (i.e., a group which is already in existence with a work orientation) involves somewhat different considerations (3). In such groups superiors and subordinates are together in the same training situation. A natural group might involve a top-level staff, a group of line employees and their supervisor, or a group of supervisors of unequal rank from a given division. Although basically the procedures employed with such a group are similar to those just described, the consultant is constrained in this by several additional factors. Here, formal "status relationships" exist among the members, and patterns of interpersonal relations have already been established. In this setting, the consultant is primarily concerned with (1) reducing the group's tensions to the point where it can identify interpersonal problems that interfere with its day-to-day performance, and with (2) introducing techniques useful for the solution of these problems.

Prior to the actual meetings of the natural work group, the consultant may wish to familiarize himself with the setting and the organizational structure of the plant (4). He may also find it helpful to have interviews with the individual participants in order to establish some degree of rapport, evaluate motivation for training, and familiarize himself with the "jargon," problems, existing relationships, and other pertinent variables. Since the success of the program crucially depends on the support of the person with the highest status in the group, it is advisable to counsel with him prior to and during the administration of the program.

When working with higher echelons of management, perplexing technical and administrative problems often arise which do not appear on the surface to be "human relations" problems. New perspectives on such problems may be gained, however, through a consideration of the impact of the human factors which generate and maintain them. The consultant can never duplicate the accumulated experience of the leaders with whom he works, but he can help them apply *their* knowledge more effectively. For example, the perennial problems of communication in a large plant are more easily solved when managers acquire insight into their *own* contributions to the failure in communication and better understand the emotional factors involved.

An important distinction between these two training patterns lies in the degree of resistances that develop. Resistance to training in artificially formed groups is considerably less than that encountered in the natural work group. This is due to the greater anxieties that are aroused in exposing one's self to those whom one encounters daily in his work than to (relative) strangers. However, the compensation for overcoming this additional barrier is that the results of training are more easily transferred to the work setting.

At the present stage of development, adequate data is not available from which to specify the optimal conditions for training. If meetings are too widely spaced, the training may have little effect since forces cannot be generated to break though resistances. If the intervals between meetings are too short, individuals do not have the opportunity to integrate new learning. The larger the group, or the greater the number of supervisory levels which the group encompasses, the more difficult it is to create the desired atmosphere. We have found that satisfactory results can be obtained in a group of from 15 to 20 persons meeting weekly.

## EVALUATION

The difficulties of evaluating work of this nature are even greater than those encountered in the clinical setting where careful records of diagnostic testing, treatment, and follow-up are available. Considering the reports of participants, as well as those of individuals with whom they work, we believe that the programs described succeed in accomplishing the specified objectives to a considerable extent. Following training, participants experience greater comfort and decreased tension in their interpersonal relationships. As in group psychotherapy, the experience of communicating with a wide variety of individuals in a permissive atmosphere produces a greater appreciation of individual differences, more insight into one's self and one's impact upon others. Consequently a clearer understanding of the bases of success or failure in human relations emerges. The sensitivities and skills acquired permit individuals to become more effective in group activities, both as leaders and as group members. Changes resulting from training sessions can filter through the organization since each participant can now improve the working atmosphere in his respective unit.

## DISCUSSION

It is to be stressed again that the group psychotherapist working in this area is not primarily interested in those individuals who show more obvious signs of emotional disturbance, but rather in the average, "normal" person subject to the many stresses inherent in our society. Thus the procedures employed are not to be confused with psychotherapy, nor are they in any sense to be substituted for it, when it is indicated. The consultant may meet more of the demands of group members in the industrial setting than he would with his psychotherapeutic groups since his relationship with group members and his goals are different. Whereas a therapist's activities are primarily confined to exploration, uncovering, reflection, interpretation, clarification, and support, the industrial consultant may also function as teacher, information giver, or as discussion leader.

The impact the consultant has, the extent to which he can be nondirective in his approach, and the amount of insight he can affect, are directly proportional to the motivation and psychological sophistication of the participants and to the amount of support given by their superiors to the program and its ensuing results. Because there is a certain threatening aspect attached to the use of this method with persons who do not regard themselves as patients, we would be untherapeutic indeed if we were to arouse more anxiety than we allay.

The *resistances* encountered in training groups are rarely different from those with which we are already familiar. It is in dealing with these resistances that the greatest demands are made upon the clinical skills of the consultant. As groups become active, the consultant has to make accurate judgments regarding the degree of anxiety that individuals can deal with constructively. The clinical skills of the consultant give him a better understanding of the underlying, deeper group dynamics, although not interpreted to the group, and enable him to guide the group toward its goals more skillfully; moreover, they stand him in particularly good stead in training other industrial trainers.

## IMPLICATIONS OF THE STUDY

The importance of effective training activities cannot be overestimated. All too frequently, people rise in administrative hierarchies primarily because of technical competence, but lack an understanding of human relations and skills needed for adequate job performance (5). The atmosphere of our industrial society with the emphasis upon technical knowledge, logic, and facts, and the social stereotypes of how people ought to, should, or might be expected to behave, leaves very little room for training in human relations. Consequently, leaders who have failed to acquire such understanding in the process of their own development can do little in this direction except through programs of the type described here. The lack of such understanding and experience is the source of countless frustrations and anxieties which have repercussions on many other persons.

The type of training described here in industry is equally applicable to many other segments of the community. In education, teachers and school administrators are faced with many of the same problems. Social group workers can utilize similar training procedures in helping informal community groups develop more effective working relationships. Programs of this type are currently under way in hospitals, government agencies, and service organizations. A more recent application is in the field of organized labor. Here, as in any organization, failure of leadership to recognize, understand, and meet the needs of the membership can result in costly program failures.

## SUMMARY

The group psychotherapist can promote valuable mental hygiene activities by providing consultative services to various formal and informal groups in his community. Although his efforts here are corrective and preventive rather than therapeutic, the principles and techniques of analytic group psychotherapy, appropriately modified, can be used effectively.

Various approaches have been described which are directed toward helping individuals in the field of business and industry to enhance their understanding and handling of problems in human relations. Minor changes in the industrial milieu brought about by these efforts can have considerable impact upon the emotional well-being and productive capacities of individuals who are involved both directly and indirectly.

## REFERENCES

1. Slavson, S. R. *Analytic group psychotherapy*. New York: Columbia University Press, 1950.

2. Powdermaker, F. B., & Frank, J. D. *Group psychotherapy*. Cambridge: Harvard University Press, 1953.

3. Laughlin, H. P., & Hall, M. Psychiatry for executives. *American Journal of Psychiatry*, 1951, **107**, 493–497.

4. Tannenbaum, R., Kallejian, V., & Weschler, I. R. Training managers for leadership. *Personnel*, January 1954.

5. Menninger, W. C. *Psychiatry in a troubled world*. New York: Macmillan, 1948.

6. Himler, L. E. The place of psychiatry in industry. Paper presented to Annual Meeting, Michigan State Medical Society, September 23, 1949. See also, The application of psychiatry to industry. Group for the Advancement of Psychiatry, Report No. 20, July 1951.

# 18. CLINICAL COUNSELING— ITS VALUE IN INDUSTRY

## Charles E. Barry

*The clinical counselor can be most valuable to both employer and employee when, as an independent agent, he uses the facts at his disposal to direct and redirect both the employee and his supervisor without being solicitous to either.*

In keeping with the concept of clinical counseling, the prime purpose is to promote the efficiency and happiness of individuals. To achieve this objective requires the insight and technical ability of a qualified counselor. Since the term "clinical counselor" may need to be differentiated from vocational or guidance counselor, there are some rather distinctive contrasts in responsibility.

Although psychology generally may be applied by counselors, the clinical counselor is especially interested in the application of its principles to the study of the individual. In the clinical sense, the individual is studied in relation to his function in a total life situation. Job activities are then a part of the individual's way of acting or reacting toward other situations in his total social environment. This includes a number of considerations, such as the person's marital status, habits, influence of mother, father, wife, upon decisions related or unrelated to the job. The clinical method must achieve objectivity by intensive study of the individual. It becomes evident that the person being studied behaves, acts, and is influenced by the environment in which he is located.

The author is Store Manager, Grover Cronin, Inc., Waltham, Massachusetts.

There can be many forces operating upon and within the individual which are not obvious to the untrained observer. Because these factors and forces play such a dominant role in the proficiency of performance, they need to be identified, singled out, and acted upon in order to accomplish favorable results. When the clinical counselor does his work adequately, prediction and control of the individual's behavior pattern will follow.

When the role of the counselor is established, our interest should be directed toward the responsibility of the employee. To what degree should the employer assume responsibility for providing counseling for his employees? The primary concern, in an efficiently operated business, is the cost. Cost being related to performance, and performance to efficiency and profit, the employer must give an accounting of all expenditures. The question then is should counseling be included in the budget of operating expense? Since people are an integral part of operating a business, their existence must be recognized as a part of necessary expense.

In an efficiently operated business, rules and policies are essential in directing behavior of employees into the most productive channels. In the process of accomplishing the desired objective, through the use of regulations, etc., conflict sometimes arises between the employee and his supervisor. Developed on another plane, the conflict may be between a group of employees and a supervisor. The difference may be minor, such as daily abuse of the relief period by taking a few extra minutes beyond the allotted time. Or it may be major, to the degree that the employee refuses to obey the company policy of punching only his own time card. These departures from established procedures become obvious to other employees and often are the cause of friction between the supervisor and employee. When no disciplinary action is taken, the employees who follow the rules are being discriminated against, and this can lead to the development of complications and personal problems. These problems, such as the extended relief period and punching the other employee's time card, involve other people, since the natural tendency is to presume that if "he can do it, so can I." When problems reach such proportions the person who feels hurt seeks a sympathetic ear. Usually the boss is the last person in whom the employee might confide.

## THE PERPLEXED EMPLOYEE

To whom then should the perplexed employee turn? In this instance the qualified counselor might be a valuable asset to the organization because he is usually objective in his approach. Employees, realizing that they can discuss their problems with a person not associated with management, usually increase their willingness to express themselves. When this arrangement can be put in effect, the investment should be considered sound and practical.

Management became cognizant of the advantages of interviewing in industry in the early 1920's, in relation to studies conducted at the Hawthorne plant of the Western Electric Company. It was during this early experiment in industrial counseling that the interviewers discovered that people expressed their feelings in relation to giving factual answers. Probably the more important aspects of this approach were the benefits derived by the employers from employees just talking freely in the presence of a sympathetic listener. The outgrowth of these findings resulted in Western Electric instituting a formal counseling program. By use of the new directive interviews, the employee now was encouraged to express his thoughts without reservation.

Discussing a problem, or reacting emotionally to a situation, is a valuable adjunct to the employee, but there may be a need of changing the environment. Talking with a counselor relieves personal tensions, but what is its possible relation to solving the problem? Since individual problems may differ from group problems and attitudes, the value of individual reactions might have definite limitations. In this process, the supervisors at Western Electric were completely bypassed. Initially, the supervisor was related to the problem.

In order to become effective, counseling must be related

to the whole organizational structure. Let us assume it should be part of the responsibility of the personnel division. It is a delegated function of the personnel division to hire, train, promote, transfer, dismiss, rate, limit, discipline, and conduct the many other activities associated with human relations. The clinical counselor, being familiar with possible causes for poor performance, should start his study of the case by obtaining all available records of the employee's personal history through the personnel department.

But beyond this, the counselor needs to gain the confidence of the employee in getting his side of the story. Why does he think his production is not up to the supervisor's expectation? If the employee is an extrovert, there will be a natural tendency to be outgoing and frank in giving his reason which seems to justify the situation. When the introvert is asked for his reason for failure to keep up, there will be a tendency to defend his status and possibly expect sympathy. Neither of these reactions is quite in keeping with the expected pattern and characteristics of the extrovert and introvert, but the so-called introvert and extrovert rarely come in a pure state. Because of this, the clinical counselor can become an important vehicle in helping both the employee and company reach a satisfactory solution. The major consideration is that the clinical counselor and employee realize that the company provides the counseling facilities in anticipation of reaching a favorable solution.

Since the employer is footing the bill, he has the right to expect a satisfactory return on his investment. This concept reverts back to the expectations of profit on every investment. If the raw material can be converted successfully into a valuable product, the individual is a prime reason for such action. It is then the responsibility of the personnel department to take the necessary steps required to bring about a change in attitude, resulting in a change in work habits.

## THE CLINICAL COUNSELOR'S ROLE

The role of the clinical counselor in business can be valuable when he becomes an independent agent who uses facts at his disposal to direct and redirect both the employee and his supervisor without being solicitous to either one. Courage to strongly recommend the most favorable course of action should be a major objective. However, it is vital that the counselor realize that the expectation is for constructive results without personal involvement. In order to accomplish this, it is necessary to make use of all available data on file, as well as enlisting the cooperation of schools, colleges, and other agencies acquainted with the background of the persons being studied. Often this information is readily available, including psychometric scores, which are valuable in relation to past and future findings.

When all the facts have been objectively studied and documented, the recommendations should be written in terms which can be readily understood by the reader. At this point, many a report is too involved and complicated for the average businessman to interpret. This is not to imply that the counselor should cater to the employer, but rather that he should attempt to create an atmosphere conducive to the common understanding of existing facts and conditions.

Since the original purpose of this paper is to establish the importance of profit in relation to performance, the personnel director should continuously be aware of this objective. Combining the information obtained from all sources, including the report and findings of the clinical counselor, the personnel director should attempt to determine the best course of action to take. When the results indicate the person in question has assets of value to the company, and he appears willing to change his attitude in favor of the company's best interest, the prospects of turning a liability into profitable action may be good.

## A TYPICAL SITUATION

Here is an example of a situation in which counseling provided an avenue for release of tensions resulting in adjustment and promotion. John X was employed as a salesman in the men's clothing department. He was interested in promotion and was encouraged to take the executive training program.

After successfully completing the course, John was promoted to assistant buyer of men's furnishings. In this capacity he was interested, cooperative, ambitious, and enthusiastic. After eight months John was promoted to buyer of the department. A leveling off of interest followed after the second year. When it was indicated that the sales volume of his department was not up to expectation, John offered several excuses—disinterested, incapable sales people, lack of satisfactory communication with the divisional head, limited advertising and buying budget. After these reasons were analyzed, it was agreed that they could be interpreted as excuses rather than legitimate facts. Improvement followed this conference, with John showing considerable initiative in the activity of the division. On many occasions he exerted himself to supervise adjoining sections of the men's division, even though this was not part of his personal responsibility. For this he was commended and encouraged to extend his interest and authority. In the interim, outside activities included taking courses related to business. There was also bowling and golfing, which provided opportunities for social contact. It should be noted that John's actions and activities became quite outgoing after his conference, in accordance with recommendations made by the division head, in conjunction with the personnel director.

In John's instance, redirection was necessary to provide a stimulus and change in attitude. Because the personnel director hired John and was familiar with his background and work history, making recommendations favorable to his development were not difficult. Much time might have been gained, in terms of the profit angle, if a clinical counselor had worked with the personnel director when it was first noted that John needed some attention.

Being qualified to make a study and recommendations, the clinical counselor has much to offer industry when his talents are used with discretion and without bias. When the purpose is objectively pursued, counseling in business should go far beyond the Hawthorne plan instituted by Western Electric, because now the clinical counselor has at his disposal the advantages of a backlog of case studies and methods developed in the fields of psychology and psychiatry. It should be possible to use these tools in favor of both the employee and employer

JUST AS YOU WOULD A CASE STUDY

to reach sound and impersonal understanding. This can be accomplished by:

1.   The use of the employee's employment history.
2.   Previous employment record of functional activity.
3.   School and college records of academic standing and participation in school activities.
4.   Psychometric results prior to employment and following employment.
5.   Home background.
6.   Marital status and relationship of home activities to job performance.
7.   Social activities, after-work habits.
8.   Financial obligations.
9.   Emotional stability.
10.  Opinion of acquaintances, of business associates, and of supervisor.

These are basic considerations which quite naturally lead into other avenues of discussion and exploration. When the experienced counselor brings these factors into play in attempting to reach an intelligent and objective solution, the results should favor the employer and assist the employee regarding the decision reached. When the counselor recommends a continuance of employment, both employer and employee should have an advantage. If the recommendation is to release the employee, the advantage may be assumed to favor the employer, since he is relieved of a liability; conversely the employee should be grateful that the company has afforded him the opportunity to discover his shortcomings and make the necessary change to another job.

In this arrangement, the employer should be enabled to see the potential of increased profit through a complete program of measured personnel function. This should begin at the employment selector's desk and continue through a series of well-integrated steps which measure performance and lead to making correction whenever necessary. Again, it is vital that the employer realize that growth in any direction begins with change. When constructive changes are made in personnel practices, through guided study and examination of the facts old and new, the results should favor the progress of the entire business.

# 19. SPOTTING THE NEUROTIC AND HELPING THE MALADJUSTED

## Silas L. Warner, M.D.

*"Everybody is a bit queer except thee and me,"* the old Quaker told his wife. *"And sometimes I even wonder about thee."* The author relates some queernesses to the work situation. He says we can probably screen out psychotics who might cause trouble, but identifying *"character disorders"* is more difficult. If the person is seriously depressed, watch out–this could be a medical emergency.

Many different specialties such as yours come to psychiatry for help and answers to their many problems. We are a new field that has many impressions, theories, and undocumented speculations, but we lack sufficient scientific data to speak with complete authority on many of the subjects that we would choose to be authorities on. There is a wide gap between understanding human behavior and altering, controlling, and harnessing the behavior for specific ends. Much of our theory is based on past behavior and only recently have we gained some notions about predicting future behavior.

The concept of the "normal" individual brings different descriptions from different disciplines. To some, it means a composite of all personality qualities into an average personality constellation and behavior pattern. To others, it means an ideal of maturity and emotional growth with an abundance of admirable attributes and stability. One New York psychologist has coined the term "self-actualized" personality to describe the optimum in maturity with special emphasis

The author is Chief, Section of Therapy and Clinical Services, Division of Mental Health, City of Philadelphia.

being placed on the creative, often independently obtained, realization of one's capabilities.

Now let us consider the opportunities, requirements, emotional gratification, and prestige that various jobs hold today. It is my contention that it is necessary to coordinate the job and the personality so that they mesh like smoothly fitting gears of a car. I further hold that there are many jobs that outstandingly mature and self-actuated individuals would be appalled by and, as a corollary, that individuals with certain exaggerated personality traits fare better at.

An example might include the manual worker who does the same mechanical motion with his hands for minute after minute, day after day, year after year, and doesn't tire of this. It is necessary to sacrifice immediate gratification in creating a finished product and be contented to be merely part of a mass production line in which the individual may not even see the finished product.

On the other hand, there is the stereotype of the traveling salesman who relies on his verbal ability and bombastics to emotionally sway a prospective buyer into buying his product. I realize this is an exaggeration of current selling techniques which presumably are based more on solid product information than on bombastics. However, it most certainly is an integral part of selling to be confident, outgoing, and convinced of one's own charm and ability along with the product's quality.

## HOW MATCH JOBS AND PEOPLE?

Now, the question that I am interested in is; if the job requirements are so different, and if personality manifestations are so unidentical, how can these be best matched. This obviously implies to me that certain exaggerations and biases in personality can be fitted to certain jobs which require those biases and exaggerations.

In other words, neurotics and sometimes even psychotics can serve at some specific jobs and even excel at them. However, the really mature, "self-actualized" individual shows his improved stability and emotional maturity by being so adjustable that he can do well at many different jobs.

When most psychiatrists speak of personality, they think of a dynamic, not static, mechanism of pushes and pulls within the mind and feelings, which results in a system of checks and balances to control the person's energy. The most efficient personality can get along well with the world outside and can also realize some of his own potentialities and capabilities.

However, every personality shows an overflow of energy in some direction and builds up personality "defenses" against this. As a consequence it appears on the surface that there is a lack of energy in this area. For example, a psychiatrist on seeing an individual who is excessively polite, to the point of being obsequious, immediately thinks of this as a defense measure to control aggressive feelings in the individual.

There are two basic ways of looking at employment policies. One is to find the man (or woman) for the job and the other is to find the job for the man. It takes a national emergency, however, to demonstrate how jobs can be tailored to the labor available.

## WAR-TAUGHT LESSONS

You can all vividly remember how employment practices changed during World War II. Women started doing manual work which was previously not considered appropriate for them. The physically handicapped, the aged, and the retired all helped. Attempts were made to tailor the job to the available individual. For example, in the case of women doing heavy manual work, lift trucks were used in lieu of muscular work. This trend has continued in industry.

Another example would be that those who have had strokes, affecting their right side, now can have left-hand operated machines. In a few years, more than half the people in this country will be over 45, and jobs will have to be fitted to recognize their declining physical vigor. This age group more than makes up for this however by more stability, less accident proneness, and better judgment. Another trend is the increased use of part-time help.

When I speak of the handicapped, I mean the mentally and emotionally ill also. Even the best screening devices can't entirely screen them out, and shouldn't.

Let me now mention the three large psychiatric diagnostic categories. These are the psychosis, the neurosis, and the character disorder. It is my hunch that most of your severe personnel problems will come from the character-disordered individual. The psychotic one who is disturbed, confused, and out of touch with reality is for the most part in a mental hospital. I doubt if you would have difficulty in screening out an overtly psychotic individual who was applying for work.

## DEALING WITH THE PARANOID

Those patients whom we see as having a "paranoid" psychosis can be difficult to deal with. They are the individuals who think that everyone is against them or picking on them. When you are inquiring about past reasons for leaving jobs and find the person left several different employers because he was being "picked on," you might suspect paranoid thinking.

The same applies to workers already in your employ who continually blame their poor performance on their supervisor or actually feel persecuted. Recently I saw a 45-year-old engineer whose work record had steadily declined over the past few months and who, when called to task for this, attributed it to his food being systematically poisoned.

When such a viewpoint intrudes on all thought and performance, it incapacitates the individual. However, if it is only a strange or eccentric idea which is "harmless" and not all-consuming, there appears to be no psychiatric reason why the person's job should be taken from him. Certain jobs lend themselves to a person who is excessively suspicious, as long as he has good control over his judgment.

## THEN THERE'S THE NEUROTIC

As for the neurotic, the salient diagnostic feature they show is *subjective discomfort*, whether in the form of free-floating anxiety or tension, mild depression, recurrent unpleasant thoughts, or body organs which do not properly function due to emotional problems.

Most neurotics, contrary to popular belief, are not spoiled weaklings who can't stand up to what you and I do, but are unhappy individuals, most of whom are productively working, and who have suffered from some form of emotional deprivation or overindulgence from their own parents. They would love to be "normal" but don't know how.

Neurotics are often submissive people who will do many extra hours of work when called on for this, because they are afraid to say "no." Others are extreme perfectionists who turn out accurate, reliable work at the price of tremendous internal discomfort if it is not perfect.

The prototype of the neurotic woman which most people hold is the frequently tearful person whose emotional control is so brittle that she is usually regarded as being very unstable and unreliable in work. This type is actually less neurotic and has more of an immature or infantile personality.

## THE CHARACTER DISORDER

This brings us to the last category, the so-called character or personality disorder. They do not come to psychiatrists on their own but are "sent" by somebody else because they are doing unsatisfactory work, can't get along with other employees, or have broken some rule or law. They are not particularly uncomfortable, but those around them are definitely disturbed by them. They have immature personalities, are self-centered and often asocial or antisocial. They are hard to treat and help psychiatrically because they are not well motivated.

These individuals are sometimes hard to detect by one interview as they are not infrequently charming or capable of making a good impression. Psychological testing and a skilled psychiatric interviewer can often pick them out. The best way for you to screen out this group is by carefully checking previous employments, adjustment there, and reasons for leaving; usually these records will speak for themselves.

If a person has frequent inadequately explained lateness or absenteeism, or can't get along with associates or superiors, and tends to always blame the other persons and doesn't appear concerned himself, or doesn't seem really reliable or truthful, it points towards character disorder. Through experience and skill, I am sure personnel people can pick out this category, although you may use different names such as "eight ball" or "nonconformist."

## EARLY CARE
## NEEDED FOR ALCOHOLICS

Three other specific categories are well worth mentioning. I refer to alcoholics, depressed persons, and those suffering from premature senile mental changes.

Psychiatrists tend to believe that alcoholism is an expression of certain personality problems or conflicts. Most alcoholics, on the other hand, prefer to think of alcoholism as a disease caused by a metabolic intolerance of the individual to alcohol. Because of this difference in viewpoints, most alcoholics prefer AA's or medical help to psychiatric treatment. Oddly enough, whatever approach is used, the amount of success is approximately the same; about 70 to 80% of all alcoholics, or 30 to 40% of severe cases, recover.

I am of the opinion that employers should insist on early care for employees with obvious alcoholic problems, while still allowing the alcoholic to choose the type of care. I think it is harmful to be too nice and give too much leeway to the incipient alcoholic whose performance is obviously slipping. If it were a tumor or diabetes, it would be quickly dealt with, so why delay in problems of alcoholism? This could include time off for a medical or psychiatric evaluation.

If possible, I believe it helps to have good liaison between the family at home and the employer. In numerous cases, it is easier to help the alcoholic's spouse not to create circumstances which lead to drinking. I do not think you will experience difficulty in establishing the diagnosis if you are aware of the possibility.

## TREAT DEPRESSED
## AS EMERGENCIES

Serious depressions occur most frequently in the 40's and 50's and are often associated with slowing down or retardation of movements and thinking processes, or with extreme agitation, pacing, insomnia, and worry. Early signs are lack of interest in normal things, poor appetite, weight loss, and feelings of inadequacy or failure. *This is a medical emergency* because of the danger of suicide (there are over 25,000 annually). An expert medical or psychiatric consultation should be obtained.

## EARLY SENILE CHANGES

If people continue to work until 65 or longer, there will be 5% or more who will show some early senile changes in their 50's and 60's. Clinically, one sees a gradual exaggeration of the individual's previous personality. If he was quiet, he will be quieter to the point of being a recluse. If he has been slightly argumentative, he could become quarrelsome and disruptive.

The other early signs include the impairment of such intellectual functions as memory, judgment, and future planning. If these people are in a stressful situation their symptoms are exaggerated. If they continue in a routine they have done for years and know well, they will usually continue to do a fairly good job. It should be emphasized that they need stability and they cannot tolerate too many radical changes, but if kept in a routine they will be worthwhile employees.

# 20. THE PSYCHOPATHIC PERSONALITY IN INDUSTRY— A PERSONNEL MANAGEMENT PROBLEM

**Emil A. Corona**
Assistant Director of Personnel
The Sperry and Hutchinson Company
New York, N.Y.

*It has been reliably estimated that individual personality difficulties represent the greatest single cause of failure on the job. But how, without resorting to psychiatric depth techniques, can management sift out those whose personalities virtually preclude the possibility of satisfactory employment experience? This article is concerned with one personality type that management often does not recognize as a "problem" until it is too late, simply because superficial characteristics seem to suggest that the individual would make a desirable employee. Of special value are the author's suggested "rules of thumb" for recognizing the psychopathic personality without the aid of psychiatric tests.*

An analysis of labor turnover very often reveals a particular type of individual who presents a formidable challenge to the personnel director. This individual's association with the firm is invariably short-termed and an inquiry into his past occupational history usually reveals a lengthy string of fickle affiliations with other firms.

The employment interview and the initial impression reveal a neat, very polite, assertive, cooperative individual who appears bright and efficient. He radiates a feeling of confidence and capability which is easily interpreted by the interviewer as indicative of desirable potential. Once employed, and within the immediate subsequent weeks, careful observation of this employee reveals an extremely interesting personality structure in function.

He displays a superficial ingratiation, circulates freely, and quickly becomes acquainted with the other employees. To the latter and his superiors, he maintains an overpolite attitude and frequently displays a deferent manner of relating to people. His work attitude is initially characterized by zealous concern and interest. He throws up a smoke screen of laudable ambitions, enthusiasm, and energy. If observed carefully, however, this display dwindles to inconsistency and finally to a bland, pervasive indifference. He makes recourse to fabulized dissatisfaction with working conditions, associate employees, and management regulations. His demands of management and of his fellow employees increase enormously. It is not at all unusual to find him taking advantage of the trusting, gullible employee impressed by his braggadocio. In return, however, he is willing to give very little in either time, effort, efficiency, or interest. But before his behavior and attitude become too blatant, he invariably turns up with a request for termination and a conviction that he can find a new, sustaining interest in some other occupational adventure. He is predisposed, of course, to follow the identical cycle elsewhere.

## WHAT PSYCHOLOGICAL
## TESTS TELL US

The term, Psychopathic Personality, has been applied to this type of character disorder and by definition describes a personality structure which, while not psychotic or neurotic, presents inadequacies and deviations to the extent of rendering the individual incapable of satisfactory social and business relations.

Psychometric examinations applied to the selection and evaluation of personnel have been very useful in detecting the psychopath. Experience has consistently shown certain typical and characterizing test responses. Intelligence testing usually reflects a high-average or superior range of endowment. Overall results on these particular tests present a pattern which displays a greater proficiency with items requiring manipulative ability than with those items requiring abstract thought formation. The thinking revealed is very often of syncretistic quality. His judgment often tests at an impaired level, but he manifests a particularly keen, over-alert attitude toward situations. His tendency is to remain at a fairly concrete level of ideational formation, but when hard-pressed and forced to respond abstractly, he resorts to fabulation in free fashion. He fully understands the nature of social and business situations, but contrives a pathological twist in exploiting them for his own purposes.

## TYPICAL PERSONALITY CONFIGURATION

Regarding the personality tests, particularly the Rorschach projective technique, which is analagous to an X-ray view of the underlying personality structure of an individual, this person is pictured as one within whom psychological conflict culminates in overt defiance in the form of antisocial expression. His ego is at constant battle with society—it is quite possible that in many cases an underlying sense of inadequacy and insecurity has contributed heavily to his maladaptive behavior. This technique further reveals that this sort of individual is constantly attempting to give the impression that his intellectual capacity is more than adequate and that he is unhampered by any social or emotional problem. However, he is more than often revealed as an unreliable person whose modes of behavior are difficult to explain by ordinary motives or incentives. He seems unable to plan constructively, and when attempts are made to do so he is incapable of following through. Social conscience is deplorably absent—his relations with other people are held to casual likes and dislikes. Deep attachments for people are seldom evidenced, and neither is he able to profit from experience.

The detection of this personality type is challenging indeed.

He plays havoc with managerial attempts to keep down employee turnover costs as well as with the more intangible measure of lessened departmental production resulting from the effects of disorganization incurred by change on other employees.

## SIGNS TO WATCH FOR

As a rough rule of thumb to guide the interviewer, we would suggest that an inquiry be made into what appears to be a lengthy, suspicious occupational history where each position has been held on a relatively short term. Further, the examiner should attempt some appraisal of the applicant's personality in regard to his affective life. That is, are his feelings felt or feigned? Is he capable of sustained interest? Has he the capacity to delay impulsiveness? Does his manner impress you as being overpolite and superficially ingratiating? Is he able to empathize with others? These are some of the components to be on the alert for, but it must be remembered that no one of these qualities, evidenced by itself, is sufficient basis for discrimination. For finer, accurate appraisal of personality configurations, the application of psychological tests is suggested.

To all those directly responsible for the selection and evaluation of personnel in industry, the recognition of this particular type of applicant will enhance the goal of management for optimum personnel efficiency.

# 21. SOCIOMETRIC DATA USED TO COUNSEL A SENSITIVE MAN: A CASE STUDY

**B. J. Speroff**
Research Associate and Project Director
Industrial Relations Center
University of Chicago, Chicago, Illinois

*In handling problem situations involving people, you need all the solid facts you can get. The author tells how needed facts about the attitudes and feelings of group members were obtained and how he used them to straighten out a situation that was causing grave concern.*

This paper, citing a single instance, shows how sociometric data can supply supportive evidence for use in a situation that requires the counseling of a troublesome individual, and how the interview was conducted.

As a means of straightening out employees and letting them get things "off their chests," counseling is being used more and more by industry. Sociometry is now beginning to be used as a tool for determining the nature and significance of interpersonal relationships on the job. The two can be used together effectively.

Essentially, sociometric devices have been applied in industry to measure morale and its byproducts. And, morale can best be appraised by studying the formation of groups and subgroups. Sociometry aims to make such appraisals by determining accurately and objectively the like-nominations, or choices, of an individual from among those in his group. The procedure developed by Moreno (1) and the modification made by Jenkins (2) are most useful in studying group structure for its cohesiveness, or the lack of it.

The procedure for assessing the sociometric status of the group is relatively simple. Each individual in a group is asked, either orally or in writing, to name the individual(s)—usually a specified number—in the group whom he considers the "best worker," "most efficient," or the like.

A picture of the nominations when charted is referred to as a sociogram. From it one can determine:

1. the number and size of cliques or subgroups within the group;
2. the level of group morale or cohesiveness (by the presence of cliques);
3. the accuracy of one's personal observations as contrasted to the objective evidence;
4. those who may be in need of counseling, guidance, testing, and therapy;
5. the potential leaders of the group;
6. whether regrouping is feasible or necessary; and
7. whether inferential information fits the facts about a worker's characteristics, qualities, and attitudes as seen by other individuals within the group.

The section head of a highly specialized industrial relations group became disturbed and anxious. One member of the group was creating problems. The high degree of group unity, cooperativeness, and team spirit started to disintegrate. Not only were personal problems and complaints on the increase, but interpersonal friction and rebelliousness were threatening to destroy the creative and developmental work of the group on joint undertakings.

This state of tension and anxiety was apparent to all the members of the group as well as to the section head. But no member of the group had discussed the problem with the individual who caused it. The main reason for this lack of action, either by a member of the group or the section head, was that all of them were aware from bitter past experience of the extreme sensitivity and susceptibility of the problem-individual, whom I will call Mr. X. Mr. X resented anything smacking of "interference" on their part.

## SITUATION DEMANDS ACTION

Such a situation was tolerated for some two months, during which time the group's performance degenerated to a bantering, bickering, nonproductive effort. Finally the section head decided to have a heart-to-heart talk with Mr. X. However, in considering such action, he soon realized how poorly prepared he was with facts and relevant information to help him understand the individual and cope with him intelligently.

Mr. X was an unusually intelligent, meticulous, and efficient worker. He was verbally adroit, skilled in sterile argumentation, self-confident even to the point of being somewhat arrogant. Over a period of years the group had always checked with him and asked for his opinion before putting the stamp of approval on any part of the group effort. The group at times became caustic, argumentative, and difficult with one another but not with Mr. X—that was to be avoided at any cost. In essence, Mr. X was a clever, highly defensive, resistant, overly sensitive individual who chose to hide himself behind a puerile facade of defense mechanisms.

After discussing the problem with me, the section head agreed to use a sociometric questionnaire to determine the group's interpersonal feelings and reactions. The questionnaire consisted of nine questions, asking group members to name the individual who most accurately, as well as least accurately, fitted the descriptive statements. The final item asked the group member to write brief descriptions of himself as his "best friend" and as his "worst enemy" would depict him.

The questionnaire was administered and the sealed responses were turned over to me. They were analyzed and sociograms were drawn up to show individuals' positive and negative responses to the questions. The section head and I then went over the sociometric data, question by question, and sociogram by sociogram.

The section head in this way gained a better and more accurate understanding of his group's feelings and reactions to one another. The findings also proved a valuable tool in that they gave us an estimate of the qualities and characteristics the group associated with each individual. Much of these findings merely served to corroborate and verify, but they did show clearly the level of morale in the section.

## GOT FACTS
## FOR COUNSELING MR. X

The survey plainly indicated that Mr. X was superior in many positive characteristics. He was considered most persuasive, confident, and dynamic. But the replies also pointed out and substantiated both the section head's impression and the group's reaction to his negative characteristics. He emerged as least-liked to work with, least flexible and logical.

With definitive evidence to support his position when he talked with X, the section head would not be in the vulnerable position of making statements which he could not support or defend. Nonetheless, his delicate task required careful handling. In the end it was decided that not he, but I should arrange for and conduct the counseling interview.

In a small private office I informed Mr. X of the purpose of the interview: to review the results of the sociometric questionnaire as they pertained to him. I told him that all data and information relevant to the discussion were available for his appraisal. Nothing was said about the reason for his being involved in this undertaking.

First, I described sociometry in general terms and told how it measures interpersonal relations. A specially prepared specimen of the questionnaire, together with the sociograms, was presented and explained. I pointed out X's strengths first, then eased into his weaknesses. It was carefully and repeatedly stated that these were the observations of his associates as they viewed their relationship with one another.

## MR. X HELPED TO SEE HIMSELF

After discussing and evaluating each of his characteristics, X was asked to read his own statement of how his best friend and his worst enemy might describe him. I deliberately and specifically pointed out that, in practically every trait or characteristic described, he had shown remarkable insight and understanding of himself. Furthermore, I said, his view of himself correlated closely with the sociometric findings.

From this point on the nondirective counseling method was employed. The man began to unravel some of his personal and interpersonal problems which contributed to the strained relations within his group. Hostility was both inferred and expressed towards every member of the group, including the section head who seemed to be the crux of his troubles. A superficial analysis of some of these feelings with respect to particular individuals was undertaken.

Whenever possible, as the man poured out his story, I attempted to hook up the sociometric evidence with statements he himself made. Towards the end of the interview he expressed a willingness to overcome his deficiencies and thereby improve his relationships with the other group members. He felt he understood the others much better.

Approximately three months later the identical sociometric questionnaire was employed on the group. A marked improvement in the general sociometric status of the group towards the problem-individual was revealed. On two of his worst characteristics Mr. X was now tied with another group member, and in a third characteristic his name was supplanted by that of another group member.

Some two months later, while interviewing the section members on another matter, each individual was asked how things were going. Without exception, each indicated that a striking change had taken place in his relations with X since the sociometric survey. It might be stated here that the group was completely unaware that a counseling interview with Mr. X had taken place.

# REFERENCES

1. Moreno, J. L. Foundations of sociometry. *Sociological Monographs*, 1943, No. 4.

2. Jenkins, J. C. The nominating technique: Its uses and limitations. Paper presented before EPA, April 1947.

# 22. PASTORAL COUNSELING WITH THE PROBLEM EMPLOYEE

**Clifford H. Peace**

Pastor-Counselor, R. J. Reynolds Tobacco Company
Winston-Salem, North Carolina

During the month of January 1955, a total of 33 employees with personal problems came to me, as Pastor-Counselor of the R. J. Reynolds Tobacco Company, for a total of 67 counseling sessions.

## AN AVERAGE SAMPLING

A young lady came because, since her seventh year, she had not passed more than two consecutive nights without screaming in her sleep to the degree that she awakened her family. A man in his middle fifties came because he had been seized by a terrifying and unyielding anxiety that was interfering with his work. Another young lady in her twenties came because she felt uncomfortable socially and wanted to discuss her dating problems, and a middle-aged woman came whose estranged alcoholic husband kept making return visits while drunk, creating great emotional distress.

During the five and one-third years in which he has been pastor-counselor at R. J. Reynolds Tobacco Company, Rev. Clifford H. Peace has held more than 3,280 counseling sessions with 1,561 employees who voluntarily sought his help with personal problems. A graduate of the Divinity School of Duke University, he is an ordained Methodist minister who has held four pastorates. During the war he was a chaplain in the U.S. Army Air Force, serving overseas for 2½ years.

The next visitor was a woman in her middle thirties, the mother of two children, whose husband had fallen in love with another woman whom he refused to give up—and this wife deeply loved and wanted her husband. Then came a man in his late thirties, whose marriage to an emotionally immature woman had gone on the rocks and who was harassed by her incessant demands that he return, feeling that he could not and should not; a man in his early sixties who had been in a psychiatric hospital was trying to readjust to his job, and wanted the help of religion in doing so; and an attractive woman of 40 who felt trapped in a loveless marriage, who had developed a strange physical malady which her doctor believed was related in origin to her emotional anguish.

A woman in her sixties, a member of whose family was in a psychiatric hospital, felt that it might have been her fault. A middle-aged Negro woman felt an overwhelming sense of guilt, which was breaking her. A man in his early thirties, a budding alcoholic, was unhappy in his job and with his boss, while another of about the same age wanted to discuss the strange and dangerous conduct of a brother-in-law, who turned out to be in the early stages of a mental disease.

I saw a middle-aged woman greatly disturbed over the conduct of an alcoholic husband, with serious physical complications, who seemed bent on destroying himself and family; a mother in her fifties who wanted to talk about an alcoholic son whose long period of sobriety had ended in a bender which cost him his job and left him stranded in a distant city; a tense, anxious, resentful man in his late thirties who had unconsciously transferred his hatred for his father to his boss; and a woman whose husband had left her, but whose feelings for him would not let go.

One session was with a man whose supervisor had called to say that this employee was depressed to the degree that it was interfering with his work—because his wife and child had left him three months before. Again, a mother of three children wanted to get from a night to a day shift because she feared that her alcoholic husband was not taking proper care of the children while she was at work. A lawyer referred my next counselee, a young wife and mother considering a divorce because of her husband's immorality, and another wife in her twenties came because she could not wean her husband away from his possessive mother.

A minister in our employ had attempted to help some people who had viciously turned on him, and he was eating out his heart during sleepless nights. A woman employee felt that the people in her department were against her, were whispering about her behind her back, and were watching her; her doctor and I are trying to help her make her adjustment on the job. A young married man came to confess a marital disloyalty so that he could face his wife and make things right with her. And there was a woman who was greatly concerned about her aged father, who had broken his hip.

It was a theft, resulting in the loss of a job, which brought a young man to my office to talk out the problem. There followed a 27-year-old wife who had left her husband because she said that she "just could not understand him"; an office worker who was wrestling with a deep, dark fear—and wanted to talk and go to the chapel adjoining my office for prayer; a Negro woman of 42, in her seventeenth pregnancy, whose alcoholic and sadistic husband abused her and her children; a middle-aged white woman who was caught in the net of an illicit love affair from which she could not extricate herself; a middle-aged father, greatly concerned about the conduct of a daughter over whom he felt that he had lost all control; a rehabilitated alcoholic, who is making good but who came by for a little encouragement; and a man who wanted to discuss means by which our city could better meet juvenile needs. Finally, there was a wife whose thought of murdering her husband had become so fixed that she was on the verge of acting on them.

These were not all of our 12,000 employees who had personal problems during the month. They were not the only ones who talked to personally interested supervisors or to members of the personnel and medical departments. These were the ones who came to the office of the pastor-counselor to talk about the things which troubled them. They have been listed just as they came. It was about an average month. During the last 5⅓ years, 1,561 different persons have voluntarily come to my office for a total of 3,280 counseling sessions of an hour each.

## RECOGNITION
## OF EMPLOYEES' PROBLEMS

Does this mean that the employees of the R. J. Reynolds Tobacco Company are more emotionally unstable than other employees? The record tends to indicate that they are not.

Of our regular employees, 60% have an unbroken service record of 10 years or more; 41% of 20 years or more; and 12% of 30 years or more. A total of 183 persons have served the company for 40 years or longer, while the average length of service is 16½ years. Our labor turnover for 1954 was just over 5%. The latest available figures show that the plants of our company have a safety record which is four times better than that of the average plant in the tobacco industry and eight times better than that of the average manufacturing plant in all other industries.

As this account of my counseling will indicate, we do have an awareness of the emotional problems of our employees and have established a facility whereby they may pursue a problem-solving approach to their emotional difficulties. There is a place where, through therapeutic listening, our people can communicate and drain off such tensions as anxiety, anger, grief, and guilt; where they may seek a clarification of their confusion in feeling and motivation; and where they can find ways of laying hold on a power by which they can live more adequately and creatively.

## AMERICA'S NUMBER ONE ILLNESS

Let us now turn from a localized view in a Southern industry to a nationwide picture of emotional sickness. Some have called emotional illness America's number one illness.

During World War II, Selective Service Boards rejected

approximately one-fourth of all the young men examined for military duty, and almost one-half of these rejections were for what the military called "emotional unfitness." A total of 1,800,000 were refused for this cause at induction, and 700,000 were later dismissed from service for the same reason (1).

It is estimated that a third of our nation's population is ill in one way or another (2). It is commonplace for general practitioners to indicate that 50–75% of all their patients are without organic disease, which is another way of saying that 50-75% of their patients are emotionally ill (3). And it is often stated that one-half of all general hospital beds are filled with the emotionally ill.

Dr. Seldon D. Bacon, of Yale, has indicated that there are about four million people in some phase of alcoholism (4), and the U.S. Department of Public Health, which reckons alcoholism as its number four problem, estimates that industry employs 1,650,000 alcoholics (5). Alcoholism may be a symptom of an unsolved emotional problem for which the drinker has found no better solution.

It is now generally known, too, that there are accident-prone individuals, who unconsciously put intent into their mishaps. One psychiatric study has revealed that 80-90% of all accidents spring from emotional rather than physical causes (6). The accident-prone employee is emotionally ill.

There were approximately 400,000 divorces and annulments in America in 1954 (7). In that same year, marital difficulties brought 21% of the people who came to see me. Those best qualified to know say that "emotional immaturity" is the leading cause of marital breakdowns.

A survey conducted in Great Britain in 1952 showed that nearly one-fourth of all absenteeism in industry was caused by emotional illness—a condition resulting in more absenteeism that is caused by the common cold and influenza (8)—while another 1952 survey in an Ohio industry indicated that only half of the employees were well adjusted and efficient, and that three out of every four who were well adjusted had a strong religious faith (9).

Even mental illness is very common. A total of 150,000 Americans entered psychiatric hospitals in 1954 (10). There are nearly 1,000,000 in mental hospitals now, and there are some 5,000,000 persons who are sufficiently emotionally or mentally disturbed to impair their happiness and productivity (11). Finally, there are 16,000 known suicides a year, and 100,000 more are known to make unsuccessful attempts at self-destruction annually (12).

## WHO IS THE PROBLEM EMPLOYEE?

Now, what about these problem persons? More specifically, what about the problem employee? Who is the problem employee?

To begin with, the problem employee is simply an employee with a problem. If he does not get help through gaining insights and finding emotional support, he may advance from an employee with a problem to an employee who has become a problem to himself. If he does not get help at this point, through feeling understood, and through gaining self-understanding, he then becomes a problem for management, but an employee never becomes a problem for management until he has first become a problem to himself. He is an employee who has an emotional problem which he can neither solve nor escape. As Dr. Bonaro W. Overstreet makes clear in the book *Understanding Fear* (13), an employee does not breed tension among fellow employees until he has first failed to solve his own inner tension. An employee does not raise problems for management to solve until after he has failed to solve his own problems.

Seldom, if ever, is the process of becoming a problem employee a voluntary process. Within the limits of the employee's understanding, and within the bounds of the spiritual resources which he knows how to use, he is trying as hard as anyone to adjust, to act in ways that will bring him the acceptance of his group and the approval of supervision which he so much needs and wants. He fails in these objectives, not because he does not try or care, but because his tangled and confused emotions alienate him from the group. Regardless of how blundering and stupid his behavior may appear to others, we may be assured that he is doing what makes sense to him in the light of his deep feelings.

## WHAT IS
## PASTORAL COUNSELING IN INDUSTRY?

Are the people who come to me problems to management? Some of them are. More of them are persons who have become problems only to themselves. Perhaps the majority of them are very satisfactory employees who simply have problems which they wish to talk about.

What may be expected to happen when a problem employee comes to me? What is pastoral counseling in industry and how does its function attempt to help the employee with a problem? It is not religion which the "front office" buys for those below a certain labor grade. If management does not consider it good for all, employees will probably consider it good for none. It is not, of course, a substitute for good labor-management policies and practices, although its quiet influence can have an effect in this area. Pastoral counseling in industry is not synonymous with arbitration in labor-management disputes. It is not an out-of-channels, over-the-heads-of handling of personnel and management matters, although it may be able to help employees and management at times to get at the emotional and spiritual causations behind unhappiness. Nor is it a coddling of sore-heads in industry, although it can be a cure for them.

Contrary to some rather general suppositions, it is not preaching little sermons or giving good advice to those who come. It is the capacity to provide empathic listening and interpretation of what is heard. It is not sitting in judgment on those who come or the conduct which they describe. The counselor tries never to condemn or to condone but, where there are guilt feelings, to help the individual to release them, as only religion can. Finally, it is not the man-of-the-cloth version of the gum-shoe or policeman. To rush in when not invited and attempt to straighten things out usually does harm.

## ADMINISTRATION
## OF THE COUNSELING FUNCTION

The pastoral counseling function is carried on in our centrally located office building, in quarters approached without going through any other company office. I have a reception room, with a receptionist-secretary, a private office for counseling, and a lovely little gothic Chapel, adjoining both offices, which is available for private meditation and prayer.

The pastoral counseling function is on a totally voluntary basis. No one *must* come, but anyone *may* come. Those who take advantage of the opportunity do so without loss of time or expense.

Counseling is, of course, on a strictly confidential basis. No one else in the company may know who comes or why, except with the knowledge and consent of the counselee. He can, therefore, talk freely without fear of its prejudicing his job interests and be dealt with as a person. Here the individual is heard as if he were the only person in the world and his problem the only concern in the world.

In this atmosphere the employee feels accepted and understood. He feels free to ventilate negative, hostile, and destructive emotions which are making him a problem person. He gains insights into causations behind his baffling symptoms, so that he knows where to begin on his problem. He examines alternatives and their probable consequences. He either regains, or learns to employ more adequately, his religious faith.

Where does Christianity come into this? For one thing, I believe that the base of all emotional and mental illness is a wrong attitude toward self, others, and the universe. The heart of Christianity, on the other hand, is a right attitude toward self, others, and God. Through this process, set in a religious atmosphere, emotional road-blocks may be removed, right relationships may be achieved, and a spiritual healing may be effected for a spiritual malady.

Because a minister is expected to say this, I shall let the well-known psychoanalyst Karl Jung speak:

> Among all my patients in the second half of life—that is to say, over thirty-five—there has not been one whose problem in the last resort was not that of finding a religious outlook on life. It is safe to say that every one of them fell ill because he had lost that which the living religions of every age have given to their followers, and none of them has really been healed who did not regain his religious outlook.

This is the premise on which our pastoral counseling program functions, and through it the emotionally ill are being healed.

## REFERENCES

1. Menninger, William C., & Leaf, Munro. *You and psychiatry.* New York: Charles Scribner's Sons, pp. 134–135.

2. Dicks, Russell L. *Pastoral work and personal counseling.* New York: The Macmillan Company, 1949, p. vii.

3. Dicks, Russell L. The chaplain's part in healing the sick. *The Pastor*, January 1948.

4. Bacon, Seldon D. Alcoholism and industry. *The Civitan*, March 1951, p. 4.

5. Fuehr, Irma. Alcoholism in industry. *The Advertiser's Digest*, February 1953, p. 8.

6. Dunbar, Flanders. *Mind and body: Psychosomatic medicine.* New York: Random House, pp. 96–111.

7. Holmes, Arnold W. *The family problems handbook.* New York: Frederick Fell, p. 98.

8. *Personnel Executive's Newsletter*, December 4, 1952. Help Wanted Division of Deutsch and Shea, Inc., 230 West Forty-First Street, New York 36, New York.

9. *Public Relations News*, December 29, 1952. Public Relations News, New York 21, New York.

10. Mercer, Charles. Inside a mental hospital. Winston-Salem *Journal and Sentinel*, January 30, 1954.

11. Holmes, Arnold W. *ibid.*, p. 68.

12. Holmes, Arnold W. *ibid.*, p. 141.

13. Overstreet, Bonaro W. *Understanding fear.* New York: Harper & Brothers, pp. 143–157.

# Part IV
# Mental Health Problems
# of Managers and Supervisors

# 23. MENTAL HEALTH IN MANAGERS: A CORPORATE VIEW

### Dean C. Dauw

A homosexual manager takes a bottle of sleeping pills because his roommate runs out on him. A senior executive is caught embezzling funds from an outside organization, is fired, and shoots himself. A female clerical worker hates her female boss and threatens to jump out of a window.

These problem cases are only a few examples of the situations that are daily faced by any consulting psychologist, psychiatrist, or career worker in the helping professions. One real question is: Are there more appropriate preventive or therapeutic techniques available in industrial organizations to handle them?

## RESPONSIBILITIES WITHIN ORGANIZATIONS

Various methods have been suggested. Bruce and Dutton (1) have recently summarized much of the relevant research. They concluded that the neurotic executive definitely needs to be helped by his organization, which should assume responsibility for him. "*Management obviously must recognize the neurotic executive before he can do irreparable damage.* Since the executive probably will have much to offer as a result of his experience on the job, it is only natural that management should try

Dr. Dauw is President of Human Resource Developers, Inc. His Ph.D. in psychology is from the University of Minnesota. He is Chairman of the Industrial Psychologists Association in Chicago.

to place him elsewhere in the organization rather than dismiss him. Assigning him to a staff position where he would advise more than direct the activities of others seems to be a likely alternative. Altering the job assignments to fit the neurotic executive's qualifications would appear to be easier in some cases than changing the individual" (1). Bruce and Dutton argue that companies need to pay at least as much attention to the executive's psychological well-being as to his physical health. Additional evidence for this point of view is furnished by Trice and Belasco (2).

Following the lead of the many authors cited by Bruce and Dutton, one could assume that future policies and situations could be improved merely by doing a better job under the current rules of the game. But the primary thesis of this article is that the previous policy which some corporations have used in dealing with their own lawyers and physicians is not necessarily the most appropriate policy for psychologists and psychiatrists in dealing with executive problem cases.

For example, a medical doctor employed by a corporation may have diagnosed a particular physical disorder, whether it be prior to hiring someone, or after he has been employed. Because of pressures within the medical profession that foster private practice fees of outsiders, among other reasons, the executive with any medical problem is often advised to see his personal physician. The situation has been similar with corporation lawyers, who may not charge a fee to a fellow employee or accept a private client from the same company. These policies may be quite valid, based on sound ethical, medical, and legal practices, but they do not necessarily serve as the best model within which a behavioral scientist can apply his profession. Before specifying exactly all the reasons why this position should be taken, consideration needs to be given to an important assumption.

## NEW FUNCTIONS

Bennis recently described how organizations of the future will function (2). He suggests that personnel and development

directors will be fulfilling six new and different functions:
1. training for change,
2. systems counseling,
3. developing new incentives,
4. socializing adults,
5. building collaborative, problem-solving teams, and
6. developing supra-organizational goals and commitments.

Personnel executives will no longer be needed merely to handle maintenance and emergency chores, but will need to actively stimulate innovation.

One of the most important roles is that of aiding the institutional influences that society possesses to nurture good citizens. We have to accept the problem of continuing socialization: training in values, attitudes, and ethics. In the past, these responsibilities have been primarily assumed by the family, school, and church. It was falsely assumed that socialization stopped when the individual reached maturity. This assumption resulted partially from the fear of socialization for adults, as if it implies a dread, yet delayed childhood disease.

To be more specific, we do not deplore socialization, but rather the conscious and responsible control of it. In essence, organizations are very powerful, if undeliberate, forces of socialization. Companies, especially large ones, do in fact teach values, inculcate ethics, create norms, determine right and wrong, and influence attitudes required for success in that environment. Managers who succeed tend to be very well socialized. Men who do not succeed, whether fired or not, may have it said: "Smith was a good worker, but he never quite fit in around here." In nonbusiness settings, such as universities, tenure may be granted to those men who most easily accept the values or norms, regardless of how openly the practice may be stated.

## CONSCIOUS SOCIALIZATION

Bennis' (3) most important point is clear.

Taking conscious responsibility for the socialization process will become imperative in tomorrow's organization, and finding men with the right technical capability will not be nearly as difficult as finding men with the right set of values and attitudes. Of course, consciously guiding this process is a trying business, alive with problems, not the least being the ethical one: Do we have the right to shape attitudes and values? It can be proved that we really do not have a choice. Can we avoid it? How bosses lead and train subordinates, how individuals are treated, what and who gets rewarded, the subtle cues transmitted and learned without seeming recognition, occur spontaneously. What we can choose are the mechanisms of socialization—how coercive we are, how much individual freedom we give, how we transmit values. What will be impermissible is a denial to recognize that we find some values more desirable and to accept responsibility for consciously and openly communicating them.

Finally, a well-recognized authority like Bennis has stated it. At last, the often unspoken viewpoint is out in the open. *Corporations do teach ethics and values and attitudes within their organizational structure by means of rewards and punishments.* The logical question is: How does this relate to the mental health of managers?

## THE INTERNAL CONSULTANT

Until top executives are able or willing to accept Bennis' fundamental assumption, they will not be able to use behavioral scientists to their best therapeutic advantage. A psychologist's effectiveness may be seriously curtailed because managers do not employ the organizations' rewards or punishments to the most effective degree in motivating subordinates with mental health problems to engage in or follow through with counseling or therapy. Historically, men who did not adapt were fired or asked to resign, a procedure that poses no difficulties for the man who is sufficiently healthy or adaptable to find and cope with a new position. The focus narrows, however, if the problem-executive is rather valuable, or not sufficiently disturbed to be fired. What then?

A company psychologist or psychiatrist may diagnose the manager's behavioral difficulty and can locate a clinic or outside therapist for the client. This procedure follows the medical or legal model, wherein the company therapist merely diagnoses and refers the man outside. This is precisely where the difficulty arises and where Bennis' assumptions need to be accepted. Any outside lawyer can draw up a will, or any physician can set a broken arm, but a neurotic cannot talk to or relate to just any therapist. Most importantly, the manager with a mental health or behavioral problem does not always have the insight and motivation to accept the referral (no matter how adroitly it is made) *precisely because* of the problem itself. He can recognize a broken arm, but he often will *not* recognize an interpersonal, behavioral problem. Thus, nothing happens. Eventually, because his behavior has not improved, as the situation worsens, the higher level manager will naturally lose his patience or tolerance and encourage the problem-executive to leave.

When the problem-executive leaves, he often begins a downward job spiral. Other personnel interviewers may recognize his difficulty. Or they may not believe the reasons he gives for leaving his previous position. It often happens, then, that the problem-executive has his initial difficulty compounded by the anxieties and depression associated with all his efforts to seek a new position.

My argument is based on experience in following up many cases of problem-executives who were unable or unwilling to accept outside referral to clinics or therapists, and thus began a downward job spiral. These problem-executives may have been more easily rehabilitated within their own company, if they had received counseling or therapy from a company-employed or company-retained psychologist, psychiatrist, or psychiatric social worker *on the premises. The fact of being on the premises is very important for both motivational and practical reasons.* Regardless of who pays the therapist's fees, whether insurance fringe benefits or other company provisions, my research shows a problem-executive will often visit a therapist on the premises, but he will not as easily walk across the street to see someone else. Admittedly, some do, but the majority of neurotic problem-executives will not do so, because of the nature of the difficulty itself.

If the problem-executive is still employed by the organization, appropriate measures can be employed to encourage him to counsel with the company's therapist. The client will know he must have his regular interviews or be fired. Thus, both practically (because of convenience) and motivationally (because of fear of being fired), the problem-executive will more readily accept either referrals or therapy.

In some cases, a company employed therapist may not be the most appropriate personality to interact with the maladjusted manager. Existence within the company does not, in and of itself, insure the best ability to establish rapport with the client. However, the company psychologist or psychiatrist may at least start the therapy. Then, he may later refer the client to an outside therapist, due to the nature of the problems encountered, his own personal desires, or other reasons. The argument here is not that a company-employed therapist alone should handle the case. Rather, it is that he needs to be present to make the appropriate referrals, using company pressures or possibility of dismissal if necessary.

## CLIENT-EMPLOYEE RELATIONSHIPS

Closely allied to the need to influence a man to accept therapy is the issue of confidentiality. This need never become a problem. A company-employed therapist can maintain his professional ethics just as easily as an outside therapist. A company doctor who finds himself in a position of conflict has only himself to blame for not establishing the ground rules adequately. On the one hand, his professional ethics require a confidential relationship with his client. On the other hand, the company (e.g., the personnel department) may pressure him for information about the client-employee. If any client expresses misgivings about the conflict, he can be assured no conflict exists. If the client still does not believe it, he may be the most appropriate person to be referred to an outside therapist. The important point is that any potential risks of ethical conflicts need to be taken as a means of initiating the rehabilitation process.

Further advantages are enjoyed by a company-employed or in-house consultant. He can often dissipate the client's anxieties more easily upon the first visit when initial determination was made that the client needed help. The client then recognizes that therapists can be warm, understanding, and accepting. In the referral process for a disturbed person who has never even seen a mental health specialist outside of a few stereotypes on TV, this recognition is a serious hurdle. Once this initial hurdle has been passed, the company therapist can decide whether to work with the client himself or refer him outside. Some clients are unable to generalize this acceptance sufficiently to be convinced that the therapist across the street is equally accepting.

These issues are also treated by Thomas Szasz in "The Psychiatrist as Double Agent" (4). He concludes that:

> The college psychiatrist doubly misrepresents himself and his role—first, by claiming that his work is like that of the non-psychiatric physician, when, in fact, he deals not with the diseases of a sick person but with the social problems of the college campus; and second, by implying that he is agent simultaneously of the student-patient whose personal confidences he respects and of the school administration whose needs for social control he fulfills. In fact, he is a double agent, serving both parties in a conflict but owing real loyalty to neither.

Szasz's view of a double agent role may be true in university mental hygiene clinics, where many psychologists have worked as interns, but double-agent dealings need not occur in industry because the therapist owes and gives primary allegiance to the patient only. Thus, if the patient does not decide to try for a job transfer, the company may still profit by gaining a well-adjusted manager.

Economically, the company may profit even more. Insurance fringe benefits that will pay for an employee's outpatient therapy by an outside psychologist or psychiatrist are becoming more prevalent. Larger corporations may find that a psychologist's salary may be much less expensive than the insurance claim costs that would have been made by outside therapists. However, this argument may well become merely academic because of the shortage of qualified mental health professionals.

## TIMELY ACTION NEEDED

In conclusion, this position is based upon Bennis' outline of how organizations actually do socialize. Secondly, it is based upon the need for organizations to accept more responsibility to aid in society's problems. Witness, for example, in the aftermath of the 1967 race riots how the larger life insurance companies pledged $2,000,000,000 in mortgage money. President Lyndon B. Johnson acknowledged this gesture as a significant step forward in social responsibility. Similarly, any company, regardless of its size or its health insurance fringe benefits, can provide professionals on the premises to aid the psychological health of the employees. By doing so, the organization will be more effectively preserving and using its good talent and, more importantly, will be rehabilitating problem-executives rather than forcing them into a downward job spiral and very possibly to an eventually permanent residence in a hospital.

As managers become more sophisticated psychologically, they may be better able to spot the problem-executive before it is too late. Regardless of how effective the preventive measures may be, the actual methods of therapeutic referral are the most crucial.

Argyris (5) has argued that the needs of the employee are basically in conflict with the needs of the organization and that this conflict is a major reason for the widespread problems of mental health in industry. However, as better research is done on all the issues at hand, Bennis' position may become more readily accepted. Then executives may become more aware that by accepting greater responsibility for aiding neurotic or other problem-executives, they will be decreasing future tax needs. The need to help these problem-people in order to improve job performance is evident (6).

## REFERENCES

1. Bruce, G. D., & Dutton, R. E. The neurotic executive. *Personnel Administration*, 1967, **30**, 25–31.

2. Trice, H. M., & Belasco, J. A. Job absenteeism and drinking behavior. *Management of Personnel Quarterly*, 1967, **6**, 7–11.

3. Bennis, W. Organizations of the future. *Personnel Administration*, 1967, **30**, 6–19.

4. Szasz, T. S. Psychiatrist as double agent. *Trans-Action*, 1967, **4**, 16–25.

5. Argyris, C. *Understanding organizational behavior*. Homewood, Illinois: Dorsey, 1960.

6. Dickson, W. I., & Roethlisberger, F. J. *Counseling in an organization*. Boston: Harvard University Press, 1966.

# 24. THE EXECUTIVE NEUROSIS

**Robert N. McMurry**

Let me start with a little story—fictional as to characters, but based on a cross section of real experience:

On the way home from Frank Wright's funeral, two of his superiors in the company were discussing his case.

One shook his head. "Frank's sudden death is an awful loss to the company," he said. "We've never had such a human dynamo—such energy and initiative. And he never let up, had no regard for hours. In fact, I'm afraid that's what killed him. The doctor told him to slow down after that second coronary, but two weeks later Frank was going full speed again. What a worker! Just think, only 12 years ago he started as a route salesman; in 5 years he was sales manager. And he was only 43 when we made him vice-president in charge of sales last year. I don't know how we're going to replace him."

"I don't want to speak ill of the dead," said the other man. "Frank was a terrific worker—tireless, conscientious, and unsparing of himself. I agree with you; he probably killed himself by overwork. But I'm not sure Frank was quite the paragon you think. In fact, we haven't anyone to take his place because he never developed a successor.

"You'll remember, from the day he came with us Frank was 'on the make.' He knew what he wanted, where he was going. He was willing to work to reach his goals, but he wasn't beyond being ruthless either. Look what he did to old Pete Williams. Pete had many limitations. But he was loyal to his subordinates and had done everything he could to bring Frank up in the organization. But Frank had no scruples about taking Pete's job from him."

The first man had listened thoughtfully. "You may be right," he said. "And now that you speak of it, I often suspected that Frank feared capable subordinates. They might do to him what he'd done to old Pete. He did surround himself with 'yes' men."

"And I'm not so sure Frank's judgment was always too good," the second said. "He's the one who was positive that we didn't need to make extensive model changes in our '52 line. And what happened? Our competition gained a lead that's going to be the devil to fight. Worst of all, Frank wasn't willing to take responsibility for mistakes. Remember how be blew up and tried to blame others when we began reviewing our failure to change models? Sure, Frank made many valuable contributions to the company, and we'll miss him. But he overreached. You know, several of the directors were worried. They thought that either he'd have to be demoted or be told to start looking for another job. Getting promoted from sales manager to vice-president in charge of sales stepped him up over his head. Maybe that feverish activity leading to his death was an effort to keep his head above water."

"Maybe," the first man nodded. Then he added, "Of course, if you look at it that way, our management is largely responsible for his death. We were so dazzled by his personal salesmanship that we failed to recognize his limitations, so we promoted him to a job that was too much for him."

Doesn't that have a familiar ring? Indeed, Frank typifies a characteristic figure in American business—the man who literally drives himself to death, who so lives his job that he gives it precedence over all other interests, even his family. Seeing little of his children and making a "business widow" of his wife, he has no time for community, civic, and church activities. These "human dynamos," as Frank's bosses called him, are self-indentured slaves to their careers.

Superficially, such men appear to be ideal employees. They have no distractions from their concentration on work. They are extremely ambitious and unusually competitive. They are frequently the best producers, especially from the standpoint of quantity. Their single-minded devotion to the job tends to attract the attention of management. (In fact, such individuals usually are careful to see that they do attract attention.) They are the contest winners, the quota breakers, the contributors to suggestion plans. They are the ones to whom hours mean nothing and who are willing to travel and spend nights and week-ends on the job. Often, too, they are intelligent, well qualified technically, and excellent personal salesmen. They can make brilliant analyses; they can compile complete, comprehensive, and carefully reasoned reports.

In consequence, they are earmarked early as "comers" and rise rapidly in the organization. Management quickly spots them as potential material for top jobs in the company.

Many men showing these qualifications *do* have genuine potential, of course. But some have basic limitations for *top management* responsibilities which their brilliance, competence, energy, and obvious devotion to the job tend to obscure. For instance, they are frequently, despite their seeming dynamism and self-confidence, persons with inner feelings of insecurity and frustration who have a strong need to deny these characteristics and often possess a surprising capacity for hatred, rivalry, and resentment. These aggressive characteristics stimulate them to great activity. Moreover, when they are promoted to positions which are too demanding, the threat of their deficiencies being exposed creates pressures which further accentuate their limitations and weaken their self-control. As a result, such men attempt to get out of the morass in the only way they know—by working harder. They become tense and anxiety-ridden, with occasional temper flare-ups when the pressure becomes unbearable. They are driven more and more to overwork in an attempt to "work off" their hostilities, compensate for their shortcomings, and conceal their inadequacies.

This spiral of anxiety-hostility-activity moves at a constantly accelerating rate until a point of tension is reached at which something must give. In Frank Wright's case it was his heart. In other instances the result is a nervous breakdown, excessive drinking, or "indulgence" vices of one kind or another. The unfortunates suffer from what may best be termed "executive neurosis." To paraphrase Thoreau, they lead lives of tumultuous desperation.

Quite aside from the unhappiness which executive neurosis causes the sufferer himself, this form of emotional maladjustment is a major problem to business and industry for two reasons:

1. Because of their obsessive devotion to their jobs, neurotic executives tend very quickly to work themselves into the top levels of business management. Because their hostile, destructive tendencies are frequently obscured by their technical competence and drive, their limitations are not usually recognized by management until *after* they have been placed in highly responsible positions. Once this has happened, it is often difficult to remove them.

2. Because the future of business and industry in America depends, in the final analysis, upon the quality of top management, it is imperative that those chosen be qualified for these undeniably difficult assignments. Although a neurotic may possess superior intelligence, technical knowledge, conscientiousness, and a willingness to work hard, he is likely to be deficient in some other equally important qualification such as:

   a.  exercise of sound judgment under pressure,
   b.  acceptance of major responsibilities,
   c.  sufficient versatility to adapt to widely varying conditions and cope with highly diverse problems successfully,
   d.  ability to build and maintain a team operation,
   e.  ability to develop a subordinate to take his place when he has been promoted, left, retired, or died, and
   f.  imagination or creativeness

And no one who is seriously lacking in any of these can be really competent to administer a large, complex, and dynamic business enterprise.

Hence it is particularly important to avoid selecting managers who have neurotic tendencies—the very men who often *appear* to be most suitable for exacting positions, and for that reason actually do reach the top-management level in disproportionately large numbers. Perhaps, therefore, it will be well to approach the analysis of executive neurosis—what it is and what can be done about it—first from the more general standpoint of management needs and pressures.

## PROBLEMS IN APPRAISING EXECUTIVES

The problem of finding qualified, professional managers to administer a business is a fairly new one. Until World War I there was relatively little need for managers of this kind; most businesses were managed by their owners. However, as a result of the trend toward the separation of ownership from management during the last 25 years—to say nothing of the rapid growth in size and complexity of business organizations—the need for professional (nonowner) management talent has become significant.

The responsibilities of the manager of a modern corporation may be compared to those vested in the captain of a ship; if he is not qualified, not only he but many others also may be injured—public, stockholders, employees, and so on. The choice of men to administer the larger business and industrial enterprises, therefore, is increasingly a matter of major concern. At the same time, business management has become a highly specialized profession because of the complex and heavy demands it makes on its practitioners, and the talents required are such that relatively few persons are qualified.

### Difficulties and Limitations

The problem of finding qualified business leaders is complicated by the difficulty of ascertaining who has or who has not actually demonstrated the kind of competence required in positions of top responsibility.

At first glance, it would appear to be quite easy to distinguish successful from unsuccessful business managers. Such factors as company earnings, growth, competitive position, and so on would seem to provide adequate criteria of management competence. But it is not so simple. One limitation lies in the fact that a manager's results, whether favorable or unfavorable, may have been due in a large measure to factors over which he had little or no control. Examples of such factors are shifts in market, competitive, or economic conditions, the attitudes (cooperative or noncooperative) of associates or subordinates, and the cumulative effects of policies and practices instituted by predecessors.

A further complication in appraising managers is that there is no one with whom a top executive can exactly be compared. No two top positions are identical in their opportunities, demands, or working conditions. Each executive is faced with unique and special problems. Furthermore, in many companies the top executive "makes his own job" in the sense that it is he, and he alone (with more or less perfunctory approval of directors), who decides what steps to take and what policies to institute. Accordingly, in most cases, the executive's course of action is largely a reflection of his own personality make-up, motivations, and inherent aggressiveness; and there just is no basis for direct comparison.

Comparison is also difficult because competence or lack of it may not be demonstrated for years to come. The executive's results today may not truly reflect, and may even differ sharply from, his long-term results. Thus, current profits or deficits do not necessarily provide a reliable criterion. Profits may be made at the expense of long-term considerations (e.g., deferral of needed maintenance expenditures), or as a result of the exploitation of the institution's good name (as when a company with established goodwill is taken over by a new management which cheapens product quality). Conversely, wise expenditures may be instituted whose favorable effects will not be apparent for months or years; or it may be necessary to plow back current income into needed improvements which may result in a diminution of profits or even their elimination for a period.

Appraisal may also be difficult because, owing to purely fortuitous circumstances, an executive may never have been put to the test. Many a man, even though he is but marginally qualified, can administer an organization under favorable conditions. It is only when the executive has to lead his company, division, or department under unusual stress that his qualities are actually tried. Fortunately for many executives, the postwar era in America has been a boom period.

But the greatest difficulty in assessing the performance of men in top management arises from the fact that they never operate under static conditions. Management responsibilities are constantly varying. Markets are in an incessant state of change. Technology is subject to radical alterations, often overnight. Government regulations, policies, and practices undergo almost daily revisions. Hence, the fundamental characteristic of the executive's job is that he must continually anticipate and then coordinate and integrate factors which are constantly changing. This means that a man who is particularly well qualified to administer a business under one set of circumstances may be quite unqualified to do so under different ones. To illustrate:

In its early days the consumer cooperative movement was primarily a protest. Early organizers of cooperatives were "men with a mission." As militant prophets of a new economic philosophy, they were consecrated to protecting the small purchaser from the alleged rapacity of entrenched monopolists. Without the obsessive drive of these pioneers the cooperative movement probably would have died in infancy. The qualities useful in getting cooperatives started, however, are not necessarily the ones required to administer them effectively today. Now that cooperatives are big business, the crusading founding fathers have had to be replaced, in quite a few instances, by professional managers whose points of view are distinctly different.

Similarly, the mere growth of a firm may in itself create entirely new and different demands on management. A small merchant may be quite successful until his business begins to expand. As long as he can maintain direct personal contact with his customers, he does well. Once his business gets so big that he has to deal *through* people, however, he may be in trouble. He may have difficulty in delegating duties, or he may not be able to pick and handle men to share responsibility with him, or he may lack that breadth of outlook and capacity to plan that is essential if he is to continue as the leader in his business.

## Pressures on Executives

Having looked at some of the limitations on appraising executives, let us turn our attention to the problems of the executives themselves. What pressures and circumstances make life difficult for them to the point where only relatively few are actually well qualified for positions of top authority? Here is a partial list:

1. Many pressures grow out of the increased tempo of modern living. A half-century ago, particularly before the advent of improved communication media and the broadening of competition, most businesses were conducted at a slower pace than they are now. With the physical dispersion of plants and division of large organizations into a number of autonomous units, problems of internal communication have become much more complex. Furthermore, as a result of modern technological developments, there has been a great increase in the complexity and variety of products, which has generated new and special problems of manufacture and distribution.

2. Simultaneously, government controls and restrictions have become greater, and governmental tax, spending, and fiscal policies have introduced new difficulties into company financing.

3. A factor of negligible significance 30 years ago, but a force to be reckoned with today, is the labor union. Labor's increased economic power and influence in the government have confronted top management with many problems totally unknown a generation earlier.

4. As a corollary to the union's growing power and influence, the attitude of the individual employee toward his job and his employer has changed. He constantly wants more in compensation and benefits and is less willing to turn

in a day's work for a day's pay. These changes in the worker's attitudes are due, in part, to the increased security and bargaining power he has gained through unionization. To an even greater degree, the attitudes express old resentments rooted in the abuses of years when employers exploited their superior bargaining power at the worker's expense.

5. Modern management also takes the brunt of the public's shift in attitude toward business. In the nineteenth century, employers were regarded as benefactors who *created* jobs. Since the depression, when this confidence was destroyed, big business has been suspect. This too, as reflected in government regulations and controls, adds to the difficulties of management.

6. Finally, the troubled international scene, with its threat of an all-out war, its shortages, its regimentation, and its manifold dislocations of normal routines, breeds uncertainties which make planning more difficult.

In brief, the major and inescapable characteristic of the top executive's role is its excruciating demands in terms of time and continuous mental and physical pressure. The top executive can never escape final responsibility. Regardless of the qualifications of his subordinates and his success in delegating operating duties, it is *he* who must face the music in case of trouble.

Obviously, the major executive cannot do everything himself or even supervise everything personally. He is always confronted with having to accomplish his objectives by working *through people*. (And the greater the number of people, the greater the number and variety of problems which can arise.) He must be able to put together and keep together an organization to do most of the work for him.

In theory or on paper it is easy to recruit, train, and lead an organization which is competent, loyal, and productive. In practice it is next to impossible because of several peculiarities of human nature. For one thing, most people regard work as unnatural, at least under the conditions of regimentation and control inherent in a business organization.

For these reasons an executive can hardly expect to create an organization, especially at the lower levels, composed of persons voluntarily exerting themselves to contribute to the firms's total welfare. The attitude of many of his employees always will be, "I only work here."

This does not mean that all employees will be antimanagement or necessarily a drag on the operation as a whole. They will simply be disinterested—neither outstandingly negative nor, on the other hand, boiling with constructive ideas. (This explains the popularity of special incentive systems and rewards designed to stimulate more than nominal productivity from the average work group. Most of them, however, are actually of only transient value, as the major effort of the employees is soon directed toward beating the system.) The point is that the executive himself must continually stimulate his personnel to creativity and activity. He cannot rely on devices to do that for him.

Indeed, managers must cope not only with disinterestedness but also, especially as the organization grows, with three disintegrative tendencies among company employees:

*Segmentation.* As the company expands, each of its principal functions—sales, production, accounting, finance, engineering, research, personnel—tends to grow into a suborganization in and of itself. Each of these "empires" gradually becomes convinced that *it* makes the major contribution to the company's success and sets out to convince top management. At the same time it strives to hide from management anything which might cause its worth to be questioned. Group traditions and intradepartmental loyalties intensify these tendencies.

*Bureaucracy.* As an organization grows and ages, it becomes primarily concerned with defending itself against outside influences. A rigid and self-perpetuating bureaucracy is likely to develop.

*Stratification.* The top executive is also forced to deal through a highly stratified middle-management group. The more levels of middle management between him and the sales, clerical, and production workers, the harder his communication problem becomes. Each level has its own characteristic social structure, traditions, and group loyalties. Rivalries develop between those at one level and the level above it. More particularly, they develop within a given level because each of the incumbents is a rival of all the others for promotion to the next level. As individuals progress upward in the hierarchy, competition becomes increasingly acute.

Consequently, in a manner parallel to the competition between the "empires" for top-management recognition and approbation, each individual at each level of middle management likewise devotes a substantial part of his time and effort to impressing *his* superiors. He does this by adapting to his superior's prejudices and predilections; by emphasizing constantly his own value; and by preventing his superior from learning anything prejudicial to *his* standing. One of the safest ways a member of middle management can insure his favorable consideration for promotion is to avoid responsibility wherever possible. If trouble occurs, he personally cannot be charged with anything prejudicial. Unless circumstances prevent it, this is a common practice among men of middle management.

*Isolation from workers.*    The most serious problem of relationship confronting top management is with the rank-and-file employees—the men and women who constitute the broad base of the company pyramid. It is they who, in the final analysis, turn out the production. The state of their morale not only determines how much they will produce but colors their relations with their superiors, particularly middle and top management. Here top management is usually faced with acute isolation.

Although in theory the chain of command from top to bottom of the organization provides top management with a two-way channel of communication, in practice this is *not* true. To begin with, the several factors which separate the top executive from his rank-and-file workers are too numerous and too great. There is physical distance; the plants, offices, and sales territories may be widely dispersed. Even if this is not the case, the top executive rarely has sufficient time to get to know his people personally. In addition, marked and serious barriers to communication also usually arise out of status as well as educational, economic, and even political and ideological differences.

Furthermore, rank-and-file employees see little opportunity for advancement. As compared to those at management levels, they also have less economic security, less recognition, and less voice in determining the conditions under which they have to work (including sick leave, paid vacations, retirement plans, benefit programs, and so on). In consequence, a sharp cleavage often develops between top and middle management, on one side, and the lower levels of workers, on the other. It is only natural that the unions' influence over rank-and-file employees should have grown tremendously in the past several decades.

To sum up, the top executive, having to accomplish his ends *by working through people*, must do so with a minimum of communication and despite frequent lack of understanding, trust, or loyalty. He works in an atmosphere where many subordinates, through self-interest or hostility, withhold from him or distort the information which he must have in order to administer the business. To make matters worse, the professional manager is himself subject to considerable pressure from above. Since he is not the owner, he is responsible to his board of directors and, in a general sense, to the stockholders.

These pressures and their attendant frustrations have a tremendous effect on him—whether he is neurotic *or* well adjusted. Just what that effect will be varies with the nature of the pressures, with the executive's own motivations and makeup, and with the amount of support he receives from various sources. But it is no wonder that if the individual *does* have neurotic tendencies, he sooner or later shows inability to cope with the responsibilities of a major management position—i.e., *inability to make the decisions demanded of him.* Either he has difficulty in reaching a decision at all (he procrastinates or makes use of some other flight mechanism); or his decisions are hasty, superficial, overinfluenced by his anxieties, or colored by his hostilities. In short, he becomes prone to errors in judgment.

## CAUSES OF EXECUTIVE NEUROSIS

Why are certain individuals able to handle executive responsibilities successfully while others, seemingly of equal endowment, show the symptoms of executive neurosis? Are there indices which will be helpful in predicting executive success or failure? A study of a substantial number of cases suggests that there are.

The differences between executives who are qualified for top jobs and those who are not lie primarily in two general areas:

1. For one thing, the individual's *constitution* plays an important part. Some persons, as a result of inheritance, not only have sturdier bodies but are also better integrated psychologically. They can endure mental as well as physical stress better than others who are less well endowed.

   Another constitutional factor is the individual's physiological energy level. This is also probably related to health, although here no empirical evidence is available. The fact remains, however, that some persons appear to be inherently more dynamic, energetic, and creative than others. For instance, many successful executives are hypomanic; that is, their energy level is very high but not excessively so. The hypomanic temperament is characterized by marked activity, self-confidence, optimism, and drive. While such a temperament is certainly not the *sine qua non* for executive success, it is found in successful executives with sufficient frequency to suggest that it is particularly advantageous.

   to stand up under pressures is the extent of their *emotional maturity*. The development of this quality is a slow and painful process, and it begins very early in childhood.

   Nearly every parent is familiar with the manifestations of a child's emotional immaturity. All young children tend to be:

a. *passive*, in the sense that everything is done for them;
b. *dependent*, as a result of their manifest helplessness;
c. *demanding*, because their needs are powerful;
d. *prone to disregard reality*, because of their lack of experience with it; and
e. largely *lacking in self-control*.

The young child is also quite *selfish* and is the complete *hedonist*—dedicated to the enjoyment of maximum pleasure and avoidance of pain.

The extent to which the individual outgrows these traits is determined largely by his early home environment. In many cases, to be sure, the subsequent environment during adolescence and early manhood or womanhood may play a crucial role—in contributing either to the *outgrowing* of infantile traits or to the *acquisition* of new neurotic tendencies—but the typical case is where the decisive influences occur during childhood.

Of the two general categories, that of emotional maturity is the more significant for our purposes, not only because it deals with facts which are better established clinically, but also because it bears on behavior patterns which are more likely to yield to remedial or preventive action.

## Adapting to the Environment

Maturation from infancy to childhood is essentially the process in which the child learns to control his primitive, infantile, and unsocial drives and to adapt himself to society and reality.

The success which the child or youth has in this learning process takes place as a result of his experience with *the immediate and painful consequences of an unsocial or otherwise undesirable act*. The more immediate and painful the consequences, the greater their impact on the individual; correspondingly, the greater their effect in teaching him to control his primitive, infantile drives. For example, the infant sees the pretty candle flame. He reaches for it and grasps the flames. The next time that he is tempted to reach for a candle flame, the memory of the first painful experience has an inhibitory effect.

As he grows older, he is admonished not to behave in certain ways—for example, not to steal cookies from the jar. If, in spite of this, he persists and is caught, he is punished. The memory of this punishment and the threat of its repetition serve to inhibit his impulse to repeat the act.

In the social sphere, his experiences are educational in much the same manner. If he grabs another child's toy, his finger may get bitten. If he carelessly leaves his new bicycle out overnight, it may be stolen. The painful consequences of such unsocial or unrealistic actions leave a lasting impression.

To be sure, love is necessary to sustain the child in his conflicts with reality and to support him while he is learning to adapt himself to it. But it can do little directly to domesticate his infantile drives; only in rare instances is a child–parent identification strong enough to curb these impulses, and it may actually do more harm than good if it goes to the extreme of protecting him from all their consequences. Most of the experiences which bring about these changes in the child's response patterns are painful. If they were not, they would not be effective—a circumstance which gives rise to the expression "the school of hard knocks." Although the child does not enjoy them, they are necessary if he is to mature into a self-reliant and well-adjusted adult.

In no person is domestication of the primitive infantile drives ever complete. Furthermore, progress made is always subject to a tendency to regress when subjected to pressure. Even when the adult is reasonably self-confident, continued rebuffs and frustrations may lead him to abandon a grown-up approach to his problems.

## Learning to Control the Environment

The extent of an individual's emotional maturity depends on another aspect of his early experience and training—the development of positive talents and qualities that will enable him to cope with and control his environment. The most important of these qualities are:

1. exercise of initiative,

2.  development of self-reliance,
3.  ability to give as well as get,
4.  ability to get along with others,
5.  development of self-discipline, and
6.  capacity for realistic long-range thinking.

Initiative and self-reliance are especially sensitive to early environmental influences. The first activities of the child are directed toward getting what *he* wants. If he is helped by his parents and others to learn to cope successfully with his environment, he develops self-confidence and self-reliance. He feels secure and capable. If, on the other hand, he is subjected to autocratic and arbitrary authority and is constantly frustrated, he is likely to abandon his efforts to master his environment and to get what he wants on his own. In that case, he will become prone to give up easily when confronted with resistance. As a rule, he will find it easier once again to become passive and dependent—as he was when an infant—and to gain his ends by pleasing or exploiting the authority figures to which he is subject. He becomes the "good child," docile and submissive, and later, as an adult, the "good soldier" who always does as he is told. Such persons make good subordinates but are rarely successful as administrators.

The child is also helped to overcome his passive, dependent tendencies by being given responsibilities. For example, if the boy wants a new bicycle, he can in many cases wheedle it from his parents. It is much better, however, if they indicate that it is up to him to earn it, either all or in part—perhaps by delivering groceries for the neighborhood store. He thus learns to do things which are unpleasant in order to reach his long-term goal. He must learn to get along with people, both the other workers in the store and the customers. As he inevitably passes candy counters, he must learn self-discipline because every 10 cents spent for candy is one less dime toward the bicycle. Also, since a bicycle is not earned as a result of hauling one load of groceries, the boy learns perseverance. Even more important, however, he forms the habit of getting what he wants by his own efforts rather than by depending on others to get it for him. In the same way, it will be necessary for him to learn to make his own decisions and to stand by them even though, in some instances, the consequences will be unpleasant.

## Facades for Immaturity

Unfortunately, in many cases the child is not encouraged to think realistically and to accept responsibility. The results soon begin to show up. As he grows older, his contacts with his environment create social needs for: (1) recognition, status, and prestige; (2) power and authority; and (3) money with which to indulge himself. In order to satisfy these needs and to conceal from himself and others his basic infantilism, he may early learn to become quite adept at justifying his shortcomings. He becomes expert at finding reasons to explain and rationalize the gratification of his infantile needs. For example:

> One young man had changed jobs three times in nine months, all within the hotel field where he had set out to become a trainee. Asked why, he had ready answers. In the first job the manager demanded that he work nights; he could not sleep well during the day, and to preserve his health he quit. He left the second position because the caliber of the hotel's clientele was questionable. The manager of the third hotel was over-demanding and asked him to work overtime occasionally.
> These explanations were all superficially plausible, but analysis of the young man's record indicated that he had been badly overprotected and had never persevered in any activity which required effort or diligence. The reasons which he gave for leaving his three positions were "good" ones but not the real ones.

If the individual is intelligent, attractive, and well-endowed physically, his way is made easier. Many infantile personalities learn early in life to be expert at exploiting others. Some cultivate affability and charm. Others learn to ingratiate themselves more directly by "catching the check" or by gifts. Still others discover the value of being models of decorum: They do not smoke, drink, or use vulgar language, and are "good" in all the superficial aspects of behavior. Others find a useful screen in religion.

These manifestations are actually a facade designed to conceal selfishness, dependence, irresponsibility, and an unrealistic outlook on life. The excuses the individual makes for his shortcomings seem designed to impress others—his family, his friends, and his employer. But this is only their secondary purpose. Their primary purpose is to conceal the truth about the individual from himself. They make it possible, in other words, for him to avoid facing the painful reality that he is not self-reliant, unselfish, and capable, as he likes to believe he is, but rather the opposite.

The end-product is an individual who may be brilliant intellectually, highly educated, experienced, outstanding in appearance and manner, superficially charming and likable, and often extremely ambitious, but who nevertheless is still essentially selfish, dependent, undisciplined, and an irresponsible child.

It is significant that in their relations to their superiors such men like to be subordinate to a man who is "strong, sound, and orthodox," because he will tell them precisely what to do. This usually relieves them of responsibility for decision-making and for initiating anything new that might necessitate readjustments or carry with it the danger of revealing their weaknesses. In their leader's "strength" they find a strong "father figure" whom they may resent but on whom they can rely. If he is a member of the "in" group, that fact gives them an added feeling of security; and if the superior has notable prestige and status, some of his glory will reflect onto them.

In their relations with others, however, persons of this type often exhibit quite a different kind of behavior. They may be hostile and aggressive. Particularly with their own subordinates, they tend to be demanding, arbitrary, and inconsiderate; and their conception of management is strictly authoritarian, command-giving. They find it easy to make scapegoats of their subordinates.

Status and all of the trappings, symbols, and insignia of

rank and authority are of paramount importance to this inherently passive, dependent, resentful type of executive. These symbols satisfy his insatiable thirst for recognition and prestige, proving that he is not really passive, dependent and weak. They are also very helpful in maintaining his authority over subordinates, for they are in effect crutches to compensate for his inherent deficiencies as a natural leader.

Passive, dependent executives are also invariably conformists. By conforming to the standards of the "in" group, they insure the support and protection of its members, both above and below them in the hierarchy. Furthermore, the new, the different, or the unorthodox is potentially dangerous. Hence, they cling desperately to the *status quo*.

Top-management positions appeal especially to men of this temperament. That is the danger. Since they are not realistic, they give little thought to the demands of the position but think only of the glamor and what *they* will get. Because they have so many of the qualities which, superficially considered, are required for the job, and because neither the individual nor management is aware of their inherent weaknesses, they are likely to be unwisely promoted. It is this type that is a grade-A candidate for executive neurosis. (By contrast, the *obviously* immature, who do not make good employees at any level, cause little trouble in business because their limitations quickly manifest themselves and they soon quit or are fired. They have not been able to develop the facades, in other words, that enable them to go up very far in the company.)

## Development of Emotional Maturity

It may be helpful to compare the candidate for executive neurosis to the man who *does* have the capacity for mature, responsible administration of a corporation. What points of difference in his training and experience make him a better bet for top management?

In the first place, this particular combination of traits is usually the product of a good constitution and sound habits formed in an environment where the child was neither excessively protected nor brutally mistreated, yet where he was constantly presented with new challenges. (The antithesis of this is a relatively stable, protected environment which requires the development of little facility in adapting to changing circumstances or modifying the environment.) The child was encouraged early to accept responsibility, to make his own decisions, and to begin actively to shape and influence his surroundings. He received the love and support necessary to sustain him during the period in which he was developing, and he grew up in a "climate of confidence" where his parents and others made it clear that they felt he could accomplish whatever he set out to do and did not give him tasks which exceeded his ability to accomplish. Hence, he did not bear, to an unusual degree, the experience of failure and defeat.

It is not surprising that many of the nation's outstanding leaders in business have "come up the hard way" and from homes in which affection and emotional support were provided. Take, for example, the environment in which Abraham Lincoln was raised, where his mother provided the support and encouragement during his formative years that enabled him to gain the strength that was useful to him in later life.

Given such an early environment, not everyone subsequently develops into a qualified administrator. Nevertheless, if it can be clearly determined that the individual early formed the habit of meeting the challenges with which he was faced, rather than taking flight from them, then it is reasonably safe to assume that he has formed the habit of coping with his environment in a positive, realistic manner. He is quite likely to be an individual who has learned to take an active, dynamic role in gaining his ends and who can do so, furthermore, with a minimum amount of anxiety. His aggressions will be found to have been sublimated in overcoming the obstacles which were placed in his path. The end-result, in most instances, is an effective, well-adjusted adult who can handle responsibility, make decisions, and generally play a dynamic leadership role.

## RECOGNIZING EXECUTIVE NEUROSIS

Some cases of executive neurosis are, of course, practically unavoidable. The limitations of human nature and accidents of circumstance may combine to conceal recognition of the trouble from management until it is too late. Most cases, however, can be avoided—and often without serious embarrassment to management or the executive.

In the remainder of this article I want to discuss the problems of management action from two standpoints: (1) recognizing executive neurosis before the sufferer reaches the breaking point and (2) taking appropriate steps once it is recognized.

### Detecting Neurotic Executives at the Subclinical Stage

A large proportion of the cases of executive neurosis which occur are the result of *improper placement*. A boy has been given a man's job. This has come about because neither he nor his management recognized that he was still a boy, actually only a child.

What are the marks by means of which emotional maturity or lack of it in a candidate for an executive position can be detected? As a rule, the key to the determination of an individual's emotional adjustment lies in a careful review of his record to date. Granted that a candidate for an executive position has the requisite intelligence, education, experience, skills, energy, and health, what special qualifications *must* he have if he is to be reasonably free from emotional immaturity? In general, he must at least have demonstrated on previous assignments (1) ability to accept heavy responsibility without undue anxiety, (2) capacity to make sound judgments under pressure without panic or undue aggressiveness, and (3) an active, creative, dynamic orientation toward his environment (that is, must not merely have passively adapted to it, but have shaped and molded it to meet *his* needs). Many other qualities—for example, ability to get along with others—are useful, but it is the above three that are the indispensable requisites of executive success.

Yet today nearly all promotions to top-management positions are based on such obvious factors as the amount and type of the individual's education and technical training, the level of his intelligence, and the length and character of his experience. To be sure, these are valuable factors to investigate because, if an individual is deficient in any of them, he obviously cannot handle executive responsibilities. On the other hand, these are, so to speak, only *screening* criteria. They do not customarily provide sufficient information relative to the qualities that make or break a top executive.

The difficulty is that accurate information about the qualities that do count is hard to get. Their nature is such that the individual cannot appraise *himself* accurately; that is, he cannot recognize the extent to which his overweight, for instance, or his excessive smoking or drinking, is a reaction to his basic insecurities. Furthermore, practically no one else has sufficient insight or objectivity to judge accurately the extent to which he has these qualities.

It is imperative, therefore, to scrutinize carefully the various methods that might be used to appraise the suitability of candidates for top-management positions:

1. As a minimum procedure, it is recommended that present methods be supplemented by the use of the "patterned interview" (in all cases) and the "patterned merit review" (in cases where the candidate is already in the organization) (1, 2).

2. Where the candidate is over 35, whether he is being brought in from the outside or upgraded from within, it is also desirable that a measure be obtained of his biological intelligence, using a test such as that developed by Ward C. Halstead of the University of Chicago (3, 4). This is designed to detect physiological changes that may have affected the structure of the brain. A condition which

contributes to the development of executive neurosis is physiological deterioration of the prefrontal lobes of the brain and, to a lesser extent, of the entire cerebral cortex. This condition is usually extremely gradual in its onset and subtle in its symptomatology. It may be the result of trauma, of infection, or particularly of age (i.e., physiological age, which bears no necessary relation to chronological age; owing to differences in constitutional factors, some persons begin to deteriorate in their late 30's while others have full use of their intellectual powers into their 90's). The more common causes of prefrontal lobe and cortical deterioration are

a.   high blood pressure,
b.   arteriosclerosis,
c.   diabetes,
d.   partial asphyxiation or drowning,
e.   blows on the head as in boxing, automobile accidents, or falls, and
f.   the histological changes whch  accompany senility (5).

Regardless of the cause of damage, a reduction in powers of learning, memory, judgment, and self-control results. Where deterioration has taken place, the individual exhibits a diminished capacity to assimilate new and abstract ideas into existing ideation systems. He does not forget what he has already learned, but he has great difficulty in assimilating new ideas and acquiring a familiarity with new techniques and procedures. When, as often happens, the subject is vaguely aware of the difficulty, any pre-existing tendencies that he may have toward executive neurosis are accentuated as a result of his worry and feelings of insecurity.

In addition, there appears an increased rigidity in habits of thinking, a tendency to become reactionary and to live to an increasing extent in the past. The individual has a desperate need to cling to the *status quo ante*. A person so affected also tends to regress to many of the traits characteristic of the child—selfishness, dependence, incapacity to accept responsibility, exhibitionism. He frequently has a lower threshold of emotional discharge. He is apt to make snap judgments without care for ultimate consequences.

A man may have been brilliant and capable of sound judgments prior to the onset of this condition. Since deterioration is usually very gradual, it is not ordinarily recognized until it is far advanced. The degree of deterioration may be quite extensive before the condition is discovered. Even then, because of the man's previous record of achievement and because much that was learned in the past is not lost (so that he carries on reasonably well), his superiors and associates may find it hard to accept the fact that he is no longer the man that he once was.

The fact that the deterioration of the prefrontal lobes and cortex is irreversible, that once the damage has been done it cannot be repaired, makes it especially important to attempt to detect and measure cerebral impairments of this character at the subclinical stage—before they become visible and acute. The Halstead tests provide an indication of the onset of this condition and of the extent of the damage, even before a neurological examination will reveal it. Retests will indicate the *rate* of deterioration.

3.  Insights provided by the patterned interview, the patterned merit review, and the Halstead tests are helpful not only in the selection of men for promotion to top management but also in appraising men who are already in policy-making positions. They are useful, for example, where a bank is about to underwrite an issue of securities or make a substantial loan to some firm. Many bank loans have doubtless "gone sour" because the bankers were not able properly to assess the personality qualifications of the executives running the debtor business.

## Alertness to Overt Symptoms

But what if executive neurosis is not detected at the subclinical stage? Fortunately, nearly all sufferers from executive neurosis exhibit clear symptoms of the condition long before the final breaking point. Hence, if management is aware of the symptoms and their significance, appropriate steps often can be taken before the breaking point is reached. The signs that management should be alert to might be summarized as follows:

1.  To begin with, the sufferer is rarely "on top of his job." Instead, the job is master. Evidences of this can be seen in such symptoms as inability to relax and to be at ease in work. Sometimes the executive has sudden, violent outbreaks of temper. Such a man is constantly under tension; he worries frequently; his behavior is marked by a nagging undertone of anxiety.

    Major decisions are hard to make. In fact, he may find it impossible to accept top-level responsibility entirely on his own. Because the position may demand that he make decisions despite his inability to do so, many decisions are made in an atmosphere of doubt, insecurity, and anxiety. Unfortunately, such judgments are also more than ordinarily prone to error. A person who is himself alternately in a rage or in a partial state of panic is not able to think soundly and objectively.

    His very weakness becomes in itself a source of resentment toward more able superiors and associates. He may constantly seek scapegoats on whom to vent his rage. He may be prone to wishful thinking without adequate regard for the long-term consequences of his decisions. Or he may desperately seek temporary expedients. For example, let us say that at a critical period in the company's activities an executive is faced with exorbitant union demands, reinforced by the threat of a strike. The easy solution is to appease the union by acceding, with the hope that a permanently grateful union will reciprocate by making no more excessive demands. The neurotic executive's need to escape a difficult decision prevents him from recognizing that such appeasement in labor relations rarely pays and usually only establishes a precedent for new demands.

2.  Such an executive also frequently lacks objectivity in judging both associates and subordinates. He is chronically

fearful that his limitations will become apparent to his superiors. Therefore, it is of paramount importance to him to conceal anything which may raise questions concerning his competence. He must not be placed in an unfavorable light in comparison with his associates and particularly with his subordinates. His primary unconscious motivation (rarely does he have real insight into his limitations) is to surround himself with persons less competent than he, so that he will not be outshone. Subordinates who are strong, aggressive, and generally competent are sensed as threats to his security and status. He either endeavors to rid himself of their presence as subordinates—by separation, transfer, or demotion—or does his best to keep from his superiors their splendid qualifications.

3. Executives so handicapped also find it difficult to cooperate with their peers and with others in the organization. This characteristic manifests itself in several ways. Often the individual is an overt prima donna. He may openly admit that his own interests take precedence over those of the others. As a rule, however, the rationalization is more subtle. The individual gives lip service to the principle of cooperation, but in carrying out his daily duties he thinks primarily of himself and his own interests. Not infrequently he is overtly sadistic. Unconsciously he hates people. His activities, therefore, tend to be disruptive rather then integrative.

4. The most obvious manifestation of executive neurosis is probably the inability to accept personal responsibility for decisions. Since the afflicted executive's decisions are made initially in an atmosphere of anxiety charged with hostility, their consequences are a continuing source of concern to him. If, because they were poorly conceived or because of conditions beyond his control the results are unfortunate, his existing anxieties are grossly accentuated. The man then has only one thought: He must evade responsibility for the catastrophe, whether it be a major or minor one. He seeks every pretext, no matter how flimsy, to

project the responsibility on other persons or circumstances. If, as is frequently the case, he is of superior intelligence and broadly experienced, he can make such explanations appear quite plausible.

This is particularly true where the difficulty is not wholly his responsibility but can be shared by several. By slanting his explanations, shifting his emphasis, and in other ways coloring the facts, an astute executive can keep himself in the clear to a surprising degree. At the same time, he can subtly attack his rivals for top-management favor.

Thus, for example, when Frank Wright (discussed in the introduction) decided not to make major design alterations in his line, he did so thinking solely of the cost of the new dies and retooling which would be required. He assumed that competitors would think as he did and act accordingly. When they did not and came out with radically new and improved designs, it left him at a serious disadvantage. But because of his own insecurities, he could not admit he had made an error in judgment, so he found it necessary to place the blame on others. He charged that his market research department had kept him improperly informed of competitive trends. He claimed that his field sales organization had not kept him advised of competitors' activities. He accused the engineering department of exaggerating the cost of designing and producing new models. While he could not wholly escape the outcome of the final decision, he carefully distributed the blame as widely as he could—even among those who might only remotely have had a share in it.

5. Other early indications of executive neurosis in an individual are the appearance of symptoms of defense mechanisms:

   a. a conviction of personal omniscience and infallibility;
   b. the development of paranoid (hypersuspicious) attitudes toward his associates and subordinates in general (they are working against him);
   c. an emotional, defensive attitude toward anyone who questions his policies or disagrees with him;

   d.  the development of hypercritical tendencies (no one
else can do anything right); and

   e.  a tendency to surround himself only with "yes men."

  In the early stages of executive neurosis the individual may
still be able to do a fairly creditable job. He may use reasonably
good judgment, even under pressure. Although he will rarely
be able to build a strong organization with good morale, he
may not be more than a marginal liability to the company.

  If, however, the responsibilities and presures of his job
increase—or perhaps are just allowed to continue—the
development of executive neurosis will lead him to the brink
of outright failure. Although the end-result of the ascendancy
of a job over its holder is a breakdown, most commonly the
individual simply quits or is fired because his performance
inescapably has become substandard. This is why some executives occupying high positions change affiliations at frequent
intervals—sometimes as often as once every year. Having
occupied top-level positions in other companies, they are usually accepted as being top-caliber executives. In addition, being
plausible, they are frequently able to explain to prospective
employers why it was not their fault that things did not work
out on preceding jobs and why it was necessary for them
to move. It also relieves their feelings to attack their previous
associates and superiors. Because it ordinarily takes a year
or more for an employer to discover the nature of a high-level
executive's neurotic limitations, the latter may remain for one
or even several years before he is encouraged to leave.

  In other, and in a sense more tragic, situations, the neurotic
executive remains on the job indefinitely. Thereupon certain
conditions may develop:

1.  Most common of these are so-called "flights." In the simplest form of flight, the individual flatly dodges the responsibilities of his position. He does not answer difficult
inquiries or takes time off from the job. He is not ill;
it is simply that when he is faced with a difficult situation
or problem, he walks off for a period of from a few hours
to a week or more, hoping that by some miracle the problem will solve itself during his absence. (Interestingly

enough, in many instances, subordinates, associates, or superiors will then handle the situation for him or it actually will solve itself spontaneously.)

2. In other instances, the individual will take flight into drinking. Drinking is essentially a neurotic escape mechanism because it rarely solves problems. Usually it creates additional ones, both on and off the job. (Actually, it is primarily a mechanism for self-destruction; the victim turns his aggressions on himself.) But even knowing this, some persons, if their anxieties become sufficiently acute, will inevitably anesthetize themselves with alcohol (6). Others overeat or become chain smokers.

3. The most common flight reaction is refuge into illness. Not conscious or willful malingering, this flight is a form of conversion neurosis comparable to the battle fatigue seen in World War II or to the hysterical blindness, paralysis, and deafness (the "shell shock") observed in World War I. Here also the sufferer has, in part, turned his aggressions on himself; they are simultaneously a device for self-punishment, a bid for sympathy, and a means of attracting attention. Victims of the battle of business usually manifest a characteristic pattern of symptoms, chiefly upsets of the gastrointestinal tract (chronic indigestion, ulcers, colitis, and so on), hypertension (high blood pressure of psychogenic origin which tends to become chronic), and various types of allergic reactions. In addition the physical stresses often lead to heart conditions.

## CORRECTIVE ACTION BY MANAGEMENT

In the case where the sufferer or potential sufferer of executive neurosis is detected before being promoted to a position of high responsibility, the problem of management action is of course relatively simple. The candidate can be passed over for promotion or harmlessly sidetracked. If, on the other hand, the case is not caught in time, management's problem may be a good deal more difficult. Often a mutually satisfactory solution can be found, however, and in any event management should not let things run their course—for the sake of the man and his family as well as of others in the organization.

## Psychiatric Help Sometimes Possible

Where the executive is already in a position over his head and is beginning to manifest symptoms of executive neurosis, it may be possible to arrange for psychiatric help. The principal problem here is that the average executive is quite reluctant to avail himself of such a service. Its very mention by his superiors, he feels, is a threat to his security and status, an evidence that he is "through" in the organization. It creates tremendous new anxieties which can be critical. It may precipitate a flight and cause him to decide to leave his position. His attitude, if verbalized, is: "The only thing for me to do is to get out before the ax falls." This illogic is comparable to the reasoning of the person who fears he has an incurable disease and, in consequence, commits suicide.

With many persons it is a severe blow to the ego to have the need of psychiatric help suggested. Nearly anyone can accept with equanimity the advice that he see a physician about an organic condition. Psychiatric help, on the other hand, suggests so many socially unacceptable and frightening connotations that the average person, particularly if he lacks sophistication in the mental hygiene field, is likely to be dreadfully frightened at the idea. Also, much resistance stems from an unconscious fear that the process of therapy will somehow become so profoundly disturbing that it will be unbearable. And, indeed, the emotional equilibrium of many neurotics, especially sufferers from executive neurosis, is so delicately balanced that any change, even of a therapeutic character, is likely to be extremely upsetting: Often the sufferer becomes the victim of still more unbearable anxieties.

For these reasons, any suggestions in this direction must be handled with extreme tact and should be advanced, wherever possible, by an authoritative figure—for instance, a physician in whom the individual has implicit confidence. At best, suggestions of this character will be difficult to accept; if improperly made, they can be devastating in their effects upon the victim's self-confidence.

A skilled medical practitioner can often encourage the individual, in the course of "talking out" his problems, to reach a decision, seemingly of his own volition, to seek psychiatric help. Where the sufferer believes that the initiative was his, much, though not all, of the anxiety associated with treatment of this character will be dissipated. And once he is in the hands of a qualified psychiatrist, the psychiatrist's skills can usually allay the anxieties enough for the patient to remain under treatment.

## Direct Management Action

In most instances, psychiatric help, because of the resistance described, will not be accepted by the neurotic executive. Fortunately, however, an informed management can do much to relieve the situation, independent of psychiatric treatment, *by altering the nature of the individual's work*. There are several ways to do this deliberately (although often it is done by management intuitively):

1.  The victim of executive neurosis can be transferred from a *line* to a *staff* position of equal or superior status, or be made a "consultant." Properly handled, this need not look like a "kicking upstairs." As a rule, the staff position eases many of the former pressures, relieving the man of the responsibility for making major decisions with their attendant risks.

    At the same time, an exalted staff position—"executive assistant to the president," for instance—allows considerable opportunity to gratify the individual's need for:
    a.  status, recognition, and prestige;
    b.  power and authority;
    c.  money; and
    d.  security.

If the staff position is of an equal or higher status than the previous office, little or no loss of "face" or earnings need take place; anxieties are not accentuated by a feeling of having been demoted.

2. Much can be done by periodic, informal counseling sessions conducted by skilled members of the company's personnel staff who are of equal status in the organization and are not line superiors of the person being counseled. This system has been markedly effective with rank-and-file employees. A notable example is the Western Electric Company at the Hawthorne works in Chicago, where "nondirective" counseling techniques have been used for a number of years. True, the procedure has not been used as much at the higher levels at Hawthorne, largely because the need for it has not been fully recognized until recently, but the same principles apply with executives as with employees of lower rank.

It frequently happens that the executive is frightened and, in spite of his efforts to deny it, insecure; that is, he is not on top of his job and fears the loss of his security and status. In such a case, he must have periodic reassurance that his situation is not too threatening, that his position is secure, that he is well regarded by his superiors, and that no one in his immediate work environment is a threat to him.

In a sense, the counselor becomes somewhat of a father to him, "holding his hand" and offering him the reassurance and support needed. (In psychiatry this is termed "suportive" therapy. No radical change is brought about in the subject's situation, but he feels better. In other words, the procedure is purely palliative.) The counselor also becomes the executive's advocate before management and may even help him with his personal problems off the job.

The second contribution of the counselor is his role as a cathartic agent. By allowing the executive to talk out his problems, he provides outlets for tensions arising from aggressions and hostilities, with a minimum anxiety because of the limited danger of reprisals; that is, everything told the counselor is confidential. By having this opportunity to harmlessly talk out his hostilities toward his superiors, associates, and subordinates, the executive comes to feel less aggressive toward them and, in consequence, not only more relaxed himself but also able to work with them more easily. Because he is less anxious, his judgment is better.

3. Where a man cannot be transferred to a less demanding type of work, sympathetic understanding on the part of his *line* superiors can also be extremely helpful.

A supporting role of this character requires exquisite tact, insight, and understanding on the part of the superior. He must be kindly, somewhat indulgent, but a strong and decisive father figure, providing needed support and counsel, recognition and praise where merited, and sympathy without moralizing or being admonitory. (Again, this is something that actually is often done intuitively by natural leaders. Therefore, some companies maintain good executive morale even though not all of those in the executive positions are particularly competent.)

## CONCLUSION

From a purely prophylactic point of view, a major responsibility of those who control the destiny of a business or industrial organization is to *prevent* the development of executive neurosis among members of their top management. They can do this by care in selecting persons for promotion and in the handling of those who are already filling such positions.

Unfortunately, critical appraisal techniques for *top-level* positions are not yet applied in many businesses. Instead, men are promoted because:

1. They have been for many years faithful assistants or "second men" to a qualified executive;
2. They were good *staff* men (but had never been tried in an administrative post and consequently had never had an opportunity either to develop management skills or demonstrate their lack of them);

3. They were highly trained technically and, because of their superior accomplishments in this field, were assumed to be equally qualified for administrative work;
4. They were "glamour boys" who had been able to "sell" themselves to their superiors;
5. They were once highly competent executives (but have since deteriorated);
6. They were good politicians or someone's "pets";
7. They inherited their positions;
8. They were recognized to be poor risks, but no one better was available.

In any group of executives who have been chosen in this manner, a large number of sufferers from executive neurosis, either actual or incipient, will probably be found.

For maximum effectiveness, the demands of each top-management position must be analyzed and evaluated in terms of:

1. Technical requirements as to skills and experience.
2. The human environment in which the incumbent must work, including:
   a. the personalities of superiors and associates;
   b. the attitudes and qualifications of subordinates.
3. The extent and character of the administrative, or decision-making, demands of the position.
4. The status level, extent of authority, and the economic opportunities of the position.

A next step is to match the qualities of the candidate or incumbent against the demands of the position. This, as already indicated, will necessitate the use of the patterned interview, the patterned merit review (for persons already in the company's employ), tests of intelligence, and the Halstead test. These examinations will be helpful in determining the individual's technical proficiencies, his cerebral integrity (freedom from evidences of brain damage), his principal motivations, the amount of drive which he possesses, and also the extent of his emotional maturity—in other words, the degree to which he is free from tendencies which may result in executive neurosis.

Rarely will the scores tally perfectly. If the match is reasonably good, the man is a promising candidate. If, on the other hand, there is little correlation between the qualifications for and the demands of the job, the man is a poor prospect. This is particularly true where a candidate shows an incipient tendency, recognizable in other forms, toward executive neurosis.

A program of evaluation of candidates for executive positions and of incumbents in them may seem involved and detailed, but its contribution should more than compensate for the time and effort involved. If properly administered, it should contribute greatly to the effectiveness of management at the top levels. It should also do much to spare individuals from the tragedy of being placed or kept in wrong positions where they experience the tortures of the damned—and all too often become chronic, pitiable victims of executive neurosis, perhaps (as did Frank Wright) even killing themselves with overwork.

# REFERENCES

1. Robert N. McMurry. *Handling personality adjustment in industry.* New York: Harper & Brothers, 1944.

2. Robert E. Shaeffer. Merit rating as a management tool. *Harvard Business Review*, 1949, **27**(6), 693.

3. W. C. Halstead. *Brain and intelligence.* Chicago: University of Chicago Press, 1947.

4. W. C. Halstead. Biological intelligence (Symposium on personality theory). *Journal of Personality*, 1951, **20**(1), 118–130.

5. W. C. Halstead, H. T. Carmichael, & P. C. Bucy. Prefrontal lobotomy: A preliminary appraisal of the behavior results. *American Journal of Psychiatry*, 1946, **102**(2), 217–228.

6. Robert N. McMurry. Can we save the man who is a victim of alcoholism? *Sales Management*, 1950, **4**(5), 41–43.

# 25. PRACTICAL GROUP PSYCHOTHERAPY AND ROLE PLAYING FOR THE INDUSTRIAL SUPERVISOR

**George A. Peters**

University of California at Los Angeles

and

**Joseph G. Phelan**

Bechtel Corporation, San Francisco

Those who are interested in the improvement of current industrial management practices are vitally concerned with the role of the first-line supervisor and how he affects employee morale, company loyalties, and productivity. This interest is a direct result of many attempts to discover how to motivate workers so that they will be eager to perform in a manner approaching their potential capacities. Many of the methods which have been developed to improve employee motivation have recognized this critical importance of the first-

---

This is the first of two articles which describe how supervisor-employee relationships may be improved. This first article introduces some of the theoretical assumptions underlying a new approach to this important problem in modern industrial management. The second article will outline the specific procedure and methods by which this new technique may be implemented.

line supervisor. In fact, one of the main stumbling blocks or limiting factors in the success of these methods has been the negative influences of many industrial supervisors. It is the effect of these negative attitudes which have prevented the successful attainment of some of the most farsighted employee-centered plans and, indeed, have sometimes produced entirely unexpected and detrimental results. These negative attitudes are an apparently unchangeable aspect of what must seem to be pathologic manifestations of the supervisor's personality. It is a fundamental problem, therefore, to determine how to change the basic negative attitudes of industrial supervisors.

There are probably many industrial supervisors who are actually in dire need of some psychotherapeutic help. With better personal adjustment, they undoubtedly would prove more efficient in their work and could establish more wholesome relationships with their subordinates. But, the costs involved in any program of intensive psychotherapy would prevent any industry from underwriting such a plan for their employees. Industry can afford to be humanitarian only so far as it directly or indirectly increases profits. Now, if there were some less expensive and less time-consuming manner of improving the character of interpersonnel relationships which exist among workers, it might herald a bold new approach to the pressing problems of the "human factor" in industry.

That the human factor is an extremely important consideration in industrial planning is attested by the following facts. There are reports indicating that comparable organizations producing the same product sometimes show differences in productivity such that one plant may have an output three times greater than another (1). Even in product development and research there is a very great premium placed upon group collaboration and cooperative work effort toward common work goals. The effectiveness of any work group is dependent upon the work habits and attitudes of the individual workers, which, in turn, seem primarily dependent upon the informal social controls which exist within the management structure.

These social controls in the informal social organization of industry are largely a product of the impingement of supervisor on the primary work unit. Thus, the nature of the interpersonal relationships which exist within an industrial concern have a very direct relationship to productivity and profits.

If some method of improving interpersonal relationships by a less costly, more practical type of psychotherapy could be developed and implemented, the results would indeed be fruitful. The very mention of psychotherapy usually brings to mind the practices of Freud and the stereotyped couch of the psychoanalyst. But this approach is not readily adaptable to the needs of industry because it involves dealing with individual patients in a private clinical setting. In recent years, however, there has been a virtual revolution in the field of psychotherapy due to the advent of "group psychotherapy" and "psychodrama." Although many of the specific techniques of this method are still being developed and evaluated, it is obvious that such group procedures now make certain industrial applications feasible. In fact, there is now an economical and specific remedy for improving the interpersonal relationships which exist in industrial concerns.

One technique which is utilized in the conduct of group psychotherapy seems particularly well-adapted to the problems involved in changing the basic attitudes of industrial supervisors. It is what might be called an Intensive Industrial Role Playing Technique. In general, it involves the creation of situations involving practical work conflicts and then allowing an individual to extemporaneously "live through" the experiences of a particular character. By playing first one role and then another, the individual gains an understanding of the feelings and reactions of all of the various personalities involved in a conflict situation. By carefully controlling the manner of group interaction and quality of emotional clashing with other participants, by the stimulus of constant evaluation of the nature of group reactions and forced adjustment to a varied and changing social reality, the individual gradually learns to operate in harmony with the needs of the group while promoting goal-directed behavior. In the process, there is constant growth of individual self-esteem, self-confidence, and general level of functioning in relation to social industrial situations.

While this procedure effectively changes attitudes as manifested in specific industrial situations, it does not significantly alter the basic personality makeup of an individual nor does it effectively generate insight into the genetics or dynamics of an individual's personal problems. In the manner in which this technique is used, it is a special method specifically oriented toward the amelioration of costly industrial problems. Only a limited amount of insight can be expected from such a short-term, intensive, and specific approach. But what it lacks in coverage and depth, it makes up in efficiency of application and low financial investment by industry.

At all times, this technique is oriented toward constructive changes in the attitudes of the participating group members. Specifically, it provides for the growth of both intellectual awareness and emotional capacity to respond to maximum advantage in a group situation. During the Intensive Industrial Role Playing Technique process, considerable attention is given to the correction of inadequate, ineffective, and unpleasantly provocative behavior. This type of behavior in a relatively intact ego is essentially a manifestation of the inappropriate aspects of certain personality defenses associated with manifest anxiety. Any reduction in the threatening nature of the conflict situation or demands of the role will reduce the anxiety and render the immediate satisfactions of the defensive system less essential to the emotional integrity of the individual. Thus, mere familiarity with a new role, and experience in handling routine problems associated with new roles, lessens the threatening qualities of such new social adaptations. This may permit recognition of certain disrupting trends and impulses and allows some voluntary selection or experimentation with new approaches that might be more in harmony with the group needs and goals. By personal role substitution and subsequent analysis of the feelings of the various personalities, an individual is given new perspective and aid in facing the realities of social interaction in an industrial situation. Sometimes, the distorted personal expectations of others become forcibly modified in such a socializing experience as personal substitution into the "shoes of the other fellow." Certainly, this tends to increase the individual's understanding of the reactions of others, serves to promote a deeper respect for the functions of others, and reveals the potential helpfulness of associates in working toward group goals.

One practical factor which may be overlooked is the selection of group participants who have approximately the same level of intellectual functioning, similar educational and cultural backgrounds, and with currently similar work experiences. Exceptions to this may be made when the current or anticipated demands of an individual's work requires the experiences of dealing with a more heterogeneous sampling of people. However, the homogeneous grouping provides for certain efficiencies in the therapeutic process.

The unique benefits of such an intensive specialized technique are somewhat offset by the special requirements for the therapist or *group leader*. This is because this technique is something different than a training lecture on effective human relations, a discussion group organized with therapeutic intent, or even a socializing experience where individuals can compare their problems with those of others. It is rather a dynamic life-like activity wherein every group member is an active participant and the group leader constantly exerts a modifying influence. The group must organize and function in relation to a group leader who must adequately understand the personality dynamics of each of the several group participants while encouraging meaningful group interaction in relation to prescribed therapeutic objectives.

The group leader must initially discover the reasons why each participant may have been prevented from using his abilities to the maximum and then, in a favorable emotional climate, provide the active manipulation which will stimulate reconstructive learning. He must be able to recognize and resolve the group resistances, hostilities, and tendencies toward social deterioration. Whether a psychologist, physician, or social worker, the skill or art of the group leader must rest upon adequate understanding of personality structure, dynamics, pathologic manifestations, treatment methods, and clinical experience. But his effectiveness in an industrial situation also requires familiarity with current industrial management practices and a knowledge of the social psychology of industry.

## SUMMARY

High productivity and good industrial relations are, to a great extent, dependent upon such factors as employee morale, motivation, attitudes, and loyalties. These are actually manifestations of the interpersonal relationships which exist in the primary work unit; in particular, the relationship between employee and supervisor. Since one of the main problems in current industrial management practices is to change or improve the negative attitudes of first-line industrial supervisors, some economical and specific technique is desired which will serve this purpose.

During the last decade, there have been rapid developments in the techniques of group psychotherapy and psychodrama. One of these techniques which seems particularly well-suited for use in industrial situations is the role-playing technique. However, this method has been employed in some industrial training programs with only spotty success. It is suggested that an *Intensive Industrial Role Playing Technique* be employed to achieve certain economies of application and to provide a specific industrially oriented type of dynamic reconstructive learning process. This new procedure places far greater responsibility upon the group leader in both the preliminary planning and the direction of the group process. His functions are broadened to include more complete *a priori* understanding of the personality dynamics, assets and limitations, and needs of each individual participant. It is believed that only with this understanding can he efficiently plan the type of group interaction necessary for constructive group experiences. To achieve a meaningful and goal-oriented group interaction, the group leader should both foster the desired mode of group interaction and resolve group resistances, deteriorative tendencies, and limiting defensive reactions. Such intensive goal-directed group experiences would then provide the desired practical psychotherapy for the industrial supervisor.

## REFERENCES

1. Brown, J. A. C. *The social psychology of industry.* Harmondsworth, Middlesex, England: Penguin Books Ltd., 1954, p. 88.

# 26. ROLE PLAYING TECHNIQUE IN INDUSTRIAL SITUATIONS

**George A. Peters**     and     **Joseph G. Phelan**

University of California          Bechtel Corporation
at Los Angeles                   San Francisco

The morale, motivation, and attitudes of individual workers are of far greater importance than such physical factors as illumination, ventilation, or rest periods in industrial productivity. There has been gradually increasing emphasis on human relations in industry (1, 2). Social scientists have found that the focal point for emergence of such basic attitudes lies in the primary work group (3,4). In particular, the breeding ground seems to be in the nature of interpersonal relationships which exist in the primary work group. Of considerable importance is the relation between each worker and his first-line supervisor. For this reason, great emphasis is now placed upon the character of employee–supervisor relationships and methods of fostering more beneficial interpersonal relationships.

Of considerable diagnostic importance in determining the healthfulness of supervisor–worker interpersonal relationships is the perspect or view the worker has of his immediate superior. His concept may be and, in fact, usually is radically

This is the second of two articles which describe how supervisor–employee relationships may be improved. The first article introduced some of the theoretical assumptions underlying a new approach to this important problem in modern industrial management. This second article outlines the specific procedure and methods by which this new technique may be implemented.

different from the impression the supervisor feels he is creating. Both the supervisor's impression and the worker's percept of the situation may be quite divorced from reality. This is because we are not dealing with objective facts but, rather, personalities interacting in an emotional climate. For illustrative purposes, Table 1 indicates in an overly simplified manner a rather hypothetical polarization of employee—supervisor relationships which might be found in a goal directed industrial situation.

It has been found that merely supplying information on proper supervisory methods or conducting special training programs on good human relations is of very limited value (5). Knowledge of what is right does not connote emotional acceptance nor the ability to put the words into action. Something bordering upon psychotherapy sometimes seems necessary to improve these aspects of personality. Indeed, the source of the method proposed in this study is in the recently developed techniques of group psychotherapy. It is an extension of the role playing technique which attempts to facilitate emphatic processes by fostering limited and temporary identifications with other personalities. That is, by playing first one role and then another in a group conflict situation, the individual is forced to place himself in a position which may not be so egocentrically demanding and thus permits greater appreciation of the needs and feelings of others. It is this understanding of the needs and feelings of others, combined with an increased ability to satisfactorily resolve the disrupting effects of defensive reactions, which is prerequisite to implementation of any factual knowledge on good supervisory practices.

## PROCEDURE

The basic group in the Intensive Industrial Role Playing Technique is composed of some nine individuals: one *group leader* or expert who is the responsible agent in planning the therapeutic process, and two alternating groups, one composed of four role-playing *participants* and one of four *observers*

**TABLE 1: Varieties of supervisor-subordinate relationships**

| Type of Relationship | General Results | Description |
|---|---|---|
| Dependent | Inefficient conformity | A supervisor may foster extremely passive, dependent, or submissive roles by his subordinates by acting in an authoritarian manner, making all the decisions, or doing all the important work himself. |
| Cooperative | Optimum efficiency | The supervisor may function as a leader who can advise, interpret, support, and is capable of understanding the problems of his subordinates. He promotes responsible action, stimulates achievement, and engenders a feeling of approval among employees. |
| Avoidance | Evasive compliance | A supervisor may fail to create a feeling of acceptance and regard for the personal worth of his subordinates. The employees react with passive resistance, feelings of resentment, and they will not wholeheartedly perform their duties. |
| Negative | Disruptive resistance | The supervisor is viewed as a threatening, disapproving, critical, or dominating person who is not to be trusted and is feared or rejected by his subordinates. Despite surface conformity and obedience there is an undercurrent of active resistance and attempts to find expressions for reactive aggression. |

(see Figure 1). The size of the group is vitally important since a participant is only capable of satisfactorily relating to a maximum of about three other personalities during a particular conflict situation. So too, the group leader must be free to follow exactly what is transpiring among the participants and a group of four approaches an optimal limit for the purposes intended.

This group would normally meet in sessions lasting about an hour. However, before the group meetings begin, all participants should receive an individual interview. While this interview is ostensibly to determine compatibility of members of various proposed groups, it also has the very important function of allowing the group leader to determine the needs, limiting pathology, and therapeutic utility of each individual. This relieves the group leader of the very great burden of attempting to diagnose each individual in the fluidity of a changing social group structure and results in the obvious economies found in the rigid structure of individual interviews. Not only does it save group time and allow for the more conventional experimental conditions of diagnosis, but it allows for the preliminary planning which is essential if costly mistakes are to be avoided and an efficient, goal-directed, therapeutic group interaction is to be maintained.

It is believed that diagnosis should be used in the sense of recognition of important psychopathological manifestations and therapeutic assets of each individual in relation to how they may limit the growth of the individual or affect the progress of group interaction. Thus, the emphatic relationships which are fundamental to successful role playing are based upon a conscious *a priori* plan-of-action related to needs of the group and determined by the manner in which the therapeutic goals may be reached with a minimum of lost time. Certainly, one of the most common causes of failure in group therapy is the attempt to lead the group without understanding of what is going on or having any clearcut plan of action for the individuals concerned. Diagnosis, in and of itself, infers appropriate therapeutic action.

The organization of an effective program utilizing the

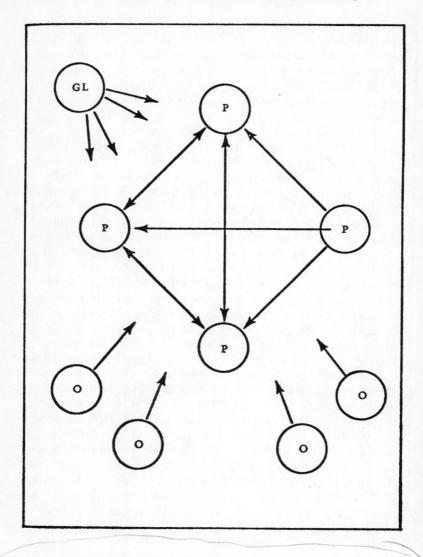

**Fig. 1.**    Structure of role playing group. P—Participant; O—Observer; GL—Group Leader.

Intensive Industrial Role Playing Technique might be as follows:

## Phase I: Planning

*Step 1: Program Orientation.*    There should be some publicity or propaganda to establish individual's expectations. This may be done by written materials which emphasize the positive benefits which will accrue to those who participate. Be careful to avoid statements which imply that this program might result in improvement of existing conditions, that it might be mandatory for some participants, or that it is directly connected with management. If at all possible, the program should be of a nature wherein individuals would be provided an opportunity to "sign up," i.e., voluntarily commit themselves. They should "expect" to learn new psychological techniques which they could employ if promoted to positions of greater responsibility. That is, there should be no implied criticism of the individual's current practices since, defensively, he may attempt to prove that what he is doing is right. This type of aroused antagonism is not the receptive expectation for new learning that is desired.

*Step 2: Individual Interview.*    The importance of clinical diagnosis of each participant as a preliminary step in planning has already been discussed. The use of psychological tests probably should be avoided; since it is time consuming, it may place some participants upon the defensive or serve to promote rumors that everyone is to be "psychoanalyzed." About one hour may be allowed for each interview, i.e., total of eight hours for a group. The interview should be a relaxed, pleasant affair with spontaneity, a free flow of thinking and feeling, and a somewhat undirected expression of events and ideas which are important to the interviewee. However, too strong an attitude of permissiveness might engender some inefficiency in the diagnostic procedure.

*Step 3. Mapping the Procedure.*    After the initial interviews are completed, the group combinations, role playing problems, therapeutic objectives, and desired modes of interaction must be determined. In a sense, it is like planning the moves in a chess game. The more successful the plan-of-action is, the less obvious the leadership or direction during the actual group process. About eight hours should be allowed for this vital portion of the program.

## Phase II: Group Interaction

The following steps are involved in each group role playing session. These steps are clearly related to the all important function of the group leader, the management of manifest anxiety as a disruptive medium in the defensive balances achieved by each participant.

*Step 1: The Warmup.*    This is merely a short introductory period to re-establish rapport and create a mental set conducive to the learning process.

*Step 2: Ego Involvement.*    When the participants are assigned roles to play in a particular conflict situation, their complacency, of course, is disturbed. The threat of role playing is anxiety arousing. But such a disequilibrium is essential to call forth habitually used protective mechanisms or defensive reactions. This, since much of human behavior is based upon reactions to anxiety and defenses against anxiety. The efficiency of habitually used defenses is lowered with aroused anxiety; they are, thus, less satisfying and more subject to critical evaluation.

*Step 3: Content Clarification.*    While there is some ventilation of feelings which may serve to reduce anxiety, the procedure should be of a nature so as to promote experimentation with new modes of reacting and adapting to stressful social situations. This demands that there be some effort to clarify the issues involved, derive possible alternative courses of action, and determine how they relate to overall management objectives. Of course, the burden of such productive thought should rest upon the shoulders of the participants, but they should not be allowed to become tautologically stalemated. While the material covered has to be meaningful and somewhat ego involving, it should be sufficiently displaced to prevent defensive "blind spots" or resistances which are but islands of incomprehensibility and nonacceptance if directly attacked.

*Step 4: Feeling Analysis.*   At this point, the group leader should attempt to promote some understanding of why various participants reacted as they did and what were the limiting factors in the conflict situation. This is where an understanding of the personality dynamics of each member of the group is of vital importance if growth is to be maximized and the chances of regression minimized (6). The group leader might best utilize the observers rather than the participants in these discussions.

*Step 5: Experimental Socialization.*   After the development or analysis of the modes of adaptation and feeling tones present in the conflict situation, some opportunity should be provided to "try again" with the added armament of an increased understanding of what is happening. By "living through" a similar conflict situation with new experimental concepts in mind, there may be some reinforcement of the new concepts prior to any healing and return to old, inappropriate defensive techniques.

*Step 6: Ego Support.*   Nearing completion of the session, the group leader should attempt to foster feelings of acceptance, the worthiness of individual contributions to the group, stimulate ego enhancement where necessary, and reduce any discomforting tension or manifest anxiety.

Since these sessions may be somewhat traumatic in the sense that they disturb a participant's equilibrium and force him to do some new learning, the participants of one session should be given the less upsetting task of being observers of the next session. However, participants who start a session should carry through the entire procedure of a session, i.e., initial ego involvement, subsequent analysis, and a second opportunity to try out new adaptive techniques.

### Phase III: Individual Ventilation

After about six Group Interaction Sessions, opportunity should be provided for individual consultation with each member of the group. This will permit some ventilation of personal difficulties and allow the group leader to determine corrective action for problems that have arisen. The original plan-of-action should be modified or extended at this time.

### Phase IV: Group Interaction

The technique may be continued for another six sessions or even further if serious problems are involved. The savings in time for the group leader (or lowered cost to industry) in comparison to individual therapy is considerable. It requires only 25% as much time and provides an unmatched, industrially oriented social experimental setting.

During the role playing process, the group leader should provide such direction as is necessary to prevent discussions which circumvent pertinent issues. He should avoid moving too rapidly over ground likely to induce resistances or demand difficult choices before the participants are ready. He should avoid premature or extensive interpretation. But most important, his leadership should not be too obvious. He must never be placed in a "teaching" position when he should be functioning as a leader or expert.

## SUMMARY

Any industry, however automated, is fundamentally dependent upon the individual worker as the key to optimum productivity. However, the individual worker seems to be an unpredictable variable in industrial management. Recently, the origin of employee morale, motivation, group attitudes, and loyalties has been found to be in the character of interpersonal relationships which occur in the primary work unit. If a method could be found to improve these interpersonal relationships, the results would directly affect productivity and profits.

It is recommended that a specialized technique of group psychotherapy, modified for use in industrial situations, be utilized to improve supervisor–employee interpersonal relationships. The method of application of this Intensive Industrial Role Playing Technique has been outlined in this article. It provides for a group leader who is a responsible agent in planning the exact nature of experimental interaction in industrially oriented conflict situations. This is achieved by individual diagnosis and subsequent mapping of a plan-of-action based upon group objectives and needs and fitted to the therapeutic utility of each participant.

The concept of anxiety management in the role playing process is introduced and its relation to adaptive learning described. The group interaction process is considered as an opportunity for ego involvement with concomitant disequilibrium of ego-satisfying defenses. Opportunity is then provided for content clarification, feeling analysis, experimental socialization, and ego support as aids in the development of more appropriate goal-directed behavior.

# REFERENCES

1. Brown, J. A. C. *The social psychology of industry.* Baltimore: Penguin Books, 1954, pp. 69–96, 124–156.

2. Maier, N. R. F. *Principles of human relations.* New York: Wiley, 1954.

3. Moreno, J. L. *Who shall survive?* 1934, pp. 103–113.

4. Haire, M. Industrial social psychology. In G. Lindzey (Ed.), *Handbook of social psychology.* Cambridge, Massachusetts: Addison-Wesley, 1954. pp. 1104–1123.

5. Bradshaw, F. F., & Krugman, H. E. Industrial morale. In D. H. Fryer and E. R. Henry (Eds.), *Handbook of applied psychology.* New York: Rinehart, 1950, pp. 302–303.

6. Spotnitz, H. Group therapy as a specialized psychotherapeutic technique. In G. Byshowski and J. Louise Despert (Eds.), *Specialized techniques in psychotherapy.* New York: Basic Books, 1952, pp. 85–101.

# Part V
# Emerging Cooperative Trends in Labor, Management, and Community

# 27. LABOR AND MANAGEMENT: NEW ROLES IN MENTAL HEALTH: WHO CARES ABOUT THE UNREACHED FAMILIES

**John J. Sommer**

*Illustrative case material suggests new case-finding and treatment opportunities when union, employer, and community agencies collaborate to develop a rehabilitation-mental program within an industrial setting.*

Modern mental health literature is replete with discussions of utilization problems. The growth of mental health programs has not been accompanied by a parallel growth dynamic involvement of all socioeconomic groups within the community (1, 2).

Many causal factors have been identified as obstacles to bringing psychiatric care to the lower socioeconomic family. Some of these factors are as follows:

1. the therapeutic model precludes involving non-middle-class families;

2. the value system and training of the middle class therapist produce social and personal distance between therapist and patient;

The author is Assistant Director of the Rehabilitation Project, Sidney Hillman Health Center, New York City.

Presented at the 41st Annual Meeting of the American Orthopsychiatric Association, Chicago, Illinois, as part of the symposium: *Are We Seeing the Right Patients?*

3.  the location and physical setting of the treatment facility are unfamiliar to the patient; and

4.  the role demands, particularly in view of the cost of treatment, are outside the mainstream of the blue collar experiences.

This author recognizes some validity in the above issues but would like to sidestep these and report instead on one experiment which seems to be having moderate success in bringing psychiatric services to blue collar workers and their families.

This paper will focus on how the auspice (in this case, the men's clothing industry) has been utilized to legitimate, support, aid, and encourage families of manual workers to seek help for emotional problems. Case presentations will illustrate how this auspice was used to maintain and restore function of the worker and his family.

The project's style of work was to develop a "syndicate of concern" which would:

1.  sanction receiving help,
2.  make the helping process visible (remove the "magic"),
3.  involve the therapeutic agent and patient in concrete tasks,
4.  permit the development of a treatment team to include "the significant others" in the patient's life, and
5.  encourage the development of goals which are feasible in the patient's real world.

## THE AUSPICE

In September 1961, the Sidney Hillman Health Center of the New York Joint Board of the Amalgamated Clothing Workers of America received a grant from the Vocational Rehabilitation Administration. Additional financial support later was received from the New York and American Heart Associations. The union contributed space, housekeeping costs, and medical services (3, 4).

A demonstration project was set in motion. Its aim was to offer rehabilitation services to the approximately 40,000 members of the New York Joint Board and their spouses.

The original protocol of the project envisaged a system in which the physicians at the Health Center would be introduced to the principles of rehabilitation services and thereby become a case-finding core. Referrals would be made to the rehabilitation team, consisting of physiatrist,[1] physical therapist, social worker, and nurse, who would offer the traditional services of rehabilitation. If the project had proceeded along these lines, this would have been, as Yogi Berra, "the dean of psychiatric baseball" would say, "the wrong mistake." It was clear that such a path of action would, at best, have made the project a highly specialized satellite of the Sidney Hillman Health Center without any real roots in the men's clothing industry.

Guided by a philosophy that any program of medical care must work with the community as well as treat the individual (5), the project moved toward a broader approach. By first viewing the demonstration through an industry-wide window, it was possible to identify key sectors that influenced the clothing workers and his way of life. These included:

1. the union and its structure of trade managers, business agents, shop stewards, and Labor Bureau (employment bureau);
2. the New York Clothing Manufacturer's Association and its network of manufacturers, management personnel, and shop foremen;
3. the joint union-management health and welfare institutions of Sidney Hillman Health Center and Amalgamated Health Insurance Company, and
4. the key public and voluntary agencies with particular emphasis on the Division of Vocational Rehabilitation.

At the outset, an advisory committee was formed which included representatives from each of these sectors. In essence a new community rehabilitation team was born. The advisory committee became a task force for finding people with medical problems and legitimating the sources of concrete help. The industry's apparatus and the project's staff cooperated in

---

[1] A physiatrist is a specialist in physical medicine and rehabilitation.

working with the patient. A treatment philosophy was evolved which has been expressed in part by Lester B. Hill, M.D. He states:

> "Treat" also means to "negotiate with, to make treaties or arrangements with, to arrive at understandings." All these meanings, too, refer to the necessary activity of the psychiatrist in mediating between the isolated and withdrawn schizophrenic and the hostile and threatening presences he fears in his human envirnment (6).

This writer believes that Dr. Hill's idea applies equally to all medical patients. The project thus serves as mediator to interpret and to negotiate at appropriate points between the patient and his institutional world.

As previously indicated, the project was developed to serve the members and spouses of the New York Joint Board of the Amalgamated Clothing Workers Union. Although in many ways this population is typical of the blue collar labor force, certain specific attributes are worthy of note:

—57% of the work force is male.
—The median age is 49.6, compared with 43.1 median age for the total work force in the New York metropolitan area.
—Of the male working population, 19.6% is over 65 years of age compared to 5.4% of the New York City working population.
—Ethnically the membership is 50% Italian, 40% Jewish, and 10% other.
—The average hourly wage rate was $2.27 per hour, placing the men's clothing worker in eleventh position among production workers in the New York City area. The skilled male's average earnings are between $80 and $90 per week, with women earning about $10 less on the average.
—17.2% of the population suffered from one or more of a group of nine select chronic conditions.
—Less than 4% of the chronically ill group had ever had contact with a community health or welfare agency (7). Thus, the population which was the target for service con-

stituted an aging, economically deprived, skilled and semi-skilled manual labor force. Many were suffering from one or more chronic conditions, yet had not used the "helping facilities" available in the community.

## CASE MATERIAL
## AND DISCUSSION

How the machinery operates and how the workers benefited from the program can best be described through illustrative case material. The story of Mr. A indicates how the entire network can be involved quickly to achieve the ultimate goal of helping a worker with an emotional problem to remain on the job.

This patient first came to the attention of the project through an urgent telephone call from a local union's business agent,[2] who had served as a member of the project's advisory committee. The content of the telephone call was as follows:

> "I just told a worker who was fired today for physically threatening his boss to 'go see a psychiatrist.' When he got very excited, I realized it was the wrong thing to do, and I remembered our program. I told him to take a walk around the block and cool off, and we would work something out. This man is 6' 3", very angry and upset. Can you come over?"

The project social worker went to the union office, and the following occurred:

> Upon entering, he noticed a man sitting in the outer office. The union official started to give details about the situation. The social worker suggested that the union member be brought in and the situation be discussed openly in front of the member. This was done. The union official recounted the worker's history of conflict with the employer and fellow workers, resulting in his job termination. The business agent felt that there were no solutions to Mr. A's problems unless the project could be of some help at this point. The social worker suggested to Mr. A that he join him for coffee in the local cafeteria to determine how the project could be of help to him.

[2] The business agent is a paid employee of the union, responsible for servicing the worker and manufacturer, particularly in relationship to their contractual arrangement.

Over coffee Mr. A was able to "unload." He stated that he was under pressure at home and at work and that it was hard for him to control his temper. Now that he had lost his job, he was even more agitated. He requested that the social worker join him on the telephone while he informed his wife of his new difficulties. The social worker suggested that he make the telephone call from the health center and that we might be able to do something about his feeling "agitated."

In a phone conversation, the wife urged her husband to cooperate. An immediate emergency appointment was made to see the psychiatrist at the health center. Both Mr. A and the social worker were present when all the facts leading up to the crisis were related to the psychiatrist. The social worker left. After the examination was completed, the social worker returned to the psychiatrist's office. The psychiatrist indicated that Mr. A could return to work, prescribed tranquilizers, and indicated that short-term therapy was warranted. In front of Mr. A the social worker called the business agent and informed him of the situation. The union representative spoke on the telephone to Mr. A. The union agent then called the employer who stated Mr. A. could return to work the following day.

The social worker was able to function in this situation because he had at his disposal the entire network of the men's clothing industry. A workable plan emerged because all the significant forces were alert to Mr. A's need and available to cooperate in development of a solution. Specifically, the forces were:

—The knowledge of "the court of first resort," (in this case the business agent) that the project existed.
—The immediate availability of a professional who could be legitimated by a union official.
—The understanding on the part of the professional of the appropriate paths of action within the union and industry setting.
—The availability of medical services at the health center.
—The trust which a union member was able to place in his union's apparatus.
—The existence of open lines of communication between management and the union.

Mr. A was obviously disturbed. Without intervention his situation might have deteriorated quickly into a pattern of a sick, unemployed, economically and socially isolated individual. But help was close at hand and quickly dispensed at the point of crisis. The entire "syndicate of concern" referred to earlier was brought into play. Short-term therapy was arranged through the Division of Vocational Rehabilitation. Thus the network's goal was successfully achieved—the goal of locating a patient in need and maintaining him in a work situation.

No matter how varied the presenting problem, the contribution of the machinery developed by this project remains a constant. The union's health and welfare program provides for a pension after a minimum of 20 years of employment in the industry. This benefit is cherished by most workers; many continue at employment under extreme difficulties in order to insure their pension rights. Mrs. W is an example.

The insurance company alerted us to Mrs. W, a 52-year-old Negro, who was receiving temporary disability benefits.

Mrs. W was born in the South, completed two years of junior college, and worked as a teacher in her hometown. After her marriage approximately 25 years ago she moved to New York City, purchased a home, and had two children. Shortly after the birth of the second child, marital conflict led to a divorce. Mrs. W assumed the responsibility for her children and home. Unable to get employment as a teacher, she located a job in the men's clothing industry, became a skilled worker, and for the previous 17 years had worked for the same company.

Five years prior to this time Mrs. W had developed an ulcer, for which she underwent surgery. Recent surgery had been performed for an abdominal obstruction. Blue collar work had always been unsatisfactory to Mrs. W's feelings about her own status. Her recent illness made the pace of work undesirable as well. Her doctors felt that return to her former job might create severe emotional difficulties and exacerbate her physical condition. Caught in the bind of financial responsibility and anxious to protect her eventual pension, Mrs. W was unwilling to seek employment outside the men's clothing industry.

The social worker reviewed Mrs. W's past history and simultaneously contacted the Division of Vocational Rehabilitation. DVR suggested that Mrs. W might be an excellent candidate for training as an office worker. The social worker contacted the business agent of the white collar section of the union, who detailed the unfilled jobs existing in the industry. A plan then was worked out to train her as a bookkeeper-comptometer operator, since this skill is in short supply. The business agent guaranteed that upon completion of her training she would

be placed ina white collar section of the union and thus insured
her 17 years of vested rights towards pension benefits.
Mrs. W was interested but confused. She wanted the program
but felt there was some kind of "charity" involved. The social
worker was able to interpret the nature of a tax supported
program and Mrs. W's basic rights for service. Mrs. W entered
on a training program and summed up her feelings about
the project: "All my life I have felt as if I had been standing
out in the rain, and it is as if someone had turned on the
sunshine."

Again, the existing union machinery, medical services, and
the Division of Vocational Rehabilitation were creatively used
to project a therapeutic program for a worker in need.

Not only has the project had an impact on the administrative
machinery of the union, but through its role of negotiator
and mediator, it has influenced patterns of medical care as
well.

Mrs. N is a 62-year-old woman of mixed Jewish and Italian
background. She had been seen periodically by the psychiatrist
at the Health Center. She was described as a constant com-
plainer who talked incessantly. Disruptive in the shop situation,
Mrs. N finally was shifted away from her regular work group
into an isolated work situation. The isolation triggered further
feelings of depression and rejection and made it difficult for
her to function at work. The psychiatrist brought the case to
the attention of the project.
The public health nurse discussed the problem with the business
agent at Mrs. N's shop. The union's agent indicated that he
was unwilling to intervene in what was ordinarily an employer's
prerogative. Nevertheless, he discussed the problem with the
employer, because two weeks later the patient's family reported
to the project that she had been returned to her former work
station and was feeling much better. Thereafter, the psychiatrist
was able to confront Mrs. N with her disruptive behavior pattern. They were able to begin to resolve (while the patient
was working) a problem he previously had been working on
unsuccessfully.

This case, too, demonstrates the importance of the strategic
location of the project, and the contributions of an industry-
wide approach to comprehensive medical care.

The problems in the three cases above are typical of the

kinds of issues faced by blue collar workers. What is unique and different is that a mechanism existed for intervening quickly and appropriately at the point of breakdown in the patient's functional performance. The individuals at specific moments had lost their ability to function within their world of work. The professional, through his knowledge of the industrial community and contact with it, was able to help mediate and negotiate a solution with the patient. Access by the professional to the worker's milieu makes possible a solution which is meaningful to the worker.

The writer does not wish to suggest that this project in any way offers major solutions to the emotional problems confronting the blue collar population. However, it does suggest the possibility for developing one style of work for mental health programs in a union-management based setting. Such a setting can provide (1) a case-finding mechanism and (2) avenues for possible solutions to the patient's vocational problems.

The working hypothesis is that trust is transferred from the familiar auspice to the professional team. This makes it possible to direct immediate attention to the presenting problem. Quick response to the patient's dysfunction coupled with the professional's free access to the institutional avenues needed to solve environmental problems makes possible therapeutic responses that mitigate the negative effect of the crisis.

The author is mindful of the fact that this treatment procedure works best with those patients who are able to transfer their trust. Those workers with negative or sharply ambivalent feelings about their place of work may require different methods for involvement in a mental health program.

It is hoped that further demonstration activity to be undertaken by this study team under grants from the National Institute of Mental Health and the Vocational Rehabilitation Administration will develop a more thorough and sophisticated expansion of the modest beachheads established thus far within the men's clothing industry.

# REFERENCES

1. Holingshead, A. B., & Redich, F. C. *Social class and mental illness.* New York: John Wiley & Sons, Inc., 1958.

2. Srole, L., et al. *Mental health in the metropolis.* New York: McGraw Hill, 1962.

3. Akabas, S. Rehabilitation demonstration. Industrial Bulletin, New York State Department of Labor, May 1963.

4. Weiner, H. J. Labor and community rehabilitation effort. *Journal of Rehabilitation.* March–April, 1963.

5. Galdston, I. *The meaning of social medicine.* Cambridge, Massachusetts: Harvard University Press, 1954.

6. Hill, L. B. *Psychotherapeutic intervention in schizophrenia.* Chicago: The University of Chicago Press, 1955.

7. Weiner, H. J., & Akabas, S. Potential demand for rehabilitation. Unpublished study.

# 28. INVOLVING A LABOR UNION IN THE REHABILITATION OF THE MENTALLY ILL

Hyman J. Weiner, D.S.W., and Morris S. Brand, M.D.
Sidney Hillman Health Center, New York, New York

For the past few years The New York Joint Board of the Amalgamated Clothing Workers of America in cooperation with management has been sponsoring a rehabilitation program for the physically and mentally ill. The essence of this demonstration project is an industry-wide approach to health problems. The union, the labor-management health center, the insurance company, the clothing manufacturers, and the recreation center for retired workers have joined forces to rehabilitate disabled clothing workers and their families.

Within the context of existing community resources, this pilot program has been able to secure more help for the physically disabled than for the mentally ill. Financial, language, treatment-approach, and waiting list obstacles all have combined to make it difficult to find and appropriately use community mental health facilities for this low-income population. Although the following presentation is not submitted as a success story concerning the rehabilitation of the mentally ill, it may be of value to share techniques and experiences

Presented at the 1964 annual meeting of the American Orthopsychiatric Association, Chicago, Illinois.

The demonstration project received financial support from the Vocational Rehabilitation Administration, the New York and American Heart Associations.

in establishing the labor union as a legitimate resource for help with emotional as well as physical problems.

This paper reports ways in which a labor union was helped to:

1. establish machinery for early case-finding,
2. minimize some of the negative consequences resulting from seeking and receiving help, and
3. participate in the vocational aspects of rehabilitation.

This project, based at the Sidney Hillman Health Center in New York City has been serving 40,000 households of working and retired Amalgamated Clothing Workers residing in New York City. It offered rehabilitation care to this population, not by creating a new resource, but rather by maximizing the use of existing community facilities. The personnel consisted of a director, two social workers, two nurses, and part-time medical specialists in physical medicine, cardiology, psychiatry, and internal medicine. Although outpatient treatment care was available at the health center for general medical care, only diagnostic service was offered for those with psychiatric problems (1, 2).

To date, more than 600 individuals have been referred and evaluated for rehabilitation services. Of these, 94 were found to have emotional problems which seriously interfered with functioning at work, within the family, and in social situations. In some cases the emotional problem was the only disability; in others, it was found in addition to physical impairments.

Strategy for altering behavior in regard to mental illness was based on union involvement, case by case. It was felt that concrete experiences rather than formal educational campaigns or seminars would lead more readily to modification of the clothing workers' perception of emotional disorder and ways of dealing with it. The union itself (the union as a social system) was identified as the target for intervention.

The project staff believed that the union subculture had notions about mental health which interfered with serious attempts at treatment or rehabilitation. It was clear that any effort to involve clothing workers in a mental health program required some change in the values and norms of the industrial social system.

## ACTION PROGRAM

The project staff believed that superimposing a traditional interdisciplinary team approach on this industrial setting would lead to its isolation. Therefore, the first 18 months of activity concentrated on building a rehabilitation network, of which the professional team was only a part, though admittedly a most significant one.

Evaluation of and service to rehabilitation patients were viewed primarily as means for involving segments of the clothing industry (the union official and indigenous leadership, the insurance company, management, and the recreation center for retired workers). The goal was direct participation by these elements in the rehabilitation process.

Two specific tasks in the rehabilitation process were identified around which professionals and labor union leaders collaborated. These tasks were (1) locating potential candidates for rehabilitation and (2) modifying or changing jobs where necessary.

Three avenues were selected as prime sources for casefinding: (1) the Sidney Hillman Health Center, (2) the Amalgamated Insurance Company, and (3) the union business agent and shop steward structure.

At the health center, physicians, nurses, and social workers began to refer to the project those physically and mentally ill individuals who had problems functioning on their jobs or at home.

The project established close working relations with the Amalgamated Insurance Company. All those with specific medical conditions who filed for union disability benefits were notified of the new rehabilitation service. Letters automatically were sent to all persons claiming sick benefits, informing them of the rehabilitation program. Between 3 and 5% of those submitting disability claims, as verified by their private physicians, listed "nervous disorder," "mental illness," "depression," or "severe anxiety."

The third major avenue for case-finding was the union business agent and shop steward. They alerted the project staff to prolonged absences from work and to the difficulties ailing workers were having in maintaining their jobs. In one local the major referral apparatus was the paid union organizer although shop stewards were involved. In another local the shop steward functioned as the primary referral source.

A professional staff member was used to underpin the various case-finding channels. Each was assigned to an official arm of the union: a local, the insurance company, or the recreation center for retired workers. Each learned to interact with clothing workers and union leaders at places other than the health center. Orientation sessions were held at factories during lunch hours and at union meetings in the evenings. Availability of the professional at the factory or at the union hall also permitted direct contact with the rehabilitation team for clothing workers who did not wish to share their problems with the shop steward or union organizer. His presence also made visible the initial phase of the helping process. Many screening interviews were held in the rear of the union hall, where a worker often invited his friends to sit in.

Guarantee of ongoing and relatively informal contacts greatly improved trust and subsequent communication between clothing workers and professionals. In effect, the rehabilitation team became accepted as a resource by what Eliot Friedson calls "the lay referral system" (3).

The union's labor bureau (hiring hall) became the vehicle for direct job placement and job transfers. On-the-job training programs also were established in clothing factories. Union officials and business agents served in a vocational advisory capacity to professionals and often were directly involved in team decisions. They knew the jobs and the special requirements in each factory.

Interpretation to co-workers also was essential if the disabled worker was to maintain his working status. Shop stewards oriented workers in that section of the factory where the disabled person was placed. This helped to create a supportive interpersonal climate and work milieu.

The pilot project reported here has barely touched on the opportunities for rehabilitation of the physically and mentally ill within a labor union and industrial context. Within limited treatment possibilities it sought avenues for involving the trade union apparatus along various points of the rehabilitation continuum, ranging from case-finding to maintenance of job.

Additional financial support from the National Institute of Mental Health and the Vocational Rehabilitation Administration will make it possible to develop a mental health treatment program in order to capitalize on the base of union involvement discussed above.

## REFERENCES

1. Weiner, H. J. Labor and the community rehabilitation effort. *Journal of Rehabilitation*, March–April 1963.

2. Akabas, S. A. Rehabilitation demonstration. *Industrial Bulletin*, May 1963.

3. Freidson, E. Client control and medical practice. *American Journal of Sociology*, **65**, 376–377.

# 29. A PROGRAM, SPONSORED BY A LABOR UNION, FOR TREATMENT AND PREVENTION OF PSYCHIATRIC CONDITIONS

**Louis L. Tureen, M.D., and Morris Wortman, M.S.W.**

St. Louis Labor Health Institute, St. Louis, Missouri

In previous reports (1–4) the functioning of the St. Louis Labor Health Institute was described in detail. To recapitulate briefly, the LHI was organized in 1945 to provide comprehensive medical and dental care to members and their dependents (numbering more than 21,000 as of this date) of Local No. 688, Teamster's Union. The professional staff providing health care for this group consists of a full-time medical director, 45 part-time salaried physicians, 18 dentists, and a part-time social worker. Consultations are available for specialties not represented in the regularly employed staff. The program is financed by a 5% payroll contribution by employers, a fringe benefit negotiated by the union.

The philosophy of Labor Health Institute from its beginning has been not only to provide a high grade of medical care, but also to practice preventive medicine. A broad concept of health maintenance underlies the LHI Program. Although optimum physical functioning still is considered the best

Louis L. Tureen is Professor and Chairman of the Neurology Section, St. Louis University School of Medicine and Morris Wortman is Assistant Professor, George Warren Brown School of Social Work, Washington University, St. Louis, Missouri.

Presented at the 1964 annual meeting of the American Orthopsychiatric Association, Chicago, Illinois.

barometer of good health, a focus on physical functioning alone with an effort to achieve health through biological, chemical, or physical nostrums is like trying to change the weather by manipulating the thermometer. A person's general state of health is seen as a reflection of all his transactions with his environment. The genetic equipment and tools that he brings to the task of coping with his environment are indisputably important, but success or failure seldom is predicated on this alone. Of at least equal significance to his health are the outcome of his efforts to achieve and maintain his integrity as an individual in his give-and-take with other individuals and attempts to maintain satisfying membership positions in his social groupings.

It is no longer a matter of conjecture that a person's mind, ways of thinking, and perceptions of his encounters with reality have the greatest significance for his body functioning. Physical exertion can make the heart beat faster, but when the exertion has passed, the normal heart rate returns. Yet, unresolved fears can keep the heart beating faster for months, years, or a lifetime.

It is our feeling at LHI, that so profound are life experiences for one's general and immediate state of health, that no member of the healing arts can practice knowledgeably or conscientiously if the symptoms presented by a patient are not related to their historical antecedents and to his current total milieu. Not only does this call for a vast coalition of experts in body functioning, but in personal and social functioning as well.

Once the notion that health is the outcome of a person's total way of doing business with his world is recognized, it also becomes clear that any institution that accepts the responsibility for health maintenance of a constituency, also must concern itself with every facet of interaction between individual and environment that can affect health. This includes the worlds of microbes and vitamins, but it also includes the worlds of values, feelings, thoughts, and beliefs. It includes the worlds of chemistry, anatomy, and physiology, but it also includes the worlds of relationships, family systems, and cultures. All these things and more influence and control the complex we call health. If we dedicate ourselves to the task of health, it is obvious there are no borders or boundaries we may not cross.

Because of its broad view of the ingredients of health, the Labor Health Institute has been insinuating itself into these various dimensions of its members' life zones: body, mind, work, play, child-rearing, family life, education, and social life, mental health, economics, community involvement, political action, retirement, etc. In each of these areas, there is room for a full variety of services and programs. A few, such as the health camp, family counseling, and political action committees, have just begun. Even though one might get the impression that these are disparate activities, they are part of an overall strategy to contact people at important points in their lives in an effort to help them with the critical task of self-realization, a prime ingredient of total health.

In this paper we shall discuss some of the theoretical considerations for a preventive mental health program now under consideration by the professional and administrative staff of LHI.

It has become evident in recent years to specialists in mental health that traditional psychiatric approaches with individual patients often fail not only to meet the needs of the individual but the needs of the community as well. It has been suggested that concern needs to be shifted to population groups, particularly to those subject to stress situations.

It has been proposed that efforts should be directed toward improving the social health of the LHI Community and toward changing conditions of the group as well as toward providing treatment for the individual patient. The contemplated mental health program described below would be aimed at reducing the incidence of mental illness, the prevalence of psychiatric disorders, and the severities of residual disabilities. Following are some of the pivotal concepts underlying the program which could be adapted to union structure and organization.

## Crisis Intervention

Deaths, prolonged illnesses, separations, divorces, accidents, abnormal births, and many other situations representing role transitional states precipitate bereavement reactions to one degree or another. Most people make a successful adaptation to those new demands. Some do so only with great difficulty. In a small percentage the adaptive effort breaks down altogether. A preventive program depends on being able to identify as many common stress situations as possible and on finding ways to help those who would otherwise fail to master them. If individuals with maladaptive responses can be identified at the point of crisis, a relatively short, well aimed, interventive effort may have more effect at that time than a great deal of effort later. It may be reasonable to assume that by the time many of our members reach the medical clinics of LHI the optimal time for preventive intervention has passed.

## Monitoring

A preventive intervention program calls for the monitoring of events related to behavior disorders. This means not only keeping in touch with that portion of the LHI population involved in bereavement situations and other crises, but also with monitoring the events affecting the basic supplies necessary for health, such as working conditions, employer–employee relations, job security, and the like. The union organization of Local No. 688 presents an almost ideal situation for such monitoring through the business office which keeps a current record of births, deaths, disabilities, and employment disturbances; through the LHI itself; and through the system of shop stewards, who are found in every place of employment. With union approval and encouragement, the shop stewards could be trained over a period of time to become key people in a preventive intervention program by spotting and reporting individuals manifesting maladaptive responses to crisis situations. Since the cultural milieu and value system of the shop steward parallels that of his fellow worker, he might become a useful aid in treatment as well as in case findings.

## Mental Health Consultation to Caretaker Groups

Shop stewards, foremen, employers, certain union officials, clergymen, doctors, teachers, undertakers, and others can serve not only as additional case-finding agents but because they embody a caretaking function in their role, also can act as helpers through the use of consultation with a mental health consultant. This type of indirect approach properly organized makes it possible for a small number of consultants to serve the front-line needs of a widespread community in a way that is not possible in a one-to-one patient–therapist approach.

### System Approaches

One might view the patient's illness as a symptom of disorder in one or more of the systems of which he is a part. The family and the place of work must be considered important systems which are sources of stress. The concept would require work with the total family to alter the functioning of this disorder in the system. Working with the whole family would provide insight into difficulties of communication and interaction, which so commonly lead to personal disturbance as well as to disruption in the family system.

This brief outline of the proposed preventive mental health program is based partly on experiences gained by the Harvard group which has been engaged in these approaches in Massachusetts communities in recent years. It seems ideally suited to a community such as Teamster's Local No. 688. The functions of this experiment would be integrated with the treatment functions of the medical and psychiatric staff. At the present planning stage it would be directed by a social worker who has special training in community health work. The setting for some of the mental health counseling and consultations would be removed from the medical facilities which could be located in the union offices or at places of work, or in the homes of members. At the present time the LHI Administration is giving the proposal sympathetic consideration. The possibilities for its eventual implementation are good.

## SUMMARY AND CONCLUSIONS

The St. Louis Labor Health Institute providing total medical care for 21,000 persons on a prepaid basis has made available psychiatric consultation and treatment for its members since 1946. Adapting goals and methods to realistic considerations of available funds and personnel, a useful program has developed for a segment of the population which ordinarily would not have access to this type of service.

As an adjunct to the psychiatric activities, it has been proposed that a preventive mental health program be developed. This program would embody certain principles of social psychiatry which require that attention be directed at the group as well as to the individual. Methods designed to prevent psychiatric illnesses would require techniques of identifying crisis situations and maladaptive responses to them, monitoring events of bereavement, use of caretakers in the community, and treatment of family and work systems.

# REFERENCES

1. Tureen, L. L. Participation of a labor union in the study of problems of psychiatry in industry. *Archives of Hygiene and Occupational Medicine*, 1954, **9**, 23–28.

2. Tureen, L. L. The role of the psychiatrist in a prepaid group medical program. *Journal of Public Health*, 1959, **49**, 1373.

3. Simon, N. M., & Rabushka, E. A trade union and its medical service plan. July 28, 1954, private printing.

4. Wortman, M. Psychotherapy and counselling in a group health agency: an integrative approach to physical and familial symptoms of stress. 1963.

# 30. THE FACTORY: SITE FOR COMMUNITY MENTAL HEALTH PRACTICE

**Antonio Blanco, M.S.W., and Sheila H. Akabas, M.B.A.**

Mental Health-Rehabilitation Project
Sidney Hillman Health Center, New York, New York

*Can industrial workers be reached by a mental health program? Utilizing a functionally directed approach during factory visits, a community mental health professional succeeded in engaging and treating emotionally ill blue collar patients. The results suggest that flexible approaches may offer new opportunities for establishing contact between mental health professionals and the community.*

A sharp bell rings at the Eastover[1] Shop to signal the beginning of the lunch period. Workers stop their sewing machines, shut off their fluorescent lights, and take out their hero sandwiches. They grab a few minutes of relaxation and shared conversation before returning to the pressure of producing men's clothing under a piece-rate system.

The employees of Eastover are industrial workers. They belong to a group which the literature on health care charac-

The work described in this paper was supported in part by grants from the National Institute of Mental Health and the Vocational Rehabilitation Administration. It was housed at and its indirect costs paid for by the Sidney Hillman Health Center, a facility sponsored by the New York Joint Board of the Amalgamated Clothing Workers of America and the New York Clothing Manufacturers Association. The Center serves workers in the men's and boys' clothing industry in New York City.

[1]Names used here are fictitious, although the factory and the cases described are real.

teristically describes as those who underutilize the services available. "Their problems of utilization of medical care are constricted on the one hand by the lack of available funds and, perhaps more importantly, by the lack of sophistication in dealing with metropolitan private and public agencies offering services. . . ". New ways of "reaching out" to bring health services to this group must be found. One possible mode of engagement, namely, an approach through the work environment will be described here.

The work was done as part of a cooperative program between a mental health project and union and management representatives of the men's and boys' clothing industry in New York City. Entry to the Eastover factory was established under the joint auspices of the union and the plant owners. Using, in part, a model developed by Youth Board workers and military mental health services (2–4), a professional mental health worker was introduced to the site of work activity of the potential patient load.

A questionnaire searching out physical and psychiatric problems was used to define the need and establish the first steps in engagement between the social worker and the employees. Further trust between the parties was cultivated through servicing social and medical as well as psychiatric needs.[2] Gradually a rewarding relationship developed, which suggests to the authors that workers can be engaged and treated successfully provided the care offered is functionally directed and meaningful to the population receiving service. The remainder of this paper will be devoted to describing the evolution of this relationship.

## THE SETTING

Having determined the basic approach, we sought to enroll assistance from the "gate keepers," namely, the key union and management figures. The project director and the social

---

[2]In order to avoid the sometimes threatening, sometimes misunderstood nature of case-finding around psychiatric illness, it was decided to offer help with the entire gamut of medical, emotional, and social problems.

worker first established contact with the union. We defined our interests, specifically,

1.  to gain a better understanding of the work environment;
2.  to examine how to reach and engage a group of industrial workers;
3.  to supply these workers with needed services.

The union agreed to cooperate in the experimental process. They started by selecting a shop which they felt was an appropriate site to carry out this study.

The factory selected has approximately 100 workers engaged in the manufacture of men's clothing. Each worker does some specialized function in the total production process. Their work is, for the most part, considered semiskilled. It requires good hand-eye coordination and the exercise of care, speed, and judgment. Most of them are paid on a piece-rate basis. The majority of Eastover's employees are Italian immigrants, many of whom continue to speak Italian as their primary language. In addition, there is a sizable group of Spanish-speaking workers who came originally from Puerto Rico and various Central and South American countries.

## ENTRY

Since the project would be operating within the factory, its activities might have some disruptive impact on the work arrangements. It was necessary, therefore, to gain the commitment of the host—the employer. The union was used as the vehicle through which to contact management. It arranged a meeting on the firm's premises where project, union, and employer representatives jointly explored methods of proceeding. The union's attendance at this meeting provided the necessary sanction to establish a legitimate role for the project in the eyes of management.

Approaching management during the planning stage further assured their involvement, if not commitment. As a result of our first meeting, an agreement was reached to hold a gathering of the whole shop. Management suggested a lunch period meeting during which we could define who we were, where we came from, and what we did, using specific examples of physical and emotional problems to clarify our function.

The program was introduced by the production manager representing the employer and the business agent representing the union. Further introductory words by the project director were followed by more specific, detailed information from the social worker assigned to the factory. His remarks were delivered in Spanish and Italian and were enthusiastically received. The groundwork had been laid.

Some comments from the social worker's diary, written immediately after the session, seem salient.

> As the project director thanked the group for their time and attention, several of the workers approached me to consult in Italian about getting help regarding their family problems. While several people looked on, one middle-aged woman described the problem she was having with her son who suffered from spasm of the jaw and was told by the physician that it was caused by "nerves." Another woman of the same age referred to her 3½-year-old daughter with an "undeveloped brain," and others inquired about treatment for their husbands' high blood pressure, injuries from working in construction, etc. They all welcomed my card with enthusiasm. . . . Many wondered whether I was a physician. They remained somewhat puzzled and to some extent confused when I identified and explained myself as a social worker. It was difficult for the people to concentrate on what they were saying because of their motive to return to work as soon as possible.

Staff assessment of the first meeting concluded that several significant features of future activities had been defined. Perhaps most important, the joint union-management introduction established the cooperative auspices of the program. Although the social worker had to nourish these contacts consistently during her later visits, the commitment of the parties had been verbalized before the entire work force. Further, the issue of health, both physical and mental, was made visible. It became a topic of discussion. This, in turn, made it easier for workers to seek help.

# CULTIVATING TRUST

The project staff felt that the introductory meeting, while helpful, was not enough to assure a flow of cases. On a previous project (5) a questionnaire seeking information on health problems had proved to be useful in establishing contact with the union membership. It was decided, therefore, to distribute a multilingual questionnaire designed to identify the existence of various emotional and physical health problems among the workers and their families—the underlying purpose to set up a dialogue between the project staff and potential patients.

Again a joint meeting among union, management, and project staff was arranged. The questionnaire was presented and their thoughts concerning the best mode of distribution were solicited. The production manager suggested lunch hour distribution by the foremen. This plan, acceptable to both the union and project representatives, was carried out a few days later. The questionnaire proved to be the "ice-breaker" in reaching the workers. A few of the women were frightened and suspicious; unwilling to complete it without showing it to their husbands. For most, however, a cooperative mood developed. Workers helped each other complete the form. The union business agent[3] and shop chairman[4] and the factory production manager circulated among the workers offering assistance. Many sought clarification, giving the social worker an opportunity to make contact with individuals and explain the program. People were able to "test out" how it would be to talk to a social worker.

[3] The business agent is a paid full-time union official who services, by periodic visit, the membership needs and union–management relations in a number of shops.

[4] The shop chairman is a union member, working in the factory, who by election or appointment is charged with handling the day-to-day membership needs and union–management relations. He is the first line in the union hierarchy.

Again, the diary provides an immediate insight:

> A particularly interesting sight was the many groupings the workers had formed, usually in pairs, helping each other fill out the forms. I observed that quite a few people weren't able either to read or write and were dictating to the person who was helping them. . . . There was no difficulty at all in getting the people's attention and cooperation. . . . It was interesting that some of the people were willing to lose time from their work to come over to ask questions.

The collection phase was spread over three weekly visits. The time interval permitted both management and workers to absorb the idea of the project and the availability of help. It also brought them into interaction with the social worker, resulting in the development of an atmosphere of trust. The questionnaire itself identified specific problems which were used as a base from which to "reach out" to involve workers in project services.

The questionnaire asked who among the workers and their families suffered from a series of physical and mental illnesses.[5] Of a total of 100 distributed, 94 were returned. The returns were separated into the categories in Table 1. Everyone who filled out a questionnaire was thanked by letter in the language of his response. Group C received notes of

## TABLE 1

| | |
|---|---|
| Group A: Positive response indicating mental health problem | 13 |
| Group B: Positive response indicating physical health problem | 14 |
| Group C: Negative response indicating no health problem | 67 |
| Total | 94 |

[5] At all times, the terms mental illness and psychiatrist were avoided. To allay fear, confusion, and resistance, terms more meaningful and acceptable to this population were utilized. The questionnaire, therefore, asked for anyone who had a "problem with nerves, worries, or a mental condition." Appointments were given to see a "doctor who examines people who feel nervous," etc.

appreciation for their cooperation. Based on staff belief that a number of negative responses were due to fear rather than the absence of a health problem, however, a postscript to the Group C letter described the existing services and suggested that the "door was open" to them should they develop problems subsequently.

Those in Group B received letters describing consultative services available for diagnosis and referral on physical problems. This, it is interesting to note, led to the unintended consequence of enrolling many eligible members into the health center. Thus, the questionnaire improved utilization of existing services. It also brought many of the workers closer to the union, since the shop chairman processed all requests for health center enrollment.

The letters sent to those who had answered positively on mental health problems (Group A) included a promise of a visit by the social worker to the employee in the shop. The alternative option would have been to bring potential patients into the office. Although the latter would assure confidentiality, it was felt that such a formally structured interview would have watered down the very process of reaching out that this project was designed to test. Interestingly enough, when approached at their place of work, patients did not seek confidentiality. They invariably felt free to discuss their problems among the "villagers."

The social worker's offers to talk behind coat racks or clothing bundles were met with amusement. A possible explanation for this is suggested by the following diary entry:

> The lunch hour had expired so I rushed over to Mr. O and while he was pressing I conducted a brief interview, checking out the effects of the medication. . . . I noticed that Mr. O felt more comfortable and this was made possible by the fact that he was talking while working. . . . This was also a unique experience for me to interview with steam blowing in my face instead of having to cope with the rays of a desk lamp.

Thus, the professional's anxiety concerning confidentiality proved ill-founded. Conversely, it was only after a "warm-up" period at the worktable that patients finally did come in for concerted treatment. Not one of those given an appointment on a first visit showed up. Trust was built up slowly. Patience turned the wary into cases. New patients from the factory arrive at the project's door to this day, although our activity in the shop ceased almost a year ago.

During the social worker's early visits to the shop, the production manager invariably accompanied him onto the factory floor. Slowly a feeling of trust developed, evidenced by the production manager's suggestion, after several visits, that the social worker could visit the floor alone. This increased independence was an important turning point. The factory personnel began to feel that the mental health worker was one of them rather than a management representative.

## PATIENT HISTORIES

The production manager's trust in the project was evidenced by his request for assistance for one of the key foremen. The foreman, Mr. Tagliato, who became the first project case, was a recent Italian immigrant. He had been an "entrepreneur" in Sicily where he made suits for the "top echelon." His children were grown and he had migrated, believing real wealth was available here. Because the owners had come originally from his native village, he and his wife had sought employment at Eastover on arrival in the United States. The patient had a history of diabetes, malaria, mild coronary disease, and chronic depression. The latter had become acute because of the problems of cultural displacement and severe disappointment with the economic reality of employment. According to management, this interfered with his work ability. They also felt guilty about having "let down" a fellow countryman.

The patient was given a mental health work-up, including a psychiatric evaluation in the employer's office. He was placed on a program of medical care, counseling, and pharmacological therapy. On each visit to the shop, the project representative stopped to check with and offer support to the patient, making the helping process completely visible. As Mr. Tagliato improved he talked with the workers he supervised about the social worker and the help he had received. Significantly the next series of cases developed among those who were closest to the process of care received by Mr. T. They felt freest to test the reality of available help.

At one worktable, each of the four female workers became a case. The first to seek help was Mrs. Zambia, a middle-aged South American immigrant who made contact around her desire for help in securing a permanent residence card.[6] These discussions led to a request from the patient for help with her sense of anxiety and loneliness. In the involutional period of life, she was suffering from severe anxiety, manifested by headaches, tremors, and acute insomnia. In addition she had serious medical problems. The combination had affected her speed at work. Paid by piece rate, her earnings were barely at subsistence level. She was concerned about who would care for her if she became ill since she had no relatives in the United States. The fact that she spoke only Spanish further increased her sense of isolation. At one point, she asked the social worker how to order a sandwich in English.

After psychiatric evaluation and team discussion[7] the patient received counseling and pharmacological therapy. She was helped to enroll in a class in English for foreigners. Her observed improvement brought requests for help from Mrs. Zambia's tablemates.

Mrs. Romero had indicated a physical problem on the questionnaire. Despite the thank-you letter, she had not requested service. Mrs. Zambia's improvement resolved her "wait and see" game. She requested an appointment of the health center.

---

[6]The usual pattern for self-referrals was for the patient to test the social worker around a nonthreatening issue and disclose the real problem only after a relationship had been established. This may be an important reason why blue collar workers do not utilize classic psychiatric services where the patient is required to identify his "presenting problem" at the time of first interview.

[7]The project's customary mode of operation involved an interview of the patient by a social worker and a psychiatrist. Then, the two professionals, in team with the clinical director and/or associate director, established a treatment plan for the individual patient.

Eventually, her "nervous stomach" was cured by clearing up a long-standing, previously undiagnosed, parasitic condition. Her work productivity was increased by a change in eyeglasses, made possible when the social worker served as translator during an eye examination.

Another tablemate sought an intermediary to intervene with the hotel workers union on behalf of her husband. Once his rights to union membership and a job were established, she presented herself for care. On evaluation she was suffering from insomnia, hand tremors, phobic reactions, and chronic depression. Supportive counseling and medication alleviated the severest manifestations of her mental health problem.

Finally the last member of the worktable, a critical bystander during this entire period, appealed for and received help for her back condition. Life became a little more bearable for these four women who, because of their problems of cultural displacement and pressured work environment, had varying combinations of emotional and physical distress. They began to understand how to make use of services to which they were always entitled.

The other cases which developed during the relationship with the Eastover shop were, in essence, comparable to those reported above. Few, if any, of the patients had had prior care for symptoms they had endured over a period of many years. The reaching-out experience had, it was felt, an ameliorative effect on the entire labor force.

The new understanding of the availability of help was translated into action on the part of the workers, most clearly in the case of Mr. Cariglio, a young Italian immigrant who was observed crying at his machine. On inquiry, management learned that the worker's wife's pregnancy had terminated in the death of the newborn baby and a hysterectomy for her following severe hemorrhaging. The emotional trauma was worsened by the fact that the husband was being hounded for payment of a hospital bill in excess of $1,000. The hospital, a private institution, had threatened, according to the worker, "to keep my wife in the hospital till the bill is paid." This young man, unfamiliar with the United States, faced this personal tragedy without funds to mitigate the intense economic pressure. He was depressed and close to a breaking point when management referred him to the project.

It is interesting to note that numerous workers in the shop also approached the social worker about Mr. Cariglio. There was an almost universal belief among the employees at Eastover that the social worker could help with Mr. Cariglio's problem.

Evaluation suggested that if the source of stress were removed, the patient and his wife would be able to recover their former tenuous equilibrium. The member's union rights included certain hospitalization benefits which he neither understood nor had fully used. The social worker, in negotiation with the physician, hospital, and insurance company, was able to secure a large partial payment for the Cariglio family. With the help of the shop chairman, a group of workers was organized to donate blood through the Red Cross. This donation replaced the transfusions given Mrs. Cariglio, further reducing the balance remaining on the bill. The cooperative effort harnessed in this case alleviated the emotional problem faced by the employee. Perhaps more important, it gave the entire Eastover work force a better self-image and sense of ability to cope with the stresses of life which, all too often, present themselves to a blue collar population.

## DISCUSSION

These industrial workers, having had no prior experience with mental health services, had difficulty starting to talk about their own problems. Approaching them during lunch or at work provided a unique way of overcoming initial resistance. They were able to continue a familiar activity while becoming involved in the therapeutic process.

The culture of the factory, which involved eating at the worktable, contributed to making the patients readily available during the social worker's visits.[8] They could not, in a sense,

[8]Our experience suggests that like the practice of eating lunch at the worktable at Eastover, most settings have their unique practices which, once identified, can offer positive help to the professional worker in doing his job. The period of group cohesiveness immediately prior to the receipt of biweekly welfare checks was identified as such by Shapiro (4) in her work with single occupancy dwellers.

stop treatment by not showing up. It was, however, quickly apparent that talking with a potential patient did not mean engagement and utilization. It would not have been enough, as is too often the case in community psychiatry, merely to move the classical model to this new setting. The problems faced by this population are real and immediate. The prospect of help must be immediate and functional in terms of these problems.

The goal of utilization was realized beyond expectation. The path was not, however, without its roadblocks! Several dilemmas were built into the situation by the nature of the original sanction. The introductory meeting had left unresolved the question of whether the social worker represented management, the union, or the patient. The project staff itself questioned the meaning of joint institutional involvement in terms of actual practice. Intimately tied up with this was the whole problem of confidentiality. Did visibility carry with it the implication of "exposure"? What was "appropriate" staff behavior in such a situation? The joint auspices pre-established certain commitments to both the union and management. Professional responsibility defined the rights and interests of the patients. There was, however, no definitive path for threading one's way through these mixed expectations and demands of the cooperating parties.

Experience, rather than theory, provided the answers. The project found that it represented all three of the parties. Sometimes the individual interests were cohesive and no difficulty arose. At other times they were in conflict and the interest of one party, often the patient, had to be served, to the ire and even detriment of the others. In a real sense, project activity was undertaken under a constantly shifting alliance dictated by the situation and task at hand. The goal was always to increase the number of alternatives available in solving the patients' problems.

Patient confidentiality remained a guiding principle, but when the worker needed a job change he had to face the risk involved in a discussion of his problem with the union and management. Utilizing the union as a case-finding resource was fruitful, but when a patient so referred questioned how the professional had heard about him, an honest response made the social worker, at times, look like the union's representative. This initial perception sometimes constituted an obstacle that had to be dealt with during treatment. Flexibility became the order of the day to achieve the objective of cooperative involvement around specific tasks while maintaining the usual code of professional confidentiality in dealing with patients' problems.[9]

As the shop experience unfolded, a pattern seemed to evolve. Each development established the preconditions for the next step in the ever-increasing arena of activity. Thirty-two visits were made to the shop over a period of a year. The visits, ranging from 10 minutes to 2 hours in length, usually took place during the lunch period. The average visit consumed 50 minutes. During these visits, 32 potential patients made a total of 107 contacts with the social worker. The average number of contacts per person and per visit was three.

Some of the contacts were merely exploratory on the part of the individual worker. Others were requests for help which could be quickly dispensed and required no further follow-up. The value of being able to offer meaningful help, immediately, can be understood in light of another entry in the diary.

> Walking back to his office, the production manager mentioned that one of the foremen was having trouble with headaches and needed certain examinations from the Sidney Hillman Health Center. He has been a member but never attended. I offered to have the foreman join me on my way back to the center, if feasible, and that I would guide him through the procedure. The production manager's face seemed to light up and he went over to the foreman and made arrangements. The foreman was very grateful for the guidance I offered him, and after he was through he came to the project's office to thank me again.

Still other contacts involved serious problems and comprised

---

[9]While this is not the appropriate time or place to explore the question, it should be noted that the total experience of the mental health program has led the staff to some questioning of the meaning and appropriate handling of confidentiality. We have come to a position of asking, "confidentiality for what?"

the group of 21 cases requiring extensive service at the project office as well as in the shop.[10] Of these, 13 were predominantly psychiatric problems, while in 8 the patient's major problem was physical in nature. The story of these cases is, in essence, a history of a developing relationship in which trust, hope, and new roles for both professional and patient became the essential ingredient in case-finding and engagement.

The awarding of sanctions was slow but steady. Following the introductory meeting, the questionnaire established the first pillar in the bridge-building process. The production manager's increased trust led him to introduce the social worker to a key foreman. Care for the foreman brought entry into his immediate work group. As word of concrete help spread, more and more people evidenced comfort in asking for care. Toward the end of the year, an employee in the shop faced a major crisis of which everyone was aware. Six co-workers, none of whom had had any previous direct contact with the social worker, requested help from him for the man in crisis. By the close of the liaison even the factory owner had sought a consultation from the project staff member.

## CONCLUSION

The experience at Eastover confirmed the project's hypothesis that reaching out into its own work environment is one way of engaging an industrial population around its health needs. But the experience also confirmed the hypothesis that improved case-finding does not assure engagement. The mental health professional must be able to respond with flexibility to the cues offered by the population. He must be prepared to take risks in a world of uncertainty. Moving into an unknown terrain can be uncomfortable and even threatening. The stepping stones are there, however. A solid theoretical framework is essential, but preset notions have no place. As a group of clients in a single-room occupancy

---

[10]Of the 13 mental health cases, 6 resulted from the questionnaire reported above, 4 were self-referrals, and 3 were brought to the attention of the project by management.

housing unit advised, "You don't need to go by the social work book with us" (4). In this program at Eastover, we too found a unique experience which led to new techniques and methods of work outside the "good book."

# REFERENCES

1. Shostak, A., & Gomberg, W. *Blue-collar world*. Englewood, New Jersey: Prentice-Hall, 1964.

2. Crawford, P., Malamud, D., & Dumpson, J. Working with teenage gangs: A report on the Central Harlem street clubs project. Welfare Council of New York City, New York, 1950.

3. Ginsberg, E. *Lessons for management and nation, Vol II, Breakdown and recovery*. New York: Columbia University Press, 1959.

4. Shapiro, J. Single-room occupancy: community of the alone. *Social Work*, 1966, 11(4).

5. Weiner, H., et al. Demand for rehabilitation in a labor union population: Part Two: Action program. Sidney Hillman Health Center, New York, 1966, pp. 9–22.

# 31. PREPAID PSYCHIATRIC CARE EXPERIENCE WITH UAW MEMBERS

## Melvin A. Glasser, LL.D., and Thomas Duggan, Ph.D.

*This first report on the landmark UAW psychiatric benefit program, stressing outpatient care, reveals that the program appears to be economically viable. During the first year of the outpatient benefit there was a utilization rate by Michigan UAW members of 6.4 per 1,000 eligible persons; the average number of visits was 8.5, and paid claim averaged $136. However, an expected decrease in in-hospital utilization did not occur.*

Over a period of more than 100 years, organized labor in this country has struggled for better wages, shorter hours, improved working conditions, pensions at retirement, life, sickness, and accident insurance, and prepayment for health care. Protection has been sought against the external obstacles to full and equitable participation of workers in the life of our society. In the last five years there has been evidence of increasing recognition of the need for programs to help deal with the internal obstacles to self-fulfillment—in substantial measure with the kinds of obstacles that are the concern of mental health programs.

Dr. Glasser is director, social security department, United Automobile, Aerospace and Agricultural Implement Workers, Solidarity House, 8000 East Jefferson Avenue, Detroit, Michigan 48214. Dr. Duggan is senior research consultant, Michigan Health and Social Security Research Institute, Detroit, Michigan.

This study is supported by Public Health Service grant MH-09249 from the National Institute of Mental Health.
Read at the 125th anniversary meeting of the American Psychiatric Association, Miami Beach, Florida, May 5–9, 1969.

But the largest single group in our population—blue collar workers—has not had equal access to services that would help them deal with what two Presidents of the United States have called "America's number one health problem" (1). This has been due to economic barriers, educational limitations, attitudes of fear and resistance developed over many years, and the orientation of many in the mental health treatment professions.

The studies of Hollingshead and Redlich (2), Srole, Langner, and associates (3), Kornhauser (4), and others, as well as its own analyses of its health care programs, convinced the United Auto Workers Union in 1964 that it was essential to break new ground in the prepayment and insured health care field. Accordingly, a decision was made to invest a portion of collective bargaining monies to make available, through prepayment, the financial resources to pay for out-of-hospital psychiatric care and thus encourage early referral, diagnosis, and treatment.

The benefit program, designed with the assistance of the American Psychiatric Association and the National Institute of Mental Health, was negotiated with 16 major corporations in the automobile and agricultural implement companies in the fall of 1964. It became operational in the fall of 1966, with the employers paying the full premiums as a part of the overall health insurance coverage.

This first nationally negotiated basic coverage psychiatric insurance and prepayment program provides for 45 days of in-hospital care, including in-hospital physician services. Provision is made for out-of-hospital care to cover all the major treatment modalities (except for out-of-hospital drugs, which have been added to the program as of the fall of 1969), with a maximum benefit of $400 per individual per year. This $400 in benefits is renewed for all members every January 1st. Workers' families are included in the program.

Because of the lack of experience with costs, and because it was hoped to remove barriers to early referral and treatment, the classic insurance industry principles were reversed. There are no deductibles or co-insurance for the first five visits to the physician or mental health center. There is a

15% co-payment by the patient for each of the second five visits, and 45% beginning with the sixteenth visit. It was anticipated that most patients would be seen fewer than ten times in a given year; experience has proved this hypothesis to be valid.

The new coverage is based on two major assumptions: Psychiatric benefits belong in basic health coverage, rather than as special add-ons to major medical and similar highly restrictive kinds of insurance; and it is possible through relatively short-term out-of-hospital therapy to assist most workers and their families who are in trouble to maintain their emotional health and ability to function. The aim is health maintenance rather than character reorganization.

The UAW psychiatric care program initially covered some 2.75 million members and their families in 77 cities in 34 states. Since then, identical or essentially similar coverage has been negotiated by unions with employers in the aerospace industry and in the steel, aluminum, and can industries. Most employers in these industries have extended the coverage to their employees who are not in bargaining units. The federal government provides similar benefits to some 7 million federal employees and family members. What was initiated as a brave venture into the unknown has grown more than five-fold in less than five years.

Because of widespread interest in the utilization and impact of these benefits, an intensive study of the first three years of experience is under way. It is not likely that sound long-run generalizations can be made until a minimum of 36 months' data can be analyzed. There are, however, a number of important implications and interesting suggestions that can be derived from the first 12 months' experience with auto workers and their families in Michigan. These data constitute a first report.

## THE UAW PROGRAM: OUTPATIENT EXPERIENCE

In Michigan there are approximately 1.1 million auto workers and dependents eligible under Blue Cross-Blue Shield for out-of-hospital psychiatric care benefits. During the first year, which began in the fall of 1966, 6,937 persons received some psychiatric care as outpatient benefits. As expected, the initial utilization rate of 6.4 per 1000 eligible persons was somewhat lower than it is expected to be as the program matures. It is of interest to note, however, that the first-year utilization rate for auto workers is about 45% higher than the rate of 4.4 per 1000 for blue collar workers in New York found by Avnet in her classic GHI demonstration project and study of outpatient psychiatric care (5).

About 60,000 additional auto workers and dependents in Michigan receive their health care, including coverage for psychiatric disabilities, through the Community Health Association of Detroit, a prepaid group practice plan. When this group, with 625 first users in the calendar year and a utilization rate of 10.4 per 1,000, is added to the Blue Shield utilizers, a combined utilization rate of 6.6 (7,562 persons) results in Michigan for the first year. This rate is exactly 50% higher than the rate found in the Avnet study.

A separate and related study of the prepaid group practice experience is being carried on as part of this overall study. Because these data on CHA are being analyzed separately, detailed breakdowns are not yet available. The balance of this analysis therefore is based solely on Blue Cross-Blue Shield information; the data were supplied by Michigan Blue Cross-Blue Shield.

## Age of Patients

A disproportionately large number of young people have used the outpatient services. While approximately one-third of the covered population is under 30, one-half of all users of psychiatric services during this period were under 30 and about one-fourth were over 40. The median age of all users was 29.7 years.

If, as seems apparent from this first evidence, the availability of this type of benefit is enabling people to seek help at an earlier age, there are important implications in terms of early treatment and possibly improved functioning of the worker and family group in later years. Even if it should be demonstrated that treatment of illness manifestations at younger ages does not necessarily prevent a later need for similar help, at the minimum this earlier utilization would mean that workers' families are exposed to opportunities for meaningful help in their younger years. Accordingly, when new symptoms of mental stress occur subsequently, they should be more likely to seek help at earlier stages in the course of the development of the symptoms.

On the negative side, it is noteworthy that there was least use of psychiatric services by persons over 65. This age group represented only 0.7% of the users. They used the benefit at a rate of 0.7 per 1,000, although this group represented 6.5% of the eligible population. Disproportionately low utilization in this group may be related to a lack of knowledge of availability of the benefit or to lesser familiarity than in younger age groups with the objectives of psychiatric care.

## Sex Ratios

It is of considerable interest that there were proportionately more male users of the benefit than in other reported programs. While sex was not recorded for persons under 20, among the adults, 51.9% were female and 48.1% male. These reflect rates of 8.2 and 8.1 per 1,000 females and males, respectively. One-year rates for women aged 20 and over in the Avnet study were 8.4 per 1,000; for men the rate was 6.6 per 1,000 (5). In the experience of the Health Insurance Plan of Greater New York, the rate for a 20-month period for women aged 20 and over was 19.6 per 1,000; for men it was 8.1 per 1,000 (6). In both studies, as well as in the UAW experience, peak utilization among women was in the age groups under 40.

That almost as many males as females used the benefit may well derive from the fact that the benefit resulted from the collective bargaining agreements, and was therefore closely related to the work situation in an industry which is overwhelmingly male in its labor force. It will be of interest to see if the proportion of female utilizers increases in subsequent years, as knowledge of the benefit becomes more widespread among union families.

## Diagnoses

What were the illnesses of these patients? Their diagnoses were recorded according to the traditional categorizations of psychoses, neuroses, and behavior or character disorders. Using this classification system, 18.9% were treated for psychoses, 55.7% for neuroses, and 35.3% for character disorders. (These percentages do not add to 100 because of changes in diagnoses for the same patient.) When the incidence of these diagnoses is analyzed within periods of this first year (October 1966–September 1967), one   particular pattern emerges. Among the psychotics, approximately 600 received their first treatment during the first quarter year and about 200 first appeared during each succeeding three-month period. Among the neurotics, slightly more than 1,100 appeared during the first quarter and about 900 during each later quarter. For the patients with character disorders, approximately 600 appeared during each three-month period.

These figures would seem to indicate a backlog of demand or need for psychiatric care before the benefit became effective, especially among what were probably the more seriously disturbed patients. This backlog, while substantial for the psychoses, does not appear to have been overwhelming among these blue collar families. Whether the individuals were receiving treatment prior to the effective date of the benefit or began treatment with the effect of the benefit is not yet known.

While it has not been possible to do a statistical analysis of presenting problems, we have reviewed a number of records and held extensive discussions with mental health professionals providing services to auto worker families. There is a rather clear indication that the problems causing concern among workers are not essentially different from those of middle- and upper-income patients, who until now have been the chief utilizers of private psychiatric services. Marital discord, children who do not get along in school or with their parents or both, alcoholism, depression (particularly in women), men who feel unable to continue functioning at work, others who resent the restrictions of the work situation—these are typical problems which cause the UAW worker or family member to seek professional assistance.

## Types of Service

Considering the fact that a variety of services was available under the benefit, it is important to review the utilization of these types of services. Again noting that individual patients may use many types of services, the distribution that appeared is shown in Table 1.

Of interest is the relatively low utilization of electroshock therapy and the substantial use of half sessions. The relatively low use of group therapy and of day care has little meaning; it is primarily a reflection of lack of available resources rather than of choice of treatment methods.

Once the first three months of operation of the new benefit passed and the high proportion of seriously disturbed persons was dealt with, there was a significant broadening of the program in terms of the use of services and personnel other than the standard psychotherapeutic session. During the first quarter only 5.4% made use of limited medical services, but this increased to 10% or higher during the subsequent quarters. Similarly, family counseling was utilized by only 3.4% during the first quarter but increased to an average of about 6% during the following periods. Psychological testing was received by 3% of the users during the first quarter but doubled during the later periods, while social services were first used by only 3.8% of the patients but by about 9% during the subsequent quarters.

**TABLE 1**

| | |
|---|---|
| Full-session therapy | 71.7% |
| Half-session therapy | 19.5 |
| Group therapy | 5.7 |
| Electroshock | 3.1 |
| Day care | .9 |
| Limited medical service | 9.2 |
| (brief sessions with a physician) | |
| Family counseling | 5.5 |
| (collateral visits with other members of the primary | |
| patient's family) | |
| Psychological testing | 5.1 |
| Social service | 7.4 |

## Number of Services and Costs

Finally, there are some overall figures. During the first 12 months of the psychiatric care benefit, the patients received an average of 8.5 services, and paid claims averaged $135.50 per patient. This may be contrasted to the allowable benefit of $400 per person. Considering this fact, the question arises: How completely was the benefit used? The first complete year during which it was available was 1967; the following figures refer to that *calendar year* rather than to the actual *first year of benefits* (October 1, 1966–September 30, 1967). During 1967, a total of 7,396 individuals received psychiatric care. Of these, 54% received benefits totaling less than $104, 75.3% received benefits totaling less than $208, and 7.2% (536 persons) received the limit of $400 in psychiatric care.

It appears that the $400 benefit for out-of-hospital services was adequate for well over 90% of the patients. It is not known at this time what percentage of the 536 persons who received the limit of $400 had completed the course of treatment and what percentage required further treatment; nor is it known how many of the latter were able to arrange for continued help.

In terms of number of services, 54.7% of these people received five or fewer services of all types, 74.2% received ten or fewer services, and 8.8% received more than 20 services.

## Treatment Resources

As to what resources these UAW members and their dependents made use of, the majority, 60.7%, received treatments from private practicing physicians, 41.6% received treatment in community mental health facilities (primarily child guidance clinics), and only 4.9% were treated in outpatient departments of general hospitals. The 4.9% is in all likelihood a reflection of worker resistance to hospital clinics, the crowded conditions in these clinics, and the unfavorable climate in which services are generally offered.

## INPATIENT EXPERIENCE

In addition to the outpatient benefits, auto workers have access to inpatient psychiatric services. In 1965 the contract coverage provided up to 30 days of in-hospital psychiatric care coverage; in 1967 the benefit was extended to 45 days. In both years the plan paid full costs in participating hospitals. It is relevant here to examine the use of this benefit by auto workers before and after the outpatient benefit became effective. For this purpose, utilization data on the inpatient benefit during 1965 and 1967 will be presented and discussed.

During 1965, 3,998 auto workers or their dependents were identified as receivers of inpatient psychiatric care. This represents a rate of 4.1 per 1,000 eligible persons. For these patients the median number of days hospitalized was 12.3, and the average amount of claims paid per patient was $466.[1] For 1967, there were 4,552 hospitalized patients, a rate of 4.2 per 1,000. These persons were hospitalized for a median of 12.6 days, and the average payment was $603 per patient.

---

[1] In the GHI study, the median days hospitalized for mental or nervous conditions was 26. However, the rate of hospitalization for this group was less than 1 per 1,000 and the median is high because of the large number of patients who used the full 30-days benefit available to members of that plan. It appears that in the GHI project, the emphasis was so strongly on outpatient care that hospitalization was used as a last resort, mainly for the most seriously ill patients. This form of emphasis is feasible only in a controlled setting such as a demonstration project provides.

These figures indicate no essential change in the rate of hospitalization, a slight increase in median number of days hospitalized, and a considerable increase in average cost—this last figure reflecting also the general increase in the cost of hospital care. The reasons for the maintenance of the rate of hospitalization, when decreases were expected with the introduction of the out-of-hospital benefit, are difficult to specify because of a number of events that transpired during this time. It is reasonable to infer that the outpatient benefit brought numbers of new patients, some of whom would become hospitalized, to the care of psychiatrists and mental health clinics. The fact that the outpatient program picked up a substantial backlog of patients diagnosed as psychotic is probably the single most important factor in the increased hospital utilization. In addition, the educational efforts of mental health groups to encourage use of mental health services has undoubtedly sensitized more people to this kind of care. Further, extraneous events such as the disastrous civil disorders that occurred in Detroit in July 1967 quite conceivably precipitated a need among some people for treatment of nervous and emotional conditions. Finally, a single year's experience is not an adequate time span on which to base a firm conclusion.

During 1965 males comprised 47.4% of the hospitalized patients and females 44.8%. The remaining 7.8% were dependents; almost all of them were under age 20 and no sex is indicated on the Blue Cross records. In 1967 the distribution was 47.3% male, 43.6% female, and 9.1% dependents. Thus between the two years there was almost no change in the proportion of males, a decrease in the proportion of females, and a corresponding increase in the percentage of dependents. These figures indicate the usual situation of an excess of male over female psychiatric in-hospital patients in both years.

This point is emphasized by inspection of hospitalization rates. For males, it was 7.1 per 1,000 in 1965 and 7.2 in 1967, only a slight increase, but in both years it was higher than the rate for females, for whom it was 6.3 in 1965 and 6.2 in 1967. With regard to median number of days hospitalized, there was again a slight increase for both sexes in 1967, but in each instance the median stay for females was somewhat longer than for males. In 1965, these statistics were 11.7 for males and 12.8 for females, while in 1967 they were 12.0 for males and 13.0 for females.

With regard to age, the bulk of the patients were adults between the ages of 20 and 64; in both years they comprised over 90% of the patients. The younger of these age groups (20–39) decreased slightly in percentage in 1967, from 47.3 to 46.9%, while the 40–64 age group increased from 43.0 to 43.5%. The under-20 group in both 1965 and 1967, and for the 20–39 year olds it changed only from 6.9 to 7.0, and from 7.9 to 8.1 for the 40–64 group.

As to median number of days hospitalized, there were increases between the two years for all age groups except those under 20. For that group the median decreased from 13.4 days to 12.3. Among the adults the changes in medians were from 11.5 to 11.7 for the 20–39 group and from 12.8 to 13.6 among the 40–64 year olds. For the 65 and over group, the use of inpatient psychiatric care was extremely low, as it was for outpatient care. In 1965 this group comprised only 0.6% of the patients and 1967 only 0.4%. These represented rates of 0.4 and 0.2 per 1,000 for 1965 and 1967, respectively.

In terms of overall costs for services received, inpatient claims totaled $1.8 million in 1965 and $2.8 million in 1967. This increase of 53% was due primarily to escalation in the costs of hospital care as well as increases in the size of the population-at-risk and median number of days hospitalized. The change in the in-hospital benefit coverage from 30 to 45 days had no meaningful cost impact.

During the first year of the outpatient benefit, claims totaled $940,000. This indicates that the cost of the outpatient care received amounts to only about one-third of the cost of inpatient care.

## DISCUSSION

Preliminary review of the first year's experience in Michigan with a uniquely designed prepayment program appears to indicate the program is functioning well in terms of getting patients to treatment resources and may have an important impact in getting a larger proportion of younger persons to seek help at earlier stages of incipient ill health.

There has been substantial utilization of out-of-hospital benefits—7,562 patients in the first year; this utilization is expected to rise as knowledge of the program spreads and treatment resources expand. There is as yet no evidence of expected decrease of in-hospital utilization resulting from the availability of out-of-hospital services. The combination of the newness of the out-of-hospital benefits and bringing into the treatment system a backlog of patients diagnosed as psychotics may account for this.

There is fairly clearcut evidence that the 45-day limit on hospitalization in an acute general hospital and the $400 limit on out-of-hospital services are realistic and feasible for the overwhelming majority of patients in the program. The introduction of a variable fee schedule by Michigan Blue Shield in the fall of 1968 may, however, sufficiently increase physician fees to require a re-examination of the present $400 ceiling.

In the first year of the program there was no concerted effort to interpret the benefits to the members of the union. This derived primarily from concern lest bringing large numbers of new patients into the treatment system might overwhelm the available resources and possibly discredit the program before it had an opportunity to develop.

A subsidiary study conducted by the Michigan Health and Social Security Research Institute in the second year of the benefit, due to be published shortly, indicates that of those eligible for the benefits, 28.9% knew or thought they had the mental health benefits, 24.9% were certain or thought they did not have the benefits, and 46.1% did not know about the benefits. These data suggest that development of educational programs for union members and their families would be of value.

Lack of knowledge of the program is in all likelihood the chief factor in the very low utilization by those over 65. They are by and large outside the usual communications system in the plants and union halls.

The study does not deal with the effectiveness of treatment; this complex question will have to be dealt with in a separate study. For the time being, the present program is based on the hypothesis that bringing emotionally disturbed or potentially disturbed persons together with competent treatment resources is likely to result in a constructive outcome.

Finally, based on the first year's experience, the evidence indicates that a program designed in the UAW pattern, when integrated with other basic health benefits, is economically viable. Cost and utilization experience have not exceeded predictable limits. There is no reason to assume that the relatively modest costs of these new mental health benefits would not occur if other blue collar groups were covered.

## REFERENCES

1. Glasser, M. A. Prepayment for psychiatric illness. *American Journal of Psychiatry*, 1965, **121**, 736–741.

2. Hollingshead, A. B., & Redlich, F. C. *Social class and mental illness.* New York: John Wiley & Sons, 1958.

3. Srole, L., Langner, T. S., Michael, S. T., Opler, M. K., & Rennie, T. A. C. *Mental health in the metropolis: The midtown Manhattan study.* New York: McGraw-Hill, 1962.

4. Kornhauser, A. W. *Mental health of industrial workers: A Detroit study.* New York: John Wiley & Sons, 1965.

5. Avnet, H. *Psychiatric insurance.* New York: Group Health Insurance, 1962.

6. Fink, R., Shapiro, S., Goldensohn, S., & Daily, E. The "filter-down" process to psychotherapy in a group practice medical care program. *American Journal of Public Health*, 1969, **59**, 245–260.

# 32. INSURANCE COVERAGE FOR "MENTAL AND NERVOUS CONDITIONS": DEVELOPMENTS AND PROBLEMS

### Simon L. Auster, M.D.

*The author reviews the evidence for the probable acceleration of insurance coverage for mental illness treatment and points out the flaws in some of the arguments advanced by insurers against the feasibility of increased coverage. He suggests some areas in which the profession should focus efforts toward attaining more comprehensive benefits, including the coverage of all accepted types of treatment and of newly emerging consultative services, as well as the pooling of family benefits. The need for peer review as a control measure is also stressed.*

Despite the data that have been accumulating over the past 20 years concerning health insurance coverage of mental illness, one keeps hearing the same kinds of questions as were asked when little information was available. What is it we are trying to insure? With reported prevalence rates of disabling mental conditions above 23% (1)—as high as 47% in the lowest socioeconomic group and at least 13% in the advantaged groups—how can service be covered at acceptable premium levels? What kind of condition should be covered— acute, or chronic as well? What kinds of treatment should be covered? Since a number of professions contribute their

Dr. Auster is director, Fairfax-Falls Church Mental Health Center, 2949 Sleepy Hollow Road, Falls Church, Virginia 22044, and consultant in occupational mental health, Division of Mental Health Service Programs, National Institute of Mental Health.

services in this treatment, how are we to determine whose services should be included? How can we get reliable statistics for research purposes?.

It is perhaps symptomatic of the state of the arts—both psychiatric and insurance—that we are now faced with the paradox of a flood of information and the persistence of these questions, each reinforcing rather than moderating the other. Nevertheless, certain developments stand out clearly. Before considering them, however, I would like to note that to avoid one source of confusion, I will attempt in this paper to consistently use the language of the insurance carriers in describing their benefit plans; they refer to "mental and nervous" conditions and disorders. Following this pattern, it should be possible to explore the present state of knowledge, the problems, and the potential of insurance coverage based on health insurance concepts.

I hope thus to avoid the pitfall of becoming preoccupied with the possible conceptual distinctions between the more blunt terms used by the carriers and those frequently employed in discussions and educational programs about insurance benefits, such as emotional disturbance, troubles, mental health benefits, etc.—terms actually selected for euphemistic purposes because of the stigma still hovering over the word "mental" (except as attached to health), and with no concern about these conceptual distinctions, if in fact they even exist.

To return to recent developments, perhaps foremost among these is that insurance carriers now consider treatment for mental conditions, both in and out of hospital, insurable at premium rates acceptable to subscribers. While 10 years ago such coverage, particularly for out-of-hospital services, was still relatively uncommon, trend-setting programs such as the Federal Employees Health Benefits Program (1962) and the one negotiated by the United Auto Workers and the automobile industry (1965) sparked a period of rapid growth that is still continuing. Most of this coverage is through major medical expense benefits having a co-insurance feature; at the present time over 90% of these, whether they comprise the subscriber's basic protection or merely provide supplemental benefits, include some coverage for mental conditions (2). More than three-quarters of these make no distinction between in-hospital expenses incurred because of general medical conditions and those due to mental and nervous conditions. Nearly 25% offer similar benefits for out-of-hospital expenses, the remainder providing outpatient benefits on a reduced level.

As a result of this increase in the number of people with coverage for nervous and mental conditions, we are beginning to get data on utilization by a very broad population. The data are intriguing, deceptive, and provoking. For example, reported utilization ranges from under 1% of the eligible population to a high of 5% (3). At the same time, payment for nervous and mental claims as a proportion of total health insurance benefits ranges from 2 to 20% with no clear relationship between cost and utilization—i.e., between the number of people claiming a benefit (as compared to the total number of services for which reimbursement is claimed), and the amount paid out.

While certain occupational groups for which policies are written appear predisposed to utilizing outpatient benefits, within any one group there can frequently be observed striking differences in utilization between subgroups—e.g., between men and women and between different age groups. These differences, however, are not uniform across contracting groups. Another fact that must be acknowledged, then, is that the diversity of utilization patterns and the complexity of the total situation suggest that it will still be a long time before we have firm statistical support for what has become in fact a widespread and accepted practice—the inclusion of out-of-hospital benefits for nervous and mental conditions in group health insurance policies.

An incidental finding is that even where the financial deterrent is significantly reduced, utilization by the better educated and socially advantaged groups continues to remain ahead of that by the poorer groups. This is often attributed to greater awareness by the better educated, indicating a need for extensive educational programs, or to the irrelevance of prevailing treatment practices to blue collar and disadvantaged groups, indicating a need for a broadened therapeutic approach. However, it also raises some important questions about the class basis for the definition of a variety of impairments as being of a primarily psychiatric nature; perhaps we are overly hopeful about the scope of impairments for which our knowledge and skill have relevance—an unrealistic hope better recognized by the people themselves than by us.

## SOME INDICATORS OF FUTURE PROGRESS

Perhaps the most significant aspect of the present situation lies in the many indicators of future developments. These suggest that not only has the period of rapid growth of insurance coverage in this area not yet come to a close; it will probably continue to accelerate. Evidence comes from several sources. It can be found in the statements of the large insurance brokers who design   and package the group policies that include specified benefits for mental disorders as being the major development in the health insurance field in the 1970s. It comes from the valuation placed on these benefits by the California Council for Health Plan Alternatives in its efforts to develop a system for assessing health insurance plans: payment for psychiatric services is considered in the same category as maternity and dental benefits and only a little lower than doctors' office calls and diagnostic procedures.

Another development of potentially major importance is the policy adopted by the National Association of Blue Shield Plans requiring participating plans to have available after April 1969, to all groups willing to buy it, a fully paid benefit for outpatient psychiatric treatment. While it is too soon to predict the impact of this policy on evolving patterns of coverage, it should facilitate further movement along the course of expanding coverage.

Perhaps most important for its implications regarding patterns of medical care is the current research on psychiatric aspects of medical practice. Several studies, done both in private (4) and group practice (5) settings, have shown rates of diagnosable psychiatric disorder in a general medical practice to be in the range of 14 to 18%. An observation in the latter study was that patients with a psychiatric diagnosis were disproportionately heavy users of general medical services. One study (6) has revealed a reciprocal relationship between high medical service utilization and psychiatric service; referral for psychotherapy resulted in diminished medical utilization sufficient to more than compensate for the costs of psychotherapy *even when long-term care was necessary.*

While the economics of private medical practice admittedly limit the ready translation of this finding from a group practice setting into a feasible form of patient management in private practice, its significance for the insurance industry is clear. In accordance with the axiom that medical care follows the dollar, absence of readily available coverage for psychiatric services will serve to continue a patient in general medical treatment for which he has coverage despite the fact that over time, the total cost of the latter may well exceed that of the former. Equivalent hospital benefits for psychiatric diagnoses and other medical diagnoses relieved the need for subterfuge when hospitalizing mentally disturbed patients lacking psychiatric coverage; the provision of outpatient benefits that permit referral of a medical patient for psychotherapy at no added cost to him should facilitate more economical and appropriate care in the outpatient field.

## NEW EMPHASES IN MEDICINE

That someone should think of doing a study of the reciprocal relationship between medical and psychiatric utilization is perhaps a consequence of a basic change that has been taking place in medical education in the past 15 years. Still predominantly limited to undergraduate medical training and at that not universal, it reflects a shift in the view of the basic nature of health and disease (7). Advances in therapeutics and technology during and after World War II, because of the promise they held, resulted in increased emphasis on the physical aspects of disease. The present shift represents a return to the balanced view of the human as an integrated organism whose social and psychological aspects are intimately articulated with his physical being and its function. It is observable most clearly in the establishment of behavioral science and community health curricula in medical schools; its impact is also felt in restructuring of programs on all levels to give the student exposure to the familial and social environments of his patients.

While the effects of this reorientation of priorities on medical practice cannot yet be fully felt, it is safe to say that the growing appreciation of the nonphysical determinants of disease and health will lead to earlier and more frequent referral of the medical patient to psychiatric services. Perhaps the increasing number of medical graduates entering psychiatric training is a result of this development. Not only will these services help reduce medical utilization but they will begin to assume significance in their own right in the average citizen's medical budget, the traditional starting point for the demand for benefits.

Beyond this, however, is another shift in priorities represented by the growing trend in medical philosophy toward preventive activities as our entire society becomes more aware of the social cost of disability in wasted human resources. It is the responsibility of the medical profession to prevent such waste from occurring on the basis of ill health; it does not seem unreasonable to look to the underwriters of health insurance for assistance in facilitating the discharge of this responsibility.

## THE "REAL ILLNESS" PROBLEM

One of the more puzzling aspects of the seemingly interminable discussion about the insurability of psychiatric care is the question of assuring that benefits be paid only for treatment of "real illness" and not for the ordinary strains of living. This same question is *not* asked when we urge people to see their physician for a complaint that may be an early symptom of a treatable, progressive condition but more often is probably a reflection of those very same strains of living. Yet many carriers do not hesitate to provide benefit coverage for the extensive X-ray and laboratory testing that may be required for the evaluation. Although regular physicians' office fees are not ordinarily covered, except sometimes as part of a supplemental benefit, a case can be made for paid-in-full coverage for a psychiatric evaluation, analogous to X-ray and laboratory studies. Such an examination takes substantially longer than the average office visit to a general physician and hence is more expensive; it should be covered if we wish to encourage the use of a service that many people are still reluctant to utilize.

A more distressing aspect of this question of the "reality" of the illness lies in its reflection on the profession; it contains the suggestion that a significant number of practitioners spend their time "treating" people suffering from ordinary strains of living. While abuse can and doubtless does occur, this simply requires that adequate controls be devised, not that coverage be denied. Denial of coverage implies either that abuse is widespread, which is doubtful, or that the clinical judgment of the profession is defective insofar as it is unable to distinguish ordinary life stresses from other conditions. This is a grave accusation.

A particularly unfortunate consequence of efforts to devise adequate and appropriate controls is inherent in the very nature of controls—namely, their institutionalization of the status quo. By requiring conformance to specified patterns of practice, indiscriminately applied controls may stifle innovation or make liars out of innovators; fortunately, the latter probably occurs more often than the former. In a field as much in ferment as ours, with new approaches being continually developed, special care must be taken to avoid closing off newly opened avenues simply because they do not fit into accepted patterns of care. The difficulty in obtaining coverage for day and night hospitalization continues to be an especially egregious example of this. Obtaining coverage for the unique requirements in the areas of services to children and outside consultation is another. Problems such as these emphasize the importance of considering the dimension of appropriateness before instituting a system of controls.

In addition, there are several other considerations, none of which is singular to mental disorder and which considered alone would not necessarily be sufficient to inhibit the development of coverage. However, coinciding as they do, they have had a cumulative deterrent effect of considerable significance.

The first is that in general, a mental disorder is basically a *chronic* disorder. While several of the conditions associated with the organic brain syndromes are truly acute, all of the disorders not attributable to physical conditions (with the exception of transient situational disturbances) are more or less chronic conditions. The personality disorders certainly are. That the psychoses and psychophysiological disorders are is clearly indicated by the injunction in the second edition of the *Diagnostic and Statistical Manual of Mental Disorders* (8, p. 52) that the diagnosis "no mental disorder" is not to be used for patients whose disorders are in remission. While the probability of relapse in the neuroses may be much less, and their major disabling features may respond to therapy relatively quickly, they too are inclined to a degree of chronicity. The behavior disorders of childhood and adolescence tend to be chronic; even with an excellent response to therapy, a predisposition to respond to stress in this symptomatic manner lingers until maturity. This factor of chronicity has been a deterrent despite the fact that, as in many chronic medical conditions, treatment may be needed for only brief periods and only infrequently—to keep the condition under control.

The second consideration is that despite the responsiveness of most of these conditions to short-term and other acute forms of intervention, the treatment model that became traditional in this country was one of long-term, intensive individual therapeutic contact. While it is being increasingly recognized that there are many conditions for which this is not only unnecessary but even contraindicated, whether or not to pursue such a course remains a matter for the clinical judgment of the individual practitioner. This creates a serious problem for the insurance carrier attempting to estimate benefit costs; he has no way of predicting whether a more or less expensive treatment program will be undertaken.

Closing the circle is the tradition of public care for mental disorders. This has served to blunt the demand for insurance coverage insofar as it provides an automatic backstop, however inadequate, against the threat of disastrous costs that has been the major stimulus to the development of health insurance programs.

Considered together, these three factors of chronicity, range of treatment possibilities, and absence of incentive constituted a potent obstacle to the natural growth of coverage. They created a situation characterized by a lack of demand from purchasers and caution by carriers. Thus initially it was only the providers of care who pressed for change. Later, through the interest and efforts of a few outstanding individuals, the labor movement began to seek benefits in this area, and the U.S. Civil Service Commission, through its negotiations for the 36 plans operating under the Federal Employees Health Benefits Program, became a major force in the extension of coverage.

## THE CASE FOR PAID-IN-FULL COVERAGE

The eventual development of total, paid-in-full, insured health benefits for mental disorder does not seem a particularly remote possibility. The evidence comes from a number of areas. The experience of the Federal Employees Health Benefits Program, International Business Machines, and other plans with a high maximum benefit has been that expenditures have not been so high that benefits have had to be reduced. In fact, in the federal program the one plan that initially offered the most generous mental benefits, and later cut back, subsequently restored the initial benefit level; another major carrier on its own initiative increased its benefits to the same level.

As supplementary major medical benefits these plans have an initial deductible and 20–25% co-insurance paid by the insured. However, Massachusetts Blue Cross is now offering a special rider to their Master Medical group policies that provides a fully paid benefit of up to $700 in a two-year period for out-of-hospital care. (This is in addition to regular in-hospital benefits.) Although the dollar limit is relatively low, this benefit requires no deductible and no co-insurance.

.Next, despite frequent references to individual cases of extensive utilization of generous benefits, often in a manner insinuating subscriber dishonesty if not improper professional behavior, suggestive evidence for the feasibility of both first-dollar coverage and no limitation on benefits is concretely available. Data on utilization in two projects (9, 10) where services were offered at no cost to the patient show that the average number of visits ranged from less than eight (9) to slightly more than 14 (10)—a spread fully within the range of reasonable underwriting costs.

Also, a potent argument exists for generous outpatient benefits since limitations in this area favor hospitalization, a distinctly more expensive form of care. This is not to say that the person who exhausts his benefits will be hospitalized. Rather, for those precariously adjusted patients who need long-term care (whether intermittent or continuous) and who are most likely to use up their outpatient benefits, there is a greater likelihood of hospitalization. This could occur because of decompensation after treatment is terminated or as a way of avoiding a termination that the therapist feels will have a catastrophic effect.

While not as important as these factors, a minor contribution to the development of a fully paid benefit is coming from the profession itself: the belief that it is therapeutically necessary for the patient to pay for his therapy is being stated with less conviction today than in the past.

## SOME RECOMMENDATIONS

Progress, however, is made slowly. While we may be moving in the direction of full first-dollar coverage, much can be done within the limits of present programs to increase the therapeutic returns on the benefit dollar.

Perhaps most important of these is that benefit coverage, whether provided under an indemnity program, a service benefit program, or a prepayment program, should be extended to cover the full range of services that may be provided in the course of evaluation or treatment for mental disorders. As listed in the *APA Guidelines for Psychiatric Services Covered under Health Insurance Plans* (11), these include not only regular inpatient and individual outpatient care, but also partial hospitalization in day and/or night programs, the full range of psychotherapeutic services including group, family, and the somatic therapies, collateral visits with family or other intimates, consultation with medical, employing, school, or agency personnel, and the services of other professionals providing care for mental disorders.

Of these, payment for inpatient and a variety of outpatient services as well as for the services of other professionals is traditional in the health insurance field. What is not traditional is payment for other services, such as partial hospitalization, of proven value in preventing the need for more expensive care. While partial hospitalization is now covered by some programs offering both inpatient and outpatient benefits, there was a considerable lag between publication of research data proving its effectiveness in staving off the need for full hospitalization and its inclusion under insured services. The role of the profession is paramount here, as one reason presented by carriers for not extending coverage sooner was that they were reluctant to include benefits in policies written for large groups if the services were available on such a limited basis as to make them inaccessible to a majority of the group members. If coverage for new services is to be provided, it is up to the profession to implement innovative programs and activities.

At the present time, group therapy and collateral interviews with members of the patient's family are covered by many policies, but family therapy as such is not. Although benefit coverage for consultation is an accepted element in traditional health insurance policies, we do not yet even know what the response of the insurance carriers will be to requests for benefit compensation for time spent in different kinds of consultation from that traditionally covered. This could include the therapist's consultation with other physicians, employers, schools, or other groups or agencies deeply involved with the patient's functioning that may be called upon to play an essential role in his rehabilitation.

Nor has the concept of consultation to organizations purchasing or negotiating health benefits been adequately explored. With 86% of all group health insurance policies being written for employment-based groups, the purchasing organization (whether management, union, or both) is in a position to significantly influence the individual's capacity to continue functioning. For this kind of organization, such consultation is particularly important: Through suggestions for changing aspects of the person's environment (whether physical or psychological), it often can relieve the need for a referral for service. In addition, it can provide the education so badly needed for dealing with the endemic fears about mental disorders that deter people from utilizing available benefits. It is only as the profession presses for recognition of these services as essential for good care in appropriate situations that both the purchasers of care and the carriers will begin to explore their inclusion in benefit packages.

Providing benefits for such services not only assures good care by placing the full range of therapeutic techniques within the economic reach of all patients, but it is also economical, insofar as the most appropriate service is also ultimately the least costly. For this reason, insurers might give consideration to the development of special financing arrangements in cases where patients turn to service programs that assure this spectrum of therapeutic activities. Such is the case in the United Automobile Workers contract, where the unique co-insurance provisions described later in this paper are suspended and full coverage is provided for services obtained through organized service programs.

## POOLING OF FAMILY BENEFITS

More innovative would be conversion of the benefit from that provided to individuals, i.e., subscriber and each dependent, to one provided to families, i.e., the family of the subscriber. Thus, rather than having each family member individually entitled to benefits, the family as a unit would be entitled to benefits equivalent to the sum of those now being provided individually. Although this approach represents a distinct shift from the traditional health insurance approach, it is cognizant of current concepts of family theory and family therapy. It stems from a recognition of family involvement in mental disorder and—particularly in the case of children—of the frequently primary role played by the parents. This approach would enable treatment to be focused on whichever family member or members the situation called for, regardless of who may have initially presented the complaint. It would make it possible to dispense with the ritual of assuring the insurance carrier—even in the case of family therapy—that contact with the family was necessary for the proper management of the patient and that actual treatment was limited to the patient.

Some plans do not limit the benefit available annually to a fraction of the total benefits: for example, a benefit available over a two-year period may be used at any time in that period and the patient is not limited to using half the first year and the other half the second. The arrangement suggested here could increase this kind of flexibility. At the present time the conscientious therapist is in a dilemma when he is faced on the one hand with a clear need for continued treatment and on the other with the subscriber's financial inability to continue unless insurance benefits are obtained through the subterfuge of listing another family member as a new patient. Combining the approach of calculating benefits for the duration of the contract with the pooling of a family benefit should provide for optimal utilization of the benefit dollar. It would also provide a truer picture of the pattern of service for actuarial purposes, as there would be no incentive to obscure actual practice.

The presence of powerful social deterrents to utilization generally provides a sufficient check on any tendencies to overuse, making unnecessary the traditional deterrent of the deductible. If anything, as suggested earlier, these social deterrents are so powerful that a more appropriate step might be the provision of *incentives* to utilization. Accordingly, another important step would be to provide first-dollar coverage through a graduated reverse co-insurance arrangement. Such a practice is currently in effect for outpatient benefits obtained through physicians in private practice under the United Automobile Workers program. The first five visits are fully covered by benefits. For the next five, 85% of the cost is covered; for the next five, 75%; for subsequent visits, 55% is covered to a maximum of $400. Similar arrangements can easily be instituted in ordinary major medical programs at no added benefit cost through the simple device of reviewing utilization and increasing the amount of co-insurance required during later interviews by a percentage that will compensate for the added cost consequent to removing the deductible.

## THE ISSUE OF CONTROLS

The issue of controls has pervaded this discussion—explicitly in terms of the limiting effect it has on innovation and implicitly in reference to problems of abuse or questionable practices. At the present time, as is traditional in health insurance, efforts at establishing controls are centered on the facility in which service is rendered, the qualifications of the person rendering the service, and a definition of the service. While stringent enforcement of these controls should limit gross abuse, they do not deal with the two other significant aspects mentioned above, the restraining force exerted on the introduction of new therapeutic techniques and the gray area of choice among accepted forms of treatment (although the latter is now controlled indirectly through dollar or total-number-of-visit limitations).

Both areas are of serious concern to the profession since they involve the freedom of the practitioner to choose from among the full spectrum of available therapies; they are also of concern to the insurance carriers because of the economics involved. Satisfactory resolution will require both professional and actuarial skills. Accordingly, we must begin to implement a system of peer review that will provide the necessary controls while not inappropriately restricting freedom of practice and that will also be acceptable to the carriers as a replacement for undesirable elements in the present system.

This kind of peer review system has already been endorsed by the APA. In February 1967 the APA Council approved a recommendation of the Task Force on Prepaid Health Insurance that each APA district branch establish a medical insurance review committee, to function either within the framework of an already established medical society insurance review committee or under the auspices of the district branch. In making its recommendation to the APA Council, the task force described the function of such committees as:

1. acting as a review body to assist insurance carriers on the professional aspects of psychiatric coverage;
2. evaluating the appropriateness of services rendered, and type, frequency, and extent of treatment in special cases; and
3. providing impartial professional advice with respect to fees charged by physicians when such fees vary from the normal or customary charges in the area (11).

It will perhaps require more innovativeness than the insurance industry is customarily called upon to provide if these suggestions are to be implemented. Yet they do no more than bring together current knowledge and understanding of therapeutic effectiveness and translate them into a form which should permit the extension of insurance coverage to enhance the quality of care available to subscribers and obtain maximum returns on the benefit dollar.

# REFERENCES

1. Srole, L., Langner, T. S., Michael, S. T., Opler, M. K., & Rennie, T. A. C. *Mental health in the metropolis: The Midtown Manhattan study.* New York: McGraw-Hill, 1962.

2. Follmann, J. F., Jr. Health insurance plan design trends—Coverage and benefits. *Pension and Welfare News*, 1969, **5**, 1–23.

3. Katz, A. H., & Hunter, H. R. A study of experience in insuring for psychiatric services with special reference to workers in manufacturing industries, Los Angeles, California: UCLA School of Public Health, 1968, unpublished paper.

4. Locke, B. Z., & Gardner, E. A. Psychiatric disorders among the patients of general practioners and internists. *Public Health Reports*, 1969, **84**, 167–173.

5. Locke, B. Z., Krantz, G., & Kramer, M. Psychiatric need and demand in a prepaid group practice program. *American Journal of Public Health*, 1966, **56**, 895–904.

6. Follette, W., & Cummings, N. *Psychiatric services and medical utilization in a prepaid health plan setting: Part I. Abstracts of contributed papers.* New York: American Public Health Association, 1966.

7. Dubos, R. J. Mirage of health utopias, progress, and biological change, 1st ed. New York: Harper Brothers, 1959.

8. American Psychiatric Association. Diagnostic and statistical manual of mental disorders, 2nd ed. Washington, D.C., 1968.

9. Akabas, S. H., & Weiner, H. J. The blue collar worker and psychiatry; A new alliance. *Rehabilitation Record*, 1969, **10**(4), 8–11.

10. Fink, R. Financing outpatient mental health care. Presented at the Conference on Mental Health Services and the General Hospital, Pocono Manor, Pennsylvania, July 15, 1969.

11. American Psychiatric Association. *APA guidelines for psychiatric services covered under health insurance plans*, 2nd ed. Washington, D.C., 1969.

# 33. PSYCHIATRIC INSURANCE—
# TEN YEARS LATER

### Helen Hershfield Avnet

*Ten years after the Group Health Insurance research project to determine the feasibility of insuring short-term ambulatory psychiatric treatment, the author describes the remarkable gains in mental health insurance in the interim. Progress has been along two contrasting lines—the "social" approach, emphasizing easy access to care with a minimal financial deterrent, and the "business" approach, with deductibles and co-insurance. Underlying some of the still unresolved problems, the author feels, is the basic schism in this country concerning how medical care should be provided and distributed.*

Ten years ago, the Group Health Insurance research project on psychiatric insurance was just getting off the ground. As of July 1, 1959, 76,000 people insured for other physician services by GHI became eligible for psychiatric coverage on an experimental basis. The experiment continued for 2½ years. While this initial effort did not pretend to furnish definitive answers, it did break down some of the fears that had been inhibiting action and it encouraged others to take next steps. The experimental benefits emphasized early short-term ambulatory psychotherapy by paying for a limited number of psychiatric services, starting with the initial visit. It was the first time such concepts were successfully applied in a community medical insurance plan.

Mrs. Avent is director of research, Group Health Insurance, 227 West 40th Street, New York, New York 10018.

Read at the Conference on Delivery and Financing of Mental Health Services, Gracie Square Hospital, New York, New York, June 4, 1969.

Now that they have been incorporated as the basis for an impressive number of subsequent experiments, people tend to forget that only a few years ago such an approach was regarded as actuarially unthinkable. Those who become discouraged with the confusions still evident in this field in the 60s may take hope by looking back at the 50s. It is startling to realize that the modern era of pharmacopsychiatry in this country dates back only 15 years, to 1954, when psychotropic drugs were first used; that the decrease in the state and county mental hospital population began in 1955; that the emphasis on care in the community—in offices, psychiatric clinics, and general hospitals—made its first real impact in the 50s, along with the notion of short-term therapy as a possible answer to many problems. These interrelated developments, plus the simultaneous mammoth drive to bring the problem of the mentally ill to public consciousness, plus the growing importance of voluntary medical insurance, accounted for the interest in private insurance financing of mental illness costs that also first emerged in the 50s.

People began to ask: Why can't mental illness treatment be included under insurance? Why? Because, they were told in effect, if mental illness is as prevalent as you've been claiming, no prepayment mechanism could cope with it at premium levels the public would pay, that's why. There were endless discussions of the special problems of financing unproven treatment of undefined illness. "Mental illness is an illness just like any other illness" was a clever strategem for overcoming both individual resistance to seeking treatment and community ostracism of the afflicted, but it was obviously not true of either treatment problems or financing problems. The GHI pilot project was an action device to cut through the binds of unproductive talk by making arbitrary decisions on sticky issues, paying for psychiatric services without waiting for definitions, studying what happened, and publicizing the findings.

The book reporting these findings, called *Psychiatric Insurance* (1), appeared toward the end of 1962. It was welcomed by the National Institute of Mental Health, which had financed the research project, as evidence that private insurance could make provision for some worthwhile degree of ambulatory psychiatry treatment. Shortly afterward, in February of 1963, President Kennedy's mental health address to Congress proposed a national network of mental health centers, for which he hoped operating funds would be provided partly by private insurance; the message referred in passing to "recent studies" demonstrating the insurability of short-term treatment and announced a goal of "having community-centered mental health services readily accessible to all within a few years" (2).

Dr. Robert Felix, then director of the National Institute of Mental Health, recalling the message two years later, said "I am convinced this goal is achievable"; and Wilbur Cohen, Secretary of Health, Education, and Welfare, spoke of 500 to 700 mental health centers projected for operation by 1970 (3).

Around the same period, the National Institute of Mental Health published suggested principles for improving what was by then called mental health insurance, in contrast to GHI's more limited term, psychiatric insurance (4). Like the GHI experimental coverage, the NIMH guidelines emphasized the importance of coverage for ambulatory treatment and urged concentration of resources on provision of early, intensive short-term therapy. In addition, the guidelines went beyond the GHI experience in recommending that "the services of all mental health disciplines" be included in the mental insurance package.

Since the term "mental health" itself has much broader implications than the term "mental illness," and since many different types of personnel can be involved in the achievement of mental health for individuals with a broad range of unhappiness problems, the role projected for mental insurance by the National Institute of Mental Health recommendations exceeded any previous conception of medical insurance responsibility.

When referring to the rest of the medical insurance complex, mental insurance protagonists should also recognize that their aspirations are not properly characterized by phrases such as "nondiscriminatory benefits—as broad as those for nonpsychiatric illness." The fact is that emphasis on early ambulatory treatment calls for more extensive coverage in mental illness than the majority of the population has for physical illness. In appraising the progress of mental insurance, it is important to keep this distinction in mind.

The history of mass purchase of voluntary medical insurance in this country has reflected a preoccupation with the dramatic expenses associated with hospitalization and far less concern with the problems of keeping the vertical patient vertical. As a result, the proportion of the under-65 population with some coverage for hospitalized illness, now claimed to be nearly 90%, is twice the proportion with office coverage of physician services (5). In the evolution of psychiatric insurance, the same type of priority order has prevailed, despite the proven value of ambulatory care in reducing the need for hospitalization. Carrying the comparison further, population segments that present special actuarial and enrollment problems to medical insurance, such as unaffiliated self-employed or other individuals, are even more difficult prospects for worthwhile mental coverage. *Whatever problems medical insurance has had, psychiatric insurance has them too—only more so.*

## THE CURRENT SCENE

Where does psychiatric insurance stand now? It has expanded remarkably in numbers covered and scope of coverage over the past few years. The information lag makes it difficult to describe precisely where we are, but one can discuss impressions of trends in terms of the hospitalization coverage and ambulatory coverage being sponsored by the various segments of buyers and sellers.

The trend in hospital coverage has been away from exclusion of mental illness; and discriminatory clauses, while still in evidence, are gradually being whittled down. It is virtually impossible to judge the extent of this change to date, but the evolving attitude seems to be that anyone sick enough to require hospitalization and able to get a bed in a nonpublic general hospital is entitled to coverage under his hospitalization policy, regardless of diagnosis.

This does not mean that there is either universal agreement as to the change among all insurers, or that those who do agree in theory have acted consistently to broaden their contractual obligations. But with further experience and further buyer pressure—the real keys to change—one should expect general implementation within a few years. The recent Joint Information Service study (6) of a sample of hospitalized mental patients showed three out of four in voluntary hospitals to be insured, with the average insurance amounting to 71% of the bill. In contrast, voluntary insurance contributed little toward the financing of mental care in public hospitals. The study did not determine the reasons for this—the extent to which those in public hospitals had no insurance, had exhausted their benefits before coming to the public hospital, or owned policies that discriminated against mental conditions or against public hospitals. In the case of patients who would have been covered had they been in nonpublic hospitals, the cry of "discrimination because of mental illness" is of course invalid; the insurers involved[1] would also refuse to pay for nonmental conditions under the same circumstances. We have to remember that nondiscriminatory hospitalization coverage for mental patients means they have no more to worry about financially than those with physical illness—no more, and no less, either. In other words, their mental benefits will depend on how comprehensive a policy they own.

When it comes to outpatient benefits, no single trend can be described. Unlike hospital coverage, where agreement at least as to general purpose is discernible, outpatient coverage, to the extent it is provided at all, has followed two paths based on opposing philosophies of the purpose of insurance.

The hardheaded business approach to medical insurance has been modified by many insurers over the years, at least

---

[1]It appears that in this respect the commercial insurers are more liberal than Blue Cross and Blue Shield.

for group enrollees, in its application to coverage of pre-existing conditions and elective procedures; but it is still far from the point of encouraging people with not-obviously-disabling emotional or environmental problems to seek help at company expense.

The social approach, in sharp contrast, works on the hypothesis that today's emotional or social problem may be tomorrow's major mental illness; therefore mental insurance must provide easy access to early help for problems that interfere with the individual's ability to function optimally.

The business approach has resulted in ambulatory coverage that characteristically provides financial deterrents both to initiation and continuation of treatment. The social approach generally minimizes and preferably eliminates any financial barrier that might stand between the troubled patient and his decision to make the first visit or to undergo short-term therapy. Between these two basic approaches there are gradations describing current realities of various coverages in effect. There are also indications that the deterrent approach softens for large groups requesting tailored-to-order coverage—except in the case of professors, entertainers, journalists, and public relations, advertising, and other groups likely to be intellectually oriented toward psychiatry.

The picture is confusing, especially if one tries to examine the multitude of ambulatory coverage variations written into plans for different companies or unions, or to differentiate between what is available for sale and what has actually been purchased, or to make a head count that eliminates duplications (for instance, Blue Shield may be listed as covering 8 million people who are already counted under a specific union or company plan). These distractions must be disregarded in selecting significant highlights of the current scene.

## Private Major Medical

The majority of the people with some degree of outpatient psychiatric protection have the deterrent type, under group major medical policies issued by commercial insurers and purchased by employers or unions or both; individuals rarely can buy it. It is conceivable that as many as 60 million persons are now in this category. Coverage is hemmed in at both ends and between; a typical policy appears to entail an initial payment, applicable to all services, not just psychiatric, of $50 to $150 or more; after that co-payment of 50% of treatment costs by the insured (as compared with 20 to 25% for other illness under the same policy); an upper limit on visits per year (usually 50) or on dollars payable; also frequently a limit of $10 per visit payable by the insurer. Coverage is generally for the services of a physician or those ordered or supervised by a physician, but some companies have agreed to pay clinical psychologists without that requirement.

## Federal Government

The federal government wears at least different hats vis-à-vis ambulatory mental coverage—as guidelines writer, as employer-purchaser, and as insurance underwriter.

As recommender of policy for the private insurance sector, it issued the National Institute of Mental Health principles previously referred to, suggesting encouragement of early, short-term intensive treatment, the mental health team approach, all types of service, and inclusion of prescribed drugs. The NIMH has followed through on these recommendations by working actively with interested groups, particularly labor unions and prepaid group practice plans, to effectuate the type of coverage wanted.

As employer, the federal government has participated in the purchase of mental insurance benefits for its employees and their dependents—7.5 million people. The psychiatric coverage originally (1962) either excluded outpatient psychotherapy entirely or resembled the typical commercial policy, with initial deterrents and 50% co-insurance. On the basis of a study of the first years' experience, the coverage was expanded to include greater amounts and more types of service; the most important change, in the plans enrolling the great majority of federal employees, reduced the patient's share of payments to 20% for outpatient psychiatric treatment. Aside from the value of the new federal benefits, the renegotiations that brought them about provided a major demonstration of what can be accomplished with a combination of facts and the pressure of large group buying power.

In its third role, as underwriter of ambulatory mental coverage, the federal government turned the other cheek. Those who drew up the Medicare provisions threw away their opportunity to practice what their colleagues in other government agencies were preaching to the private insurance sector and adopted the hardheaded business approach to ambulatory coverage—50% co-insurance and a $250 limit per year after satisfaction of the general deductible.

The significance of government behavior in the role of insurer may have escaped the attention of those who warn voluntary insurers, in effect, that "the government will do it if you don't watch out." But what *will* "the government" do? Apparently, when the chips are down, no more than voluntary major medical, so far as benefits are concerned. The government can of course force the universal purchase of insurance, but that is a solution addressed to a different problem—that of reluctant buyers.

## Blue Shield

What about Blue Shield? Until recently, its role has been as underwriter-on-demand by large, nationally scattered groups of employees, such as the federal workers. A new development, about which little is publicly known as yet, is the announcement by the National Association of Blue Shield Plans that beginning in April 1969, outpatient psychiatric treatment must be available as a paid-in-full benefit to insured groups willing to buy it. Because of the recency of this requirement, it is difficult to find out how it is being implemented. The mention of paid-in-full benefits seems to imply a leaning toward the social approach rather than the deterrent approach of major medical. But that remains to be seen. In any case, this directive to all Blue Shield plans must be regarded, even before implementation, as a milestone of potentially major significance in the further development of ambulatory psychiatric insurance.

## Social Approach

The social approach to mental coverage is being pursued by a variety of sponsors, now including a Blue Cross plan and the prepaid group practice plans, in addition to the union plans that dominate this arena. In varying degrees, most plans placed in this category emphasize early crisis-oriented treatment and encourage the mental health team approach to therapy. In common with major medical, most of them either exclude psychoanalysis specifically or place upper limits on reimbursable amounts, which accomplishes the same thing. Aside from that, no two plans are exactly alike and all are regarded as experimental.

In terms of numbers of people currently covered, the largest of these plans is that of the United Automobile Workers. It is outstanding for the coverage it provides, the nearly 3 million people it includes, the research planned on its experience, and the influence it is having on expanded coverage being purchased for other large groups, notably the United Steelworkers union. It is estimated that about 15 million people have been affected to date. UAW's first year of experience with the Michigan portion of its constituency, admittedly insufficient for definitive impressions but nevertheless of interest, was recently described by Glasser (7). It held some surprises for the sponsors. Hospital utilization did not decrease as expected with the introduction of ambulatory coverage, and it cost three times as much as ambulatory care. Most patients, particularly adults, used private office care despite the fact that the plan offers financial inducements to encourage use of centers or clinics. This of course would be partly related to the availability of good and convenient clinic care, as well as to lingering personal preferences for individual private care. The total costs to the plan, per eligible person, were under two dollars during the first year of operation, including hospitalization; for ambulatory care the cost was well under 50 cents. These figures would be expected to rise as more of the membership becomes aware of the benefits and their need for them. The fact that fewer than 1% used benefits during the first year despite the absence of any initial financial deterrents is not regarded as surprising, in view of the domination of the group by blue-collar workers and their dependents; no special educational program was used by the union to recruit them as patients.

There is a world of contrast between the UAW plan and another union plan—relatively mature, but small—operating in Los Angeles since the early 60s for the Retail Clerks' Union (8, 9). It offers coverage to 50,000 people through its own clinic. During the first year there were eligibility and coverage restrictions and practically no utilization. A patient recruitment program was introduced that talked in terms of emotional or social problems and counseling instead of mental illness and psychiatric treatment. Benefits, available on a self-referral, walk-in basis from a mental health team, were expanded to include not only unlimited individual and group psychotherapy and psychological testing but also family counseling, marital counseling, premarital counseling, and parent-child guidance, plus educational evaluation and vocational guidance; occupational therapy and social service assistance were also available to hospitalized patients.

On this basis, the annual utilization rate had reached 5% of the population by 1965 and was maintaining this level two years later. The annual cost to the plan per eligible person had reached $12.30 by 1966 for outpatient care. Another $3.70 per capita was expended for in-hospital care. In addition, there is a nominal charge to the patient. Thus, aside from this charge, plus whatever long-term hospitalization was required beyond the plan allowance, plus whatever use was made of private care outside the clinic, plus drug expenditures (and not to mention other services connected with the total care of mental disorders), the costs for "mental health" came to $16 per eligible member, with 5% of eligibles using services.

With the apparent exception of the Health Insurance Plan of Greater New York—which, following the initial period of experimentation, is charging a premium rate of $10.80 per capita or $32.40 per family annually, for an expected 1% clinic utilization rate—this is higher than any other known recent experience with psychiatric insurance.[2]

It is difficult to evaluate what, if anything, the Los Angeles union's experience might signify to other insurance plans without knowing how many of its members went outside the clinic for psychiatric treatment. Nevertheless, it may be significant that even the broad range of mental health services offered, which greatly exceeds what many of us would have thought of as psychiatric services, brings only 5% of the eligible population to the clinic in a year. This contrasts with the 1 or 2% per year generally found to be under psychiatric treatment but is still far from the 10% said to be the minimum proportion in need of psychiatric help at any one time.

## COMMENTARY

Evaluation of progress in this field depends on expectations. It is easily the most complicated component of the medical insurance complex. In retrospect, more has been accomplished than would have been thought possible only a few years ago.

[2]On the basis of its pilot experience it was reported that in a year's time, an HIP population of 60,000 would be expected to yield about 600 patients under treatment at one center, who would require about 9,000 services to be provided by a full-time professional staff of ten (10). This would indicate an average of 900 services per year rendered per professional, or, given a 45-week year, 20 services per week, 4 per day. Assuming the premium represents an income of $600,000 from 60,000 people, and assuming a fourth goes for drugs, for psychiatric personnel services in hospital, and administration, this leaves an income of $50 per clinic service.

Unit costs of clinic services for the Los Angeles plan during 1968 were $30.86 per visit and $39.76 per clinician treatment hour (11).

As with all of the scant data on experience in this field, the figures on the two plans are not really comparable. Nevertheless, they are separately and in combined consideration relevant to any eventual evaluation concerned with the economics of the mental health center approach to treatment.

Mental insurance has increased tremendously and has apparently progressed further than the community mental health center program it was supposed to help support. The lessening of insurance discrimination against mental illness treated in community hospitals and the accompanying increase in the number of general hospitals accepting mental patients is now taken for granted. The question of private support for public hospitals is still fuzzy, as is the whole issue of public versus private responsibility for care of mental disorders.

In ambulatory coverage, major impetus has come from evidence that limited, crisis-oriented psychotherapy is not only insurable for large general population groups but can "stand on its own merits and need not be dismissed as something to do until the real therapist comes" (12). Although brief therapy is still anathema to many psychiatrists and has not yet been endorsed in the insurance guidelines issued by the American Psychiatric Association, both of the principal current approaches to ambulatory coverage characteristically rely on this technique. Contrary to former beliefs, it has been found that members of blue-collar families are responsive to such therapy—hence the growing investment by large, single-industry, national groups in programs with this emphasis. In addition to single-industry or company coverage, nonprofit community insurance plans and some prepaid group practice plans are offering or preparing to offer such coverage to employed groups and their dependents in the general population. And even the commercial companies, which account for most of the coverage in effect so far, seem to be developing flexibility to accommodate real demand for less deterrent benefits. Current activity is being interpreted by some as a ground swell of interest that could make mental insurance the big medical insurance development of the decade.

All this happy talk is not to imply that basic issues have been resolved. Indeed, some of the problems that 10 years ago were inhibiting action on psychiatric insurance have in some respects deepened. Discussion of the need to define mental illness, which we could formerly sidestep with the phrase "any condition treated by a psychiatrist," is now challenged by phrases like "social psychiatry," "preventive psychiatry," and "the mental health team approach," which implicitly defy any thought of treatment delineation.

Underlying this and related problems is the schism that divides the various factions in our society not only on the question of mental insurance but, more basically, on the whole question of how all medical care should be distributed. Public health, university, and labor leaders who vocalize their desire for change want to replace the present dominant system of private fee-for-service care with a network of community medical centers employing salaried physicians and other health team members, as in prepaid group practice.

From this viewpoint, the mental health field can be regarded as the vanguard, with comprehensive mental health centers providing impetus toward eventual involvement of the whole medical complex. In some quarters this has resulted in simultaneous demands for voluntary mental insurance as a financing mechanism and resentment at any success in that direction which reinforces the dominant fee-for-service system. The consequence is confusion.

The reporter who attempts an objective evaluation of progress in mental insurance is confronted with the contrast between the objectives of an important segment and the realities of the present situation. After years of advocacy of prepaid group practice, such practice covers only 2% of the population. The majority of physicians, including psychiatrists, are in fee-for-service private practice. The majority of insurance subscribers, given a choice between salaried group practice or fee-for-service plans, have chosen fee-for-service plans. Given a choice between private or clinic care under psychiatric insurance, the majority have chosen private care.[3]

[3]Aside from the UAW experience, GHI, on request, has provided one group (since February 1968) with a choice between private office treatment and treatment at a good private psychiatric clinic that is specifically mentioned in the literature distributed to the group. During the first year, the majority of the patients used private office treatment.

Six years after President Kennedy's announcement of federal support for community mental health centers that would blanket the whole population, the program has just about gotten started and shows signs of modifying its goals. The quality of the psychiatric clinics that have continued to blossom apart from the mental health center movement is variable, and individual clinics may or may not offer an equitable alternative to the individual patient. Thus, in the real world, average psychiatric insurance buyers and sellers can at most offer their constituents a choice; even if they wanted to they could not bypass the fee-for-service system.

Other basic problems concern the priorities that society will assign to competing demands. What priority will be given to mental health care, as opposed to removal of socioeconomic conditions said to cause mental illness? Will the priority for mental health insurance be high enough to finance aid for all the environmental and personal problems now classified under mental health? Developing attitudes toward society's responsibility for helping the individual adjust to it will call for major financial commitments in the future—commitments much larger than either public or private sources seem ready to undertake. How and where, then, do we, or can we, draw a line between medical care and social care, between public and private responsibility, between the need to educate people as to the value of mental treatment and the need to conserve resources? These are all questions that will have to be faced eventually.

In the meantime, there are likely to be continued efforts, along the lines already drawn, to improve the scope of benefits and increase the number of people eligible for insured short-term psychotherapy. It cannot be expected that those efforts will be directed toward the vast number who still lack coverage for nonmental conditions. The principal target will be the people who already have fairly comprehensive medical insurance coverage, including out-of-hospital care. For such groups, nondeterrent psychiatric benefits would be a logical next step.

It may or may not appear that way to the decision makers,

however. Management, which tends to regard medical insurance for its employees as an expense rather than an investment, has more often than not been cool to the whole notion of paying for psychiatric coverage. Union officials, for their part, do not always see the need for mental benefits; some of them echo the feelings of many of their constituents—they still think you have to be crazy, to see a psychiatrist. Furthermore, the attention of both labor and management may be diverted by competing urgencies—e.g., the local Blue Cross plan, which charged $64 for a family hospital policy in 1959, wants $200 now. What effect will that have on the rest of the medical insurance budget? Again, it is a question of priorities.

One economist claims that "the outlook for family income is so excellent that the nation should be able to pay its way for the health care it needs and wants, whatever may be the method chosen for assessing and meeting financial costs" (13). On that basis, the continued growth of comprehensive medical insurance, including psychiatric insurance, will be assured when enough medical insurance purchasing agents are seriously convinced that we "need and want" it.

One final observation: Apart from psychiatric insurance, I have been struck by the fragmentary nature of available data and the difficulty of obtaining answers to simple specific questions concerning mental health activities, even on local matters, even from agencies whose job should include knowing them. It no longer makes much impact to read hackneyed claims about mental illness being the number one health problem. In this complex field, which has changed so much in so short a time, there is an urgent need for a definite program to provide regular review and coordinated appraisal of current progress and problems. Only through such means will we be able to develop realistic perspective on the present and realistic goals for the future.

## REFERENCES

1. Avnet, H. H. *Psychiatric insurance*. New York: Group Health Insurance, 1962.

2. Kennedy, J. F. Message from the President of the United States related to mental illness and mental retardation. *American Journal of Psychiatry*, 1964, **120**, 729–737.

3. Cohen, W. J. New directions in mental health legislation. Read at the Conference for Leaders in State Mental Health Planning, American Psychiatric Association, Washington, D.C., February 20, 1965.

4. National Institute of Mental Health. Improving mental health insurance coverage. Public Health Service Publication No. 1253, 1965.

5. Reed, L. S., & Carr. W. Private health insurance in the United States, 1967. *Social Security Bulletin*, 1969, **32**, 5.

6. Scheidemandel, P., Kanno, C. K., & Glasscote, R. M. *Health insurance for mental illness.* Washington, D.C.: Joint Information Service, 1968.

7. Glasser, M. A., & Duggan, T. Prepaid psychiatric care experience with U.A.W. members. *American Journal of Psychiatry*, 1969, **126**, 675–681.

8. American Psychiatric Association. *APA guidelines for psychiatric services covered under health insurance plans,* 2nd ed. Washington, D.C.: American Psychiatric Association, 1969, pp. 27 and 30.

9. Employee benefit plan review. Chicago, Illinois: Charles D. Spencer & Associates, March 1965.

10. Goldensohn, S., Daily, E., Shapiro, S., & Fink, R. Referral and utilization patterns in the first year of a mental health center in a prepaid group practice medical program. *Medical Care*, 1967, **5**, 36–43.

11. Wagner, P. D. Joint union-management mental health programs. Los Angeles, California: Retail Clerks Local 770, Mental Health Development Center, 1969 (processed).

12. Campbell, R. J. Discussion of brief psychotherapy in an outpatient clinic: Evolution and evaluation. *American Journal of Psychiatry*, 1968, **124**, 1225–1226.

13. Upgren, A. R. Address read to the Group Insurance Forum of the Health Insurance Association of America, Philadelphia, Pennsylvania, February 25, 1969.

# 34. PSYCHIATRIC SERVICES IN A CALIFORNIA GROUP HEALTH PLAN

## Edward L. Green, M.D.

*Provisions for the treatment of mental illness under various kinds of insurance coverage have undergone dramatic change, which the author outlines. He also describes the expectations, patient and contract characteristics, and results of establishing psychiatric services in the Southern California Permanente Medical Group, a large group health plan. Utilization rates (which are much higher than in the UAW program) and the problems encountered over an eight-year period are included.*

The similarities among group health plans, the Blue Cross and Blue Shield organizations, commercial insurers, and various union and company health programs have been obscured by our usual view of them as competitors. Health care (including psychiatric) has become a complex intertwining of these organizations as well as volunteer, private, social, and governmental agencies. Both prepaid groups and the insurers share many features in common: Especially fundamental is the collection of premiums or dues in accordance with the prestated conditions of a contract.

Dr. Green is chief of psychiatry, Southern California Permanente Medical Group, 4900 Sunset Boulevard, Los Angeles, California 90027.
This is a revision of a paper read at the 125th anniversary meeting of the American Psychiatric Association, Miami Beach, Florida, May 5–9, 1969.

The history of health insurance is contemporary in that hospital expenses have been insured on a group basis only since 1934, surgical expenses since 1939, and other medical costs since 1944 (1). Psychiatric conditions have been the last major diagnostic category to be included. Bennett and associates (1) reported that 70% of 153 companies offering health insurance excluded mental illness in 1945. In 1967, 99% of the new group major medical policies written by the commercial insurers covered nervous and mental disorders treated in a hospital (2).

In 1965 the National Association of Blue Shield Plans reported that 75% of their membership was covered for inpatient services and about 13% for outpatient services. Of the Blue Cross Association's 64 million members, 95% achieved some form of coverage by 1967 (3). During this past decade industrial plans, union coverages, and the group health plans have also made dramatic changes. Most of these advances are documented in detail in the Joint Information Service study by Scheidemandel and associates (2), which outlines many of the specific provisions of the large plans, although not those of the Kaiser-Permanente organizations.

Within the group health movement, the St. Louis Labor Health Institute, an organization serving the Teamsters Union, has provided continuing neuropsychiatric services since 1946. Both neurological and psychiatric conditions are referred to this service, which was staffed on a part-time basis for many years (4).

The first major experiment in providing large-scale outpatient care occurred in 1959, when Group Health Insurance, Inc., in New York City sponsored a project to demonstrate the insurability of mental illness by offering short-term psychiatric treatment to 76,000 members (5).

Since then there have been a succession of plans offering liberalized benefits for the treatment of mental illness. In a few instances retrenchment was found necessary; one of these occurred when the National Association of Social Workers withdrew a benefit that was used to subsidize psychoanalysis, although this had probably not been the intent of the insurer. Because of similar experiences, insurers have been guarded:

The Joint Information Service (2) quotes the following excerpt from a 1965 article in the *Weekly Underwriter,*

> Covering mental illness under major medical is dangerous. Many insurance companies have sad experiences in insuring out-of-hospital psychiatric treatment, and most companies now cover only in-hospital expenses. Some companies have retreated from even this position. But the trend is now toward greater coverage, through cautiously worded limitations on coverage.

The growth of coverage for mental illness has been followed closely by professionals in the field and has been documented by at least 30 articles relating to the general topic. In addition there have been articles on the psychiatric provisions of Medicare, including a special section in the August 1966 issue of this journal, which incidentally contains the following statement by a federal official: "In this area of coverage in which little insurance experience exists, it was considered necessary to acquire actual program experience before any of us could judge the actuarial effects of this kind of outpatient coverage" (6).

## FACTORS LEADING
## TOWARD GREATER COVERAGE

President John F. Kennedy's message on mental health drew attention to the general inadequacy of care for the mentally ill and the mentally retarded. The federal government responded by passing legislation authorizing the construction of community mental health centers. It also provided its own employees with health insurance plans that in many cases included liberal psychiatric benefits. Many unions and progressive industrial organizations also dedicated themselves to improving mental health services.

Journalists and legislators (7) documented some of the shocking conditions still existing in our public facilities, and the public became more aroused to the needs of the mentally ill. The long-time educational efforts of such organizations as the National Association for Mental Health helped to dispel some of the taboos in public discussions concerning the treatment needs for the mentally ill. As more individuals had therapeutic contacts, the educational efforts merged with experience to give a credence that was not accomplished by education alone.

The development of social and community psychiatry enabled the mental health field to make dramatic changes in attitude. The development and endorsement of crisis intervention techniques by competent and respected clinicians caused many therapists to re-think the old issues of long-term versus short-term therapy. Within the field of psychoanalysis there was a marked shift; psychoanalysis as a method of therapy is now recognized as having limited indications rather than being seen as the ultimate or exclusive method of treatment (5).

Long before the new theoretical structures were laid down, many agencies and clinics had been treating patients for short periods of time, usually less than eight sessions, but the therapists were often dissatisfied because they did not have a sufficient theoretical framework to justify this approach. Unfortunately, in many settings once-a-week therapy was viewed as a one-fifth analysis and the inappropriate transference of psychoanalytic methodology led to therapeutic difficulties that reinforced the dissatisfaction.

There was a shift from the hospital base of psychiatric practice as more psychiatrists were trained and entered private practice. As more patients became involved in treatment that could not be extended because of the "middle class squeeze" (too poor for psychoanalysis, too rich for clinic care), therapists necessarily accumulated experiences proving the value of short-term therapy.

In the same decade psychiatrists became increasingly familiar with the psychotropic drugs; pharmaceutical houses produced hundreds of new drugs, many of which were remarkably superior to the sedatives and stimulants previously known. Without the advances in technology, the changes in attitude of the psychotherapists, and the increased prestige of the mental health professions, it is unlikely that insurance coverage for mental illness could have moved along as quickly as it has.

## SOME BARRIERS
## UNDER INSURANCE CONTRACTS

Neither an insurance mechanism nor a group health plan can create funds to perform medical or social functions, no matter how noble the objectives. There must always be a balance between what the consumer is able or willing to pay and the cost of meeting his needs. As an example, many children are in need of psychiatric residential treatment services, but the cost for a single patient would so drain the resources of most funds as to prevent other members from receiving their share of a less costly but valuable service such as outpatient care. Each setting must set its own priorities as to how care is to be distributed: This will naturally vary with the self-conceptualized goals of the agency.

Since it is still an economic impossibility to cover care for every degree of emotional disorder, as clear a definition of the coverage as possible is an essential. Though we have made some improvements from the time when some policies specified that nervous conditions were covered and mental illnesses were not (1), we still have to struggle with some lack of clarity, which the following examples will illustrate.

It is common for many plans to limit treatment to "acute" conditions. Most psychiatrists have been trained with the psychodynamic orientation that practically all illness is an outgrowth of the earlier environment and in this sense is chronic. However, the term "acute" acquires more relativity as we give increasing recognition to the importance of stress not only as a precipitant but also as the determinant of an illness or crisis state.

In the past there was much concern about differentiating between social maladaptation and mental illness. Some insurance coverages will not be honored if the "diagnosis" is stated in terms of an interpersonal difficulty such as a marital problem. Yet in our experience we find that most of our patients present their problem as interpersonal; they are as much in need of psychotherapy as those who come with complaints relating to intrapersonal problems.

Control of utilization is seldom achieved through diagnosis, particularly in a field noted for its difficulties in nosology. Clinicians, whose basic motivation is to help patients, will attempt to help no matter what the diagnostic label may be. All humans function on several levels, any of which can be given a diagnostic label such as character disorder, phobia, anxiety reaction, etc. The diagnosis that will most help the patient is the one that will be chosen from the complex presented. General hospitals that excluded alcoholics have learned this lesson well: The alcoholic is admitted not because of his alcoholism but because he has acute gastroenteritis or an electrolyte imbalance. Our plan, which excluded alcoholism from psychiatric coverage, found that when the coverage for federal employees was changed to include alcoholism and the therapists were asked to list those patients who had such a problem, they comprised at least 5% of the case load.

A contract provision that is a holdover from our Puritan ethic is the provision exempting payment for a claim arising out of a self-inflicted injury. Suicidal patients obviously have a psychological difficulty for which they should not be punished, so this exemption is a basic contradiction to providing overall care. It would be possible to stretch this interpretation from the wrist slasher to the LSD user, the diabetic who fails to take insulin, the cardiac who refuses to observe restrictions, etc. The confusion resulting from this provision can best be removed by removal of the restriction itself.

Clear specifications can be written concerning the number of days of hospitalization to be covered, the number of hours of psychotherapy, dollar maximums, lifetime benefits, etc., and it is through such specifications that control can most easily be achieved. Exclusions, like limitations and exceptions to the warranty of a new car, tend to be less explicitly and emphatically stated, but these unpopular restrictions also require clear definition.

Other basic essentials for establishing a sound plan for insuring of mental disorders were well stated by Whitehall in the session on health insurance and psychiatric coverage at the 1957 APA annual meeting, abstracted by Davidson (9).

# THE EXPERIENCE AT SOUTHERN CALIFORNIA PERMANENTE MEDICAL GROUP

## The Expectations

In 1961 the Kaiser-Permanente group health plans in southern California simultaneously established a department of psychiatry and agreed to offer outpatient psychiatric services to a contracting union (10). This union was Retail Clerks Local 770, the majority of whose members work in supermarkets but which also includes pharmacists and clerks working in drugstores. The employers, therapists, union hierarchy, and physicians in the existing organization, as well as the newly hired psychiatrists, all had a set of expectations and anxieties concerning the new venture. The one point of agreement was that they all wanted an efficient organization that would deliver high-caliber services at a reasonable cost. The Avnet study (5) had not yet been completed, and we had little reliable data upon which to base our expectations.

The therapists, who expected to be overwhelmed by applicants, were anxious about the adequacy of their past training to meet the needs of this supposedly new kind of group. The employers, the union, and the group physicians were concerned about the cost involved. (One of the administrative officers said: "This may be the first year that the doctors pay into the partnership instead of receiving a profit!") The employers feared that utilization would be promoted and that the psychiatric service would be abused and would therefore be unnecessarily expensive. The potential patients were the least vocal; in fact, our repeated efforts to survey them to gain their opinions were largely failures. From this I inferred that they wanted to have as little to do with us as possible.

The community at large had heard of the health plan's organization for services and many people expected that there would be a mass oriented, inferior quality, "quickie" approach to mental health, emphasizing group therapy. These fears were partly dispelled when the senior training analyst of one of our two Los Angeles psychoanalytic institutes, Philip S. Wagner, M.D., was appointed as the first chief of psychiatry.

## The Function of the Department of Psychiatry

We had to establish a working relationship among all of the interested parties; our most positive approach to this was through providing direct services and some consultative services. There might have been a considerable advantage in structuring our services in a less traditional manner by using a community psychiatry model that might have made more effective use of the large number of nonpsychiatric physicians and many of our other employees as well. But the orientation of the medical group physicians did not permit us to do this, even though we recognized that the majority of psychological illnesses are still treated by the nonspecialist.

With the advancing knowledge in the field of community psychiatry, we have had a desire to implement a program that would be more in keeping with this philosophy, but group health plans face a unique problem in this respect. Although we deal with a relatively stable population, this population is scattered over a wide geographical area and we therefore cannot work with schools, social agencies, the police, etc., in ways that a community mental health center based on a catchment area can. For this reason our approaches to such agencies are almost always associated with a particular health plan member rather than on a continuing consultative effort with a whole organization. Our community is essentially the medical group community, and we have to restructure concepts of community psychiatry to fit the needs of this group.

Occasionally there is an exception. The department had a rewarding experience with the personnel board of the City of Los Angeles when we were able to persuade the board to use a different kind of rejection letter in cases involving mental disorder. The previous letter had induced high anxiety in those who received it because the applicant perceived the letter as a statement that virtually certified his "insanity."

We have also considered work-related consultation within factories, government agencies, school systems, etc. In discussions with other psychiatrists having similar contracts, it has become quite apparent that psychiatric consultation of this sort would not be welcome in most of our settings. Most corporations and government agencies, like families, are unwilling to admit or do not recognize the degree of mental illness existing in the employed population; when the illness is recognized, the common attitude is to have the treatment take place away from the scene. Many of the plant physicians have an industrial orientation and while they manage to cope with undiagnosed mental illnesses, they fear the patient who has been given a psychiatric label. The experiences of Weiner (11) have been to the contrary, but the clothing industry has a functional organization that lends itself more readily to such intervention because of the long tradition of a guild-like union, with greater cohesiveness among the working population and a familial pride in the skills that are represented.

Our population is accustomed to specialty care, and they do not conceive of us as a social agency. Consequently they expect us to provide them with direct psychiatric services rather than to have their treatment conducted by an intermediary. Although we offer a psychiatric training program for our interested physicians, it is a rare patient who receives psychotherapy from anyone outside of the department of psychiatry.

## Patient Characteristics

Our patients come from many walks of life, but the majority fall into classes IV and V on the Hollingshead and Redlich scales (12). They do not fall into the poverty range because most maintain their employment, through which they are eligible for health plan membership.

We see proportionately more men (46%) than many clinics, presumably because the benefit seems work-related. This is a slightly higher percentage than reported by Avnet (5) and is comparable to that in the study of UAW members reported by Glasser and Duggan (13).

About 20% of our caseload are juveniles; of these, two-thirds fall into the adolescent age range. We hospitalize about 10% of our caseload each year. The usual reasons for hospitalization are suicidal or homicidal impulses or grossly psychotic behavior, but many of those hospitalized do not carry a psychotic diagnosis and it is a coincidence that 10% of our patients carry such diagnoses.

We have been analyzing demographic data of all patients seen during a two-year period; a paper (14) is in preparation that interrelates such factors as age, sex, diagnosis, racial background, income, educational level, etc.

## The Coverage

The largest group we now serve, federal employees numbering 85,000, consists largely of postal employees. These workers are entitled to 45 days of hospitalization per calendar year and an unlimited number of outpatient visits. Their prepayment arrangement permits 20 individual office visits without charge; beginning with the 21st visit there is a $5 fee per visit.

The next largest group consists of State of California employees, including the university system, but these members have only a hospital-based program with us. This consists of 45 days of hospitalization per calendar year and up to 10 outpatient visits to facilitate the hospitalization, prevent it, or for follow-up. These 10 visits may not be used for nonemergency outpatient therapy.

United Auto Workers members are entitled to the same hospitalization benefit and receive up to 10 individual office visits yearly without charge. They may have unlimited additional visits at a charge of $5 per visit.

Our other groups are of a smaller size and all have plans based upon one of the above three basic patterns. In all plans, day or night care can be substituted for total hospitalization with a formula that equates one day of partial hospitalization (day or night) to one-half day of 24-hour care, e.g., 90 days of day care in place of 45 days of complete inpatient care. The total number covered by the various plans amounts to about 150,000 members.

## Utilization of Services

In 1968 our federal patients utilized services at a rate of 23.6 per 1,000 members per year, and UAW members had a rate of 21.8 per 1,000 per year. This figure is almost four times the overall rate reported by Avnet (5) and the blue collar rate reported by Glasser and Duggan (13). Our speculation is that this higher utilization relates to the referral to our services by other group physicians and to the fact that our patients more readily avail themselves of our specialized services because this is a pattern with which they are already familiar. Presently only one major group, the United Auto Workers, is permitted self-referral but most people from this group are still referred by physicians. In actual practice, many patients simply ask their internist or family physician to refer them and he readily obliges.

## The Problems

Three-quarters of the patients have problems related to their marriage or their children. Only one-fourth of the patients come to us with a self-directed complaint of inner tension, anxiety, depression, etc. Kadushin (5) reports similar results in his survey of New York City patients as far as "social problems" were concerned, but these patients also reported many more "biosocial" and "inner emotional" problems. On the basis of presenting problems many of our patients would be considered unresponsive to traditional psychiatric treatment, but since we have a contractual obligation to meet the needs of our population as far as possible, the group health plan must devise means of reaching these patients. In practice this has usually meant more of an emotional involvement, a greater focus on precipitating events, and increased activity by the therapist but otherwise relatively little modification of basic psychodynamic techniques.

## The Mode and Length of Treatment

About three-quarters of the visits to the clinic are recorded as individual visits, but in practice the clinicians often see two or more members of a family when an individual visit is scheduled. We are seeing an increasing number of patients in group therapy as our patients and staff become more comfortable with this modality, but scheduling difficulties have been a limiting factor because the postal workers are customarily off duty on rotating weekdays.

Our raw data indicate that more than half our patients who came for a single consultative type of visit and also the collateral visits of various relatives who were not subsequently involved in the direct therapy but were seen to provide information. They are also distorted by the fact that cases remaining open at present have not been averaged in. Nonetheless, there are substantial numbers of patients who benefit from being seen on such an extremely short-term basis. Although we used to view such treatment as "failure" we have come to take a second look at these interventions, and we now feel that many families have quickly made substantial gains. Cummings and Follette's (16) data based on a sample of patients from the Northern California Permanente Medical Group show that even a single psychiatric consultation reduces medical utilization and therefore by inference may have promoted a sense of well being.

In the Avnet study (5) terminated cases averaged about 10.3 individual visits. In a 1960–1961 study of private practice patients in Monroe County, New York, the average number of visits of those who received treatment was four per patient (17).

## The Therapists

At present we have the full-time equivalent of 7.8 psychiatrists, 5.8 social workers, and 1.6 psychologists on our staff. Associated with this staff are two other staffs that service community clinics sponsored by the Kaiser Foundation and are devoted to parent-child guidance. All the social workers, psychologists, and psychiatrists work as psychotherapists but there is an automatic selection that favors assigning the more disturbed patients to the psychiatrists because they are on emergency duty in rotation. Thus any acutely disturbed patient not previously known to the department is automatically channeled to the psychiatrist and becomes his assigned patient. We do not do a formal social work intake or routine psychological testing batteries, although we do use the Minnesota Multiphasic Personality Inventory (MMPI) as a screening device. (We do not use the computer services because we have a consultant who is able to supply us with more meaningful interpretations than the original static scores or the current computer ejaculates.)

We avoid waiting lists and assign a patient to one therapist with whom he will work from the beginning of his therapy to the end unless this is contraindicated by subsequent developments. This therapist will also work with any members of the patient's family who require services unless there is good reason not to. We intentionally avoid formal team intakes and discharge staffing. Consequently much responsibility is placed upon all members of the department, but there is a cohesive group and consultation is readily available.

## SOME RESULTS

It turned out that we as therapists were not overwhelmed by applications for therapy and that we had been overly anxious about our abilities. When we removed many of the obstacles to having a patient reach us, we found that we were equipped to offer services to all of those who requested it. The Retail Clerks and our later groups did not abuse the service, and we felt that we disproved the old adage that one must pay until it hurts to receive benefit from psychotherapy. The employer, as represented by supervisory personnel, began to see merit in our functioning and on occasion referred employees to the clinic and even transported them to us.

In the areas where we have worked closely with physicians, the understanding of our function and cooperation with us have improved markedly. Those physicians who expected instant one-hour cures have also come to view us in a more realistic fashion. (In our planning for new facilities we hope to distribute our psychiatric staff in such a way that there will be a geographical proximity to the other services. This will make the referral process much less formal and permit many more day-to-day interchanges between mental health professionals and other health workers.)

Although the union that comprised our first contracting group has now set up its own independent clinic, the concepts upon which the psychiatric service was provided are still vigorously supported by the union leadership.

The administrators of our health plan have less fear that we are going to bankrupt the plan: the fact is that it has been proven over an eight-year period that our department can function without taking resources from the health plan at large. As already noted, Cummings and Follette's statistics (16) indicate that the reduction in medical utilization by patients seen in the psychiatric clinic greatly offsets the cost of providing psychiatric care.

The patients have become considerably more accepting of psychiatric services through the years. This may be due to the increasing acceptance in the community at large but is also related to word-of-mouth referrals from one worker to another. We have even had some instances where a worker has taken a job in order to receive psychiatric benefits provided by the clinic.

The community at large has come to know us partly through the patients' contacts and partly through such measures as offering annual symposia to which we invite our professional colleagues. We frequently invite outside speakers to our weekly staff meetings; through this device we have been hosts to hundreds of professionals in our community. The skepticism that remains is largely that of traditionalists who are skeptical of brief therapy approaches in general or those who view treatment with a different philosophy than we do.

# REFERENCES

1. Bennett, A. E., Hargrove, E. A., & Engle, B. Voluntary health insurance and nervous and mental disease. *Journal of the American Medical Association*, 1953, **151**, 202–206.

2. Scheidemandel, P., Kanno, C., & Glasscote, R. Health insurance for mental illness. Washington, D.C.: Joint Information Service, 1968.

3. Action guidelines, health insurance coverage for mental illness. New York: National Association for Mental Health, Inc., 1969.

4. Tureen, L. L. The role of the psychiatrist in a prepaid group medical program. *American Journal of Public Health*, 1959, **49**, 1373–1378.

5. Avnet, H. H. Psychiatric insurance. New York: Group Health Insurance, 1962.

6. Hess, A. E. Medicare and mental illness. *American Journal of Psychiatry*, 1966, **123**, 174–176.

7. California Assembly, Sub-Committee on Mental Health Services, Assembly Interim Committee on Ways and Means: The dilemma of mental commitments in California, a background document. Sacramento, 1967.

8. Marmor, H. The current status of psychoanalysis in American psychiatry. *American Journal of Psychiatry*, 1968, **125**, 679–680.

9. Davidson, H. A. Health insurance and psychiatric coverage. *American Journal of Psychiatry*, 1957, **114**, 498–504.

10. Wagner, P. S. Psychiatry for everyman. *Psychiatry*, 1967, **30**, 79–90.

11. Weiner, H., & Brand, M. Involving a labor union in the rehabilitation of the mentally ill. *American Journal of Orthopsychiatry*, 1965, **35**, 598–600.

12. Hollingshead, A., & Redlich, F. C. *Social class and mental illness*. New York: John Wiley & Sons, 1958.

13. Glasser, M. A., & Duggan, T. Prepaid psychiatric care experience with UAW members. *American Journal of Psychiatry*, 1969, **126**, 675–681.

14. Stout, H. G. Demographic differences in a prepaid psychiatric service, unpublished paper.

15. Kadushin, C. *Why people go to psychiatrists*. New York: Atherton Press, 1969.

16. Cummings, N. A., & Follette, W. T. Psychiatric services and medical utilization in a prepaid health plan setting, Part 2. *Medical Care*, 1968, **6**, 31–41.

17. American Psychiatric Association: APA guidelines for psychiatric services covered under health insurance plans, 1st ed. Washington, D.C. 1966.